Pushing Cool

Pushing Cool

Big Tobacco, Racial Marketing,
and the Untold Story of
the Menthol Cigarette

KEITH WAILOO

The University of Chicago Press
Chicago and London

The University of Chicago Press, Chicago 60637
The University of Chicago Press, Ltd., London
Published 2021
Printed in the United States of America

30 29 28 27 26 25 24 23 22 21   1 2 3 4 5

ISBN-13: 978-0-226-79413-6 (cloth)
ISBN-13: 9 978-0-226-79427-3 (e-book)
DOI: https://doi.org/10.7208/chicago/9780226794273.001.0001

Library of Congress Cataloging-in-Publication Data

Names: Wailoo, Keith, author.
Title: Pushing Cool : big tobacco, racial marketing, and the untold story of the
   menthol cigarette / Keith Wailoo.
Description: Chicago : University of Chicago Press, 2021. | Includes
   bibliographical references and index.
Identifiers: LCCN 2020056563 | ISBN 9780226794136 (cloth) |
   ISBN 9780226794273 (ebook)
Subjects: LCSH: Menthol cigarettes—United States—History—20th century. |
   African Americans—Tobacco use—History—20th century. | Menthol
   cigarettes—Marketing—United States. | Target marketing—United States. |
   African American consumers. | Consumers' preferences—United States.
Classification: LCC HD9149.C43 U678 2021 | DDC 338.4/7679730973—dc23
LC record available at https://lccn.loc.gov/2020056563

♾ This paper meets the requirements of ANSI/NISO Z39.48-1992
(Permanence of Paper).

For Alison Isenberg

Contents

Prologue

Pushers in the City of My Youth

I grew up in New York City in the 1970s in the era of *blaxploitation*—a term coined during my early years, describing a new genre of Black-themed films like *Super Fly* (1972) that trafficked in garish stereotypes of urban street life filled with criminality, sex, and new heights of coolness. Curtis Mayfield's "Freddie's Dead," one of the film's hit songs, was also the soundtrack to my early years. Bemoaning the death of a junkie "ripped up and abused" by drugs, it was a lyrical tragedy broadcast across the airwaves, a melodic warning about one man's downward spiral into drug abuse: "another junkie plan, pushing dope for the man." I first learned to be wary of pushers looking to get kids like me "hooked on dope" from these stark stereotypes, but growing up in the Bronx and Queens, I spotted real pushers soon enough. Street-corner hustlers as well as older teens trafficked in everything from marijuana and heroin to cocaine and quaaludes (which I first heard mentioned in my Bronx elementary school). One of my friends, intending to be funny by riffing on my name, called me Keith Quaalude.

At some point between life in the Bronx and in Queens (where we moved next), I also became alert to another kind of push: the messages emanating from cigarette billboards. They were everywhere. New York was saturated with tobacco posters on buses and subways. Massive billboards lined streets and highways, featuring their own stark and stereotypical fantasies that pushed a popular and legal drug. Many of these ads promoted menthol cigarettes, known for the minty cool sensation they produced on the throat. The brand names are etched in my memory—Kool, Salem, Newport, and the now-defunct More. I remember the signature waterfall imagery, the smooth-looking Black men and women, and the carefree Black groups featured in the Newport ads.

Not far from our LeFrak City apartment in Queens, a new oversize 14-by-48-foot cigarette billboard appeared in 1976 at Woodhaven and Queens Boulevards near a busy shopping center. To me, it was just an ad, an unremarkable sight in a city bathed in outdoor advertising. It was only much later that I learned just how elaborate was the web that landed this particular sign in this specific neighborhood. Purchase Point, the Park Avenue company responsible for the Woodhaven billboard in my Queens neighborhood, boasted to the American Tobacco Company about its magnificent placement. Brightly illuminated, the bulletin loomed day and night over "the busiest area in Queens where within three blocks you will find four major department stores," near "two of the largest private housing developments in Queens . . . (Park City and LeFrak City)." Purchase Point estimated that the "daily effective circulation"—the number of people seeing the tobacco ad every day from roadways—was 75,000. The number did not include "the estimated 20,000 pedestrians that pass this area daily nor the viewing available from the Long Island Expressway."[1]

Nor was this billboard unique. Surveying New York's expansive billboard menagerie, an advertising manager for the American Tobacco Company boasted that he had just driven by "72 of the 127 [oversize] thirty-sheet posters . . . located in Manhattan, Bronx, Queens and Brooklyn." This extensive coverage meant that American Tobacco's "competitive position in New York is good," but he bemoaned that R. J. Reynolds, an arch competitor, was "using almost all of their out-of-home media . . . to introduce [a new menthol brand] More cigarettes. The effect is overwhelming."[2] Unknown to me, these images, with their waterfall motifs and cooling messages, had arrived in my neighborhood after careful deliberations, extensive testing, and outreach to Black civic groups and communities—efforts crafted by Madison Avenue firms, psychographic consulting groups from Chicago to Princeton, and tobacco executives from Richmond, Virginia, to Winston-Salem, North Carolina.

In 1970s New York, all these pushers—of cocaine, pot, quaaludes, and cigarettes—stalked neighborhoods, but in different ways. Of course, I knew that smokers were also addicts, even if of a less threatening sort, hooked on a legal drug. I also knew that many New Yorkers worried about so many cigarette ads, seeing them as another dangerous drug push. Only a few years earlier, when I was ten, cigarette ads had been banned from the television and radio airwaves. City ordinances had been enacted to keep cigarette billboards away from schools. All this I knew well. What I was less aware of was how recently these billboard jungles had sprung up. They multiplied quickly in the aftermath of the 1970 TV and radio ban as part of the tobacco industry's push to make up for the loss of national media channels, saturating urban markets closer to the points of purchase.

But why my neighborhood? And why menthols? From scanning *Ebony* and *Jet* magazines—Black-themed periodicals I read at my grandparents' house in the Bronx—I knew that menthols were pushed as a "Black thing." *Ebony*, which in 1972 questioned whether the rash of new Black-themed movies like *Super Fly, Cotton Comes to Harlem*, and *Shaft* were "culture or con game," also ran ads for all the major menthol brands.[3] The Newport ads were particularly striking, with their Menthol Kings making a direct appeal to togetherness, amusement, and Black identity. "After all," asked Newport, "if smoking isn't a pleasure, why bother?" At the time, I could not have known how the tobacco industry targeted *Ebony*, or how the magazine participated in the push to connect Black smokers to menthols in exchange for much-needed advertising revenue. Nor could I have known that this intense drive toward racial advertising was only in its adolescence; the push was no older than me.

I had no inkling that the billboard hovering over Woodhaven and the ads in *Ebony* were the product of something larger—the web of relentless, enterprising executives, researchers, and marketers who invited would-be consumers to see ourselves in a new light. These marketers studied not only the flow of people in the city but also human behavior and racial group identity; the social researchers tracked changing habits in neighborhoods like mine; the admen shaped the therapeutic, calming imagery of More, as well as the other prominent brands of Kool and Salem; and myriad other consultants closely evaluated the effects of these messages on viewers' preferences, brand choices, and sales. Nor did I understand how Black media outlets, civic organizations like the NAACP, politicians, and urban leaders (including some of the politicians whom I admired) channeled these messages, while also relying on Big Tobacco's economic support for their enterprises. All were caught in the web that cigarette companies, and menthol makers in particular, had spun.

Looking back now, I see that my youth coincided with a particular chapter in menthol smoking's racial history, an era defined by blaxploitation not only in film but also in tobacco marketing. It was an era in which menthol sales reached new heights, accounting for 30 percent of all cigarettes sales. The two trends—menthol and blaxploitation—went hand in hand. *Ebony* said about films like *Super Fly* that Black viewers would have to decide for themselves whether the imagery and message were "reflections of a glorious people—or trick-mirror, fun-house distortions of black truth."[4] Within a few years, the cultural high point of blaxploitation subsided on-screen, but tobacco marketing pressed on in the city.

New York's ever-present billboard scene soon receded from my life, but only because my family moved to suburban New Jersey during my high school years. The sheer absence of billboard fantasies in a town named Maplewood was remarkable. The rustling waterfalls of Kool, the promise of mentholated Salem, the Marlboro Man—so relentless and dense in the city—were absent from my new leafy-green surroundings, even though they were readily visible in the nearby city of Newark. As I later learned, this urban-suburban divide in pushing tobacco and menthol was no accident. It was a product of careful study and social design, a disparity in the push that had a troubling racial and marketing logic. In the early 1980s, for example, the

Figure P.1. A Salem cigarette billboard, viewed from Park Avenue in Newark, New Jersey, around 1979. The urban billboard era of pushing menthol brands and dominating urban vistas spanned three decades, coming to an end only as a result of local activism and legal action in the late 1990s. Credit: Duke University, Resource of Outdoor Advertising Descriptions (ROAD). Courtesy of the Out of Home Advertising Association of America.

William Esty ad firm for R. J. Reynolds worried about its competitor brand "Kool's strength . . . concentrated in those markets in which a high proportion of Black consumers reside," and they told RJR executives that their "Salem Spirit" campaign could "gain brand share by focusing its couponing activity on poverty markets." Their study ranked Newark as the number one such metropolitan poverty market, with some 33 percent of people living below the poverty level.[5] Of course, the suburbs also had their problems, their drug users, and their economic worries. Tobacco researchers and consultants studied them, too, examining every social opportunity to sell. But the focus on "poverty markets" aligned neatly with the industry's menthol strategy in this age of blaxploitation. No matter how regrettable poverty might be, marketers saw people in need, social alienation, or drug use in cities as opportunities to shape cigarette markets in general, and menthol markets in particular.

The experience of coming of age in this peculiar era of blaxploitation surely informs the questions I ask in these pages, many years later—questions about the geography of racial markets; questions about how menthol smoking found its way into the Bronx, Queens, and Newark, and into Black amusements, magazines, and consumer preferences; and questions about how these perverse images of Black masculinity and identity were created, and how this campaign was sustained for so long, with what effect. What I learned in researching this book and by delving deep into the heart of the tobacco industry's archives is how these pushers and their supporters, as well as many influencers unknown to me in the 1970s, shored up these preferences, and how this house of menthol was built and maintained. Deception as a feature of commerce, life, and psychology was at its peak.[6] Finally, I also learned how the foundations of this campaign were eroded, how the billboard era came to an end, beaten back by social developments beyond the industry's power to control. Reflecting on these years of pushing cool, I still hear "Freddie's Dead" playing in my head—a distant backbeat to the strange history of the menthol cigarette and the tragic business of making racial markets in America.

Introduction

The Crooked Man
Influence, Exploitation, and Menthol's Expanding Web

"Why do black people love menthols so much?" wondered comedian Dave Chappelle, playing the host on a quiz show called *I Know Black People*. In the memorable 2004 skit, Chappelle challenged "contestants who claim to know black people and put their knowledge of African American culture to the test." His questions, like his comedy, mixed wry humor with edgy social commentary designed to expose ignorance, challenge stereotypes, or (in this case) reinforce truisms.[1] American popular culture is, of course, replete with condescending humor about Black people's consumer preferences, like the stale stereotypes around, say, watermelon or fried chicken. For Chappelle, menthol was not just another hackneyed racial trope; it carried the aroma of authenticity, apparently highlighting a dimension of modern Blackness. But to say that "Black people" writ large loved menthols was, indeed, a crude stereotype. Most Black people did not smoke cigarettes at all. The stereotype had emerged from the fact that, as his viewers on Comedy Central likely knew, those Black people who *did* smoke disproportionately preferred menthol brands when compared with white smokers or other groups.

Challenged to answer the menthol question, a young white female contestant on Chappelle's show fidgeted uncomfortably, unsure of what to say. As the clock ticked, she muttered hesitantly, "I don't,

1

I don't know." Just then the bell pinged, and the host exclaimed, "That is correct!" Audience laughter broke out. Then Chappelle, with impeccable timing, knowingly added, "Nobody knows. Nobody knows for sure." Every other contestant's answer to the menthol question was greeted with the same pinging bell, no matter how tentative, wild, or imaginative their response. "That is correct! No one knows," Chappelle repeated. In this telling, the love of menthol smoking was authentically of Black culture, a mysterious flavor preference that neither whites, nor Chappelle, nor anyone completely understood.

This notion of a deep connection between Black people and menthol cigarettes has broad cultural appeal, but it is misleading and overblown. Chappelle's answer, "nobody knows," is also wrong. A truer-to-life skit would have put different people onstage as contestants in the imagined game show. It would have been fun, for example, to imagine Chappelle quizzing the 1960s marketing expert Ernest Dichter, or the Philip Morris economist Myron Johnston, or even John H. Johnson, the former publisher of *Ebony* magazine, for their views on how the love of menthols came about. Most of them were deceased by the time of Chappelle's show, but they would have had stories to tell. They had been there at the inception of the trend that Chappelle's audience took as a given. Many of them would have recalled the era before menthol had become a Black preference. As motivation researchers, market analysts, and powerful media figures, they had participated in the crafting of these preferences over the past six decades. They had helped to build menthol's racial market in different ways.

A few years earlier, Philip Morris's Johnston had been pulled out of retirement and forced to defend his role in the deceitful craft of targeted marketing—compelled to answer questions not on television but in a legal setting. Johnston had been deposed in a lawsuit contending that his studies lay the groundwork for the kinds of racial exploitation that made menthols so desirable for Black smokers. Had Chappelle staged such a skit with Johnston, the wry comedy might have turned grim and contentious. But what might have emerged would have been fascinating testimony from the men and women who worked so hard to create, nurture, and sustain this preference over many decades. By 2004 Johnston and the many other influencers who shaped these affinities were appearing in deadly serious courtroom settings. Their testimonies revealed that the affinity of Black smokers and menthol cigarettes had been a major project of tobacco capitalism since the mid-1960s. And their activities on behalf of the industry provided pages and pages of answers to the question Chappelle posed. They knew, or had good theories to explain, how the social conditions, psychological worries, health concerns, and shrewd marketing tailored to the status anxieties of specifically urban Black people explained menthol's rise.

If advertising analysts from the firm Computer Field Express (CFE) had appeared on Chappelle's show, they would have told the story of menthols and Black America as a tale of exploitation. As CFE advised their client Liggett & Myers in 1971: "The Afro-American segment . . . is open to exploitation"; they lived in an urban landscape that was opening "new opportunities in the menthol cigarette market."[2] In the lingo of Madison Avenue advertising, *exploitation* was not an immoral behavior—it was a business reality. Exploitation merely meant that Black people, expanding in consumer and social influence with increasing centralization in so-called inner cities, were a market segment ripe for an aggressive sales push. In 1971 the marketing of menthol cigarettes in cities had been fierce already, for almost a decade. With a national ban on television and radio advertising of tobacco products about to take effect, the competition moving to billboards and public transportation was about to become even more intense. To participate in this exploitation, the CFE analysts explained, Liggett would need a brand that resonated with Black concerns, and to do that they would need to understand the social psychology of Black people—to "know Black people," as Chappelle put it. Building menthol markets involved studying the people, understanding the urban context including its particular drug scene, said CFE. It meant being attuned to human psychology, particularly African American consumer psychology. Branding also required understanding changing racial attitudes in the 1970s. In the view of the marketers, Americans were riven by identity conflict and political tensions. Some people were afflicted by "the Vietnam disease," still believing in the possibility of military victory. The youth of the "generation gap" felt they had "a better sense of values" than their elders. And people enamored of "the drug scene" clamored for "the legalization of marijuana." At every turn, identity was driving buying behaviors. It was in this last group—those in the drug scene—that CFE saw a growth opportunity for menthol smoking.

Moreover, the CFE analyst would have explained to Chappelle that the success of menthol was not about the pull (the "love" of menthol among any one group), but about the shrewdness of the push. As CFE concluded from surveys, the US public was divided on "the Negro problem." Some 9 percent of those surveyed believed in Black militancy and 22 percent hoped for better interracial understanding, as reflected by their support of interracial marriage. But a majority of Americans, 55 percent, embodied a "backlash" against these liberal trends, and another 5 percent expressed "militant, anti-negro racism." In the middle, so to speak, were so-called racial "crossover" segments—"negroes who would be white" and "whites who would be negro." Because these racial and social attitudes shaped their product preferences, all people's brand choices were prone to exploitation along these lines. The tensions were particularly obvious in menthol branding. As the market analysts told Liggett, a carved-up nation shaped the "carved up, segmented, and fractionated" menthol cigarette market. It had become a common refrain across the tobacco industry: to understand preferences for menthol brands (Kool, Salem, Newport, and so on) and to build those preferences, one needed to study not just Black attitudes, but also white attitudes toward Black people. Above all, one needed to understand how the smoking choices were defined by fundamental psychographic, social, and personality drivers peculiar to each group—men, women, Blacks, whites, ethnic groups, and so on. A misguided sales pitch to Black buyers ran the risk of turning off whites, who made up the majority of overall menthol smokers. In short, this was a complicated, varied, and ever-shifting racial market. Kool had become an industry leader in tapping into Black buyers. But whites also smoked Kool. Salem, by contrast, led in overall sales but lagged in the African American market, while other menthol brands trailed Kool in the Black sector. As CFE analysts saw matters, Brown & Williamson, the maker of Kool, apparently understood African American needs better than others and had figured out how to present Kool as a cigarette of choice and as a balm, a salve, and an antidote for what troubled Black Americans. One could not sell menthols without navigating this racial terrain.

How did this racial logic emerge? *Pushing Cool* centers on the analysts, marketers, scientists, and psychologists and their theories of health and race in the rise of menthol smoking. The story begins not as a tale of racial psychology but of a cigarette tailored to health anxiety in the 1920s—a tale in which race or innate love of menthol played no part. Indeed, if one had asked tobacco consultants, market psychologists, or insiders prior to 1960 "why do Black people love menthols so much," they would have been dumbfounded by the question. What "Negroes" had to do with menthol smoking was not even a question worth asking, never mind a truism of the menthol market. In their time, menthols were unquestionably about health reassurance. *Pushing Cool* follows the twisting path of how menthol's health promise became racialized or, rather, how the health promise became layered with new racial meaning as psychology researchers turned (four decades after the invention of menthol cigarettes) toward the embrace of racial marketing in the 1960s. In 1964 Brown & Williamson's Kool led the industry into this new urban market. Kool's rise coincided with the formation of the postwar "inner city"—a term that signified how cities and urban cultures were changing. Once Kool pushed into the urban Black market, other competitor brands soon followed. Why did this shift happen when it did? And why did menthols gain traction? At a time when many businesses fled the city, Big Tobacco flooded in and stayed behind, seeking to create new markets there, waging an increasingly intense battle to define menthol in racial terms.

Menthol's first market was not an ethnic one, but rather a health market. Only in the 1950s did the logic of menthol marketing shift, first to an intensification of health reassurance, then to youth marketing, and then finally—in its third chapter—to racial themes. As this narrative suggests, the logic of menthol marketing was deceptive, tricky, and ever-changing. The chapters ahead examine how the industry would refine its health messaging (menthols as a "healthy smoke") while turning aggressively to cultivate these new market segments—women's markets, youth markets, and then increasingly racial and ethnic urban buyers.

Tobacco companies did not act alone in the push. Their success hinged on shrewd partners—consultants like CFE, marketing firms, and social scientists coaching the industry on how to exploit opportunities. The psychologists in this enterprise knew that cigarettes thrived best in places of tension and anxiety. Big Tobacco's partners in Black communities also played a role in menthol's rise—newspaper publishers and powerful civil rights activists who allied themselves with the industry rather than recoiling from their outreach. Tobacco merchants eagerly worked with all of these influencers to study both health anxiety and racial ideals, to theorize race and masculinity, to sell menthol smoking as a feature of Black free choice and self-determination, and to engineer a stunning and worrisome transformation in consumer preferences.[3] The scheme's success can be told in numbers. In the 1930s, menthol cigarettes accounted for a mere 2 percent of the smoking market; by 2008, menthols represented more than 30 percent of cigarettes smoked in the United States. As late as the 1950s, one study suggested that Black smokers did not even like menthols, contrary to Chappelle's quip. But by the 1970s and into the twenty-first century, Black Americans made up a disproportionate segment of this booming consumer market. The story of how this transformation happened goes well beyond targeted marketing, to tell a sweeping tale of urban transformation, social entrapment, exploitation, and the rise of a form of racial capitalism that resulted in the long-term extraction of health from Black communities.[4]

To grow the market for menthol cigarettes required layered exploitation. And for this the industry relied on both in-house experts and hired consultants—to develop razor-sharp theories about buyers' likes and dislikes, and to study their psychological profiles and social status anxieties. The relentless challenge was how to tailor their products to keep these buyers coming back for more and also to recruit new smokers. In selling menthol cigarettes, consultants and companies crisscrossed and blurred the lines between cagey selling and deceit. Of course, nicotine was the most crucial element in the success of tobacco products, the primary addictive ingredient. But experts knew that menthol's impact on the body, the distinctive sensation it produces, also carried a potent meaning for smokers—a meaning they worked hard to exploit.

Menthol itself is a deception—a chemical obtained from the oil of the peppermint plant that delivers a distinctive cooling sensation in the nose and throat. The substance was a trick upon the senses, creating a perception of coolness and the feel of opening airways without actually changing temperature or enhancing airflow. Critics today see such flavorings as deliberate enticements to young smokers, and they worry over how the menthol sensation encourages deeper inhalation of tobacco smoke. Industry defenders of menthol cigarettes insist that their popularity among Black or white smokers is fundamentally about taste preferences. They see menthol's popularity as shaped by a pull; critics focus on the push. What many observers have not appreciated, however, is just how long, changing, and sophisticated the history of the menthol push has been. Long before the racial push, the original deception was in advertising menthol as a "safe" cigarette and also as a "therapeutic" for "smoker's throat." That is, menthol was presented as the answer to the very dangers associated with the increasing prevalence of cigarette smoking. Tobacco's hired consultants and its social scientists, psychologists, and health experts have long understood that these health meanings drive menthol's appeal. And so the question we should ask about the menthol push is when, where, and how did the industry first discover this health appeal? How did they cultivate it? And when did this artful health marketing cross the line into exploitation and predatory racial manipulation?

As I looked closely into the industry's menthol project, I came to understand that menthol's history is layered with trickery that takes one's breath away—both figuratively and literally. I also came to see menthol's ascent as exemplary of the broader story of racial capitalism in America. That is, it is a story of race and the economy of cities, of the racial profits to be made in the smoking business, and about the devices created for extracting wealth from Black communities even as they also extracted health from Black bodies.[5] The business tactics that helped companies develop Black menthol markets were not specific to African Americans. Yet the industry's commitment to understanding the African American social condition (in order to shape smoking preferences) is at once fascinating and frightening. If their studies of Black life had been done for any other purposes than for the selling of tobacco products, the depth of thought devoted to understanding race, the city, and society might be admirable. They studied the difficulties that Black people in cities confronted. They looked closely at the challenges of poverty, drug use, residential segregation, and urban decline—doing so to a remarkable degree. Big Tobacco's interest in these issues was not focused on ameliorating social ills, however. Their brand of racial capitalism looked at urban distress and social vulnerability in search of opportunity. With greater social adversity came the capacity for greater profits.[6]

Audacity defined the scheme. Sometimes, consultants' theories about race and menthol were keenly astute about racial attitudes, social changes, and taste. At other times, they were maddeningly offensive (such as views on menthol as a mask for Black body odor). Other theories they espoused were outlandish, even laughable—the kind of irreverent racial tropes that comedian Dave Chappelle might skewer or deploy. As CFE told Liggett in 1971, for example, menthol smoking had gained a foothold in Black America alongside the rise of heroin, and the analysts matter-of-factly saw some promising synergies. Other analysts of the time had also noted this convergence in drug use. CFE endorsed the idea that menthol branding should ride the wave of emerging so-called *hard drug* lifestyles. The leading brand "Kool . . . has attracted a group of indolent, young, psychedelic, 'drug-taking' Blacks," the company's analysts explained to Liggett. Kool had created a "drug franchise" and had acquired an image of being for "drug-prone male Blacks . . . unambitious, loafing and lazy in nature, with no interest in class."[7] To understand Kool's appeal, then, was to understand this culture of drug use in the 1960s and 1970s. In their view, LSD, heroin, or marijuana use was not a social crisis or a human problem. Nor were drugs merely symbols of youth rebellion and counterculture protest, as many saw them. To these consultants, heroin use was a type of urban consumerism that suggested market synergies and opportunity. How to leverage these synergies, that was the question. Kool users, according to CFE, "bite for the heavy, pungent, impact of an icy cooling taste—that is a 'half-way' house toward marijuana and heroin." As the analysts further explained, "Kool has the sense sharpening, the 'feel' that is the essence of menthol['s] narcotic image." This suggested an opening for a new Liggett brand. For Black people in the "drug culture," CFE advised, they might even be lured to a new menthol brand name that spoke unabashedly to their situation: "We . . . know that a direct, non-subtle approach to advertising pretty much 'works.' 'Halfway' is a possible name [for a new brand]."[8] If Kool was already a halfway house to other forms of drug use and if Kools were already integrated into marijuana and heroin drug cultures, then why not make the pitch explicitly in a new menthol brand? Shocking as CFE's proposal was, this outlook was quite commonplace. Studying the simultaneous use of menthol and other drugs was just one of the many crafty schemes that consultants envisioned for embedding the taste for menthol.

As tobacco consultants might have explained to Chappelle's audience, the active substance in menthol cigarettes carried several social or psychological meanings—and not only to Black people. Long before menthol marketing's racial turn, Kool and the first menthol brand, Spud, had spent decades homing in on menthol as a remedy to health worries. That health deception never stopped. Menthol had always packed a powerful health promise based on the drug's cooling sensation. As CFE informed Liggett, people "smoke menthols for specific health remedies of colds, sore throats, coughs, throat irritations, and cure of the bad mouth feel of staleness."[9] People without health worries also loved menthols. For many smokers, however, menthol's cooling sensation *felt* healthful, and companies had pitched them as health promoting for decades. The cooling "healthful" quality had been a long-standing marketing deception. To be clear, menthol cigarettes carried no true health benefits, yet their rising popularity starting back in the 1920s hinged on their image as a "safe" type of smoking and as medication. Throughout the decades, the industry and its analysts worked hard to reinforce these therapeutic associations. Indeed, this view gained increased salience in the 1950s when the connection between smoking and cancer became established. Worried smokers looked to the industry for reassurance, flocked to menthols, and turned menthol brands into lucre. The therapeutic promise remained an important part of cultivating new markets. Even nonsmokers knew about the signature cool sensation when menthol entered the mouth and appreciated "the 'numbing, anesthetizing' effects of menthol on the throat." As CFE pointed out, smokers had internalized the advertising messaging. They had psychologically conjured menthol as a "medicinal drug," seeing it as a drug with "narcotics [themes] involving psychological lift." So the lift of menthol—as a drug, a medical salve, and a racial preference—worked across multiple registers. The downfall of many menthol brands, said CFE, was because they promised none of the specific health/throat benefits (anesthetizing, numbing, freezing) "credited to Kool."[10]

What about women and other groups of menthol smokers? Did they also love menthols? Were their anxieties also exploitable? With R. J. Reynolds's Salem Menthols used heavily by white women, a common theory in the business held that they were drawn not to the drug appeal or the "lift" purportedly pulling Black smokers to Kool, but to the hygienic and breath-freshening qualities of this lighter menthol brand. Stereotypes of race and gender pervaded the industry. CFE pointed out that Liggett's new brand, Eve, had sought to exploit this feminine menthol appeal. But Eve's difficulties highlighted that gender or race marketing, by itself, did not ensure success. Eve turned out to be deficient in other registers; it "has virtually no image other than that it is a new, highly feminine, flower-loving, possibly perfumy menthol brand." To sell effectively, one needed to understand feminine as well as masculine anxieties at a deeper level, not to mention how gender and health worries intersected.

Everywhere, regardless of race and gender, the issue of health reassurance remained an undercurrent to menthol's appeal. At their core, menthol brands offered one thing that normal cigarettes could not—a health promise. Menthol cigarettes were a singular type of commodity. Commodities, as Igor Kopytoff once explained, were never fixed; they were "inevitably ambiguous and open to the push and pull of events and desires, as [they] shuffled about in the flux of social life."[11] Branding menthols was all about exploiting unstable situations for profit. As CFE analysts put it, "Benson and Hedges has a menthol class position but the essential health component has escaped [its maker] Philip Morris." The cigarette psychologists were ever-alert to the pulls and pushes of desires, and ready to provide balms for these anxieties of identity and health.

For CFE, then, it was not love but opportunism of different kinds that created menthol markets. CFE's frank incitement to predatory exploitation was blatant and unapologetic, but also quite typical of tobacco's business culture. To associate the "high" of menthol with heroin and marijuana in the consumer's psyche, the new menthol product called Halfway must be presented "in a nonsubtle way." Today such corporate targeting comes across as a devious, indeed shameful, plot. In 1971, however, there was no shame. CFE's frank invitation to exploit along lines of race and drug use to make new markets was commonplace chicanery. Decades later, when confronted with such studies in court trials taking aim at the deception, CEOs like RJR's Andrew Schindler tried to distance themselves from such practices. But at the time, few in tobacco's business culture would have been embarrassed by the idea of a menthol called Halfway. The history of menthol smoking cannot be fully understood without studying closely the history of that corporate culture—a marketing culture reaching for new heights even as it dove to new depths of deception.

These schemes of menthol marketing can be found in the industry's records, which reveal hundreds of such behind-the-scenes examples of corporate race work. Some of it is blunt and laughable racial theorizing. But many researchers and consultants offered astute analyses of Black life that lay the groundwork for inventive forms of market exploitation. Of course, these market-making practices, many of them indeed shameful and blatant in their manipulation, were not unique to Big Tobacco. Other industries like alcohol manufacturers were busily wrapping their webs around Black urban consumers as well. They turned to the same pollsters, psychology consultants, and advertising firms that served cigarette interests. Pharmaceutical companies worked from a similar playbook in the 1960s, 1970s, 1980s, and 1990s as they branded new drug products to influence physician prescribing behavior and forge new patient markets.[12] Indeed, the parallels across these drug-selling sectors in the selling of race products and the making of race are striking. Whether the products are prescription drugs—such as Ritalin, OxyContin, or BiDil, later billed as a race-specific drug for treating heart failure—or menthol cigarettes, the strategies of influence making, building markets, and shoring them up (the push) were similar.[13] These practices might remain hidden for decades, only visible to the public in the advertising. It would take nearly two decades, for example, for Purdue Pharma's sophisticated push of OxyContin to produce a nationwide opioid crisis, followed by investigations of their practices that would pull back the curtain. Then came criminal charges and admissions of culpability.[14] Disclosure revealed how deceitful tactics and skillful marketing to physicians helped to build those drug markets, and eventually create a heavy toll in addiction and lost lives. Big Tobacco, of course, had led the way in developing and refining these audacious strategies of market making.

In studying how menthol markets emerged, my attention became fixed on hundreds of researchers in operations like CFE and how industry insiders studied group psychology in a canny and calculating way. In business records, human crises (drug use, economic distress, fears of cancer, poverty) were opportunities. These approaches to market making defined the cigarette industry. Finding and exploiting vulnerabilities became keys to unlocking new markets. To make this scheme work, a vast and growing cadre of consultants—CFE and many others—was necessary. They worked out of public view. Their private corporate communications were never meant for wider circulation, but lawsuits in the 1980s and 1990s dramatically altered this private-public divide. In the 1998 Master Settlement Agreement, seven companies agreed to change the way they marketed tobacco products, pay over $200 billion to the states filing suits, and finance a $1.5 billion public health campaign. In the aftermath, millions of documents provided to state attorneys general led to the creation of an archive at the University of California, San Francisco. The Legacy Tobacco Documents Library, created in 2002, has since been renamed the Tobacco Truth Industry Documents and permanently houses the internal corporate documents produced during the litigation.[15] Today these once-private schemes are searchable by any citizen. They provide the raw material for new, previously untold stories of how menthol brands leveraged social crises in cities and found partners who helped to woo new consumers and secure new markets. In opening private corporate practices to the public view, a vast archive of business stratagems (some cynical, some laughable, some predatory, and some of them brimming with crass stereotypes) has since received extensive scrutiny. And over the past decades, a rich literature has blossomed focused on the industry's schemes and tactics—its manipulation of nicotine levels, its efforts to reach a youth market, its strategies for building political influence, and so on. Through this archive, new questions can be posed and answered: Was CFE alone in hatching such a devious scheme to pitch menthol as a therapeutic "lift" or a drug of choice? What other forms of predation did consultants and industry promote, and how did menthol's targets shift over time? How vast was the plot to shape inner-city markets in this fashion? And what precisely were the turning points on the industry's crooked path (as menthol makers first rose in the 1920s and 1930s, as they confronted 1950s news about cancer and smoking, and as they sought to market along racial lines in the 1960s)?

Predatory Influencers and the "House of Menthol"

Increasingly strict regulations of cigarettes from the 1950s onward played a surprisingly important role in creating these urban markets. It was exactly in those years of expanding anti-cigarette laws, rising taxes, and bans on television and radio advertising that tobacco firms proved to be masterful at finding new ways to compensate for lost menthol markets by cultivating new ones. When the youth market was threatened by advancing regulations, they turned attention to the Black inner-city market. Here is a critical irony of this story of menthol as a racial product: with every victory by government in regulating cigarette ads targeting youth and the general public, these developments led tobacco companies more and more to exploit racial markets. When television ads were banned, urban billboards sprung up and ads in Black newspapers flourished. Regulators were, in a sense, unwitting influencers. Uneven government actions shaped the market in new ways, helping drive companies aggressively into the sphere of racial marketing and urban exploitation. Along the crooked mile, the industry also cultivated political supporters in the Black community. The story of racial capitalism is not, therefore, a one-sided affair of white exploitation or government pitted against the private sector. The rise of menthol smoking could not have occurred without government. Early in the twentieth century, in fact, the federal government's breakup of the American Tobacco monopoly had created the opportunity for the first company selling menthols to arise. Throughout the following decades, menthol smoking could not have prospered without such regulatory influences or without allies.

To understand menthol smoking's traction in Black urban America, one must grapple with the influence of men like *Ebony* magazine publisher John H. Johnson, the NAACP's Benjamin Hooks, and even, most recently, the staunch civil rights activist Al Sharpton. These stalwart supporters of racial equality and justice also, perversely, helped secure the tobacco industry's hold on its Black franchise. Invited to opine on why Black people love menthols so much, they, too, would have much to say. At different times in menthol smoking's history, they pushed back against tobacco restrictions, defended the industry, railed against banning cigarette billboards, and (most recently) lobbied aggressively against a proposed ban on menthol cigarettes. As vocal industry supporters, they adeptly portrayed menthol smoking as a legitimate Black preference rooted in Black consumer taste.

Moreover, they often insisted that banning menthol cigarettes would therefore be discriminatory and even racist—this was Hooks's argument regarding billboards in 1990. Decades later, Reverend Sharpton alleged that a proposed menthol cigarette ban would produce an underground market and that the resulting police actions against Black smokers would only have one tragic outcome: putting Black lives at greater risk. At other times, civil rights advocates argued that a ban on workplace smoking would be racially discriminatory. A full history of pushing cool in America could not be told without close attention to these free choice, pro-menthol arguments and to the potent role of Black publishers and civil rights groups (often funded by industry) in this exploitative game of racial capitalism. Their influence stretched from newspaper advertising to the halls of Congress, and they remain major forces sustaining menthol cigarettes as race products.

Whatever the role of Black publishers and civil rights figures in menthol's ascent, the road to menthol fortunes started within the industry—with the work of people like the Philip Morris economist Myron Johnston. These insiders and influencers figure prominently in this study. Johnston spent decades dissecting the racial, psychological, and social logic of menthol smoking, or tracking, as he once called it, the "strange happenings in the menthol market."[16] By the early 2000s, his work would become evidence against the industry in lawsuits alleging corporate deception. But for much of his career, Johnston worked quietly out of the public spotlight, helping the industry giant to break into the lucrative menthol market. As Johnston once explained, the positive social image of Black youth in the 1960s had expanded the base of Kool. In those years, he observed, "young blacks were the trend setters and young whites were copying them in everything from clothing styles to music to language and behavior patterns. This, plus the generation gap, is why Kool became the brand of choice among young white menthol smokers." But by the 1970s, Kool's drug associations undercut this appeal, and in the increasingly conservative climate of the 1980s, Johnston sensed a shift in racial attitudes that were cutting into Kool's fortunes, while rebounding to benefit Philip Morris. Now that "[race] relations are more strained,"

Johnston wrote in 1985, white youth seemed less inclined to emulate Black consumption trends. Kool was losing white smokers, and Philip Morris's Marlboro, which had struggled to make inroads with its menthol brand, was seeing a rise. Race underpinned sales trends: "[Young] Marlboro smokers who might otherwise have been tempted to switch to a menthol have stuck with Marlboro, while other young whites who might otherwise have started on a menthol have rejected the black image of menthols and have started with Marlboro instead."[17] The tobacco business was filled with students of race and smoking like CFE and Johnston. These researchers conducted psychographic studies of smokers, scrutinized their social attitudes, generated psychological profiles of important consumer segments, and produced insights into health worries, vulnerabilities, and aspirations that shaped messaging. Supporting the industry were companies with names like the Institute for Motivational Research, the Psychological Corporation, and Marketing Research, Inc.—an army of experts that grew in numbers and influence as the menthol market expanded.

Race and race-making was their business—one of the primary focuses of this influence network. Reading their schemes, one is simultaneously fascinated and repulsed by their sweeping studies of race. Yet the intelligence they gathered was rich and formidable. Researchers gathered insights from the streets and studied responses to brand images and billboard signage. They asked shopkeepers about local purchasing trends and followed closely racial attitudes, down to the neighborhood level at times. Visiting West Harlem stores in the 1950s, for example, a Black interviewer hired by the Roper Organization sought to gather local intelligence for their client, Philip Morris. The interviewer learned from one African American proprietor, Mack Austin, why the company should put pretty Black women on cigarette posters: "See, colored people seeing those get the idea that the company is giving those [Black] kids a break—which means that they are giving the colored people a break—and I think that's a smart public relations move."[18] But Austin also stressed the importance of placing those ads within sight of white viewers. Such interviews highlighted what advertising imagery meant to people, and how deeply tobacco imagery was entangled with the broader politics of representation and respect. Researchers used such interviews, focus group discussions, and social analysis to extract useful intelligence, and the data also informed and shaped marketing strategies.

Gathering such data, industry experts tried at every turn to tap into the social psychology of the moment. In so doing they learned, for example, that menthol was not only about selling Blackness to Black people but also about trafficking in whiteness, femininity, and masculinity, as well as constantly navigating racial hostilities. As CFE explained to Liggett in 1971, "Kent Menthol . . . [the Lorillard brand] has a natural allegiance for the civilized White 'male supremacist.'" How, analysts asked, should companies use such knowledge? Menthol marketers studied America's racial affinities and hostilities in strikingly intimate terms—for the purpose of selling more smokes. According to CFE, one option available to Liggett was to follow the Philip Morris Marlboro model when it shrewdly turned the minor feminine brand into a product with a stark white, masculine image in the 1950s. But in 1971, they counseled, this white masculine strategy carried too many risks. Across the years, such consultants understood that success in branding involved artfully navigating these white and Black perceptions of self and other. Often, however, theories of menthol crossed over into the absurd, as when one infamous 1970 Lorillard memo titled "Why Menthols" suggested that stereotypical Black body odor was an explanation for menthol appeal—that is, they wondered if Black people turned to menthols as a response to the racist belief that they were "possessed by an almost genetic body odor . . . [and] smoke menthols to make their breath feel fresh?"[19] Cigarette psychologists and social scientists absorbed and worked with all of these racial theories in their studies of race and taste.

To me, these corporate professionals are akin with the "ghost-readers" described in William Maxwell's *F.B. Eyes*—men employed in J. Edgar Hoover's FBI to closely read African American literature, anticipate political unrest, and even nurture a deceptive "counterliterature."[20] Big Tobacco's readers of Black culture were a more scattered and decentralized bunch, looking not to shut down unrest, but to channel it. As with Maxwell's FBI story, public disclosure made it possible to visualize this work and the webs of influence, but only after millions of documents were opened up by either FOIA requests or lawsuits.[21] Many of the sources for this book comes from this Tobacco Truth Industry Documents archive, offering unprecedented insight into the machinations of preference formation. Other sources included the personal papers of influencers like Ernest Dichter, founder of the Institute for Motivational Research and renowned consultant across multiple industries, as well as the papers of critics such as Vance Packard; newspaper coverage over the century; medical and scientific writing on menthol as a drug, medicine, and flavor; evidence gathered in congressional hearings, regulatory settings, and other court cases; the vast advertising and business literature; and archival collections relating to billboard advertising and Kool jazz festivals.[22] Through these sources, we can follow the issues that the industry studied during the menthol cigarette's rise. We learn what they were discovering about menthol's meanings from focus groups, and what billboard placement and imagery meant to viewers. We also learn how they monitored radio call-in shows, tracked the rise of local movements resistant to their products, and worked to combat rumors harmful to their products. Through these sources and archives, we can see the American society that the industry saw and also examine how the network of psychologists and social scientists expanded to sustain menthol smoking in that changing society.

These influencers included industry-leading figures like Dichter, pollsters like the Roper Organization and Gallup, market research companies, psychology firms, social science outfits, and many others. Their strategies ranged from man-on-the-street interviews to so-called "depth interviews" or psychographic studies, as well as deeper sociological study of how behaviors were influenced. They studied consumers' ability to recall radio jingles, as well as consumer responses to imagery, their health fears, and many underlying concerns. These firms' questions and strategies evolved with the times; so, too, did their targets.[23] It was these scientists, for example, who helped industry identify the menthol smoker as a social and psychological type in the wake of what they called the "cancer scare" and to develop a strategy of selling menthols using promises of safety and security. But in time, what had begun as a menthol *health* project transformed into a sophisticated and sweeping *racial* project capitalizing on the forces shaping Black life in the "inner city." It is here that the "house of menthol" would be built, with devastating implications to this day.

Toward a Menthol Ban

In following the strange trajectory of the menthol cigarette through American business and consumer culture, I ask five questions.

First, how did menthol smoking's rise (long before its racial turn) depend on an underlying and deceitful therapeutic promise? This question is taken up in chapters 1 and 2. From the very start, marketers knew that health anxieties figured prominently for smokers, with the first upsurge of mass smoking in the 1920s producing worries over throat irritation. The health concerns created an opening for menthol cigarettes. Two decades later, the rise in smoking rates after World War II was accompanied by another set of concerns, this time over cancer. Once again, health anxieties benefited menthol cigarette makers like Brown & Williamson, who understood the therapeutic meaning associated with their product. The deceptive therapeutic message was suggested in advertisements, when Kool's well-known cartoon Willie the Penguin promised smokers relief from "Smoker's Throat," or when Willie promised in the 1950s: "When April showers make you cough like crazy, refreshing KOOLS taste fresh as a daisy! Got a cough, Switch from 'hots' to KOOLS as your steady smoke for that clean, KOOL taste!"

One cannot fully understand menthol smoking's upward trajectory without studying how menthol makers trafficked in the imagery of a "clean" smoke, providing a medical salve. As chapter 2 shows, the "cancer scares" created additional opportunities for menthol brands to burnish these "health"-oriented appeals, aiming them particu-

Figure I.1. Willie the Penguin, the mascot of Kool from the 1930s into the 1950s. The cartoon figure illustrates the way advertising equated smoking Kool cigarettes with therapy and relief, an enduring and deceptive promise underpinning the menthol appeal.
Credit: From the collection of Stanford Research Into the Impact of Tobacco Advertising (tobacco .stanford.edu).

larly at the health-anxious consumer. On the basis of those appeals, menthol cigarettes climbed from less than 5 percent of the cigarette market in 1955 to 15 percent by the early 1960s.

Second, what explains the turn in menthol marketing toward themes of youth, race, and gender in the 1950s, and why did the corporate competition for poor, urban, Black smokers intensify so aggressively and rapidly in the 1960s? In the 1950s R. J. Reynolds's new Salem Menthol appeared, and its fortunes rocketed upward, forcing Kool, the older Brown & Williamson brand, to refine its outmoded pitch. As chapter 3 shows, Kool surged back in the 1960s, surpassing Salem to become the industry leader—doing so by way of a bold new campaign aimed at Black Americans. The shift was aided by the rise of a new cadre of marketing psychologists who drove menthol advertising toward population segments vulnerable to the menthol appeal. But government policies also played a major role, as restrictions on youth marketing increased after the 1964 Surgeon General's report *Smoking and Health*—intensifying menthol marketers' drive into the inner city. The year 1964 would be decisive in menthol's racial pivot as the industry responded to the rising tide of legislation and regulation on youth smoking by cultivating other markets. For Kool, the most dynamic

Menthol Percent Share of Cigarette Market, 1950-2016

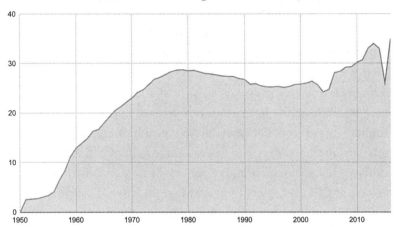

Figure I.2. Menthol cigarette sales as a percentage of the total cigarette market, 1950–2016. The shift to menthol smoking coincided with growing evidence of the health dangers of smoking and with the industry's new approaches to health and racial marketing.
Credit: Data compiled from *Printer's Ink, The Maxwell Report,* and FTC documentation.

new franchise became African Americans; for Salem, the target remained white women. By the late 1960s, however, the entire industry had come to see urban Blacks as the primary growth segment.

Third, as the competition became more centered on questions of race, the inner city, and the ghetto, what other actors assisted in building the industry's web of influence? As chapter 4 shows, building deep connections to Black communities involved far more than aggressive marketing; it also involved robust support for Black fashion and education in the 1960s and 1970s, sponsorship of urban jazz festivals, advertising in struggling Black newspapers in the 1980s, winning support for urban economic partnerships with organizations like the NAACP, and buying silence by political donations to prominent African American elected officials. The embedding of preferences thus went far beyond advertising; it involved cementing these relationships and building a web of influencers. This web allowed menthol marketing to withstand criticism and to shore up menthol smoking in times of industry stress. Even with the nationwide ban on television advertising of all tobacco, menthol advertising would surge in cities, finding new opportunities and catalyzing the rise of the urban billboard, shaping urban vistas as a symbol of the industry's dominance.

Fourth, how did the work of these influencers (the pollsters, market researchers like Dichter, advertising executives, economists like John-ston, psychologists, and social scientists) embed new tastes, and how did they create and project new forms of "authentic" Black identity? Over time, the industry dedicated vast resources to a peculiar kind of "race studies"—a perverse mirror of the type of multidisciplinary university scholarship that gave rise to the academic field of African American studies. This corporate brand of race studies examined not only drug culture as CFE did; they studied whiteness, white alienation, suburban youth emulation of racial styles, Black masculinity, urban social structure, street-corner influence making, responses of Blacks and whites to racial imagery, and more. They studied all of these aspects of race in the United States in order to understand the consumer's mind, and also to better sell menthol cigarettes. The so-called "inner city" became a primary topic of study. As the Chicago protester and billboard vandal known as Mandrake later astutely observed, companies "try to package the image of being champions of the downtrodden, the image of credibility," when they were really "the pushers of drugs of illusion which has the side effect of diminishing the opportunities for real success."[24] Such criticism only became prominent in the 1980s—long after menthol smoking had become embedded and tied to Black identity.

Fifth, how did the movement to ban menthol cigarettes emerge and expand in influence? As chapter 5 shows, the political and legal currents shifted in the 1990s when critics took to the courts and when state attorneys general also took aim at the industry's marketing practices. By the 1990s, state governments faced with rising Medicaid costs found that they were now responsible for covering the health care costs of thousands of men and women whose bodies had been devastated by decades of cigarette consumption. The industry's private gains had produced massive public burdens and the legal bill was coming due. Public health activism against the industry and its targeted marketing flourished, buoyed by local outrages—most notably the intense

SURGEON GENERAL'S WARNING: Cigarette Smoke Contains Carbon Monoxide.

Figure I.3. Kool advertisement overlaying the cigarette brand with the marketer's carefree vision of Black male coolness, circa 2005.
Credit: From the collection of Stanford Research Into the Impact of Tobacco Advertising (tobacco .stanford.edu).

backlash in 1990 surround R. J. Reynolds's new Uptown brand, aimed explicitly at Black smokers. Here was another turning point. With the industry lurching from scandal to scandal, pressure for more restrictions (including possibly a menthol ban) came into view. In their defense of now-besieged markets and products like menthols, the industry would rely again on a web of supporters they had cultivated over the years, among them influential congressmen like New York's

Edolphus Towns, leaders of the NAACP like Benjamin Hooks, and Black newspaper publishers. Their arguments continue to resonate today, in still-unfolding clashes with public health reformers in cities, states, and at the federal level over proposed bans to menthol cigarette smoking.

The chapters of menthol's journey through American commercial culture follow the outlines of the English nursery rhyme that starts: *There was a crooked man and he walked a crooked mile.* The rhyme is an allegory, according to some sources, about the making of strained political alliances between England and Scotland. In this book, however, the *crooked man* is menthol itself—the chemical obtained from peppermint oil that gives the feeling of coolness to the nose and throat, a drug that warps and "perverts" sensation. Menthol found its way into myriad products to become a recognized article of commerce principally because of its strong therapeutic associations. As the rhyme continues, *He found a crooked sixpence upon a crooked stile,* or a fence. It was, after all, a chance happening—the cancer news and the "health scares" of the 1950s and 1960s—that produced unexpected new fortunes for menthol makers. The *crooked stile* was the jagged and uncertain line separating Blacks from whites, urbanites from suburbanites, that became the setting for new commercial pitches. The famous rhyme continues by shining a light on the crooked man's fellow travelers: *He bought a crooked cat and it caught a crooked mouse,* describing the industry's embrace of Black civic groups, its use of jazz motifs (literally cool cats), and urban coolness as a marketing strategy in the 1970s. The new Black urban landscape beckoned; and, at the very moment when "inner-city" economies were declining, jobs were disappearing, and employment options were dimming, tobacco became a more vital, visible presence than ever before. Menthol's *crooked mouse* was the powerful Black civic organizations like the NAACP and well-positioned, influential politicians whose support allowed menthol cigarettes to evade bans and criticism, to become further embedded in Black communities. The rhyme concludes, *And they all lived together in a little crooked house,* thus putting onstage the web of supporters who built over the years this "house of menthol," a slogan developed by Brown & Williamson. The "crookedness" in menthol's history is not merely corruption, but something far broader. Menthol's path was truly a twisting tale, with sharp turns, chance occurrences, and unlikely brokered relationships.

Should menthol cigarettes be banned? When Dave Chappelle aired his menthol skit in 2004, this question had just begun to surface in cities and states. Calls grew in subsequent years. In debates about banning this brand of cigarette, the question of exploitation remains a central question—that is, whether a Black preference for menthol smoking was cultivated through malignant practices or whether these preferences came about by the exercise of free choice (an argument made publicly by the industry). The word "exploitation" (a term used privately by influencers themselves) captures both meanings. This book can be understood then as a cultural history of market making and exploitation.

This question of exploitation and how preferences and markets were created carries enormous importance today as cities and states enact menthol bans, and the nation moves toward implementing one as well. Since 2009, when President Barack Obama signed a new law that banned flavored cigarettes and handed the Food and Drug Administration (FDA) jurisdiction over tobacco products as drugs, the ban question has loomed large. But the 2009 law itself was a stunning example of the enduring power of Big Tobacco's web of influence and the broad reach of exploitation. When Congress banned flavored tobacco products, the law exempted menthols (which, the *New York Times* reported, "masks the harshness of tobacco and accounts for about one-quarter of the market").[25] Some members of the Congressional Black Caucus had orchestrated the exemption.[26] The legislation moved the question of menthol cigarettes' fate to the FDA, where the agency's deliberations have been marked by legal threats from industry, political threats from industry supporters, and stalemate. Meanwhile states and localities, and indeed entire nations, have banned menthol cigarettes and taken aim at flavored e-cigarettes. In 2016 the Canadian Parliament banned menthols, following provincial bans in Alberta and Nova Scotia. In June 2017, San Francisco passed a ban.

Hundreds of cities and two states have followed. The UK announced a ban to take full effect in 2020.

As the conclusion describes, opponents of such bans portray these prohibitions as an assault on the freedom to choose, and more pointedly they have warned of the consequences to Black lives should bootleg menthol cigarettes become subject to police and law enforcement oversight, invoking the police killing of Eric Garner while being restrained merely for selling cigarettes on a New York street corner as a warning for what a menthol ban might mean for Black people. Whether such statements unfairly exploit Garner's death, or whether they reasonably describe the threat of banning menthols, remains heatedly debated.

The truth, of course, is that the suffocation of Black lives has been happening not only by police chokeholds, but also by menthol smoking. One is a shocking, violent sudden attack; the second has been a slow assault unfolding over decades, a slow deprivation of breathing brought about by an economic logic this book seeks to describe. The history of menthol is therefore a layered tragedy. I close the book by asking what it means that cigarettes were at the scene not only of the murder of Eric Garner, killed by a police chokehold in 2014 while pleading, "I can't breathe," but also that menthol cigarettes were there when George Floyd was killed in 2020 with a policeman's knee on his neck.[27] In the months surrounding his death, the COVID-19 pandemic also assaulted the breathing and disproportionately ended the lives of African Americans. Nothing about how menthol arrived at these tragic scenes was accidental or inevitable. Along menthol's long road, we meet many travelers whose deceptions aided the push—the rise of menthol smoking in these urban settings. The story of how experts and industry worked to shape preferences adds up to a strong argument—a specifically *historical* case—for banning the menthol cigarette. But in order to make that case, we must go back to where the crooked road begins.

1

Selling the Menthol Sensation

On a June day in 1934, Madison Avenue adman Carl Spier ventured onto the Yale University campus in New Haven, Connecticut, in search of physiologist Yandell Henderson. The adman was seeking help in defending his client's Kool cigarette brand against a scurrilous rumor. Working for the influential advertising company Batten, Barton, Durstine & Osborn (BBDO), Spier had come to Yale on behalf of the Brown & Williamson Tobacco Company, whose Kool mentholated cigarettes had appeared on the market only a year earlier but now stood accused by competitors of carrying risks to human health.[1] Spier had hoped to talk with Henderson, whose laboratory of applied physiology had developed considerable expertise in analyzing the human body's responses to gases, drugs, and other substances like the cigarette. But the renowned Henderson apparently wanted no part of the meeting and sent his junior colleague Howard Haggard in his place. It was a rough first meeting as the scientist eyed the adman suspiciously. Despite the tense beginning, the session launched a fraught long-term affair between the advertising representative and the human physiology expert, a partnership forged in service of defending the Kool brand. Over the next few years, the relationship would also illuminate for Haggard and Spier the role of science in sustaining an industry deception.[2]

Rumors that menthol irritated the throat and that it amounted to a kind of "doping" threatened to destroy the fledging brand; this was Brown & Williamson's worry. Working to clear Kool, here was Spier's question for the laboratory: Was the menthol in B&W's Kool cigarettes a dangerous additive, was it harmless, or was it perhaps (as many believed) health promoting? The laboratory's answer had implications not only for B&W but also the entire tobacco industry because every company was fending off charges that "smoker's throat" (a rising tide of throat irritation) was caused by rising rates of smoking. Every company sought to outdo the competition in the battle to reassure consumers that their product carried a remedy that relieved.

Spier's visit to Yale carried an air of urgency. Besides the accusations from competitors, B&W faced the threat of government regulation. But more important, B&W was a small company swimming with the giant sharks of the tobacco industry in one of the country's largest commercial sectors.[3] Cigarette sales were booming. Kool was a tiny player in this million-dollar market, a niche product. At the time of Spier's Yale trip, Kool accounted for less than 2 percent of cigarette sales nationwide. It was no threat to industry leaders like Lucky Strike or any of the Big Five companies. Nor was Kool the first menthol cigarette on the market—that honor went to Axton-Fisher's Spud, which was first marketed in the mid-1920s. Spier understood that the question of menthol's effect on physiology was complex and could not be answered in one sitting. As Haggard explained, it would be months before the lab issued a report. Spier was willing to wait. He would stay in close contact with the Yale lab, as the menthol question hung in a thick mist over the company, the physiologist, and the American smoker for months, and then years, to follow.[4]

It was not Kool's minuscule sales that constituted a threat to the industry giants eying the upstart firm cautiously; they worried about Kool's health message. B&W's marketing pitch claimed that Kool would soothe and calm the throats that had been irritated by all those other brands. By the early 1930s, throat irritation had become such an industry-wide worry that every brand aggressively pitched its own forms of "relief." Lucky Strike, for example, promoted itself as easier on the throat because its tobacco was toasted. For its part, the makers of Kool offered menthol smoking as a distinctively therapeutic break from the normal smoker's routine, like sucking on a menthol lozenge or gargling with mouthwash. Kool was medication mixed with tobacco. Of the Big Five companies, Philip Morris seemed to resent the B&W marketing message the most, annoyed by the implication that their own product had caused the irritation that Kool would relieve. To retaliate against such claims, Philip Morris allegedly spread—through the medical press—its own rumors about menthol as a harmful irritant. This devious charge, and the damage it could do to the Kool brand, had brought Spier to Yale.

Spier and his client hoped to use scientific expertise and the reputation of Henderson's laboratory to put to rest these competitor-generated rumors of menthol as an unsafe irritant. The first meeting began with mutual suspicion partly because Spier resented being handed off to Henderson's junior collaborator Howard Haggard. In turn, Haggard looked skeptically at the adman; the scientist distrusted Madison Avenue's willingness to say anything and to use science in any way possible to make a sale. Spier's annoyance eased somewhat when Haggard explained that he was there in Henderson's place simply because he, Haggard, had the expertise to conduct the research that could settle the menthol question. But Haggard remained on guard. He explained that he been burned once before by a deceitful advertising firm when the William Esty Company had misused one of his published findings in an advertisement for Camel cigarettes. The Haggard-Spier meeting thus began, as Spier recounted, "with a slightly acrimonious thrust at the Esty Co." for turning the lab's published work on the effect of smoking on sugar content in the blood into the catchy claim that "Camels give you a lift."[5]

Haggard would have no part in selling the menthol sensation to smokers, he declared. He was only interested in the truth about menthol rather than slick advertising, believing that the advertiser would respect that line in the sand. As Spier described the discussion, the lab was "willing to put the resources of Yale . . . behind any study that

Figure 1.1. Howard Haggard of the Yale Laboratory of Applied Physiology, whose laboratory studied menthol effects for Brown & Williamson. The drug produced a "perversion of sensation," he concluded.
Credit: Yale University, Harvey Cushing/John Hay Whitney Medical Library.

tended to bring forth a general truth about mentholated cigarettes." But Haggard refused to conduct research for the purpose of contributing to marketing pitches or enhancing sales. "As Dr. Haggard put it without prompting from me," said Spier, "'We would like to convince ourselves of the exact truth about menthol so that we could take the witness stand and give it as our opinion that menthol in cigarettes has absolutely no harmful effect on smokers.'"[6] Spier's eyes must have lit up at the thought that the Yale laboratory's "exact truth" might produce such a sweeping claim of menthol smoking's safety, one that might stand up in any court.

Their first conversation began like an opening gambit in a chess match, and then evolved into a tentative and suspicious dance between truth and deception; before it went sour, the relationship would play out over years starting in the 1930s, with important implications for how menthol smoking gained a foothold in the market and how menthol brands defended against attacks.[7] Although neither party knew it at the time, the questions of menthol's harmfulness, the role of science in its defense, and the industry's marketing deception would continue for years, winding from the Yale laboratory and one day—decades into the future—truly ending up in the courts. When the legal case against menthol was finally heard, the types of relationships forged in New Haven would receive careful scrutiny.

But what was the truth about menthol? To Haggard, the "exact truth" was that menthol was itself a deceptive chemical. This deception has much to do with how menthol smoking found its niche amid the industry's internal battles over smoker's throat. Another truth is that in these early years, the collaboration of admen and scientists was critically important to crafting defenses of the product, studying which smokers were vulnerable to the menthol appeal, and laying the groundwork for tapping into the health worries of the time.

In the Company of Drugs

"Menthol itself is not a drug that has been much gone into," Spier explained in a June 1934 letter to BBDO executives after the Haggard meeting.[8] There was broad consensus that menthol was a drug, and a tricky one at that. Beyond that, Spier acknowledged, "No one knows very much about the actual effect of smoking [menthol] on the system." Many questions remained: How benign was this substance being added to lozenges, medical kits, and many other products, including cigarettes? What were its exact effects on the throat, the nasal passages, and health? How potent was it? And, most importantly, how safe was it, especially if inhaled and passed over the mucous membrane of the throat into the lungs?

Used as medicine for decades before, menthol was well known to doctors and the general public as a drug that produced the sensation of cooling on the mouth and throat. In the heyday of germ theory and bacteriology, it was also known as a germ killer with mild antiseptic powers. But perhaps menthol's most notable quality was its ability to deceive the brain with that feeling of coolness in the throat, nose, and some other parts of the body—a physiological response that convinced people that their parched throats were actually being "cooled" or their congested airways widened. In reality, the temperature of the throat did not change at all and the level of congestion remained unchanged; menthol played tricks on perception. Haggard later concluded that menthol was "a perversion of sensation" that produced no actual drop in temperature and no widening of the airways, and yet left a distinctive feeling of relief.[9]

As of 1934, products also used menthol to mask flavors with its distracting, cooling sensation, even as its physiological character and the source of its effect were open to debate. Was menthol an effective drug or a deceptive one, or both at the same time? In truth, the answer was "all of the above." Haggard, Spier, and the consumer products regulators who were keenly attuned to all kinds of flagrant deception and drug pitches in the marketplace knew that menthol's identity was complex and could be spun in multiple directions. At the time, however, there was no single regulatory standard other than truth in labeling for judging such drugs. And since menthol was relatively benign especially compared to other more toxic substances on the open market, few would have worried about policing the drug. Yet precisely in these years, policing deceptive practices in various kinds of consumer affairs was becoming an increasing focus of government regulation—whether via the FDA's attention to drugs and mislabeled products, the newly created FCC's concern about communications deceit, or the FTC's focus on false advertising. Menthol as a product was seen as artfully distracting but unproblematic, falling far below any regulator's concern.

In 1934, then, there were very few reasons for government agencies to police menthol claims. It was widely used, and its cooling quality had been popular with doctors and patients for decades. Since late in the previous century, Americans could buy menthol products at any drugstore. Nor was menthol merely a "flavor" or an additive. Doctors hailed it and consumers embraced it as a drug in itself, a mild painkiller that might also ward off germs or, as one renowned user noted, dilate the throat. For the famous opera tenor Enrico Caruso, menthol was part of a standard preperformance ritual. Before taking the stage, Caruso scrubbed and cleansed his teeth, followed by a gargle with salts and a vaporizer. Then came the delicate application of "menthol and Vaseline on absorbent cotton attached to long sticks."

HOW I TAKE CARE OF MY THROAT.

Caruso Knows How-to Sing Even if He Has a Cold— Often Eats an Apple Before He Sings—Gargle of Salt and Water Most Helpful.

"WHEN I AWAKEN IN THE MORNING I TRY MY VOICE."

Figure 1.2. In this 1914 *Boston Globe* article, the famous tenor Enrico Caruso described how he used menthol to "dilate the throat," followed by a cigarette, before taking the stage for a performance. Credit: *Boston Daily Globe,* June 21, 1914.

As one reporter in Caruso's dressing room described the practice, the great tenor swabbed his throat "as a gunner would a cannon." "Dilates the throat," Caruso told an interviewer. Then to the amazement of his visitor, the robust man lit up a cigarette, "inhaling every blessed puff of it!"[10] For the great tenor, menthol was essential care for his powerful voice box. He found that such rituals allowed him to sing even when he had a cold. Even so, some British physicians bemoaned the practice of using such sprays on singers' throats, "especially in Paris, where the physicians seemed to treat all their singers with a cocaine spray," observed one skeptic. It led to addiction and ruined the most beautiful voices. "Menthol was almost as bad as cocaine," he concluded.[11]

Caruso was not unusual in practicing this type of self-medication that mingled menthol with other commodities like the tobacco cigarette, delighting in the sensation as they interacted. Enterprising companies had been mixing drugs and touting their innovations for decades in a commercial atmosphere with little regulation or oversight of these products. Novel concoctions were the stuff of patents and business innovation. Despite increasing government attention to drug regulation beginning in 1906 with the passage of the Pure Food and Drug Act and the 1927 establishment of the Food, Drug and Insecticide Administration (later renamed the FDA), there remained in every household an array of drugs—some mixed commercially, some compounded by doctors, others made up by their users—that today might be regarded as makeshift or dangerous. At the turn of the century, opiate painkillers still remained available as a treatment for colds. "I believe personally in taking an opiate to start with," wrote one anonymous author in the *New York Times* in 1901, describing their approach to treating colds. But since opiates induced sleep, the writer confessed that "the man who moves about may find much relief from sniffing up a little menthol snuff now and again." Maybe a peppered "cubeb cigarette" might help, too.[12]

Menthol was one of the more common drug products that consumers turned to for distinctive and fast sensory relief for colds and congestion; and since coughs and colds were omnipresent, menthol had become a mass-market item with plenty of appeal. A "cold," broadly defined, was a serious thing. Both experts and laypeople alike connected cold symptoms with major causes of mortality—pneumonia, tuberculosis, the flu (an outbreak of which had killed tens of millions worldwide and over a half million in the United States in the 1910s). The man or woman with a sudden spasmodic cough could never be sure whether their body might harbor the germs for tuberculosis or whether it was only a "chest" cold.[13] Tuberculosis, with its telltale cough and pulmonary symptoms, was the leading cause of mortality in 1900. But coughing, phlegm, and congestion could also be a sign of impending pneumonia, another leading cause of death in children and adults. Whatever the cause of the cough, "the patient's mouth and nose must be kept scrupulously clean, by the use of suitable disinfectant sprays or washes of a mild character," warned one

Canadian doctor in 1919.[14] All across North America, medicines like oil of eucalyptus, thymol, and menthol acquired an important role in self-care. It was always prudent to treat colds and congestion quickly and aggressively. The question confronting congestion sufferers was not whether to treat the ailment, but with what. Which combination of drugs would fortify the body, and put relief and peace of mind within reach? As one author noted in 1903, every medicine cabinet should have a few bandages, two thermometers, a glass syringe, and of course a menthol pencil to apply the anesthetic oil or crystal on a painful spot.[15]

In the early years of the twentieth century, then, the typical American medicine cabinet could contain a stunning range of products—everything from the fragrant to the vile. Many a medicine contained cocaine, morphine, and alcohol. In this context, menthol was deemed by medics to be a good, if weak, *materia medica* in its own right. It was also useful as a mask—as a soothing, minty, sensory distraction to cover the bad taste of a more foul-tasting medicine, helping it to go down easier. Deception and distraction were, in a real sense, part of the essence of the drug and central to its medical uses, and also central to its role in cigarettes. Menthol was a drug with many facets—a substance that could be mixed with almost any other product to mask or alter its identity.

In the atmosphere of limited drug regulation that prevailed in the early twentieth century, where novel mixtures were patentable and quickly commodifiable, there were few restrictions on who could innovate a new menthol product. New uses of menthol and menthol combinations, some noxious and some mild, appeared everywhere—in the doctor's office, at the bedside, at the local druggist.[16] One Manchester, Kentucky, druggist loudly crowed in the late 1890s about a newly concocted cure for congestion and inflammation (catarrh) that combined menthol and cocaine (a drug recently discovered in the mountains of Peru, cultivated from coca plants, and being incorporated into many consumer products and patent medicines). At the time, most observers saw menthol and cocaine as alike in many ways, medically speaking. Both were anesthetic painkillers at the forefront of medicine. While they differed in potency with anxieties about cocaine's addictive potential quickly rising, both were deemed vital to medical care.[17] In both, anesthetic action was local—a highly prized novelty. Cocaine deadened pain on the mucous membranes of the nose and throat, as well as on the eyes. Doctors hailed it as revolutionary; as one news report in 1897 noted, when former president Ulysses S. Grant lay dying of throat cancer in the 1880s, cocaine "rose to world-wide fame when it touched the aching throat of Gen. Grant and bade his pain be still. It came in time for him as it has for thousands of similar sufferers since."[18] It was also now possible to conduct new eye surgeries without putting the patient under general anesthesia.[19] The era thus produced an odd family of local anesthetics—chloroform, ether, morphine, eucalyptus, cocaine, and menthol—each becoming essential to the doctor's, surgeon's, and (in many cases) layman's tool kit for soothing pain. Menthol, like cocaine, was deemed effective at dealing with worrisome ailments of the upper airways.[20]

For the doctor of the 1910s, cocaine, menthol, and chloroform were classified together on a continuum of painkillers.[21] They also intermingled—the strengths of one complementing the other, or masking it. Menthol appeared in multiple varieties—as a snuff, as a lozenge, as menthol pencil, and also as menthol sprays for bathing the sickroom in a soothing mist.[22] This cavalier mingling of products continued even after the Pure Food and Drug Act of 1906 defined a new, if modest, federal oversight over the drug market. The act focused on truth in labeling rather than judging the efficacy or safety of drugs. It singled out a handful of eleven problematic substances (cocaine among them), mandating that products containing any of these ingredients be labeled appropriately so that consumers knew what they were taking. The new labeling law made no actual restrictions as to cocaine's use.[23] Menthol fell far below the regulatory radar. The American drug market remained mostly unregulated, with a steady business in selling relief.

The idea of incorporating menthol into cigarette smoking owed much to the lay public's long familiarity with menthol stretching back decades. But the invention of a menthol *cigarette* in the 1920s was catalyzed by something specific to the decade: the post–World War I popularity of cigarette smoking in that pivotal decade.[24] Before the war, prohibitionists had taken aim at morphine, cocaine, alcohol, and the cigarette for strict controls and bans. Amid the success in banning alcohol and other drug controls, the cigarette industry was in crisis and under attack. The 1910s was no time for industry innovation; survival itself was uncertain. Henry Ford called the cigarette a "coffin nail" (he characterized alcohol similarly), insisting that smoking undermined industry by damaging American men's capacity for work. Ford spoke for millions of others. In some states, alcohol and cigarettes both seemed fated for banning. Kansas, a hotbed for alcohol prohibition, banned cigarettes in 1910. At the same time, an empowered federal government turned its sights on breaking up trusts and monopolies, taking aim at the giant American Tobacco Company. The Supreme Court validated its breakup into five large competing firms—often labeled the Big Five. The new companies born in the wake of the antitrust action included Liggett & Myers, Lorillard, and a newly formed American Tobacco, as well as three new independent subsidiaries of American Tobacco—United Cigars Stores, R. J. Reynolds, and British American Tobacco.[25] Champions of antitrust actions argued that the end of monopoly capitalism would lead to new competition and innovation. Indeed, a decade or so later, the first menthol brand emerged from one of the new firms—a spawn of anti-monopoly reform.

The First World War would be a catalyst for menthol smoking in other ways, for it transformed and normalized cigarette smoking in general. Slated for prohibition only a few years earlier, the cigarette found a new purpose and redemption in the adversity of war. As historian Cassandra Tate has noted, even as the moral climate and the need to preserve grain for bread ushered in alcohol prohibition, cigarettes dodged the ban, becoming a commodity tied to supporting the troops abroad.[26] In war, Wayne Wheeler of the Anti-Saloon League drew a clear line between alcohol and cigarettes. "Tobacco," he said, "may be a private or personal bad habit, but it is not in the same class as intoxicating liquor."[27] Suddenly with soldiers "over there," organizations like the Salvation Army switched from vilifying smoking to supporting troops by becoming one of the world's largest distributors of cigarettes. If the war strengthened the case for alcohol control and led to national prohibition in 1919, it weakened the moral case against the cigarette because of the urgent need for giving battlefield comfort to fighting men.[28] As a result, a cadre of young soldiers returned home as avid cigarette users, ushering in a new era for smoking in the 1920s. At the same time, a younger generation of women began to reject restrained prewar roles and fashions that they characterized as grim and humorless, and for them, too, moralizing about women smoking seemed decidedly old-fashioned. Why not have women's smoking cars on trains, they asked. Why must women put up with "conductors with Puritan prejudices"?[29] By the booming and giddy 1920s, the cigarette had been redeemed, and the Big Five were flourishing.

The war had also enhanced the value of mentholated products on the front and at home, expanding consumers' familiarity with menthol's "cooling" and therapeutic effects. Whether used to treat soldiers and citizens afflicted with coughs and chest congestion during the 1918 influenza epidemic, or to relieve and distract victims of gas attacks (using a menthol-soaked rag in the mouth), the appeal of menthol was bolstered by two of the era's most pressing concerns: war and disease.[30] After the war, one company (the maker of Musterole mentholated ointment) played to popular fears of the flu, for example, warning readers of the *New York Times*: "Don't Let That Cold Turn into Flu," and highlighting Musterole's use "in our training camps during the 'Flu' epidemic."[31] Menthol was a vital weapon in the battle for good health, Musterole preached: "At the first sign of a cold, get out the jar of good old Musterole and rub it gently on the congested parts."[32]

With more men smoking and women's rates rising as well, smoking-related discomforts like parched and irritated throats also increased, opening a completely new niche for menthol as a balm for smokers. (It would take another two decades for cancer to surface as a major smoking-related disease, again expanding the market for menthol.) So worrisome was the "smoker's throat" in the 1920s, that already by 1924, cigarette ads sought to outdo one another, promising that this brand or another would go easier on the throat, reducing coughing and irritation. Promises to relieve the smoker's cough or the smoker's throat expanded along with smoking rates. American Tobacco, the maker of Lucky Strike, explained that its special "toasting" process "removes all 'bite' and harshness, hence never any throat irritation."[33] In the growing mass consumer marketplace, cigarettes promised many things—luxury, excitement, glamour. But a new niche was opening for the cigarette brands that could reassure or those that promised smokers relief.

It was only a matter of time before some savvy small businessman thought to combine menthol and tobacco; given the intersecting trends (rising rate of smoking, a growing awareness of the capacity of menthol to soothe, and a business environment that made it safer for smaller cigarette firms), menthol and tobacco seemed destined to meet. The message that menthols provided a soothing answer for parched throats would have been ill-suited to the 1910s, but it was perfectly tailored for the coughing smoker of the 1920s and 1930s. If Enrico Caruso had discovered how to combine menthol with the cigarette in his own personal ritual of self-care, how long before some enterprising cigarette maker did the same and turned a profit?

According to industry lore, the first menthol cigarette was invented in Mingo Junction, Ohio, in 1925, just fifty miles west of Pittsburgh. A longtime resident, Lloyd "Spud" Hughes, had suffered from colds since childhood; his mother had always dosed him liberally with menthol. Spud Hughes, like Caruso, also loved to smoke, rolling his own cigarettes. And so, one fateful day, "he compromised by mixing a few menthol crystals with a package of tobacco and leaving the whole to mature overnight in a baking powder can."[34] At first, Spud kept the homemade menthol cigarettes for himself, but soon he started sharing them with the railroad men and miners who came to his father's restaurant. They became regular customers, and word spread quickly. Later that year, Hughes was granted US Patent No. 1,555,580 for his simple method of "impregnating the tobacco with a solution of menthol and alcohol."[35] A year later, he signed a contract with the Axton-Fisher

Tobacco Company of Louisville, Kentucky (hundreds of miles south on the Ohio River), to manufacture the brand that bore his name, Spud. Axton-Fisher then bought Spud outright, and the mentholated brand soon became a "change of pace" cigarette for anyone seeking a temporary break from their regular smoke routine—whether because of colds, congestion, or throat irritation. When the irritation disappeared, smokers could return to their regular brand.

Menthol itself was abundant. Its availability in the United States relied on a supply chain that originated with Japan's peppermint crop and ended with a wide range of consumer products and health salves. A global commodity, menthol came from Japan as oils (popular in England) and as crystals (Japan shipped nearly half a million pounds of it to the United States each year).[36] According to the US Department of Labor, imported menthol remained cheap; it was accessibly priced (around $4.30 per pound) at about one-third the price of opium.[37] Some US observers worried over the nation's rising dependence on Japan for a substance that was now being so widely integrated into an increasing number of products. So, by the mid-1920s, the US Department of Agriculture's Bureau of Plant Industry set out to encourage "home-grown [i.e., domestically produced] menthol."[38] The US Department of Agriculture, in turn, was concerned with ensuring that the menthol supply stay strong, to be used in cold medicines that depended on delivering that distinctive feeling of relief to sufferers. Axton-Fisher was thus well positioned to enjoy the benefits of this expanding menthol production. New opportunities for finding cheap menthol abounded. In 1926 a plant opened in Porterville, California, with the hope of growing peppermint domestically—the oil from its leaves producing the menthol to be used in "salves, ointments, cough drops, and other medical preparations."[39]

The Therapeutic Pitch

Menthol products carried an essential health promise, claiming to penetrate the body with therapeutic relief, and the mentholated cigarette echoed and amplified that promise.[40] By the time Carl Spier visited Howard Haggard's office seeking clarity on whether or not Kool was safe to smoke, almost every American had familiarity with the sweeping therapeutic and protective claims made by menthol products ranging from lozenges, sprays, balms, and ointments. Marketing for these products did not merely promise relief of symptoms. They offered buyers exaggerated, ultimately doubtful, yet extraordinarily precise claims about how menthol worked to remedy their health concerns. "When applied over the throat and chest," proclaimed a Vicks VapoRub advertisement in the *St. Louis Post-Dispatch*, "the body heat releases vapors of Menthol, Camphor, Pine Oil, Thyme and Eucalyptus, that are inhaled with each breath through the air passages to the lungs, loosening the phlegm, and soothing the inflamed membrane."[41] There was, of course, no evidence at the time or today to support such claims, and (more to the point) there was no agency empowered with policing such unsupported claims; it was left to the buyer to decide whether the notion that menthol soothed inflammation or loosened phlegm was believable or not. Many believed, slipping into the menthol trap. A 1919 advertisement for another mentholated ointment asked users to imagine the menthol experience as a penetrating action with the power to heal: "Notice how much easier it is to breathe freely through the re-opened air passages. Notice the disappearance of that miserably stuffy, clogged sensation." This was how the product Turpo could "penetrate every nook and crevice of the respiratory organs—the nose and mouth" and "drive away a cold."[42]

Such portraits of menthol doing battle with congestion continued to gain wide prominence in 1920s consumer culture, appearing in ads for soaps, creams, and ointments like VapoRub as well as snuffs, sprays, lozenges, and pastilles.[43] Luden's, a Reading, Pennsylvania, company, pitched its signature menthol cough drop as a preventive suitable for seasonal and year-round use, noting that "thousands of people during the past winter learned their extraordinary value as a preventative of coughs, colds, and sore throat."[44] Courting smokers from another angle, Luden's also advertised its lozenge as a welcome relief and, in a nod to cigarette smokers, as a taste enhancer. "If you smoke for pleasure—and who doesn't—try this new way to keep your

Figure 1.3. Luden's cough drop advertisement, circa 1928. Menthol (whether in a lozenge or in a cigarette) was widely advertised as therapy for the smoker's cough, with the promise that "your 11th cigarette tastes as good as your first."
Credit: From the collection of Stanford Research Into the Impact of Tobacco Advertising (tobacco .stanford.edu).

smoke-taste keen and appreciative," a 1928 advertisement suggested. After ten cigarettes, a Luden's cough drop would refresh the mouth, throat, and nose.[45]

As many scholars have observed, therapeutic messaging was everywhere in the 1920s. Along with the birth of modern advertising came distinctive, reassuring psychological appeals straddling the line between claims that science could support and the catchy promises of relief concocted by admen to push products. As historian Roland Marchand has noted, consumer culture of the 1920s was rife with this type of therapeutic messaging (whether implicit or explicit).[46] Advertising for menthol products, including cigarettes, followed these same themes. As a salve for the ill effects of normal smoking, the menthol cigarette embodied exactly the logic that Stuart Ewen said defined corporate capitalism: it "hoped to profit by the attack on its own failures."[47]

The age of Kool as a Black-themed cigarette brand with an appeal targeted to the racial anxieties of the 1960s and 1970s loomed decades into the future; in the 1920s, the menthol pitch was targeted at another set of anxieties and niche markets: smokers with parched throats, those who feared congestion, and people seeking throat relief across every race, gender, and age. In this era of mass marketing in magazines and radio, advertisers also used "common man" or "common woman" testimonials to appeal to a range of customer segments. In one Luden's ad in the *Journal of Education*, a Mississippi teacher's "original letter" described a sore throat caused by her squeaky overused voice in the classroom, and the "vexatious colds [that were] aggravated by catarrh and chalk dust." The Luden's pitch promised that such irritation would be quickly alleviated by the menthol cough drop.[48] Marketers of menthol products, spanning from Luden's cough drops and Vicks VapoRub to Spud menthol cigarettes, employed these "common man/woman" motifs in their efforts to build credibility and markets.[49]

Menthol advertising employed a familiar gimmick—offering largely unsubstantiated (and unregulatable at this time) claims about the physiological mechanisms behind the menthol sensation. Ads asked viewers to visualize menthol action. Absent regulations, it was left to the viewer to decide whether these claims were credible, or merely fluff, deception, and hype. Companies described menthol's action on the body with compelling clarity, and with an eye toward allaying specific fears. It was precisely this misuse of his physiological science by admen in the "Camels give you a lift" advertisement that

Haggard found so annoying. Menthol ads spanned a wide range. Some were understated, sticking close to known effects and echoing the words of medical experts: for example, menthol provided quick pain relief, was an antiseptic, and was "effective in allaying irritation" such as that from a mosquito bite.[50] But other ads went beyond what was supported by any known evidence. They promised, for example, that a menthol salve, ointment, or lozenge might protect the body against worsening health by entering the pores, stimulating circulation, opening the airways, breaking up congestion, or preventing a cold from becoming a flu (none of which had any scientific basis). These claims went unpoliced. Drug laws generally took aim at more toxic and nefarious substances like cocaine, and the regulatory agencies—only two decades after the 1906 Food and Drug Act—exercised little jurisdiction over these mundane fibs and claims of advertised nostrums.

With a wide-open terrain to promise menthol as curative, these ads craftily asked consumers to envision menthol as a powerful and soothing decongestant and a counterirritant, loosening the phlegm and soothing inflammation.[51] One 1919 advertisement asked users to imagine the menthol experience as the drug opened their airways: "Notice how much easier it is to breathe freely through the reopened air passages. Notice the disappearance of that miserably stuffy, clogged sensation." Such ads invited readers to feel palpably and to imagine the drug action of menthol products penetrating the "nooks and crevices" of the nose and throat, doing therapeutic battle with a cold and driving it away.[52] And as Musterole preached to African American readers of the *Chicago Defender* newspaper, the drug action could be understood as counterirritation: "Colds are merely congestion. Musterole is a counterirritant." The shrewd ad then vividly pictured how the product "stimulates circulation and helps break up the cold. Enters the pores then a cooling sensation brings welcome relief."[53]

Axton-Fisher's Spud entered the menthol market in the 1920s as a beneficiary of these inflated, widely publicized, therapeutic associations of menthol; and the deception continued to underpin menthol smoking's appeal. Yet the early years were difficult ones. Three years after its creation, Spud remained a small novelty item, a gimmick, a "trick cigarette." As *Fortune* magazine later commented, "The three heads [of Axton-Fisher] did not know whether Spuds could ever be lifted out of the class of trick cigarettes; they did not even know why Spud smokers liked Spuds."[54] All of this changed dramatically in 1929, when adversity would again prove (ironically) to enhance the fortunes of mentholated smoking. A cash infusion apparently from an investor to Axton-Fisher early that year, prior to the great stock market crash, allowed the company to launch a national advertising campaign that would set Spud on a new path.

Economic calamity would also be good for smoking. In hard economic times, people smoked more and the industry prospered not only *in spite of* hard economic times, but also *because of* the fact that hard and anxious times drew people even more to the cigarette with its self-medicating nicotine lift. Even with the nation in economic free fall, Spud cigarettes were doing well and Axton-Fisher looked like a new market force. "While the graph of industry in general was sweeping ever lower during the depression, this company's sales and profits moved in the reverse direction," announced *Fortune* in 1932. Net sales climbed steadily from $3.9 million in 1928 to $6.2 million in 1931.[55] "Twenty years ago, before people smoked so much that their parched throats cried out for relief," explained *Fortune*, "Spuds could hardly have been so great a success."[56] People in hard times were smoking more than ever, and in this context the therapeutic message of mentholated cigarettes retained its appeal.

Less than a year after *Fortune*'s flattering write-up of Spud, Brown & Williamson leaped into the menthol cigarette market with a new brand: Kool. More than any other cigarette, Kool hung its hat on the therapeutic idea. It promised "throat comfort" in a series of magazine and radio advertisements. Kool's earliest advertising copy stressed menthol's decongesting "beneficial head clearing qualities," but then soon switched to the cigarette's ability to soothe the throat. Ads exhorted viewers, "In between the others rest your throat with Kools."[57] As an occasional smoke wedged in between other normal cigarette brands, Kool's share of the cigarette market remained small—about 1.9 percent of the cigarette market in 1934. By contrast, the big national brands like Camel, Lucky Strike, and Chesterfield each claimed just over 30 percent of the market that year.[58] But Kool's sales soon surpassed those of Spud, and by 1937 Kool's market share had climbed to 2.5 percent.[59]

If you were a menthol smoker in the mid-1930s, whether you were a teacher, a lover of literature, a woman or man, an urban or rural resident, you were part of a tiny market; but your very existence highlighted a nagging industry worry. The smoker's cough was everywhere. Everyone was promising throat relief and less harsh tobacco products, with each product subtly undercutting others. Lucky Strike (the popular non-menthol brand) counseled, "Don't rasp your throat with hot irritants," while Lorillard promised that there would be "Not a cough in a carload" when using Old Gold.[60] Philip Morris (long known for a distinctive Turkish blend) introduced a milder blend as a salve for irritated throats.[61] Amid all this worry over harshness and coughing, R. J. Reynolds, maker of Camel, hired "a new hard-hitting advertising agency (William Esty)" that threw a new idea at smokers—that it was those other companies who engaged in tricks and gimmickry, but not the makers of Camel. "It's fun to be fooled . . . it's more fun to know."[62]

Tiny though it was, the market of smokers drawn to mentholated tobacco challenged mainstream brands directly, exposing their promises of throat relief as a charade. Seeking to join the race to reassure, other companies cautiously introduced their own menthol brands. Even American Tobacco, with its industry-leading Lucky Strike and its own campaign of toasted reassurance, considered entering the menthol cigarette market.[63] In 1934 Lorillard tested out the third mentholated cigarette to hit the Depression-era market—Polar—making it available in the New England region.[64] But the company remained uncertain about this path, worrying about whether the industry's heavy reliance on menthol supplies might not drive up the commodity's price.

But was menthol smoking safe? Wasn't menthol itself irritating to the throat, contrary to the promise? Opinions differed about the tricky substance. A 1930 study by Chicago MD Noah Fox had alleged

that menthol, "even in dilutions as low as 0.5 per cent, proved irritating to the mucous membrane, causing a swelling rather than a
constriction of these tissues as is popularly believed."[65] The science remained uncertain. Lorillard executives were not fully convinced that
menthol was harmless, asking "several people closely associated with
the tobacco industry . . . whether the continued use of Mentholated
Cigarettes would have any harmful affect [sic] on the smoker's throat
and the system in general." There was precious little data on these
questions of harm. Lorillard had only received vague reports of harms
from those who "indicated that there might be something to it."[66]

How Menthol Tricked the Senses

Despite the initial frostiness of Haggard and Spier's meeting, it did
not take long for Haggard to agree to assist Brown & Williamson.
Thus began a testy relationship between the scientist and the adman
over questions of truth and deception on the question of menthol
cigarettes. Haggard praised the company for its "simple non-claiming
advertising" of Kool, a precondition of his involvement. The Yale laboratory had been bruised by its former work with William Esty, and
Haggard explained bluntly to Spier that he believed advertisers had
questionable ethics. His complaint was with Esty, not the makers of
Camels. Haggard laid aside his suspicions of Madison Avenue to be
of service to the B&W company, which he saw as more trustworthy.
His relationships with the advertiser and the cigarette maker would
be tested in months to come, as the Yale laboratory delved into the
study of menthol's effects.

Haggard was being drawn into a struggle with huge commercial
stakes and he knew it; what he could not have known was the depth
of animosity building up between tobacco companies as they battled
one another to reassure smokers while undercutting the competition.
Nor could he have known the scale of corporate tensions surrounding
the menthol question, with no small amount of conniving. Firms were
at each other's throats, so to speak—questioning each other's claims
publicly and seeking other ways to cast doubt on competing brands.

Spier had come to the Yale lab as part of this corporate jousting. In the adman's view, science offered two things of distinct value: findings that could be used both for aggressive marketing and also evidence in a company's legal defense should any claims be made about Kool's dangers. Asked by his bosses whether the contract for research services should be signed by *both* Haggard and Henderson, or only by one of the scientists, Spier noted that "if any law suit against Brown & Williamson were ever started, two professors, two signatures on a piece of testimony are better than one."[67] What Haggard naively perceived as the "search for truth" in his laboratory, Spier saw as a crucial weapon in promoting a product and in defending the company against attacks and innuendo.

In these battles to reassure smokers, one particular claim about Spud menthol stood out for its grandiosity. In far-reaching terms, Axton-Fisher embellished menthol's action and antiseptic properties, but also claimed grandly that Spud was a "menthol-cooled" therapeutic smoke—a statement that drew special attention across the industry.[68] The company alleged that the smoke was air-conditioned and thus a lower temperature than normal cigarette smoke: "Spud's smoke is proved 16% cooler by science."[69] This statement by a Kool competitor stood out, and Spier hoped Haggard's studies could address it. But even as B&W turned to the Yale lab, Axton-Fisher was pushing the claim even harder by offering to send any curious customer the company's own scientific report on these matters. The booklet titled *Theory and Facts of Cigarette Smoking* walked readers carefully through a thicket of issues, from why people smoked at all to the fallacy (they argued) that nicotine caused irritation. The mail-order booklet carried a simple marketing message in support of Spud: menthol was beneficial to health, menthol produced a "refrigeration of smoke," and this control of temperature was "the most reliable indication of mildness."[70]

Almost immediately, these claims of cooling came under attack from competitors as a kind of trickery if not outright deception, even as government regulators remained reluctant to police these types of competing claims. If the government was reluctant to act, competitors were not; the Spud claim awakened their skepticism and animosity. In one in-house memo for American Tobacco, chemist J. A. Bradford dismissed Axton-Fisher's claims that mentholated Spuds burned at a lower temperature. Any difference in cigarette burn temperature was likely due to the moisture content of the tobacco and the burn rate, he protested. Menthol itself was "of infinitesimal importance" and not "nearly so powerful a refrigerant as plain water."[71] For scientists like Bradford, Axton-Fisher's claims (for example, that visible smoke did not carry irritating elements) were either exaggerations or flatly ridiculous. The Louisville, Kentucky, company's claims "failed utterly" as science, said Bradford. Menthol was no coolant; it was more accurate to call it a chemical trick upon the senses—a trick magnified by Axton-Fisher's "refrigeration" advertising. As Bradford insisted, menthol created a "sense of cooling" without actual cooling, amplifying this effect by "direct stimulation of the nerves" on the mucous membranes of the nose and throat. His own studies suggested that the temperature of these air passage actually increased by one or two degrees while the trick of menthol did its work. Nevertheless, the American Tobacco Company chemist acknowledged, "It must be admitted that the publication has attractiveness and credibility to the lay mind, notwithstanding its many contradictions and inaccuracies."[72]

Stung by accusations of trickery, Axton-Fisher took out two advertisements backing away specifically from its medical claims and admitting that its product should not be seen as a medical prescription for better health. Menthol cigarettes were not cold medicine. "If you have a cold see your doctor! . . . A cigarette manufacturer is not a physician." The company nevertheless stuck to its promise of refrigeration, protesting that Spud smoke, although not "a remedy for throat or nose irritation, coughs or colds," was "cooled by menthol."[73] The message: for actual ailments, a smoker should see a physician; for relief, smoke a Spud. The ad featured a physician looking into a man's throat.

These questions about Spud had implications, of course, for Kool—which is why Spier had come to Haggard's door in a dance involving university science, legal defense, and the making of new markets. But inviting a scientific study of menthol was itself a gamble, for who knew what Haggard might learn about menthol as an irritant or as a harmful additive. Would the Yale scientist's study support B&W's insistence that menthol was not an irritant? Would a study confirm that its cigarettes carried credible physiological effects and therapeutic benefits, as the company hoped? Experts like Haggard welcomed the opportunity to conduct science on consumer products, as he and Henderson developed the field of "applied physiology" to be of maximum benefit to companies. His laboratory sought out exactly these commercial opportunities—a chance to show the importance of physiological science to product evaluation. But the Yale scientist also wanted to retain control over how his findings might be disseminated, and to limit the use of the findings in generating sales. It was a difficult balance to sustain. For his part, the adman promised to abide by Haggard's rule; yet he remained ready to seize on any findings that would make good advertising copy or bolster claims that would stand up in court if menthol smoking was ever challenged. Menthol science was, in Spier's view, a tool for stabilizing this fractious business competition.

Haggard threw cold water on Axton-Fisher's exaggerated claims about Spud's refrigerative and germ-fighting properties.[74] The company had offered vivid examples, pointing to the fact that men working in its factory, exposed to higher-than-common amounts of menthol vapor in the air, suffered fewer colds. By implication, menthol prevented colds. Echoing a general view on germs yet pointing to no specific studies, Haggard deemed this claim potentially true: "I suspect that the gentlemen mentioned as supervising the preparation of Spuds . . . may have been actually freer from colds because of the menthol." On other issues, Haggard criticized the quality of the science in Axton-Fisher's consumer booklet. "Our findings do not support many of the points," he wrote in September 1934. Spud's claims were "founded on some very badly controlled experimentation." For example, it was definitely not a refrigerant; the cooling sensation on the throat was deceptive. As Haggard put it, "Menthol feels cool because it paralyzes the nerve endings that give rise to the precipitation of heat. There is actually no real cooling." In truth, Haggard's own understanding of how menthol created its effect on the throat was theoretical. Whether the nerves were "paralyzed" as Haggard said or "stimulated" as Bradford insisted remained speculative; however, both men knew what menthol did *not* do. The claim that menthol mixed with tobacco produced a lower-temperature smoke was rubbish. Haggard concluded that the Axton-Fisher deception was "an attempt to get around the physiological effect of menthol and to imply that its action is on the smoke before it reaches the mouth. Our findings are to the contrary."[75]

Over the next year, Haggard's menthol study produced a middle-ground portrait of the drug: it was not dangerous, likely beneficial, but also no coolant, and many of its effects were illusory. The drug's "cooling" action was well known to impact only some parts of the body (mucous membranes) but not others, such as the skin. Haggard's laboratory delved more deeply into menthol's effects by separating the chemical from the cigarette's other ingredients. But because it was "impossible to use . . . the human throat for this work," he explained to the B&W legal department, Haggard "turned to an even more susceptible membrane, the eye of the rat."[76] "It is a well known fact," he noted in his final report, "that the conjunctiva of the eye is more sensitive to irritation than is the mucosa of the upper respiratory tract."[77] His study would look for evidence of irritation. Treating the eyes of sixty caged rats with solutions of menthol eight times daily over five months, Haggard detected no signs of redness or irritation, concluding that menthol was not irritating or harmful. Other rats were exposed to continuous menthol vapor over six months. "During the first three days of exposure . . . they kept their eyes shut most of the time but they gradually became accustomed to the menthol" and appeared to be "as healthy and comfortable as the rats in the control cages." He saw no systemic effects. Contrary to another study conducted on menthol in 1930, Haggard concluded that there was "no physiological effect except transient and harmless paralysis of the nerves."[78]

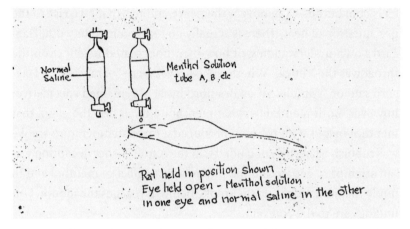

Figure 1.4. An illustration from Howard W. Haggard's 1935 *Report of Investigation to Determine the Physiological Effects of Menthol Derived from Smoking Kool Cigarettes,* showing his menthol experiments on rats.
Credit: Image courtesy of Truth Tobacco Industry Documents (https://www.industrydocuments.ucsf .edu/tobacco/).

Brown & Williamson received Haggard's findings as good news. B&W's law firm was pleased to learn that menthol was not a long-lasting drug—it "does not accumulate in the body but is rapidly eliminated." The idea of a rapidly eliminated drug was reassuring. In an atmosphere in which toxic patent medicines continued to proliferate, when new "doped" marijuana cigarettes catalyze public fears and police actions, and as calls increased for the regulation of products from hormone-based "organotherapies" to insulin and even radium-water remedies, menthol's fleeting effects seemed moderate by any measure.[79] A few years later, it would take a deadly scandal involving a new type of potent antibacterial drugs, a sulfa drug, to produce new federal drug safety laws, requiring (among other things) toxicity testing before marketing. In the meantime, the therapeutics market was largely self-policed: corporate self-regulation, as well as advertisement and undercutting the competition, prevailed as the primary way to shape the marketplace. In this context, the menthol cigarette maker sought both to promote menthol's therapeutic effects aggressively while gently reassuring smokers that menthol, once it "cooled" the throat, did not linger in the body. Haggard's work blended labo-

ratory observations of menthol's effects on rats with his own speculation about a range of other neurological matters, most of which he
simply did not have the methods or expertise to examine. The overall
effect was to downgrade menthol as a "drug" in an era of rising drug
anxieties; as B&W now explained, it had "no more systemic effect
than would be expected from chewing gum flavored with peppermint
oil . . . one of the flavored oils of which group menthol is a member."[80]

Nearly two years into their relationship, in April 1936 Spier returned gingerly to the issue that had triggered Haggard's suspicion the
first time they met: Could Brown & Williamson use Yale's findings on
menthol's safety to advertise their product? As Spier explained, "We
think the well-informed physician knows enough about menthol . . .
[but] the less well-read doctors" might benefit from knowing about
some of the Yale findings. Otherwise, these less-informed doctors
might be "unwittingly doing mentholated cigarettes an injustice" by
warning patients away from them unnecessarily. The proposed ads,
produced as part of a series, would be placed only in professional
medical journals, including the *Journal of the American Medical Association* and *Oral Hygiene*, Spier explained. Wary of Haggard's prickli-
ness on this question, B&W reassured him that their "determination
not to capitalize publicly on your report is just as firm and unshaken
as when we asked you to make the original study," but it was just
that the competitive circumstances and rumor campaigns had convinced the company that it was time to act — to set the record straight.
"There is just enough harm being done [to] mentholated cigarettes
by incorrect professional opinion to make us feel that some definite
action such as this should be taken."[81]

The adman's request infuriated Haggard; this was precisely the
deceit and exploitation he had feared from slick advertisers. He had
insisted from the beginning that neither his name nor Yale's would be
used to sell menthol smokes. Yet now "it is exactly this exploitation
you are now suggesting," Haggard protested. His only motive in taking on the study was to help show that "the menthol in the cigarettes
was not detrimental to the health of the consumer," but now that
the advertisers wanted to turn his science into a sales pitch, Haggard

dashed off a letter to H. M. Robertson in the legal department at B&W, naively seeing the admen as the problem and the cigarette maker as ethically scrupulous.[82] "I cannot help but feel that this move on the part of your advertising agency . . . was motivated by them rather than by you," Haggard wrote, believing that the cigarette company would sympathize with his annoyance at the Madison Avenue advertiser's tactics.[83] Meanwhile, Spier backtracked modestly, coming up with an alternative request. Would Haggard agree to a footnote in Kool advertisements saying, "Source — Studies and report regarding menthol in Kool cigarettes made by the Department of Applied Physiology of a leading university." Anonymizing the name Yale was no better, Haggard responded angrily to Spier: "There are in this country only two departments of Applied Physiology, one here and one at Harvard." The suggestion was also deceitful and was "perhaps consistent with the somewhat uncertain ethics of the advertising business"; moreover, the attempt to use his science in selling Kool was not in the spirit of their original understanding, Haggard insisted.[84]

Spier resented the accusation of having "uncertain ethics," although in truth the phrase accurately captured the shifting way in which the industry used, appropriated, exploited, and repurposed science for commerce. To start, Spier insisted that nobody at the firm was aware of how few such laboratories existed and could not have known that anonymizing the laboratory would be a meaningless charade. Haggard's ethics accusation stung— "it is not pleasant for us to read." Yet Spier labored to preserve their valuable association, hoping it would not end with "distrust on your part and a sense of being unfairly accused on ours."[85] It was at this point that B&W executives intervened to safeguard the relationship with Haggard, informing him that they had scrapped the planned advertisements. B&W instructed Spier and the advertising agency to let the matter drop.[86]

Only now did it dawn on Haggard that menthol trickery came in many forms. He knew that menthol worked by a clever deception of the senses: the cool feeling was subjective, unrelated to temperature, and had no effect on phlegm or congestion. Menthol worked on the mind, on perception. There was little evidence as to its therapeutic value for colds, but enterprising companies were everywhere pushing these strong claims, checked only by their own sense of business ethics and by their competitors. It bears noting that many smokers remained unconvinced by the menthol promise. Even as Spud and Kool slowly gained market share, many consumers regarded menthol in cigarettes as an off-putting and distasteful trick. Looking back from the 1950s, for example, one British physician recalled how, in his younger days, a practical joke he enjoyed was to push a menthol crystal inside a cigarette and offer it to a drug house salesman, just to watch his shocked reaction after one puff. The dustup at Yale highlighted, however, that the small-niche menthol product—although distasteful to some—was attracting attention because of this trickery of the senses. The trickery extended, of course, to the gimmick of how that sensation was sold as therapy for the smoker's cough.

Into the Smoker's Psyche

The taste for mentholated tobacco was not love at first puff, Spud advertisements admitted disarmingly. The appeal had to be learned, acquired through extended use and several stages of consumer re-training of their senses. While Howard Haggard worried about menthol's effect on the throat, a different set of tobacco industry consultants in psychology and marketing were more interested in influencing the consumer's mind—on shaping the personal meaning and health associations of the product. That is, they sought to imbue the menthol smoking experience with explicit health meanings. In a nod to theories of behaviorism and behavioral conditioning influential in psychology at the time, Spud's first national advertisements instructed potential users that the taste had to be learned by a kind of Pavlovian reeducation of the senses. The advertisers understood that the battle to establish Spud was as much about shaping the meaning of the menthol sensation as it was about therapeutic relief—be it real or promised. As early as the 1920s, Edward Bernays had used psychological insights on oral fixations and gender symbolism with the goal of shaping mass smoking behavior.[87] Spud's advertisers followed this strategy, explaining directly to smokers how to retrain their psyches and how to learn to love the taste of mentholated tobacco.

Three steps were necessary for someone to become a Spud smoker. First, one needed to set aside the initial surprise and skepticism after the first puff, explained one ad. "Certainly, it's cool! That's the menthol. But wait." Second step: "Smoke through one pack." In doing so, the advertiser explained that with repeated use, the taste of the menthol itself would dissipate, but the coolness would remain. The third step involved starting a second pack, which promised "no noticeable menthol sensation at all. Instead a swell cool tobacco taste." In this telling, the menthol taste itself was initially distracting and off-putting—an experience that first had to be endured. The goal was to learn to ignore the taste (a reconditioning of the nose, tongue, and mouth) and to appreciate the cool sensation that followed on all the mucous membranes. Once your throat had become conditioned by menthol, "you've arrived . . . at full tobacco enjoyment," but with a mouth that felt fresh and clean.[88] Axton-Fisher portrayed this three-step process not only as the path to "mouth happiness," but also (perhaps counterintuitively) as a "little argument with Old Man Habit" on the road to a truer enjoyment of tobacco. In other clever Spud ads, placed in *Literary Digest*, the three stages of reconditioned taste were presented as if they were acts in a play—Monday at your office; Thursday at home with a book; and Saturday at a party, "curtain falls on the mouth-happy ending."[89]

Even as menthol cigarette marketers encouraged this self-training, they continued to bathe menthol with associations of therapy and relief. Looking back over these early decades of menthol pitches, one executive at the Ted Bates advertising firm (which would later take over the B&W Kool account) explained that "while 'health' copy has been featured in the majority of the successful campaigns, probably because it lends itself well to aggressive advertising, the therapeutic approach in and of itself, is no guarantee of success."[90] The menthol sensation could be double-edged; it had no inherent meaning. It could be appealing; it could also be a deterrent; it could also be a prank, as in the case of the guileful British doctor mentioned above.

Like picking up a taste for OLIVES

SPUD
takes a little trying!

Frankly, the first Spud does taste mighty cool. But, after half a dozen, your surprise wears off. And by the time you've smoked a pack, all you're conscious of is pure tobacco flavor. *Fine* tobacco flavor! But your mouth keeps a *fresh, clean taste* ... no matter how much you smoke. That's "mouth-happiness!"

SPUD
MENTHOL-COOLED CIGARETTES
20 FOR 15¢ · 12 5¢ IN CANADA)

© *The Axton-Fisher Tobacco Co., Inc., Louisville, Ky.*

Figure 1.5. This 1934 advertisement for Spud, the first mentholated cigarette brand, encouraged the smoker to "retrain" his taste buds and learn to love the taste of menthol. Like picking up any new taste, they promised, "Spud takes a little trying."
Credit: From the collection of Stanford Research Into the Impact of Tobacco Advertising (tobacco .stanford.edu).

The challenge was to give the sensation psychological significance and thus personal meaning for worried smokers. Effective advertising required credibility—"believable copy." As historian Roland Marchand has observed, the aim of advertising in this era in the rise of corporate mass marketing was not to project accurate representations of users but to project ideals, wishes, and aspirations that might appeal in a mass consumption society. If the science of applied physiology added value, legitimacy, and legal cover to products like menthol cigarettes, so, too, would the field of psychology add value. Cigarette manufacturers of this era understood well that the smoker's mind was not at rest, that they were often anxious, wary about coughing, and searching for reassurance. For the marketers and admen, psychology, like Haggard's physiology, offered a science to reassure and coax. Psychological theories in particular offered insight into the smoker's mind, and theories of the smoker as a person, that might shape advertising imagery and ease the worry.

Menthol advertising was devoid of explicit racial meanings, speaking to a set of anxieties that rippled across the mass smoking market. The menthol smoker, when pictured in ads, was always white, of course. If no African American people appeared in these ads, it was in part because the white user was the presumed norm. It was also because the era's dominant characterizations of Black life were overwhelmingly negative and profoundly stigmatized, and therefore not aligned with mass cultural ideals and aspirations in the view of advertisers. Race did figure in branding, however, in a particularly racist fashion as Black stereotypes were used in branding tobacco products to this mass market. Some tobacco firms were all too happy to employ the noxious imagery of Blackness in branding—with product names like Nigger Head Chewing Tobacco and Nigger Hair tobacco. These products sat easily on shelves of grocery stores, as did other household products with caricatured Black figures like Aunt Jemima. It was only in the 1940s that such explicitly racist gestures to American consumers began to be protested by the NAACP, resulting in small victories like the discontinuation of several brands, including American Tobacco Company's Nigger Head pipe tobacco; other products lasted into the 1960s.[91] Other examples of racist branding withstood social criticism, remaining staples of American consumer culture.

Spud's advertisements, by contrast, projected the image of a man (Anglo-American, nicely dressed, seemingly earnest and discerning) striving for middle-class satisfactions and coping with workplace and social anxieties. From the pages of the African American *Chicago Defender* to the *Literary Digest*, and from the *Detroit Free Press* to the *Baltimore Sun*, Spud advertisements encouraged smokers across lines of race, class, and region. "Do long hours unleash your cigarette appetite?" they asked readers of *Literary Digest*. "Do you smoke away anxiety?" their ad asked *Time* magazine readers. "Then you'll appreciate Spud's greater coolness," because "even after hours of waiting and smoking, a Spud tongue and throat are still moist and cool . . . tobacco enjoyment still keen, not killed."[92]

If there was any class tilt to Spud advertising, it seems to have been toward the sorts of people interested in literary, theatrical, or business concerns. Some of the Axton-Fisher ads were aimed, for example, more narrowly at the theatergoing set or discerning readers of the *Literary Digest*. These ads took a comical turn—comparing the fledgling menthol cigarette company's rapid growth to the trajectory of the poor boy Dick Whittington and his cunning cat, Puss-in-Boots, who carried him on a journey toward power and wealth. "But look where the lad is now . . . Counting its friends by the millions. *Cool smoke* made Spud the story-book success of modern cigarettes."[93]

At the same time that tobacco executives were seeking insight into the consumer's mind, academic psychologists offered their own brand of assistance in much the same fashion as Yale's Haggard. They reached out to the industry, keen to apply their own insights on the buyer's mind to commerce. Writing to R. J. Reynolds in 1933, the Psychological Corporation, "a nation-wide organization of psychologists," offered to conduct "consumer surveys on products, advertising, and sales appeal" as well as "counsel on the psychological aspects of sales."[94] Playing for relevance in consumer culture in precisely the style of Yale's physiology laboratory, these psychologists also hailed from the nation's elite institutions.[95] Among the Psychological Corporation's directors were Yale's President James Angell and Professor R. M. Yerkes, Princeton's Howard C. Warren, and other men of national scientific standing. The very idea of a "psychological corporation" highlighted the aspirations of the profession in this moment, as these scientists who studied mind and behavior sought both to incorporate and to build deeper relationships with major businesses—promising that their understandings of the psyche, needs, desires, and anxieties of smokers would build profits.

The Web of Scientific Reassurance

All this menthol gimmickry created worry for executives at the powerful Philip Morris firm, a company without a menthol brand of its own. Skeptical of competitors' mentholated claims, the firm had been pouring energy into reassuring smokers that their brand had developed a formula for going easy on the smoker's throat, preventing the telltale smoker's cough. Philip Morris also sowed seeds of doubt about the promise of menthol, undercutting those fledgling brands. Kool's manufacturer strongly suspected that Philip Morris was responsible for spreading the most harmful menthol rumors—that it was in fact an irritant, a form of "dope," or unsafe in some way. PM was also investing considerable energy in studying menthol—primarily to protect its own brands, partly to undermine the appeal of menthol cigarettes, but also to explore menthol's potential value should its popularity continue to rise.

Menthol smoking exposed fissures among the tobacco companies, each of which pursued distinct strategies in the race to reassure their customers that *their* products, and none other, had the secret (such as the ill-fated PM additive diethylene glycol) to avoiding the smoker's cough. PM executives in the 1930s believed that their chemists had discovered a solution to throat irritation with an improved preparation process substituting the chemical diethylene glycol for glycerin as a moisturizing treatment for tobacco. In much the same way that B&W hoped to promote menthol smoking via outreach to physicians, Philip Morris anticipated that it could take its diethylene glycol story straight to doctors and mental health professionals. As company insiders explained, the "philosophy behind our advertising" could be summed up as "when smokers changed to Philip Morris cigarettes, every case of irritation of the nose and throat due to smoking, cleared completely or definitely improved." Backing that statement with science was a driving passion, for "that statement alone and its acceptance has a value far in excess of the cost of operation of the Research Department," explained the company's researchers.[96] The researchers were particularly proud of their ability to sell this message to physicians so relentlessly that "our competitors discontinued its advertising in the medical field because they felt Philip Morris so predominated . . . that it was a waste of advertising." Like the psychologists, some medical editors were all too willing to partner with the industry, trusting that their reassuring science was sound and sincere. Indeed, PM's message dominated the medical journals and conventions. They organized presentations at scientific meetings to such an extent that "Philip Morris is called the doctor's cigarette. By far the majority of doctors and dentists are Philip Morris smokers and a great proportion of them are recommending Philip Morris to their patients."[97] In a stunning coup, Philip Morris even won over the American Medical Association with its claims on vanquishing throat irritation, securing valued advertising space in the AMA's flagship journal. As the research department saw matters, the prestigious medical journal had become "the backbone of our medical advertising campaign."[98]

The industry's white-coat strategy of scientific reassurance was taking shape. White-coated medical allies had become powerful voices in the battle to present evidence to reassure smokers, working in tandem with physiologists and psychologists. Famously, doctors also appeared in advertisements to calm smokers' worries.[99] Unlike Haggard, who at least sought to mark clear lines between science and advertising, many signed on to help in sales. The AMA's former president Wendell Phillips assisted Philip Morris by agreeing to survey physicians on the psychological dynamics of the smoker's cough. Asked by Phillips whether his patients experienced any improvements by switching from their usual brand to PM's glycerin-treated cigarettes, one New

York psychotherapist, Sol Ginsburg, offered his observations on several cases, touching on both physiological questions (throat irritation) and psychological ones (whether the smoker's mental outlook had changed). One twenty-eight-year-old housewife with "compulsion neurosis" and a long-term hacking cough had shown marked initial improvements, Ginsburg wrote. "Within one week after she had started to smoke Philip-Morris cigarettes, the hacking cough had become remarkably relieved . . . however, during the third week of the trial, following a severe psychic upset, the cough recurred." Ginsburg urged Phillips to be cautious in taking lessons from this single case. The patient's "very deep transference to me" may well have accounted for her original improvement—so that her behavior could likely be "the result of suggestion."[100] Such psychological experts believed that relief came in many flavors; even if diethylene glycol or glycerin or menthols did not actually ease symptoms, the smoker's mind (rather than any particular chemical) often held the key to relief.

There was a glaring and tragic irony in Philip Morris's plan to promote cigarettes treated with diethylene glycol; the chemical they trumpeted as a solution to throat irritation would turn out to be toxic, a poison to the system. But in the battle to reassure, the company insisted that the chemical had the backing of science. PM had won over the physicians, many of whom trusted their claims about the new chemical and accepted their campaign in much the same way that smokers did. In their view, diethylene glycol was a novel product of extensive scientific development, and therefore by definition beneficial. For many physicians and scientists, that claim was enough to win their support. These medical and scientific men like Yale's Haggard and the AMA's Phillips were also well positioned to amplify the pitch.

At the same time, Philip Morris's consultants and scientists planted seeds of skepticism about menthol action, wooing physicians to undercut Brown & Williamson's and Axton-Fisher's claims. One in-house scientist, Dr. Hamner, briefed PM's advertising firm on the case against menthol. Assessing Axton-Fisher's menthol booklet, Hamner concluded that Spud's "menthol-cooled smoke" claims were preposterous. By contrast, he explained, Philip Morris's treatment with "Diethylene Glycol blends the smoke, makes it smooth. 'Spotty' smoke is always irritating." Nor was menthol a refrigerant, Hamner protested. "If I wanted to pick the worst possible refrigerant I would pick menthol," he said. The only reason it felt cool was "because menthol affects the ends of the nerves that take a message of coldness to the brain." Finally, Hamner criticized one of menthol's more deceptive uses on the consumer market—it was often used to conceal and mask other off-putting tastes in products. "Mentholated cigarettes are probably made of fair tobaccos . . . the use of menthol gives great opportunities for fudging. Menthol so kills all individual tobacco flavours that inferior tobaccos could be used and not noticed."[101] Menthol, in this telling, was a deceitful mask covering over something far worse in a product.

Hostile toward menthol makers throughout the 1930s, Philip Morris also planted the seeds of doubt about menthol in the medical news. In the corporate game of undercutting the opposition, PM remained a step ahead of B&W in courting physicians, in games of reassurance, and in sowing doubt about the menthol brand. In one notable act of trickery, Philip Morris planted its negative views on mentholated smoking in a Q&A section of *Modern Medicine*. Answering a reader's question about whether continuously smoking mentholated cigarettes had any ill effects, the journal answered by citing "considerable research . . . done under the auspices of an important tobacco company [that] tend to show that menthol increases the irritant properties of cigarette smoke. Measurements of the temperature of smoke from cigarettes with and without menthol do not show any difference."[102] When B&W's George Cooper saw the report, he insisted that *Modern Medicine* reveal its source. When Cooper learned that the journal's source was none other than Philip Morris, he dashed off an angry letter to PM's CEO Othoway Chalkley citing Haggard's study in Kool's defense. Angrily he accused PM of crossing a line in stealthily spreading such harmful information. "I am surprised . . . that your company should have furnished any such data in disparagement of competitive goods," Cooper wrote. "You know from time to time very serious charges have been made with respect to one of the ingredients in your cigarettes which you advertise as beneficial. Our policy has been . . . not to promote the extension of such rumors even if we thought . . . this particular ingredient was harmful. I would certainly have expected the same treatment from your company."[103] Cooper did not say it, but he was likely referring to PM's use of diethylene glycol. More to the point, Cooper accused PM of violating an unwritten rule of corporate gamesmanship. Brown & Williamson would not indulge speculation about the dangers of diethylene glycol, and, in turn, Cooper hoped that PM would not denigrate the menthol cigarette. This was the corporate agreement that Chalkley's firm had broken by planting the *Modern Medicine* information. Despite being caught in the act, Chalkley refused to apologize.

By the time that Cooper wrote to Chalkley, chemical additives like diethylene glycol were under new kinds of extreme scrutiny. In these years, US regulatory agencies from the FDA to the Federal Trade Commission (FTC) and the Federal Communications Commission (FCC) were casting a more watchful eye on these additives and the often dubious scientific claims endorsing them. Even so, the government's actual market controls on products and claims remained weak.[104] After the anti-monopoly breakup of American Tobacco in 1911, regulatory oversight of the new multi-company industry had waned and new patent products had flourished. Menthol cigarettes had emerged in the wake. But now, New Deal–era agencies in the 1930s were asserting slightly more oversight authority, even if they paid attention mostly to the egregiously false and scandalous excesses of the consumer marketplace. As companies courted doctors and scientists for protection, and undermined one another, the FTC remained laissez-faire — as it would for decades, for example, watching but not intervening in the 1950s horse race often called the "tar derby" as companies sought to reassure smokers that their brand, and not that of their competitors, had the lowest tar levels (the chemical substance produced when tobacco is burned).[105] For the tobacco industry, the stakes of these drug claims and counterclaims had risen markedly through the 1930s, touching not only on the smoker's cough but also on matters of life and death.

Then in 1937, a nationwide drug scandal changed government oversight, with rippling implications for diethylene glycol, additives, and PM's cigarette claims. Sulfa drugs (potent antibacterial medicines used to treat a range of infectious diseases associated with high mortality) had been discovered and brought aggressively onto the market in the mid- and late 1930s. But in 1937, one company's sulfa elixir compound killed more than a hundred people, most of them children. The cause of death was the elixir's toxic solvent—coincidentally, diethylene glycol, the same substance Philip Morris was using to condition its tobacco. The shocking deaths provoked national outrage, and a call for expanded government oversight of drug makers to protect consumers from unsafe, toxic drugs. The regulatory landscape shifted suddenly by introducing new requirements for toxicity testing for drugs. The company had tested diethylene glycol for fragrance and flavor, but not for toxicity.[106] The irony, of course, was that the new requirement that drug companies test their products for safety did not apply to the tobacco industry, which skillfully maintained exemption from new laws by convincing politicians that tobacco was neither food nor drug, and thus not subject to FDA oversight.[107] In the wake of the sulfa scandal, new standards for evaluating drugs were established for other firms—not tobacco companies. But even so, other federal agencies were compelled by these events to look more closely than ever at all therapeutic claims in the marketplace, and at the use of toxic, dangerous, or deceptive products—including tobacco.

Despite the momentary scandals and the conniving wars within the industry, the strategy of scientific reassurance for the worried smoker continued on. Regulators, although now attuned to the dangers of additives, remained loath to intervene. It would not be until the 1950s that regulators would take a more aggressive stand against the therapeutic claims of cigarette makers, for example, banning "low tar" promises on cigarettes because they deceitfully implied a correlation with better health. Through these critically important early decades in the 1920s and early 1930s, then, a potent argument about mentholated cigarettes as health promoting was being crafted and widely circulated, supported by scientists, and flourishing unchecked.

At the same time, an enduring set of relationships (a web of scientific expertise) took shape as the industry cultivated a cadre of experts to support their products, and to reassure. Most of these relationships—like that of Spier, Haggard, and Brown & Williamson—remained outside government or public purview. These strong institutional relationships, hallmarks of big corporate capitalism in the early twentieth century, were being forged by the industry with elite organizations and institutions—shoring up the industry's therapeutic claims. The relationships ran in multiple directions and served many purposes: between Yale's Haggard and Brown & Williamson to fend off accusations but also for touting products; between the AMA's Phillips, Ginsburg, and Philip Morris to collect evidence to bolster therapeutic claims; between the Psychological Corporation and other cigarette firms to study consumer psychology; and so on. The collaborations involved respected institutions like the AMA and Yale, and scientists at the nation's most prestigious research universities. Philip Morris's research department understood that "the results of our work form the foundation of our entire publicity campaign, and it is believed we cannot leave any opening for attack."[108] For example, in defending diethylene glycol, the company had worked closely with Columbia University scientist M. G. Mulinos on the questions of toxicity and irritation. When PM executives learned that Axton-Fisher had approached the same scientist, offering him $20,000 a year to work with them instead of PM, they responded with more generous compensation to the Columbia scientist and his laboratory. Going further, PM also established a Philip Morris fellowship for tobacco research at the university. Across the industry, investing in medicine, physiology, and psychology made good long-term sense: "Experience has shown that research pays dividends."[109] All of this effort was devoted to a vast and durable web of reassurance.

How a Drug Became Merely a Flavor

The deep irony of menthol smoking was this: if the cigarette marketplace had produced health ills, the same market claimed to be able to relieve and cure those ills with medically treated tobacco. Many smokers accepted the conceit. Menthol smoking came into its own as a therapy; it was also a hedge, an explicit admission that there was something unhealthful about smoking that might require medication. In the early years of mentholated smoking, few observers would dispute the notion that Spud or Kool were medicated cigarettes, and that menthol was a "drug" (as Haggard had described it). But the common portrait of menthol as a drug was shifting slowly, particularly as drug regulations increased and as the explicit health claims and reassurance of menthol makers came under scrutiny from competitors. It was as a drug that menthol had become embedded in American consumer products more generally. With colds, flu, and congestion omnipresent, and with worries about the smoker's cough and throat irritation climbing along with smoking rates, menthol smoking's appeal had grown. Industry built markets around the fact that the drug worked by a clever trick of counterirritation and the claim that it brought health benefits. Meanwhile, the question of who would police these claims—or whether the industry's reliance on men like Howard Haggard was all that was needed to assure the public—had become a growing public concern by the late 1930s.

Ironically, the most heated criticism of menthol as a deceptive substance came not from government regulators of the 1930s but from inside the tobacco industry. Menthol had come into medical and social awareness as an antiseptic (germ-killing) agent and as an anesthetic (painkilling) drug. It was Haggard at Yale who saw its claims of cooling as deceptive, but it was a PM scientist who pointed to its role as a mask for other noxious elements—a way to conceal off-putting tastes and odors. Philip Morris seeded medical and consumer doubt about menthol as an irritant. By the end of the 1930s, whatever these scientists might say, several generations of consumers had come to view menthol products as healthful and protective, even restorative. Following Spud and Kool, Polar had come into the market riding on the coattails of these long-standing therapeutic promises. As new menthol cigarettes emerged, leveraging health claims to build markets, the question of how to police these "cough relieving" claims

Figures 1.6 & 1.7. Ads from 1940. Menthol smoking increased based on a deceptive promise that the "cooling smoothness" of Spud or Kool was therapeutic for people suffering from colds. In time the health promise became less explicit, but psychologists and marketers continued cultivating these spurious health associations in creating menthol markets.

Credit: From the collection of Stanford Research Into the Impact of Tobacco Advertising (tobacco .stanford.edu).

remained a topic of heated discussion both inside the industry and outside.

If the First World War and the 1920s had laid the groundwork for the rise of smoking, its accompanying cough, and a new market for menthol smoking, then the Second World War would repeat the trend: sending menthol smoking around another corner and further down another profitable road. The war interrupted peppermint supply chains as hostilities with Japan sharply curtailed the trade. Manufacturers searched hastily for other sources of peppermint. Finding suitable alternatives would not be easy; each strain of peppermint plant carried its own combination of sweetness, bitterness, and minty sensation, depending on where it was grown in the world. Some marketers turned to Brazil for menthol. The decline of Japanese menthol supplies also awakened a new interest in synthetic chemistry, opening the possibility of menthol that was synthetically produced in laboratories. Here, again, another science—not physiology or psychology but biochemistry—became entwined with the future of menthol.

As in the earlier conflict, the Second World War became a bonanza for recruiting new young smokers who would become the lifeblood of commercial success for years to come. With millions of young men (and women) stationed abroad, cigarettes were again a popular mass pastime—they reassured worried, tired, and fearful troops. They suited the needs of soldiers, a captive market.[110] Not surprisingly, smoking rates among men spiked in the 1940s and continued rising. New advertising strategies followed, attuned to the wartime appeal. Kool, for example, showed its longtime mascot Willie the Penguin now dressed in US Navy garb calling soldiers to "Ten-shun!" and striving to convince men and WAC women to try Kool when they had colds, but also to carry on with menthol smoking after getting well—because "if they tasted so fresh and soothing then . . . wouldn't you be smart to smoke them all the time?"[111] Increasingly, Kool smokers were encourage to "make Kool your steady smoke."

In the midst of war, menthol's supposed therapeutic qualities began to attract closer scrutiny only because the Federal Trade Commission began taking on expanded responsibility for monitoring deceitful advertising more generally. To be sure there were many critics. Daniel Crean's 1941 polemic against the industry in a booklet titled *The Cigarette Racket: You Are Being Drugged!* was little noticed—a one-man operation under the guise of the Tobacco Control League, drowned out by the tempest of world war. His message was clear enough, however: "the unwary consumer of cigarettes, unprotected by urgently needed legislation, is at the whim and mercy of any unscrupulous manufacturer who might see fit to adulterate cigarettes. It is not sufficient that nicotine, furfural, pyridine, and acrolein take their horrible toll of damaged lives—diethylene glycol can now be found among this lethal group."[112] Crean's complaints had little impact. In the early 1940s, however, such substances were attracting closer, if more measured, scrutiny as the FTC became the first federal agency to challenge the industry's menthol claims—criticizing B&W for promising to protect the throat, promote decongestion, and clear the head when there was no evidence to support these pitches. These appeals simply were not credible. As most knew by now, and as Haggard had noted, menthol was a "perversion of sensation"—a drug that "worked" by a clever distraction, by convincing smokers that their nasal passages were opening when, in fact, no such change in the airways had taken place. With this understanding widely established, the FTC issued a cease-and-desist order against B&W—the company could no longer make explicit therapeutic claims about menthol as a source of relief.

It was not merely that the federal government's regulatory skepticism had grown; it was also that by 1940 the definition of what constituted an effective drug was changing. The standards for what defined an efficacious drug was shifting, with a flourishing consumer drug market defined by an array of new products—ranging from the mild to toxic and from ineffective to lifesaving. In 1900 menthol was a drug as defined by the popular standards of the day—a new antiseptic that also carried a painkilling promise. But by the 1940s, with other strong antibacterials on the market—from the sulfa drugs to penicillin—few physicians thought of menthol as a potent germ killer anymore. Nor did scientists regard it as a remarkable painkilling agent, especially with many new potent synthetic opioids on the booming postwar pharmaceutical market. Seen through this lens, menthol was defined less as a drug in the popular or therapeutic sense and more akin to a taste, an enhancement of flavor.

These new drug markets had strengthened the need for wariness about deception; these realities also challenged menthol cigarette makers to find new selling strategies. In this regulatory setting, tobacco companies would be challenged to defend, for example, menthol's therapeutic advertising or else to get rid of unsupported health claims. Henceforth, explicit promises would be replaced by implicit healthful associations in pitching menthols. The FTC's scrutiny of Kool advertising highlighted one of the many ways that the US drug market had changed—thus changing the very meaning of menthol as a drug. A new avenue of marketing was opening. Menthol, once promoted as a potent cold-relieving drug, would be championed as a flavor. But industry now sought different ways of delivering the health promise more quietly. Despite being downgraded, menthol continued to gain prominence as a familiar household ingredient and a common ingredient with a masking appeal. For users, the most distinctive aspect of menthol remained the way it made people's throats and airways feel. But if selling menthol cigarettes as a defense against colds was no longer possible, then how would industry market the menthol sensation?

For those in industry seeking to avoid regulatory scrutiny, a necessary step in the defense of menthol smoking was to treat menthol not as a drug, but as a mere flavor—albeit a flavor that still carried strong if implicit therapeutic associations. By the early 1940s, with menthol's promise still strong, even Philip Morris had decided to stop undermining competitors' menthol brands and join the bandwagon—shifting course by purchasing Axton-Fisher, and with it Spud, in 1944.

∴ ∴ ∴

Over the course of their long-term consulting relationship, Howard Haggard had given adman Carl Spier and his client Brown & Williamson most of what the cigarette company had sought for its menthol push. The Yale study provided the reassuring protection of science, with a defense against competitors' claims that menthol was a hazard.

In the quarter century from 1925 to 1950, the door to menthol smoking had opened; the menthol market was not defined by any specific class or identity group but by a broad-based appeal. Wherever smokers had coughs, congestion, or throat worries, menthol smoking offered to help, even if temporarily. By and large, menthol was an occasional smoke—a salve. Tobacco industry insiders along with the admen, physiologists, physicians, psychologists, and many others had worked to establish and stabilize such tobacco markets, enrolling medical organizations in the effort, sending free samples to troops in wartime, and forging relationships with scientists to defend their products. The business atmosphere of the 1920s and 1930s, following the breakup of the tobacco monopoly and rising smoking-related health worries, had fostered menthol's market. More than anything, smoking itself had opened the door for the mentholated cigarette with its claim to assuage throat ailments. By the early 1940s, the stealthy backhanded efforts of PM to undermine menthol (as B&W alleged) had subsided. In a remarkable shift of strategy, Philip Morris (a former champion of diethylene glycol as its own answer to the smoker's throat and the fiercest critic of mentholated cigarettes) became a menthol champion itself—lurching in a new direction by acquiring Spud. Now a menthol cigarette maker, Philip Morris sought to adapt the first menthol brand to this new era.

By the early 1940s, however, Haggard's annoyance with the science-industry-advertising relationship—and his worries over his own exploitation—had turned to resentment and resistance about the marketer's push. Haggard's initial conclusions about menthol had been mostly exculpatory even if his initial conclusions on menthol irritation were ambiguous. As he wrote, "With the possible exception of irritation of the mucosa [minor in his view], and some slight antiseptic action, the effects from inhalation of menthol are subjective."[113] What vexed the Yale scientist, however, was the advertising company's continued efforts to use some of these findings in marketing. In Haggard's view, the problem of deceitful misuses of his science resided with the slick advertisers, not with the cigarette companies or their products. In 1938 he appealed to be released from the agreement with B&W and Spier's BBDO, earning the right to publish his own findings on menthol physiology. BBDO agreed that "this is the course to follow . . . [and that] any articles . . . would refer to mentholated cigarettes in general and not mention Kools by name." The publications would be aimed at medical audiences, and the advertiser reserved the right, once published, to quote from the report, which would "have a lot more weight with the public than quoting from our own literature."[114]

Importantly, the agreement that allowed Haggard to publish his findings and the marketers to quote from any publication also kept invisible to readers the long-standing relationship between the scientist and the tobacco company. Haggard's article would not need to acknowledge his years of close work with the tobacco industry. Thus, although he, BBDO, and Brown & Williamson formally parted ways, no one reading his 1941 article in the *Archives of Otolaryngology* would know about his years of close consultation. No reader would suspect that his laboratory's findings on the absorption of menthol, how concentrations of menthol acted on the respiratory system, or the effect of continuous exposure to menthol vapors had been nurtured by years of contract research for the industry. Medical readers would, however, be impressed by Haggard's apparently objective findings: "Menthol added to tobacco in the amount now present in cigarets on the American market exerts no toxic or irritant action."[115]

The next decades brought new threats and opportunities for the menthol cigarette makers, in which novel health worries—cancer foremost among them—would help menthol manufacturers further expand their strategy of implicit therapeutic marketing. Moreover, as mass markets appeared to fragment, they also turned toward targeted identity-based appeals. Menthol's second act in the American tobacco marketplace, like its first, would benefit from a health crisis—with menthol brands again positioned to promise relief to anxious smokers. Within a few years after the end of the Second World War, with studies drawing a clear line from smoking to cancer and threatening the industry, menthol health messaging and profits soared. Assuaging the psyche of anxious smokers in the cancer-conscious era, if also deceiving them, would build the niche menthol-smoking market into something vastly more profitable. And a new cadre of experts would be called upon to help companies with the challenges, and the opportunities, of this new era: to study the psychology of cancer fears, to bolster the image of menthol as protection and therapy, and to understand how these worries resonated with different groups. Investing in this web of supporting actors—physiologists, psychologists, admen, doctors, and many others—was critical to the enterprise of using menthol to turn adversity and anxiety into profit.

2

For People Susceptible to Cancer Anxiety

Vance Packard looked past the radio microphone, his focus on the man he deemed a menace responsible for a "strange and rather exotic" strain of consumer manipulation in America.[1] Packard's radio combatant that day was Ernest Dichter, who figured as the villain in Packard's new best-selling exposé, *The Hidden Persuaders*. The year was 1957, and the place was an NBC broadcast studio, set up for a debate about ethics, commerce, manipulation, and "the art of persuasion."[2] For his part, Dichter seemed oddly pleased with the attention Packard's book had drawn to his marketing techniques—a method of tapping into the buyer's psyche to sell everything from hair products to cars and menthol cigarettes. Dichter shunned terms like manipulation or seduction to describe his methods, preferring the label "motivation research," a term he claimed to have coined; Packard saw it as hidden exploitation, aimed at children, trafficking in dangerous products—cigarettes among them. Menthols loomed large in the charade.

In the tense back-and-forth, Dichter, author of *The Psychology of Everyday Living* and founder of the Institute for Motivational Research, broke his calm only once.[3] "In one of your chapters you talk of the psychoseduction," Dichter objected. "It is a very good title . . . ," but before he could finish, Packard interjected to correct him. The audience surely needed to hear the rest of the title. "Of children," Pack-

Figure 2.1. Vance Packard, the author of *Hidden Persuaders* and a harsh critic of market psychologists and manipulative advertising aimed at adults and children. Seated at a bookstore signing, 1958.
Credit: From the Photographic vertical files, Portraits, 1855–present (01212), Eberly Family Special Collections Library, Pennsylvania State University Libraries.

ard said. Packard's chapter was on the psychoseduction of children. In calling attention to the psychological techniques used by advertisers, Packard worried about more than just candy, hair products, and toys pitched to children. "My little eight-year-old girl is now singing the jingle of Pall Mall [cigarettes], 'don't miss the fun of smoking,'" he complained. "It is being conditioned into her mind that it is something that is fun."[4] To Packard, artifice also drove menthol sales.

As the journalist saw it, Dichter's techniques of consumer psychology were being used to deceive not just adults but the most vulnerable minds, children's. It was a worrisome new stage in marketing, singling out specific groups, seducing them with false promises, feeding on both high-status appeals as well as group anxieties and vulnerabilities. In many ways, the youth market seemed ideal—presenting the pros-

Figure 2.2. Ernest Dichter in 1963. The founder of the Institute for Motivational Research, he and a growing cadre of market researchers provided rich insights for the tobacco industry about menthol, race, status anxiety, and the range of psychological concerns that underpinned brand preferences. Credit: Photo by Larry Ellis/Daily Express/Hulton Archive. Courtesy of Getty Images.

pect of long-term users. But the industry cultivated men's products, brands with feminine appeal, and also (somewhat more ambivalently, as we shall see) appeals for Black smokers. Packard's outrage, however, settled on the appeal to youngsters. His book documented that postwar US consumerism had generated a cadre of Dichters—an entire industry of market researchers spawning jingles and ads intended to make every American home, via the new medium of television, a place to traffic in new desires. Packard complained that the most serious offense of these so-called "depth manipulators" was "that they try to invade the privacy of our minds."[5] He accused consultants of "psychoanalyzing little girls, for example, to find out their attitudes toward their hair," so that they could foster their innermost anxieties about beauty and then sell beauty products.[6] These motivational techniques were novel and ascending, Dichter confirmed—replacing an era of what he termed "buckshot advertising" with new targeted outreach aimed at the "mobilization of human needs."[7] Packard objected, countering that these hidden persuaders were nurturing dangerous behaviors in a new generation. Among those behaviors, smoking had become deeply worrisome by the mid-1950s.

Dichter refused to play the role of villain on NBC radio or elsewhere; he had heard these complaints about devious marketing many times. These were the worries of Puritans, Dichter believed—humorless people long accustomed to the denial of the pleasure and who needlessly shunned buying as if it were a shameful indulgence. As he saw it, his critics were deeply uncomfortable with the psychological satisfactions of postwar consumer society. They did not understand the complexities of human psychology or the stabilizing impact of consumption on people and society. So even though new findings warned that cigarettes raised the risk of cancer, Dichter saw the human desire for cigarette smoking in positive terms; and even as Packard and others decried the "conditioning" of youth into smoking by using slick marketing on television, Dichter saw an industry catering to human impulses. To the psychologist, the cigarette was a positive outlet for pent-up anxiety, a symbol of identity and rebellion, and part of the individual's constant struggle for status and personal stability. The very feel of the cigarette in the mouth provided psychic satisfaction; it was no different than chewing gum, he insisted, sidestepping Packard's claims of the seduction of youth.

The architect of theories about human motivation, Dichter saw product choices as opportunities for self-making and, in the case of youth, for rebellion. Yes, "chewing gum is used by youngsters to rebel, to revolt against their parents," he admitted. "At the same time as a clinical psychologist I know that revolt and rebellion of this type is almost unavoidable . . . it has to take place at a certain point." He saw the youth market as a cauldron of natural urges that were dangerous if suppressed; and products could be helpful, even therapeutic, tools to help young people adjust to the turmoil of growing up. In his view, chewing gum—decried by some as a bad habit—actually promoted psychologically balanced youth. Its value was to "organize" a rebellious streak. NBC's moderator, Clifton Fadiman, could not help finishing Dichter's thought—children chewed gum, he explained, to "provide a legitimate channel for releasing this aggressiveness or re-bellion. What do you think about that, Mr. Packard?"

"It sounds rather oversimplified," the journalist responded curtly. For Packard, Dichter's views about anxious citizenry, including chil-dren, who needed to be soothed psychologically by a new world of products was nothing but a cynical justification for marketers, admen, and companies to manipulate the public for profit. As Pack-ard explained, "I know that . . . one of the chewing gum companies did conduct a test in a mining town and they tried to see if they could eliminate dissatisfaction [among workers] by chewing gum, and they professed success." Where Dichter saw consumers channeling "natu-ral" desires and realizing their dreams through consumption, Packard saw corporate manipulation, but, worse, consumers being controlled and deceived. But for Dichter, the study of motivation was a duality. "The human mind" was both "a projector and a receiver of the things which surround it."[8] To study the motivation for smoking—or any consumer motivation—was to explore both the push and the pull of desire, the inner drives of people projected outward, and the way outside pressures molded those drives and anxieties. He made no apologies about being a molder of perception or pitching products tailored to the psychological anxieties of the time; nor would Dichter shrink from working with companies to understand how vulnerability created new markets for smoking mentholated cigarettes.

This debate over chewing gum sales, cigarettes, and youth un-folded in a changing political environment with health anxieties on the rise. Americans had recently learned that cigarette smokers had higher cancer rates than nonsmokers. The moment added a new chapter to the history of menthol smoking, as the tobacco industry responded to the critics in two ways—by denial and also by pushing filtered and menthol brands in a play to hedge their bets. Industry executives grew keenly interested in what men like Dichter could tell them about rising cancer anxieties and how they shaped brand choices. The first major report linking smoking and cancer had been announced a few years before Packard's book appeared. Soon after,

R. J. Reynolds capitalized on the moment with a new brand of menthol cigarettes, Salem—joining an increasingly crowded field, with Brown & Williamson's Kool, Philip Morris's Spud, and Lorillard's Polar. With smokers seeking security, market analysts studied this new landscape of worries to learn whether women were more concerned than men; whether class, social status, or age determined who was worried; as well as other demographic indices. They keenly looked for any evidence of how health worries affected brand choice. The circumstances, they learned, were ripe for a rise in menthol smoking.

Health, not race, provided the best market-making opportunities for menthols in the 1950s. In surveys, focus groups, depth psychology analysis, and psychographic studies, psychologists probed how adversity reshaped smoker preferences, trying to discover why menthols seemed to be rising as a brand choice. What they learned was that menthol smoking rose *because* of the cancer findings and the anxiety that followed. Moreover, researchers began to see the new menthol smoker as a particular kind of social being—a personality type prone to being rattled by the cancer news, but a person who could be coaxed by promises of more safely engineered cigarettes to stick with smoking despite their worries. Filtered cigarettes and menthols were filling a space in these smokers' lives. Menthol smokers' numbers were growing; they made up an increasing percentage of smokers. Who were these menthol lovers? Were they squeamish sissies? Hypochondriacs? Women more than men? What drove them? Were they looking for a "health cigarette"? The insights of men like Dichter were critically important in this moment of market turmoil—a moment of high smoker and industry anxiety that would guide tobacco companies toward seeing menthol use as deeply connected to postwar health worries.

At this juncture, Black smokers seemed no more likely to embrace menthols than any other group; nor were companies in the 1950s particularly interested in the kind of targeted menthol marketing along racial lines that would define the 1960s. Those possibilities were not yet imaginable by Dichter and others in his line of work. Even where Black smokers showed an affinity for a particular brand in the 1950s as they did for the Philip Morris brand, companies often looked past the opportunity to target—wary, as we shall see, of white backlash and being stigmatized as a "Negro brand." There were other more lucrative markets to exploit—the youth market and, for menthol makers in particular, a newly emerging, health-conscious smoking market. In the 1950s, health targeting would remain the key, as it had for menthol makers since the 1920s. Even with the dire cancer findings, the bad news, and consumer uncertainties—indeed, precisely *because* of this turmoil—marketers of menthols sensed opportunity.

Tapping Anxiety

In Dichter's view, the cigarette was no different than any other consumer product; it carried an abundance of meanings and fulfilled different psychological needs. Smoking played a stabilizing role in the psychology of everyday life. "Psychologically, smoking is chiefly a substitute," he had once insisted. But it was also a "conditioned reflex"—a reaction when people needed to control such basic drives as hunger, loneliness, anxiety, and the need for companionship.[9] Packard and Dichter both believed that Americans in the 1950s had good reason to be anxious, whether about the economy and jobs, the communist threat and the Cold War, or the fate of their children. As historian Daniel Horowitz has observed, affluence (a new, uncertain economic prosperity after decades of depression and war) itself produced anxieties.[10] The two men, however, differed on how they thought those anxieties should be channeled or exploited. And they differed in their thinking on the role of consumer products like menthol cigarettes, chewing gum, or status goods in addressing these anxieties of modern American life.

A European émigré during the war years, Dichter believed that the market, and its various new products, calmed social turmoil and channeled anxiety. If political passions tore a nation's people apart and forced them to extremes, as they had in Nazi Germany for example, the satisfactions of consumerism could be a stabilizing salve—so Dichter believed.[11] "What I try to do personally is to combine the socially desirable goals, I call them, with the commercial goal," explained

Dichter. "They are not identical but they are often combinable."[12] Motivation research provided the tools to align consumerism and the social good. Dichter aimed to study people deeply enough to learn their wants, so that industry could feed their desires while giving them relief, ease, and calm amidst the turmoil and worry of modern life. For Dichter, this is where smoking, and menthol smoking in particular, fit into American society.

Anxieties and insecurities had always been central to the smoker's relationship with cigarettes, as experts like psychologist Steuart Henderson Britt of the McCann Erickson advertising agency knew. For Britt, a psychological consultant and one of Dichter's competitors, two facts stood out about smokers in 1950. First, "almost all people have terrific feelings of insecurity," he wrote, and these feelings were often tinged with underlying fear, hate, and prejudice. Second, people also needed "symbols of prestige, in order to bolster up their own ego-deflated selves." These unflattering facets of the insecure modern consumer were bedrock concepts underpinning the new field of consumer motivation. "If ever there were a need for significant studies of social behavior, now is the time," observed Britt. The insights were as relevant for understanding status, prejudice, and insecurity among smokers as for understanding citizenship more generally. These insights from social sciences, he said, were being used everywhere—from the "ingenious study" of Paul Lazarsfeld on "how voters make up their minds in a presidential campaign," to Howard Odum and Harry Estill Moore's "important studies on regionalism." To understand how markets behaved, said Britt, it was necessary to study social movements as well, and marketers "ought to know more about the problems of minority groups, and the ways in which prejudice acts in relation to important segments of our population."[13] For Britt as for Dichter, these social-psychological drivers underpinned all "principles of motivation" and were particularly salient for modern marketing.

Motivational researchers understood that inner conflicts were impossible to put to rest; understanding the consumer's inner turmoil was key to mobilizing buying. These were theories well suited to understanding how smokers were responding to increasingly bad news about the product they used daily. According to Dichter, the smoker's true motivations resided deep beneath surface appearances. He saw smoking behaviors (and particularly brand choice) being driven not by addiction or nicotine, but by status and fear. A "glamour girl smoked with a long dark holder," for example, both to be alluring and to say, "Don't come too close." Smokers carried within them many conflicts, and among the most important was "an underlying guilt feeling . . . a buried feeling that smoking is not only harmful physically but also has the taint of immorality." The task of the depth psychologist was to understand why smokers persisted in the habit despite these health worries, and to explore why the psychic drive to smoke "is difficult to defeat by warnings or preachment."[14]

Dichter earnestly sought to learn as much as possible about these psychological drives and to use that knowledge to help companies develop, market, and sell products tailored to meet consumer needs. Some characteristics like insecurity were inherent to all humans, Dichter believed; but different groups—like those rebellious teenagers who took up chewing gum or cigarettes—exhibited behaviors, choices, and preferences that particularly interested motivation researchers. Men, women, youth, and people across regions and ethnic groups thus shared certain propensities, but enacted them in different ways in their product choices.

If consumers of the 1950s were anxious, so, too, were tobacco executives. To James Goodson, the vice president in charge of sales at Brown & Williamson, the market had become "capricious."[15] Unlike in previous decades, the postwar market had become fickle, dividing in unpredictable ways. Consumers were relentlessly changing brands, and these habits of "the fidgety consumer" provoked much industry concern. Did the proliferation of cigarette brands itself create "switch-happy consumers," Goodson wondered. Or did this fickleness stem from the health fears—the fact that "the cigarette campaigns have become increasingly riddled with warnings and appeals to fear . . . promoted on the grounds that they contain less nicotine, or travel the smoke further and thus protect your throat"?[16] Whatever the reasons, brand loyalty was in flux; sales were fluctuating, long-standing solid brands were suffering, and new brands were rising. The mass market of smokers was becoming "segmented" and fractured along unfamiliar lines.[17] At B&W, Goodson looked hopefully to psychology as a stabilizing factor: "It may be said that somewhere—whether in terms of psychologists' probing of the subconscious . . . [or] a preference for the color of one package over another predicated upon seasonal style . . . there are in fact explanations of buyer caprice."[18]

At Philip Morris, sales expert George Weissman turned to Elmo Roper's polling firm for help in understanding consumers' fickle beliefs and hard-to-predict behaviors, with attention to some obvious fracture lines in society—class, sex, and race. For the Roper Organization, a leading political and public opinion firm, ethnicity, sex, and other markers of identity proved the most salient for making sense of which personality types preferred certain brands.[19] After extensive surveys of smokers, Roper explained to Weissman that, among PM's competitors, R. J. Reynolds's Camel brand was "a man's cigarette" ("more than any other brand," he added parenthetically).[20] Camel was popular with people in their thirties and forties, and "strongest in the lowest economic levels, having more than usual appeal among Negroes." Chesterfield was "popular with both sexes," as well as with people of "relatively high economic level orientation. . . . Definitively a white person's cigarette," explained Roper, taking note again of the ethnic contours of brands. Lucky Strike was a "man's cigarette" with appeal to the very young; "with 15–24 year olds, it's the number one brand." (The idea of naming fifteen-year-olds as potential consumers didn't seem to bother Roper despite growing public criticism of cigarette marketing to minors. Such an admission, of course, would have only confirmed Packard's fears of the psychoseduction of youth.) But Lucky Strike was also "appealing to the lower economic levels . . . [while being] strong with Catholics and Italians . . . [and] thought of as having a good flavor, along with being strong and hard on the throat." In Roper's view, brand choices and social identity were deeply interconnected, even if the link between them posed myriad puzzles. Why *did* Camel appeal as a man's smoke, and why did Lucky Strike catch the fancy of minors? These were not easy questions. Moreover, few of these connections seemed stable; so, if a group experienced turmoil and flux in status, if there was a shift in postwar prosperity, or if new worries appeared, these markets and brand choices would fluctuate.

Roper's study also found that smokers viewed brands "from a health standpoint" in the early 1950s, and that the health angle had become a submerged but compelling reason for brand choice, brand switching, and fickleness. "The primary stated reasons for smoking or being interested in smoking filter tips are reasons of health," the pollster explained. Filter tips were themselves a fairly recent innovation—their use increasing in the United States from less than 1 percent of cigarettes in 1950 to 19 percent in 1955, and heading toward 51 percent in 1960 and 82 percent in 1970. These stunning upticks highlighted how smokers were attuned to any promise of making tobacco smoke safer.[21] Driven by similar health appeals, king-size cigarettes—which pulled a higher ratio of air to tobacco smoke than did regular cigarettes—also saw steady increases in sales. Analyst Harry Wootten figured that in one year alone, from 1952 to 1953, despite a moderate decline in overall cigarette sales, kings expanded dramatically from 18 percent of US sales (71.9 billion cigarettes) to 27 percent (103.9 billion); "health talk," he noted, was a major factor.[22]

Health fears cut across many groups, but perceptions of smoking's dangers varied across identity categories—as Roper learned in a 1953 study of smoker habits. Just over a quarter of African Americans polled saw Philip Morris (along with Camel) as the least harmful cigarettes; by contrast, only 7 percent of white smokers characterized Philip Morris cigarettes this way.[23] Strikingly, noted Roper, some brands had acquired the character of a "health cigarette," but the survey was not in the position to explain why.[24] Deeper studies might answer this question. The Roper study suggested that Black Americans were slightly more attuned to health concerns than whites, with 15 percent of African Americans surveyed responding that they favored PMs because they were "better for your health." Only 9 percent of whites favored PMs for health reasons. Black respondents stood out in one other way—they were much more likely than white respon-

dents (11 percent to 1 percent) to say that PM "gives you a kick"—
presumably a sensory response but possibly also a linguistic finding
indicating that Black users in 1953 saw nicotine as packing "a kick."[25]

Roper advised the company to exploit such gaps in racial and
health perception; here was a new style of thinking focused on market
segments, an approach that opened the door to menthol's ascent. But
the opportunities of this era were not merely race-focused; nor were
they simple or one-dimensional. Rather, brand preferences seemed to
be informed by many different factors—thus demanding deeper psychological insight. Health concerns intermingled with gender concerns. Cancer worries were informed by other aspects of personal
or social identity, explained Roper: "We are inclined to think that in
addition to the health motivation there is also a style motivation, or an
aesthetic motivation," or a desire to be different that underpinned, say,
the choice of filtered cigarettes. In Roper's view, for example, women
were more inclined than men to smoke king-size cigarettes, and while
a part of the reason was taste, "we are inclined to think a large part
of it is for style or esthetic reasons."[26] Consumer psychologists and
pollsters advised that, for now, these intriguing links between health
beliefs, race, and gender offered the keys to future branding. In 1953,
studying these trends was one thing. It was another thing altogether
to use this knowledge to guide branding, shape markets, and to push
the industry toward a profitable future in uncertain times.

"Cancer Scare" as Market Opportunity

Industry insiders and consultants called it the "cancer scare" (a term
they used to draw attention to a psychological impact—"the worry"—
that came in the wake of epidemiological evidence linking tobacco to
disease). The "scare" loomed large for Dichter, Roper, Weissman,
and all those studying smoker choices and worrying over the fate of
the industry. The scare had begun in 1950, when a study by Ernest
Wynder and Evarts Graham in the *Journal of the American Medical
Association* announced a strong association between smoking and
lung cancer, making the case that smokers were far more likely to

develop the disease.[27] Then, in 1952 British epidemiologists Richard Doll and A. Bradford Hill showed that lung cancer in white men had quadrupled over the past twenty years — a finding that stunned many in the industry.[28] Their symptoms may have started with a cough and labored breathing, but would have progressed to the spitting up of blood, and pain in the chest sometimes radiating down through the arms.[29] In former years, tuberculosis would have been suspected. But with TB declining, the prime suspect for these lung ailments shifted to cancer. If detected late, little could be done other than supportive care as their ability to breath deteriorated.[30] The awful fruit of two decades of rising smoking rates was being manifest not in smoker's coughs as in the 1920s and 1930s, but in a longer-term outcome of cancer. *Reader's Digest* followed with a widely read exposé, "Cancer by the Carton," and the news media echoed the findings relentlessly.[31]

The industry sought to allay the fear and address the sales turmoil by denying the link between smoking and cancer, and also by characterizing the event as a "cancer scare." In time, the relentlessly bad cancer news became an opportunity for menthol makers to capitalize on the adversity. Initially, however, the industry took psychological aim at the outcry as an overreaction. Yet with millions of Americans aware of tobacco smoking's deadly associations, the threat to future profits was palpable. ABC television newsman (and steady smoker) Walter Winchell reacted to the reports like many others, uncertain about how worried he should be and puzzled about how, if at all, he should change his behavior.[32] Other public figures in positions to shape opinion were also hesitant to interpret what these findings could mean for smoking rates and industry profits. Harry Wootten, the widely read tobacco industry analyst for the marketing trade magazine *Printer's Ink*, observed that "the so-called cancer scare is a psychological fact that no one can evaluate accurately."[33]

Even as doctors and public figures approached the findings with caution, few Americans could dismiss outright the news linking smoking and lung cancer. The surgeon Alton Ochsner announced that the safest path amid the new uncertainty was moderation, counseling the public to "smoke no more than half a dozen cigarettes a day, and have a chest x-ray every six months (better yet, every three months) after age 40."[34] It says much about the heavy-smoking norms of the day that six cigarettes per day counted as moderation to the physician. Like Ochsner and many avid smokers, Winchell fixated not on whether to quit smoking cold, but instead on what he called reducing excessive smoking. Unlike the industry, he did not dismiss the shocking cancer findings because the "association between excessive smoking and cancer of the lungs" was all too clear to him. The hope was that moderation might bring safety. What, then, was his advice to listeners? "I still smoke about ten cigarettes a day," he explained.[35] His hope was that the industry, whose good intentions Winchell trusted, would solve the problem of unsafe cigarettes by making them less dangerous. He would be watchful about how the industry responded, even as he continued to smoke. Like others, the journalist looked for reassurance.

Rattled by the findings, the tobacco companies charted a multi-pronged approach—refuting the findings and downplaying the "scare," diverting criticism by citing other reasons for rising cancer rates, and seeking to study which smokers were most worried and to reassure them. The major tobacco firms formed the Tobacco Industry Research Committee (TIRC) in a joint effort to wage a new information campaign. The TIRC employed a strategy of refutation and denial, insisting that the "science" behind the association of smoking and lung cancer was flawed and dismissing the "scare talk" as an irrational moral panic.[36] The group tried to muddy the smoking-cancer link by asking whether the science of causation was truly as definitive as promised. Disease rates could be rising for "many other aspects of modern life," such as air pollution. Staffed by "scientists of unimpeachable integrity," the TIRC stressed that there was "no proof that cigarette smoking was one of the causes" of lung cancer.[37] The "no proof" defense would become their mantra for many decades. As Packard later told the story in his 1957 exposé, "the industry was thrown into a tizzy by the now famous cancer scare, which in the words of one spokesman of the advertising agencies put the 'cigarette industry in one hell of a fix.' . . . There was turmoil as the cigarettes groped for more reassuring images."[38] Beyond the TIRC's refuting of the cancer-smoking link, the industry also sought to deflect the anxieties and redirect fears—thus feeding new brand preferences such as kings, filters, and menthols. It amounted to a strategy of therapeutic reassurance.

While other brands suffered losses following the dire news, Kool's menthol niche began to grow based on its "therapeutic" appeal, observed J. W. Burgard, a marketing executive at B&W in 1953. "We have seen new cigarettes such as KOOL . . . and more recently, the filter tip brands, established at a premium price in the face of overwhelming competition," he observed, "solely because their advertising held a promise of some unique advantage." Still, B&W's advertising consultants at the Ted Bates firm warned that "the therapeutic approach in and of itself, is no guarantee of success" unless accompanied by "dramatic, believable copy."[39] Bates & Co. had won the Kool advertising account in 1948 and orchestrated the postwar remaking of the brand. They kept the cartoon mascot Willie the Penguin, featuring him in a new pitch to readers of the Sunday comics in 1951 and 1952. Some ads showed the playful Willie making a familiar health appeal—for

Figure 2.3. By 1951 Brown & Williamson used Willie to encourage people to "Smoke KOOLS as your steady smoke . . ." The shocking evidence linking smoking to cancer in these years would help the company to convince many smokers to switch from using menthols occasionally to a regular preference. Cancer fears, they learned, drove the upsurge in menthol and filtered cigarette sales. Credit: From the collection of Stanford Research Into the Impact of Tobacco Advertising (tobacco .stanford.edu).

Willie the Penguin
earned his degree
By explaining KOOLS pleasure
to every M. D.

Doctors learn fast—
they're nobody's fools
And thousands have switched
from "hots" to KOOLS!

When patients complain
their throats are raw
And plain cigarettes
taste like old burning straw.

Put them on KOOLS—
that's what to do
For that clean KOOL taste
will always come through!

Figure 2.4. Into the 1950s, companies continued to misleadingly highlight menthol's "therapeutic" benefits despite the Federal Trade Commission's insistence that companies cease and desist from such unsupported claims. In this 1952 cartoon, Willie pitches the idea that doctors appreciate the value of menthol smoking.
Credit: Image courtesy of Truth Tobacco Industry Documents (https://www.industrydocuments.ucsf .edu/tobacco/).

example, curing his penguin girlfriend's autumn hay fever problem with menthol smokes, and promoting Kool as "your steady smoke."[40] Another campaign showed the affable penguin earning his medical degree, lecturing to physicians, and "explaining KOOLS pleasure to every M.D." The doctors in the ad learned fast, switching patients (their throats raw from plain cigarettes) to the "clean KOOL taste."[41] As Bates analysts saw matters, these therapeutic campaigns needed the proper staging and storyline to break through with consumers; the doctors and the hay fever enhanced the drama, giving the health theme a reassuring believability.[42]

Kool's health promise was resonating, it seemed—and thus the old medication motif could be adapted to a new terrain of fears in the 1950s. The lung cancer news was having "a widespread effect on smokers," explained *Business Week* in 1953. In the battle for smokers, understated health pitches of various kinds seemed to offer the best way forward.[43] The pitches needed to be direct enough to reassure skittish consumers, but not so overt as to attract rebuke from the FTC. As the magazine explained, the long cigarettes and filter tips were "pushed heavily by the cigarette makers on the protection they afford against tars and nicotine." In a year that could make or break the industry, smokers seemed drawn to the "better safe than sorry" pitch. Midway through 1954, cigarette sales industry-wide had dropped 4.7 percent from the previous year. Sales of almost every brand had declined. Philip Morris alone sold over 2 *billion* fewer cigarettes in the March quarter of 1954 than it had a year earlier, a drop of nearly 30 percent.[44] But Kool sales were up. Filters were ascendant. And companies like Brown & Williamson sensed that the strategy of reassurance—centered on menthols and filters, and filtered menthols—was paying dividends. "As a result of the cancer scare," Packard later wrote in 1957, "virtually every major tobacco marketer brought out a filter-tip brand, and in four years filter-tip sales rose 1800 per cent."[45] Across the industry, firms observed the methods of competitors, emulating tactics that promised to stabilize markets, shoring up sinking brands, and seeking to capitalize on opportunities presented by the scare.

One year into the market turmoil, intensive polling—along with depth interviews, psychological studies, sales analyses, and other market research—suggested that the smoker's psyche was damaged and fragile but still malleable and transmutable into profit. The surging brands had one thing in common: they effectively made some design innovations or somehow promised smokers that the industry had their good health foremost in mind. Pall Mall, for example, highlighted its king-size brand as a design that "traveled the smoke farther"—its sales climbed from 11.5 to 12.2 billion cigarettes.[46] As Lorillard's president Robert Ganger explained in late 1952, three intersecting trends explained the rise of king-size long cigarettes: First, with rising federal, state, and municipal taxes on cigarettes, "a bigger cigarette for the same tax means that the consumer gets more for his money"; second, the longer, thinner shape apparently appealed to women as a "more graceful [and] therefore more flattering" design; and finally, there was the health appeal. "The longer length travels the smoke farther—resulting in a slight filtering and softening of irritants."[47]

It did not require a great deal of sophistication to see what was happening in the menthol market. Psychologists like Dichter, journalists like Packard, pollsters, social scientists, and most observers understood that people made product choices "subconsciously, including about health considerations." Accordingly, as Roper noted, much of the "health messaging" around these cigarettes remained hidden and implicit. Across the industry, it also seemed clear that explicit reassurances would not work, say, by directly claiming that smoking did not cause cancer. Rather, the moment called for obfuscation (by claiming that not enough was known) and distraction (by pointing to other likely causes). The tobacco industry also embraced fully the power of the implicit health promise. As the Roper firm acknowledged to Philip Morris executives, "Curiously, cancer is almost never mentioned as a reason for concern over smoking. . . . It may be hidden in some other reasons people give for thinking cigarette smoking is harmful, but it is almost never mentioned specifically."[48] This unspokenness and the smoker's unwillingness to acknowledge the threat, or their tendency to speak in euphemisms, opened the doors to a kind of manipulation below the level of consciousness; this was Vance Packard's most urgent concern in *Hidden Persuaders*.

Health messaging worked in complex and confounding ways, as one Indiana man named Earl Chamberlain explained in a 1954 letter sent to R. J. Reynolds. For one, it was easier for smokers to talk about cancer fear than cancer itself. "Even though this 'cancer phobia' may not be even remotely related to the smoking of cigarettes," Chamberlain observed, "the fact remains, the public is rapidly accepting it as an established fact and it therefor behoves the cigarette manufacturer to do everything in his power to promote a feeling of safety if his business is to maintain its high level of production."[49] Rather than reacting with anger or dismay about the fact that cigarettes carried harmful health effects, such observers worried that the "cancer scare" itself might even be more dangerous than the cancer. Writing in *Popular Medicine* in 1955, one psychologist insisted wryly that all this cancer talk might itself produce an alarming psychological malady: "I am much less concerned about the possibility of heavy smokers contracting lung cancer than I am with the almost certain damage caused by worrying about it."[50] Others argued the industry was overreacting to the news by pushing filters so heavily. As one testy writer exclaimed in *Fortune* magazine, "With all the postwar health advertising and the talk of lung cancer, it seems as though the manufacturers have jammed the filter-tip cigarette down the public's throat."[51]

Where many commentators saw the "cancer scare" itself as a threat, marketing psychologists like Ernest Dichter sensed opportunity. To them, health anxieties about smoking were, in themselves, unremarkable. The more interesting question was consumer differentiation — that is, understanding who was and was not susceptible to these cancer anxieties, and how cancer was itself accentuating and giving definition to new market segments of smokers. Trained as a Freudian, Dichter proudly styled himself as a leader in applying psychological insights on human nature to the business of selling products. Packard's 1957 account described how Dichter's Institute for Motivational Research had built a large following among a range of businesses by convincing them that their true products were not cars or milk or cereal, but rather *security*:

> Its fee for studies ranged from a few hundred dollars for a simple package of tests to $25,000 for a real run-down on a sales problem. The institute's gross in 1955, according to one report, ran about $750,000. . . . [Dichter] lists on his staff more than twenty-five resident specialists, including psychologists, sociologists, anthropologists. Among his clients are . . . such blue-chip firms as General Foods, General Mills . . . American Airlines, Carnation, as well as several major advertising agencies. To all of these firms, he trum-

peted a main idea . . . [that] any product not only must be good but must appeal to our feelings "deep in the psychological recesses of our mind." He tells companies that they've either got to sell emotional security or go under.[52]

For Dichter, all psyches were driven by common psychological motives (sex, security, and so on). The secret to benefiting from the cancer "scare," then, was in realizing that all products triggered quite different drives and worries, acquiring different meanings for the user depending on age, ethnicity, sex, and class.

There was profit to be made in fear. As smokers' cancer anxiety heightened in the early 1950s, the utility of psychological studies increased—as did controversy over motivation research. Wasn't it just fearmongering by another name? Menthol manufacturer Brown & Williamson's Burgard denied this in 1953: "Contrary to popular belief, advertisers do not instill fear in consumers to make them buy. They simply recognize its existence and do their best to profit by it."[53]

The cancer scare had created a new landscape of smokers' fears, opening a new market opportunity for previously niche products like filtered cigarettes and Kool menthols. Almost immediately, Kool became a beneficiary. The menthol brand that promised "throat comfort" and "beneficial head clearing qualities" through the 1930s and 1940s had found a new significance. As Bates analysts observed, menthol appealed to "the basic human motivations, the strongest of which is the desire for security."[54] As other companies struggled with declining sales, Burgard and B&W seized the opportunity to position menthol smoking as a psychological salve.

In a time defined by anxiety in all directions (business anxiety, cancer and health anxiety, brand anxiety, and anxieties about group status, for example, in the burgeoning civil rights movement), the market psychologists found plenty of consulting work and ample opportunity to prove their worth. As Elmo Roper explained to Philip Morris executives, the work of mobilizing anxieties for the purpose of selling cigarettes meant studying worries intimately—the motivation behind them, how they played out in brand preferences, and how different groups manifested them in group-specific tendencies. Exploiting anxiety also meant a new kind of targeting: more focus group interviews, more targeted marketing efforts, and greater attention to segmenting markets. Psychological reports offered clients a way to weather the storms caused by cancer, but also to see how new market segments were taking shape amid the fear. As Dichter put it, "No matter what happens, people will probably go on smoking," and so "the advertiser who will help the smoker in his re-examination of smoking will have the edge. He must prove that he is on the side of the smoker."[55] Psychological positioning was the key to branding and promised to help companies survive the bad health news, develop new markets, and perhaps even profit from the hard times.

Menthol Smokers Remade

In riding the cancer news to higher sales, B&W was more lucky than shrewd. In 1953 the firm's Kool (with therapeutic associations dating back to the 1930s) along with Viceroy and Raleigh saw sales climb close to 32 percent.[56] For all of these brands at the small subsidiary of British American Tobacco, the "health" marketing had strengthened sales, but in different ways: by equipping Viceroy with filters; by turning Raleigh into a king-size product; and simply by holding steady with mentholated Kool—selling about 3 billion cigarettes combined in 1953 and 1954. Two years after the cancer findings had rocked the industry, B&W enjoyed "one of the most successful years since its invasion of the American market in the 1920s," observed the analyst Wootten.[57] Still, Kool remained a minor player in nationwide sales, capturing only about 2 or 3 percent of the overall market.

If there were specific populations driving the trend, the data remained sparse. A 1954 Roper study for Philip Morris, for example, was commissioned to look specifically at brand preferences among Blacks. It found a surprising uptick among certain users: Kool had become the choice brand among 5 percent of Black smokers, exceeding the brand's overall market portion by a few percentage points.[58] At the time, few company insiders commented on the tiny disparity—time would tell whether it reflected any specifically racial differences in consumer psychology or associations about health and the meaning of menthols. Much more striking at this juncture was the overall development of a diverse menthol segment, spanning multiple groups who shared a desire for health security.

With health worries rather than specific group smoking trends driving menthol's rise, B&W's success with Kool caught the attention of the other major tobacco companies, setting off the postwar era's first major skirmish in a war for menthol smokers. In 1956 R. J. Reynolds dove headlong into the menthol fray with an eye-catching new product called Salem that combined two health motifs: mentholated tobacco and the filter tip. RJR's product also added a new twist to the menthol appeal—it offered the skittish smoker levels of menthol considerably lower than those of Kool, championing it as "a breath of springtime" rather than a bracing winter chill. Its new radio jingle (precisely the kind of pitch that Packard disliked) announced, "That's Salem / Fresh, mild, mentholated / That's Salem / Green and white pack / That's Salem / With the most modern filter / Smoke Salem / You will be enchanted."[59] Out of the gate, Salem set sales records. Its rapid rise caught B&W back on its heels. But within months B&W answered the challenge by fitting its Kool brand with its own filter, thus launching a war between the brands that would carry on for decades.

Executives at Philip Morris also responded quickly to Salem's appearance, fitting its languishing Spud brand with a filter tip within weeks of RJR's entrance to the mentholated market. PM's Weissman had high hopes for their own rebranding effort. The company had, after all, just completed a bold and far-reaching brand transformation, perhaps the most famous in tobacco's history, with Marlboro. As Weissman noted, "The Marlboro name had such feminine connotations that a strenuous compensatory effort, the super-masculine brand image of the Marlboro man, was needed to bring the Marlboro name up to the level of popular acceptance."[60] Having successfully turned the feminine, niche Turkish-flavored brand into a filter-tipped smoke associated with rugged men, sailors, athletes, and of course cowboys, Philip Morris now contemplated either rebuilding Spud or creating a new menthol brand altogether. In a 1956 letter to the company's CEO, Joseph Cullman, Weissman explained that there were now multiple pathways into the new menthol market: "One path takes menthol content as heavy, if not heavier, than Kool. The second path indicates a cigarette with a perceptible menthol flavor but mild enough to be attractive to Kool, as well as non-Kool smokers."[61] PM decided to roll the dice on a new brand named Alpine, turning once again to Roper's surveys to guide their strategy.[62] They would also rely on the advice of Dichter, who was "most enthusiastic about [the] possibility of attracting an audience even much wider than the current Kool audience."[63]

"Whether Brown and Williamson was just 'dumb lucky' and was 'in the right place at the right time,'" or whether their success was the result of careful study, Weissman could not tell.[64] Success in the new menthol sweepstakes depended on some combination of planning, influence, chance, and the group psychology of smokers, he believed. Emulation of competitors also laid the groundwork of success. Salem's quick leap ahead of Kool and Spud after 1956 encouraged others in the industry to jump into the market, convinced that there were profits to be made. Liggett & Myers entered the race with its menthol Oasis brand in 1957. Its commercials began running on a television program called *Club Oasis*, featuring popular guests like Dean Martin and Jimmy Durante, the same year that *Hidden Persuaders* appeared.[65]

If there was a hidden driver to this sudden uptick in menthol smoking, it was rising cancer consciousness. As smokers sought and firms offered protection, cancer loomed in the background. Like the crooked man who walked a crooked mile in the old rhyme, menthol manufacturers had found their crooked sixpence in cancer—a worrisome chance encounter, a death sentence for many, but also an opportunity bringing menthol makers unexpected riches in threatening times. But the looming cancer threat also helped transform the "menthol smoker" into a consumer type worthy of intense study. For psychologists and market experts, the menthol smoker transformed from a curious temporary medication-oriented minor consumer to a discernible, high-growth, consumer type embodying a lucrative market trend. As such, tobacco firms looked to social science experts to further sketch out the profile of this anxious consumer type whose behavior, personality, and fears were being conceptualized as a new market identity: the menthol smoker. For Salem, Kool, Alpine, and Oasis smokers, menthol seemed to be much more than a temporary source of relief in times of congestion; menthols were becoming long-term companions.

A Road Not Taken: Dilemmas of Branding and Race

Why did menthol markets, or any market brand, not racialize at this juncture? Simply put, the industry saw market opportunities elsewhere. In the early 1950s, for example, Philip Morris learned from Roper that African American buyers were avid buyers of their signature non-menthol brand. This posed a dilemma for executives at PM, for in 1950s America, they saw any courtship of a Black market as double-edged and filled with racial peril. As PM saw it, an aggressive courtship of Black smokers could provoke a white backlash they did not wish to invite. Thus, as market behaviors fragmented, such companies looked again to the pollsters, the social scientists, and the psychologists for guidance. The reigning theories of race relations at the time told companies that not all smokers were cut from the same cloth, and that race mattered in branding. But how? The path to cultivating racial markets remained uncertain. While the segmentation of preferences invited a targeted approach to sales, this type of targeting (marketing to ethnic minorities via emerging ethnic radio or Black magazines and newspapers, to children via cartoons and comics, to women, or to men) were also filled with dangers.

Two years before creating the Alpine menthol brand, Philip Morris faced a racial dilemma that shaped their views on both the perils and possibilities of racial markets. In 1953 a Roper survey alerted George Weissman to the fact that the Philip Morris brand was selling strongly among Black smokers in the US South. Throughout the region, as the movement for racial integration gained steam and as a white backlash brewed, PM sales among Black smokers expanded. The popularity was a surprise and a curiosity, posing a double-edged challenge. On one level, loyal customers were to be cherished and courted in such uncertain times. Only a foolish company would ignore such a trend, in such a growing market segment. As many pollsters advised, feeding ethnic consciousness, just like nurturing health consciousness, mattered in sales and marketing. And yet PM worried.

As Roper had informed Weissman at the time, "There is no group [other than Black consumers] among whom Philip Morris shows such a tremendous increase in popularity."[66] But the Philip Morris brand also maintained an appeal across multiple classes—at the "highest and lowest economic levels." It appealed to women and men, with "a slightly higher proportion of Philip Morris' smokers [being] women." This question of race was a new one for the firm and called for careful handling. According to *Advertising Age*, Black smokers' increasing brand consciousness—thought to be a by-product of rising postwar incomes—had been a boon to some brands like Camel cigarettes.[67] Facing this unexpected windfall from Black users, PM turned to Roper for insight. The pollster stressed caution, warning that while the brand was in an "enviable position to be doing so well among Negroes," it was also an "uncomfortable position."

Roper warned the company to avoid the trap of "having a large proportion of its eggs in one basket." Having its leading brand identified as popular with Blacks, or (even more problematically) moving toward marketing directly to Black smokers, posed multiple risks.[68] Whatever might be gained by building on an African American following could lead to losses elsewhere if white smokers recoiled from the brand. PM's dilemma highlighted the complexities of how brand usage by one group shaped social meanings that could impact usage in other groups, and thus drive up sales or undermine them. The question for PM was what to do with such a southern Black following at this fraught, uncertain moment in the struggle for civil rights. The company's decision highlights the racial calculus of branding in 1953, as compared to a decade later.

Roper saw many reasons for caution in building a Black-themed appeal. For one, African Americans were lighter smokers than whites, on average using fewer cigarettes per year than whites. This fact blunted the overall impact on PM sales. In the longer run, Roper advised, there were other, more promising growth markets; a smarter strategy would build not on Black smokers but on the "handsome gain among young people." The uptick in young smokers charted a steadier and safer course into the future. "From a long-term point of view," Roper concluded, "this gain among young people is probably more valuable than the gain among Negroes, for the habits of young people . . . tend to be indicative of [a] trend."[69]

Yet the consultant admitted that the trends among southern African Americans was appealing and warranted deeper study; and so Roper sent a few Black investigators into Harlem to learn if people on the streets of Black New York had any clues to this southern appeal. Harlem was an obvious choice—an iconically Black area of the city, and indeed the nation, with a nexus of newly migrated African Americans from the South. Roper's 1954 study (*Progress Report on Negro Market Study*) targeted Harlem stores in a series of interviews with proprietors who were seen as "style and thought leaders." They were also in a position to observe what brands Black people smoked and to opine on why. In reporting back to PM, Roper warned of many uncertainties in the findings as they related to Black brand motivations. The art of measuring consumer preference was not so clear-cut: "When respondents tell us what motivates other Negroes, or why Philip Morris appeals to others, are they actually telling us about themselves, or are they telling us how they think other people feel? And if they are telling us how others feel, are they right or wrong?"[70] Nor did Roper's staff conduct what Ernest Dichter called "depth psychology" interviewing, delving for individual and group anxieties. Despite these limitations, Roper's interviews—hit-and-miss, sporadic—proved useful in orienting the company to the new racial possibilities. The interviews also exemplified a new trend of sending researchers into neighborhoods to gather local intelligence—a practice that would shape brand decisions for decades to come.

The pollster discovered that almost every "man on the street" had a theory about smoking preferences and Black consumer psychology.

Among the most animated of Harlem store managers was Mack Aus-tin, a thirty-five-year-old running a small magazine, tobacco, candy, and soda shop. Austin emphasized the power of images of people who looked like him in posters and brand advertising. "Brother, I got no idea in this world why people buy the brands they do—people don't say why, and I don't ask. That ain't my job," he at first demurred. "It's a habit is all—once you're used to something . . . once you start on something, it ain't easy to change." But when pressed on what moti-vated Negroes to buy certain brands over others, he opened up to the interviewer (a young Black writer). One thing that made a difference was putting an attractive young Black woman or a baseball player or musician on a poster, he said. In his view, this was a gesture of respect—viewed as a visual nod of acknowledgment by the company and appreciated as a small step for racial progress because it provided work to the models in the poster. The gesture would be repaid in con-sumer dollars. "They all help, 'cause colored people are glad to see when some of the big companies are doing something for the race—it means things are moving ahead a little, and it makes you feel a little better."[71]

Mack Austin's views were echoed elsewhere in Harlem and the city. A thirty-year-old man in a Midtown luncheonette explained, "Chesterfield made a smart move bringing out those posters with pictures of Monte Irvin and Henry Thompson (Negro baseball play-ers). . . . Now, I'm a no-special-brand smoker myself, but because of the decent way those things were done, I find myself asking for Ches-terfields a lot more than any other brand." Even a white shop owner observed that image had everything to do with brand appeal: "If one outfit does something special for the group . . . like Arthur Godfrey with those colored fellows on his [television] show"—the white co-median Godfrey, whose program was sponsored by Chesterfield, had welcomed Black musicians to perform—"then people don't forget it. That's all I got to say. . . . Just say it's my theory."[72]

Viewers saw the placement of Black faces and persons on posters and television as an intentional statement. Everyone knew that these racial pitches were double-edged, however, because even as they visibly courted Black smokers and gestured toward tolerance and accommodation among whites, they risked hostility from less-tolerant whites. Such accommodations on matters of race relations were fraught. In May 1954, the US Supreme Court had handed down its decision in the *Brown v. Board of Education* case, ruling that "separate but equal" public accommodations were unconstitutional. Jim Crow segregation was ruled illegal; but a white backlash brewed. In an era of such festering battles, such images or integrated messaging (or any blurring of racial lines) carried powerful meanings for men like Mack Austin as well as for white viewers. Making matters more complicated for Philip Morris, the company employed African American as well as white workers at its southern plants. These racial lines were being contested in workplaces, on television, on billboards, and across consumer culture. Little wonder that for whites and Blacks alike, visual advertising took on important symbolism, with the potential for shaping consumption, brand preferences, or backlashes.[73]

A marketer's act of placing Black faces in ads in the early 1950s signaled respect, accommodation, and a bow to racial progress—but at what level of visibility? And with what market effects? It was one thing to run ads only at the local level in Harlem or on radio or in newspapers for Black audiences. It was quite another thing, marketers believed, to do what Arthur Godfrey had done by featuring Black musicians on nationwide television. From people interviewed in Harlem, Roper heard that Black viewers were alert to the difference:

> None of the cigarette companies—or any other companies, for that matter—has used Negroes in their advertising in the general market media. They're always on posters in Negro areas or in ads in special Negro circulation media, but never on the highway billboards, or in the large circulation magazines. This, I think, is a general weakness. And I think the company that does something about this will be noticed.[74]

The Roper interviews, conducted by a young writer from *Ebony* magazine, churned up these and other useful insights. Roper reported back to PM executives that for many African Americans, brand appeal and loyalty hinged on the company's willingness to associate visibly with positive Black images and ideals, and to do so in places where whites would see those associations. For the "man on the street" in Harlem, those projections were read as racial progress and could translate into brand identification and higher sales.

But why, without such visible advertising, were PM's sales rising in the Black South? This question still perplexed PM executives, and they looked to Harlem for answers. One grocery store owner in New York (a man with a business degree) explained it simply: Philip Morris had employed Black people, and its employment practices had helped sales. "They'll tell you, 'Yeah, I don't buy Camels 'cause they won't hire me' or 'Well, give me one of them Philip Morris. As long as cigarettes are the same, I might as well buy the one that's trying to help our race.'" Those jobs could be anywhere—in sales positions, as models in ads, or in the cigarette factories. Thus, placing ads in Black newspapers were effective because they were seen through the lens of employment opportunity. One thirty-year-old manager of a luncheonette pointed to a recent story in the *Pittsburgh Courier* about Philip Morris hiring Black workers: "Nothing but just another ad . . . bet they paid to get the story in the paper." But did it work? "Sure, it's effective." People wanted to believe in something, anything—even if it was just a case of "some colored salesmen—and maybe a few girls rolling cigarettes for a pat on the back and twelve cents an hour."[75] The straightforward secret to Philip Morris's appeal, in this view, was that the company created jobs for Black people—in factories, in sales positions, and sometimes on billboard posters—when R. J. Reynolds did not.

If Harlem citizens took note of PM's hiring of Black employees, so, too, did whites in the South, generating an angry backlash for the company. The segregationist White Citizens' Council, for example, took aim at Philip Morris for what it saw as the company's integrationist policies, its support of the Urban League, and its advertising to Black smokers. One WCC pamphlet decried the company for spending "huge sums each year advertising in the negro press" and for what

- 3 -

In just a few seconds you can **prove**

PHILIP MORRIS
IS DEFINITELY **LESS** IRRITATING
than the brand you're now smoking!

1 . . . light up a
    PHILIP MORRIS

*THEN, just take a puff — DON'T INHALE — and
s-l-o-w-l-y let the smoke come through your
nose. Easy, isn't it? And NOW' . . .*

2 . . . light up your
    present brand

*Do exactly the same thing — DON'T INHALE.
Notice that bite, that sting? Quite a difference
from PHILIP MORRIS!*

NOW **YOU** KNOW WHY **YOU** SHOULD BE SMOKING PHILIP MORRIS!

PHILIP MORRIS CAMPAIGNS FOR
NEGRO MARKET

In line with its support of the Urban League
by large contributions to the work of this
race-mixing political, economic pressure
negro agency, the makers of Philip Morris
Cigarettes spend hugh sums each year advertising in the negro press. The above is
but one example in its campaign to make
Philip Morris the "negro cigarette."

Marlboro Cigarettes in a new, non-crush
package and spent $2,200,000 advertising
them. Deceptively, no mention is made in
the ads that Marlboro is put out by Philip
Morris. Instead the words "Made in Richmond, Va., from a new Marlboro Recipe"
are used. Marlboro saved the day for PM
last year. Without its 6,000,000,000 sales,
the company would have taken a licking it
richly deserves. In line with its deceptive
policy, there is not one word on Parliament

Figure 2.5. In 1953 the White Citizens' Council attacked Philip Morris for what they saw as a
"campaign to make PM the 'negro cigarette.'" Such companies, wary of attacks like this from
segregationists aiming to use images of Black men smoking PMs against the company, saw political
risks in courting Black markets too explicitly. Youth markets were far more lucrative and promising at
the time, but this marketing calculus was always a fragile one.
Credit: Image courtesy of Truth Tobacco Industry Documents (https://www.industrydocuments.ucsf
.edu/tobacco/).

they saw as "its campaign to make Philip Morris the 'negro cigarette.'"
An advertisement showing a Black man enjoying the smoke provoked
particular revulsion: "As more Whites learn of the pro-negro policies
of Philip Morris, Inc., that cigarette is becoming more irritating — not
less. . . . Let Philip Morris have the negro market it worked so hard
and spent so much money for — but it should not have the patronage
of any self-respecting White Citizen." The message was clear: courting
Black smokers and organizations in the South risked a nasty response.
The popularity among African Americans was double-edged, lending

ammunition to the White Citizens' Council campaign to label PM as a Negro and integrationist brand. As Weissman observed at a 1956 regional sales meeting in Florida, "For some reason or other, and I can't attribute it, we had a good share of the Negro market . . . [but] we are also on boycott, I might say, in certain sections of Mississippi by the White Citizens Council, because of our contributions to the Urban League."[76] Decades later, Weissman acknowledged that "the Ku Klux Klan hurt Philip Morris by starting a rumor that the company was a supporter of desegregation," and he alleged that "most of the rumors were spread by [competitors] Liggett and Myers and some Reynolds' people."[77] Thus for PM, building a base of Black customers invited peril. For them, the movement for racial integration and the segregationist backlash easily matched in ferocity the storm over cigarettes and cancer, threatening to destabilize markets even more. Along both axes (race marketing and health reassurance), the psychology of smoking was, indeed, tumultuous.

But adversity created opportunity. From the streets of Harlem, Roper's interviewers collected, condensed, and passed along to PM a range of helpful theories about Black purchasing psychology. The *Ebony* magazine writer explained, for example, that segregation made Black purchasing behavior symbolically meaningful, with some purchases more important than others, particularly for better-off African Americans. Segregation locked many buyers out of purchasing opportunities available to whites, leaving better-off Black buyers searching for what might be called opportunities for "compensatory gratification":

"Negroes have been downtrodden economically and socially for so long," he explained, "and have been so often accused of wanting everything flashy and loud—that they consciously, or otherwise, want to impress people with the fact that they have taste and are discriminating—that they are dignified and sophisticated. And one of the easiest ways to do it is to align themselves with a cigarette pack—something they show everywhere—that is quiet and tasteful and rich-looking."[78]

Brand choice touched on these questions of respect and status — central concerns for the Black consumer at this moment. Of course, the desire for respectability (and the quest to escape racist stereotypes of loudness, flashy behavior, and ostentatiousness) had long been a middle-class Black ideal.[79] In this context, a dignified design on a pack of cigarettes or a smart image on a poster signaled so much. "This may all sound pretty far-fetched to you," he concluded, "and remember, it's just a theory of mine — but I really think there's something to it."[80]

This notion of compensatory gratification signaled how brand choice, segregation, and the quest for respect intertwined. Elsewhere in town, a middle-aged Black woman explained, "When a Negro gets a little money, he has no choice except to buy something. He can't go to the big resorts — he knows he's not welcome on the cruises and so on, so what can he do except buy something with his few dollars?" Years later, *Ebony* publisher John H. Johnson would trumpet similar views, suggesting that this idea of Black compensatory buying behavior was something of an in-house philosophy, a perspective guiding the magazine and its devotion to middle-class Black readers. Marketing outreach on Black college campuses also worked in similar ways. "I remember there was a guy on campus working for Philip Morris," recalled one Black writer in another Roper interview. "He used to bring samples around to the dorms . . . and naturally we smoked them because they were free. . . . And he used to talk about how good the company was on the race relations stuff — you know, hiring and all that . . . and I think he got a job with the company after he left school — I'm not sure. . . . Maybe that's the reason why so many of us [friends] smoke them."[81]

Whatever its origins, the "compensatory gratification" theory made it into Roper's report as an explanation on how to court Black buyers in a society where segregation and second-class legal status had left its mark on the Black purchasing psyche. These theories, of course, were merely variations on the themes of ego deflation, status, and identity that researchers believed drove smoking trends. In the end, the storefront proprietors and writers all trafficked in a similar game as Ernest Dichter—building their own theories of emergent "Negro taste" and acknowledging that hidden signaling was crucial to winning anxious customers across the color line. What these observers were telling the tobacco industry (via reports funneled back from the street through consultants and, from them, to executives) was that minority/majority group smoking preferences intermingled deeply with politics, behaviors, social movements, and health beliefs; no single factor stood alone, and the impact on brand popularity would remain in flux precisely because social relations and health concerns were also in flux.

The dilemma of smoking and marketing cut across health and race, but also gender. Indeed, the health scare appeared to activate intense gender effects. Masculine norms, for instance, like the desire to appear fearless might explain why some men smokers downplayed having any worries about cancer. But one marketing report for the women's magazine *Redbook* observed that "while smoking had been considered a man's activity, with the increasing number of women smokers 'feminine and masculine way [*sic*] of smoking' were found with some cigarettes being 'more for women, others more for men.'"[82] Interestingly, the leading brands also had the strongest gender associations along masculine/feminine binaries, with Camels and Lucky Strikes, for example, seen as "masculine, strong, and irritating" to the throat. Advertisers and companies keenly studied these association (by race, gender, and so on) for some kind of edge. By the end of the decade, this view of smoking as a form of identity self-management "to bolster ego-deflated selves" (as McCann Erickson's Britt put it) had come to predominate within the industry.[83]

There were so many lines of identity to explore, so many angles to exploit, and yet so much danger in targeted brand appeals, that Philip Morris executives followed Roper's advice. The appeal of PM cigarettes among southern Blacks would be studied and psychologically dissected, but not cultivated and pursued as a racial branding opportunity—at least not in the 1950s.

Into the Depths of Self-Deception

A youth market beckoned; but so, too, did a new health-anxious market smoker. As Dichter and Packard debated the psychoseduction of children at NBC radio in 1957, executives at Liggett & Myers awaited a report that would provide one of the most detailed profiles to date on the psychological and social drivers of the menthol appeal—highlighting that the rise in menthol smoking was driven by consumer *self*-deception, as smokers searched for safety or some way to compromise with their cigarette habit even if it meant embracing deceptive promises as reassuring truth.

Produced by the Market Planning Corporation (MPC), a subsidiary of the consulting firm McCann Erickson, the "motivation study" was based on 750 two-hour-long "depth interviews" conducted in May 1957, "supplemented by personality tests aimed at uncovering deeper, persistent aspects of personality organization." Designed to inform Liggett's launch of Oasis, the MPC report amassed a remarkable data set at a time when the market and consumer behavior was still "in a state of flux." As MPC noted, "Both the upward spurt in the sale of [Kool] and the unusually quick acceptance of [Salem] lead one to suppose that the potential market for mentholated cigarettes is increasing, and that still more people may turn to this type of cigarette for either occasional or fairly steady use." The motivation survey (conducted with the assistance of two clinical psychologists) sought to understand not only the menthol appeal across these two brands, but all other aspects of smoker and brand psychology.[84]

The report confirmed what motivational psychologists and their critics had known for years about smokers: insecurities about their identity and their health brewed within their psyches. Smokers lived amid a mass of inner conflicts, the MPC psychologists explained, with their personal choices deeply connected to social turmoil and worries imposed from the world without, and driven by insecurities from within. The report also confirmed what insiders at Philip Morris were already concerned about—that racial tensions in the country created challenges for PM in the South. Southern whites told MPC, for example, that the PM cigarettes were for Black smokers: "They're known around here as a cigarette that Negroes smoke. . . . You won't find whites smoking them. They [PM] gave money to the NAACP, you know." As another white respondent commented on the PM brand, "Northerners smoke them . . . segregationists don't."[85] Leaving these racial and health turmoils aside, however, smokers as a social type were "less inhibited than non-smokers" and "more able to indulge their pleasurable impulses," MPC psychologists concluded. They tended to be more optimistic, with a more relaxed, trusting, and outgoing attitude toward life. They tended to seek new experiences in life more than nonsmokers. Yet many were agitated and "in considerable conflict about smoking," the firm concluded. And they were struggling with a fundamental paradox provoked by the cancer and health news: "caught between pleasure from smoking and extreme self-criticism of their 'smoking habit.' The vast majority wish they could stop." Ambivalence and uncertainty about the habit defined the smoking experience.[86]

MPC aimed to help Liggett understand these psychological challenges, and how these obstacles could be turned into opportunities by following the strategies of Kool and Salem—playing to the smoker's need for novel kinds of reassurance. In the old days, companies might reassure with slogans like "Not a Cough in the Carload." Now, something new was required. Menthol appeared to be a psychic salve to these rising health worries—a pathway through the turmoil, a road to new markets. Evidence continued to mount that smoking carried grave health consequences. Between May 1957 when MPC field interviews began and the report's completion in October, more worrisome news had come out linking smoking to cancer and heart disease. Other scientific studies took aim at the industry's claim that filtered cigarettes were safer, and Congress launched an investigation into their safety and marketing.[87] Menthol makers treaded carefully in this new regulatory climate, hoping to avoid the scrutiny now aimed at filtered cigarettes.

Listening to the smokers as they worked through their own worries and often psychologized their own behaviors, MPC's "depth studies" saw smokers as troubled people looking for a way to continue their habit safely. Smokers' reactions revealed complex, and sometimes unexpected, psychological responses to the cancer and heart disease news. As MPC psychologists noted, the respondents sometimes offered artful rationalizations for why they continued smoking ("It's okay if you don't smoke to excess," or "My doctor smokes, why shouldn't I?" or "I'm young yet, it won't affect me now").[88] Psychologists also learned that most people had not resolved their inner conflicts about their habit. In the face of health threats, some people did quit the habit if they could overcome the addiction. But many others looked for a way to reconcile the fear of smoking and their need to smoke. The smoker's need and desire drove the habit (it was like "sucking on a pacifier . . . or taking a tranquilizer"; "many described feelings of panic and inability to think, coordinate, or function" without a cigarette). The act of smoking was, itself, a reassuring personal choice, noted MPC (it was an "autonomous, self-initiated, self-controlled action which serves to reassure the individual that his needs are taken care of").[89] Smoking was a salve for anxiety and "filled a certain psychological need for most heavy smokers," and it was also a way to "drain off tension." The cancer news had introduced a new world of conflict for smokers prone to thinking of their habit as calming, relieving, and reassuring. (Notably, this was the kind of language smokers themselves used; and the MPC report observed just how much this psychologizing language had penetrated the culture based on "popularized articles on psychology [and in] various TV shows, movies, and popular novels.") The report amounted to an "immense compendium" of the way this profound psychological conflict was unfolding in 1957, reshaping brand choice.[90]

For men and women alike, smoking was a "compensation in periods of tension," and menthol cigarettes were playing a small but quickly expanding role.[91] Smokers (whether they admitted it or not, whether they were male or female, Black or white) were seeking protection. The tension was particularly fraught for many men, who were afraid to show any signs of being squeamish about the health threat. "For the man, [smoking] can be a symbol of masculinity, something which is done despite the implied threat to health." MPC gleaned from its psychological profiles that the men who stayed true to their regular unfiltered cigarettes amid the cancer scares were "more masculine in the stereotyped sense of athletic activities and . . . showed overt resistance to fear."[92] It was deep in these anxieties surrounding health that menthol brands were making a mark among those who sought new ways to deflect, channel, and relieve their fears even as they performed their identities for others via brand selection.

In psychological terms, MPC understood menthol smokers as a group that was "susceptible to genuine anxiety about their health." Deeply alert to the surrounding health concerns, they "were very aware . . . of the dangers that smoking implies," and yet they maintained strong cravings—every bit as powerful as the cravings of any heavy smoker. They "seem to be much more aware than the average person, and even more aware than the filter smokers, of the ways in which their bodies react to things. They are always talking about 'how they feel.'" They were not so health-obsessed as to be labeled hypochondriacs, explained MPC to Liggett, but "they clearly have less confidence in their physical well-being." In a word, menthol smokers were worried and psychologically vulnerable.[93]

For these near-hypochondriacs, said MPC, the cool sensation carried a personal therapeutic compromise. "While menthol smokers do not think they actually do good, they still believe they do less harm," explained the firm to Liggett. Switching to menthols actually enhanced consumption, permitting a heavy smoker to smoke "more steadily and frequently than he feels he could (or should) smoke other types of cigarettes." Menthol also gave people with the strongest cravings permission to continue with the habit, to indulge. They could "go on smoking when other smokers might have to cut down or quit temporarily." And menthols also carried the added benefit of "soothing irritated respiratory passages." "It keeps a cool feeling in my throat all day," noted one steady user. Menthol smoking was becoming a salve on many levels—not only for the medicated feeling it left on the nose and the throat, as it had for decades, but now also as a new type of indulgent relief for the anxious mind.[94]

The MPC survey portrayed menthol smokers as a class unto themselves—a newly emerging group defined not by any single demographic factor such as race, age, or sex but by a cross-cutting, intense, and almost freakish desire for security. As psychologists saw matters, these were new people emerging at the place where cancer fear and smoking met. The archetypal menthol smoker (as defined by his or her search of therapeutic protection) was the Kool smoker. As the oldest brand, Kool was "connected in people's minds with the relief of colds and respiratory ailments," the study found. Users stressed the medicinal benefits of heavy mentholation: "I use mentholated cigarettes only when I have a sore throat," commented one smoker. Kool smokers were "the most alarmed of all brand groups about the recent research on the connection of smoking and cancer." Personality tests confirmed that they were also "a good deal less self-confident and less optimistic," "more likely to worry 'out loud'" about their ailments, and "more likely to be conservative in brand choice." In Kool smokers, health anxieties appear to have predated the cancer news—as smokers, they had worried about their health for a long time. But they were "very susceptible to alarm." For them, "the image of menthol in general is comforting to these people." But the taste of menthol also gave them a boost—the impression of a "tonic," a "lift," or a "kick."[95]

The rise of Kool and Salem in the 1950s (and of menthols in general) suited the moment with the looming cancer question surrounding cigarettes, with postwar consumerism and advertising making full use of the new television medium, with rising anxieties about status, gender norms, and racial turmoil driving product pitches (for men, women, Black buyers, and white consumers seeking different kinds of "social gratification" or security through the products they used). Among the social gratifications of smoking was the fact that "for both men and women, smoking is a sign of adulthood, of independence, of vigor, and of freedom from restriction. For the man, it can be a symbol of masculinity, something which is done despite the implied threat to health. For the woman, smoking may connote stylishness, sophistication, modern emancipation." Gender norms also played a

salient role in the shaping of brand choice and the making of consumer groups. In this context, menthol smokers seemed their own
distinct demographic group. MPC found that men and women were
pulled in some cases, prodded in others, to Kool's menthol promise
of protection. Male Kool smokers were more likely than the women
to be nervous and "seriously alarmed about the cancer news," MPC
found. It was a sign of their worry over cancer, the firm observed, that
these men had embraced Kool menthol smokes despite the existing
feminine, "sissy" connotation of smoking the less tobacco-heavy,
mentholated cigarette. Menthol, it was said, was for women. Where
women "were positively attracted to Kool, . . . men were, in a sense,
forced into the choice."[96]

If menthol smokers were all categorically insecure, the types of
insecurity varied between those who smoked Salem and Kool, observed MPC analysts. The Salem smoker sought medicinal relief, but
not to the same degree as the Kool smoker. As one respondent noted:
"Salems do not have so medicinal an image as Kool, and [are] not as
likely to be ticked off as a remedy useful only when one is ill." But
Salem smokers were not without anxiety. They voiced concern about
"the physical effects of smoking they observe in themselves," even
if they did not speak openly about the threat of cancer. According
to this portrait, Salem was an "in-between" cigarette — distanced from
the strictly medicinal image, while still evoking therapeutic qualities.
Salem as a brand "suffer[s] less than Kool from the stereotyped notion
that menthol smokers are fuddy-duddies and neurotics, because they
are mild and more in-between." One interview subject thought of Salem smokers as "more like ordinary people," perhaps even a bit "more
sophisticated, genteel and self-assured" than Kool smokers, who the
speaker imagined to be "dowdy, frumpy and timid . . . and they look
like penguins." They "choose Salem for pleasure as well as symptom
relief, while Kool users choose Kool almost solely for its 'medicinal
value.'" These milder therapeutic associations reflected Salem's advertising campaigns, which downplayed the medicinal imagery and
emphasized "springtime freshness."[97]

Whether menthol smokers chose Kool, Salem, Spud, Oasis, or

Alpine in this burgeoning market, these were people compromising with their health fears or looking for safety in one way or another, MPC concluded. Filters offered one kind of hedge, and MPC noted that once smokers made the switch, they were not looking back. "There is little chance for an all-tobacco cigarette to win back people from the filter or mentholated fields with their built-in apparent symbols of greater safety," explained the analysts. "Moreover, after the filter smoker has made a health compromise initially, he tends to discover additional benefits which serve to confirm the choice of a filter cigarette even if the idea that filters are healthier should be undermined." For his or her part, the Kool smoker "is willing to absorb any amount of menthol to be soothed; the filter smoker will accept loss of flavor to be saved, but the [Salem] smoker hates to give up pleasure for reassurance. He wants all three things"—a smoke without "uncomfortable after effects," a therapeutic smoke but "not a medicinal cigarette," and some "enjoyable tobacco flavor." Health promises came in several forms, then. Kool had given "mentholated cigarettes a 'medicinal' connotation and in typing [its smokers] as 'sissies' and 'hypochondriacs.'" Salem, MPC analysts believed, represented something else—"a satisfying and unprecedented compromise of several conflicting demands . . . it seems safe but not forbidding."[98]

More than any other marketing psychology report, MPC provided a deep and thickly detailed snapshot of the moment in 1957 when menthol began to rise in popularity, buoyed by health promises and health anxieties. Drawing heavily on smokers' own words, the report highlighted a market in turmoil. Yet it also highlighted how consumer trends might be directed or even engineered by an elaborate deflection of health worries, and the promise of social status and gratification, and above all the promise of security. This psychological understanding of smoking had become thoroughly mainstream in the tobacco industry, as many experts and lay observers accepted the basic idea that consumers' inner, often hidden, drives and conflicts determined their choices and behaviors. As smoking psychologists insisted, every aspect of smoking (the number of cigarettes smoked, the time and place of smoking, the way it was held, the choice of filter, whether one smoked alone or in company, the length of the cigarette, and so on) spoke to these inner conflicts. "Smoking tends to relieve tensions built up between people, tensions arising from anxiety, hostility, fear," MPC told Liggett & Myers. But smoking "may also hide these feelings."[99] If Liggett's Oasis was to be a contender in the menthol sweepstakes, the consultants explained, it would need to study closely why Salem and Kool were succeeding, listen to consumers' health worries, nurture their self-deception, and deflect their fears with compelling promises of safety.

Policing Hidden Health Persuasion

With the 1957 publication and popularity of Vance Packard's *The Hidden Persuaders*, the strategies of men like Ernest Dichter became less concealed and more widely debated, and thus politically contentious. Critics decried these arts of persuasion, with particular outrage surrounding the targeting of youth with hidden messaging. For Packard, Dichter's approach reflected marketing deception at its worst—an immoral kind of manipulation that led gullible people down a path of ruin, children foremost among them. "What is the morality of playing upon hidden weaknesses and frailties—such as our anxieties, aggressive feelings, dread of nonconformity . . .—to sell products?" asked Packard. "What is the morality of manipulating small children even before they reach the age where they are legally responsible for their actions?"[100]

In the 1950s, while some forms of market deception came under scrutiny, others did not. Packard's book (working in combination with the still-worrisome cancer evidence) catalyzed Congress to hold hearings on false and misleading advertising. But when legislators looked closely at cigarette marketing, they focused in on the filters (their false and more implicit promise of safety); there was no comparable attention to the equally false, but often hidden, therapeutic promise of mentholated smoking.[101] This would be a recurring theme in the decades that followed: while regulators took aim at false advertising and deceit in tobacco advertising and while they increased scrutiny over advertising to youth, menthol's health promise often escaped scrutiny. Hearings in 1958 focused squarely on the filter-tip cigarettes, with the House of Representative accusing the FTC of lax oversight and lashing at the industry for doing "a grave disservice to the smoking public, initially blatantly, and more recently, very subtly publicizing the filter-tip smoke as a health protection."[102] In the stinging rebuke, menthol brands were not called to account because their health appeal apparently flew well below the regulators' radar.

In many ways, the intensified criticism provoked industry to redouble its efforts to reassure, seeking to develop newer growth markets; regulators, meanwhile, intensified their assault on these games of illusion. In 1953, for example, the FTC accused Liggett & Myers of using false, misleading and deceptive advertising, "specifically that the cigarettes are milder, cooler, soothing, relaxing, leave no unpleasant aftertaste and have no adverse effects on the nose, throat or accessory organs."[103] These health promises were fatuous, the FTC insisted. Televised fraud was not limited to the tobacco industry, as the makers of Mentholatum and Infrarub ointments drew fire for falsely promising relief of pain without pills.[104] By early 1957, the FDA sung from the same script as Packard, announcing a crackdown "on the multi-million dollar rash of falsely-advertised 'tranquilizers' . . . experiencing a wave of popularity as peace-of-mind pills."[105] Relief from anxiety was being sold in many forms, and skepticism about this deceptive promise of relief ran high.

Despite criticism, these games of illusion persisted, and menthol smoking thrived. As *Consumer Reports* noted in 1957, although the cancer news had "brought many changes to the industry," the new cigarettes with lower nicotine levels, lower tar levels, filters, and menthol were really no safer than older types.[106] Indeed, these cosmetic changes had created vast illusions of security and protection for the modern cigarette consumer. Nor did the FTC's rulings on deceitful advertising do much to compel motivational researchers and advertisers to rethink their manipulation of the consumer's anxious psyche. Dichter remained unapologetic. He was now more widely known than ever because of the publicity brought on by Packard's book, becoming something of an acclaimed figure in consumer psychology. Given a bigger soapbox, he insisted that his field of motivation research was misunderstood. Experts did not manufacture or plant ideas; rather, they studied the landscape of existing anxiety and learned to profit by it. As he explained to the *Wall Street Journal* in 1958, "People smoke, not because of the taste of cigarets, but because smoking provides them with certain psychological satisfactions they can get in no other way."[107] In his view, smoking was a necessary response to problems existing in society—stress, work, worry, and so on. The study of psychology, far from being deceptive, merely revealed people as they really were, the psychologists insisted. It was an argument that provided tobacco companies with a strong defense against their increasingly vocal critics. Companies were merely giving people what they were asking for. Testifying before Congress in 1961 about deceptive advertising, Dichter acknowledged, however, that brand distinctions were illusory. As he noted, in business "the competitive edge goes to the company that can create the illusion of a desirable difference."[108] "Motivation research attempts to probe these nebulous areas . . . and much of the resentment against it comes from the fear of seeing ourselves as we really are," he explained elsewhere.[109] This type of probing had produced a now-extensive psychological profile of a new consumer type—the menthol smoker, a profitable nexus of different kinds of people who gravitated toward the illusory promise of security.

Critics of these tactics abounded. Even as Dichter's profile rose, some admen decried the motivational researcher's "mumbo jumbo" that defined so much of consumer culture in the 1950s. "I honestly believe that this dreary dependence on the glass crutch of pseudoscience . . . has been an important contributory factor to the current business decline," bemoaned one advertising executive, Charles F. Adams, in 1958. "All the motivational mumbo-jumbo, all the Freud-happy figures assembled since Herr Doktor Dichter was knee-high to a couch cannot make the public's taste-buds tingle or its ego pant for a new car," said Adams. Yet, in the very next breath, Adams echoed the very elements of human psychology that drove

Dichter's work: "It [the public] will buy only when its basically selfish instincts—health, comfort, devotion, emulation, security, hunger, and the other ancient needs are appealed to."[110] Adams did not see that even he, who decried Dichter, was actually using the very language of psychological motivation and the selling of health security that Dichter had cultivated.

The industry's social scientists made profound contributions to menthol's positive health associations, going further than merely studying people as they "really were"; they were creating the menthol smoker. One could not have menthol smokers without menthol cigarettes; nor could these new menthol brands thrive without marketing them with smoker health anxieties in mind. Psychologists, marketers, and industry consultants thus modernized menthol smoking for the cancer era by identifying, studying, creating, and cultivating the menthol smoker as a new consumer type. By the dawn of the 1960s, marketing experts had become quite adept at these games of motivation. In the new decade, new opportunities (also stirred by new rounds of anxiety in smoking, health, and society) would turn their attention to group anxieties, group psychology, and other menthol markets—first youth smokers, then Black smokers.

Interestingly, defenders of these marketing tactics (and even some critics) held consumers responsible for being duped. Industry analyst Harry Wootten downplayed the power of marketing manipulation, suggesting in 1960 that it was the consumer who projected his or her own desires onto products and "read into . . . filters['] special health benefits even without reference to tars and nicotine." Even some critics of industry blamed people for being fooled. As one physician Charles Lieb warned, "A substitution may do nothing more than give the user a little mental consolation of a 'fool's paradise' existence and an excuse for continuing to smoke." The oil of menthol did not relieve, he argued; it only "added another source of irritation to their [cigarette's] composition." Any smokers who believed that menthols were safer or less irritating were "the victims of wishful thinking or auto-suggestion."[111] What few critics understood at the time was the importance of psychologists in helping industry identify precisely who was prone to "wishful thinking" and "reading special health benefits into" filters and menthols. This class of smoker, susceptible to a deceptive health promise, would be the focus of ceaseless research going forward.

As MPC had explained to Liggett in 1957, personality tests revealed that "menthol users tend to be optimistic people who really hope their needs will be satisfied. . . . They are more likely than the average person to feel that menthol will really benefit them." They were more credulous than non-menthol smokers, "not show[ing] so much skepticism as non-menthol users about the healthful attributes of menthol."[112] By the early 1960s, large teams of psychologists working with companies like Philip Morris, B&W, Liggett & Myers, and R. J. Reynolds came to understand "the menthol smoker" as one of the many classes of smokers driven by health fears and social anxieties. The rise of menthol, these consultants confirmed, hinged on a promise made by companies and accepted by users. But the false promise

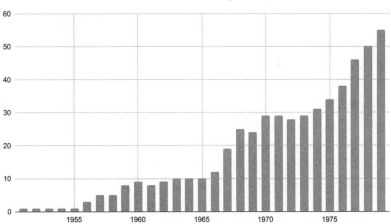

Number of Menthol Brands by Year, 1951-1979

Figure 2.6. Proliferation of menthol brands, 1951–1979. In the early years, the number of menthol brands climbed modestly from three in the early 1950s to ten by 1965. After 1965, however, came a steep increase. By the end of the 1970s, there were over fifty menthol brands, highlighting the fierce competition to shape this new market, with a significant urban focus.

Credit: Dov Grohsgal, data compiled from *The Maxwell Report* and the Tobacco Merchants Association of the U.S. Directory of Cigarette Brands.

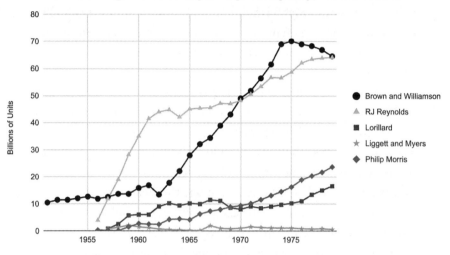

Menthol Cigarette Output by Company, 1951-1979

Figure 2.7. Menthol Cigarette Output by Company, 1951–1979. Salem's ascent was steep in the late 1950s with Kool's sales flat. But competition between Brown & Williamson's Kool and R. J. Reynolds's Salem became fiercest between the mid-1960s and mid-1970s, with the two companies vying intensely for primacy in what was becoming known as the "inner city."
Credit: Dov Grohsgal, data compiled from *The Maxwell Report.*

of menthol, MPC found, was also a work of self-deception—a lie that many smokers were willing to make to themselves in order to justify continuing with the habit.

: : :

Menthol smoking as a widespread practice cutting across many demographic groups blossomed in the space created by bad cancer news and the health anxieties that followed. What did people, anxious about the world in which they lived and fearful of the threats around them, look for in a cigarette? Many were seeking filtered cigarettes; others looked to menthols. Within the menthol markets, researchers understood there to be many segments that might be shaped and further segmented by brand and identity. Manufacturers of menthol cigarettes—Brown & Williamson, R. J. Reynolds, Philip Morris, Liggett & Myers—defined their markets in different ways with their products, Kool, Salem, Philip Morris, and Oasis. Increasingly, they each relied on psychology research to guide their understanding of the fickle smoker and to hone their health messaging. A fundamentally psychological view of the menthol smoker took hold. As MPC saw it, many smokers of the 1950s "try to evade issues raised by cancer research. . . . [T]hey have been searching for a cigarette that will do the least harm, and they believe in the possibility of finding it."[113] These concerns would not disappear. Indeed, soon enough, other shocking reports elevated public concerns even higher, bringing menthol makers more good fortune. To turn crises into opportunities required shrewd "suggestion"—the art of alluding to health gains without saying outright that menthols were a safe harbor. Cultivating these associations would be a central business concern for decades down the road.

As early as 1952, a major study observed what Ernest Dichter also knew—cigarettes carried "a psychological satisfaction sufficient to overcome health fears."[114] By the end of the decade, cigarette profits suggested that this psychological strategy of offering protection had worked. Writing to the president of American Tobacco, one industry insider explained what was now obvious industry-wide: "Salem, with both filter and menthol, was able to take advantage of health claims which had been made or inferred for other brands without, itself, being implicated in such claims." The study found that "the menthol filter market rests on the same consumer psychology as the straight filter market, that is, the search for 'protection.'"[115] From this point forward, industry would devote growing resources to studying menthol's implicit and explicit health meanings for diverse consumers.

By 1960 menthol brands accounted for 14 percent of cigarette sales in the United States, or 64 billion cigarettes.[116] Menthols were "the fastest growing segment" of the segmented market; Salem led the way, with Kool in second.[117] As one journalist explained, menthol sales were "burning brightly" because "they are said to give the smoker a sense of healthful medication."[118] Brands proliferated. Now, six other mentholated brands shared shelf space with the two leading brands. When combined, "mentholated and high filtration brands [accounted for] roughly 30 percent of the overall market."[119] The tobacco industry had emerged from the "first cancer scare" with the knowledge that adversity could be good for some sectors of the business. When American Tobacco sought to reshaped its menthol brand in 1961, they turned once again to Dichter for insight. And in the 1960s, when cancer fears spiked again, the industry was prepared to track new aspects of the menthol appeal and then cross deliberately and aggressively to marketing along racial lines. Why they crossed that line in the 1960s, but not in the earlier decade, is the focus on the next chapter.

3

Building a Black Franchise

On September 18, 2000, Andrew Schindler, CEO of the R. J. Reynolds Tobacco Company, waited in a Winston-Salem, North Carolina, law office. He was preparing to be grilled about how his company's long-ago targeted advertising and years of deceit about the safety of cigarettes connected ultimately to the ailments of an African American man named Ezell Thomas. He also faced a claim that, in a perverse game of corporate blame-shifting, other companies had been made to pay the costs for the cigarette industry's "fraud, misrepresentation . . . and fraudulent concealment." It was an extraordinary moment in a complex corporate blame game, in which the toll of decades of smoking was coming due. Major players vied to point fingers, with smokers like Mr. Thomas seeking to hold accountable companies like RJR for decades of deceit.

In the Thomas case, the questioning came from Richard Forman, a lawyer representing not Mr. Thomas but the Owens Corning company, which had settled thousands of cases with workers whose lungs were damaged by years of exposure to asbestos-containing fiberglass products. Their product was widely deemed liable for the massive toll of lung-related diseases. But Owens Corning insisted that blame should be shared. Two consumer products were on trial—both associated with long-term scarring of lung tissues, coughing, shortness of breath, and death from a range of diseases. Eighty percent of people exposed to asbestos also smoked, claimed the company. Owens Corning had joined the Thomas suit as a plaintiff to compel Big Tobacco to pay its fair share; their move signaled a moment when the tide was turning against Big Tobacco.

Tobacco capitalism confronted legal crises of stunning magnitude in these years, and in trial after trial, the evidence pointed to years of deceit about smoking's harm. Not only were former smokers who had taken up the habit decades earlier holding the industry responsible for years of dishonesty and resulting disease, but also governments and private companies like Owens Corning sought to hold Big Tobacco to account for the rising cost of caring for hundreds of thousands of people like Mr. Thomas. State governments had successfully made the same argument starting in 1994—that years of deceit had cultivated smokers like Mr. Thomas, and now the states were left to pay the hundreds of millions of dollars for caring for them through their Medicaid programs.[1] In the Thomas case, Owens Corning insisted that a major portion of blame for asbestos-related lung damage and death, which the company had acknowledged and paid for in settlements, rested with R. J. Reynolds's cigarettes. Not only was the cigarette to blame, argued Forman, but RJR had hidden the dangers for decades while mobilizing the shrewd tactics of admen to lure people like Mr. Thomas to tobacco products like its Camel menthols.[2] A bill was coming due for decades of corporate marketing built on false reassurance.

Forman sought to put RJR at the scene of a long-term crime by reading a memo outlining a predatory plan to push menthols in Black St. Louis. He transported the CEO to the scene in 1967 on the streets of St. Louis where, he alleged, RJR launching a plan to entrap Black smokers. The memo came from RJR's own files. Dated November 9, 1967, it was titled "Camel Menthol and the Negro Market," and presented one consultant's view of the opportunities for pushing Camels using the influence of barbers, bellhops, and influential people to shape community smoking preferences. The document had been written by consultant George A. Dean, who worked at the advertising firm Dancer-Fitzgerald-Sample, Inc. (DFS), and was addressed to J. A. Albanese, a marketing executive at RJR. Forman quoted one revealing section for Schindler. "Negroes tend to gravitate to groups," said the DFS report. They spent more time "with their respective groups than the average white man." It noted that every such group had "individuals who lead the others because they (a) are more in-the-know, and/or (b) they are more forceful." The corporate influencers themselves had found people of influence in the community. "These are not leaders in the sense of being president of the PTA or a local civic organization, but might well be a barber, a numbers man, a bellhop, a bartender or a taxi driver who likes to show how smart he is with his pals and associates," wrote Dean. "Some are established 'king fishes' while others only work at it."[3] Dean outlined a plan to distribute free samples of Camel menthols to these "king fish" to shape smoking patterns in St. Louis. In unveiling the memo, Forman sought to expose the vast web of cigarette pushers working with RJR who were responsible for Thomas's condition. He was seeking an admission from Schindler—an indication of culpability for this illicit push: "Were you aware that R. J. Reynolds was using an ad agency that used this kind of approach to market cigarettes in 1967?"[4]

Schindler rebuffed the lawyer's attempt to place himself at the scene of this chicanery. He dodged responsibility. "As I said previously a few minutes ago, in 1967, I was in the Army. . . . I have no idea what R. J. Reynolds was doing seven years before I joined the company with regard to its products or its marketing." Forman faced a difficult legal challenge, indeed. Plaintiffs' lawyers seeking to connect the dots and fix corporate responsibility for death and illness long after an ad campaign or a smoker's decision to try a brand often had such trouble. He pressed on: "Do you agree that the approach recommended in this letter is reprehensible?" The question provoked anger from Schindler. "For me to sit here 33 years later reading a couple of paragraphs out of some memo that somebody wrote to [*sic*, from] Dancer-Fitzgerald . . . for me to render some sort of judgment as to whether or not this is a good idea, bad idea, a reprehensible idea is totally inappropriate. I have no idea what these folks were doing or what the company did with this 33 years ago."[5] Schindler's defense amounted to a sidestepping and denial that had become commonplace in an industry under intense attack—denying knowledge of the Dean scheme, distancing RJR from any such plan. Such reports were from a bygone era, he suggested. They bore no relationship to the company's current policies, let alone to the cardiovascular disease, stroke, and other ailments suffered by Ezell Thomas.

Whether successful or not, Forman's legal gambit and others like it were having an impact. By shining a glaring light on DFS's "Camel Menthol and the Negro Market" plan, cases like the 2000 Thomas–Owens Corning liability case (and many others in the decade before it) were exposing the hidden history of influence making—shining an intense light on obscure events and nurtured relationships that, in fact, signaled a new stage of Big Tobacco's inner-city predation. In contrast to earlier decades, the 1960s saw menthol brands pivoting hard to cultivate urban Black markets. The shaping of menthol preferences stretched from boardrooms through firms like DFS to "king fish" and spilled out onto the streets of St. Louis. Even when cases like this proved unsuccessful (and the Dow Corning–Thomas case did, in fact, fail), the evidence amassed pulled the past into the present and pushed CEOs and juries to reckon with how smoking preferences had been shaped. By the 1990s and 2000s, the business tactics of the 1960s haunted the tobacco industry, state governments, and ailing former smokers alike. Trials and media reports showed that the DFS marketing plans were not at all unique; indeed, they had proliferated in the 1960s and 1970s amid a fierce and intensifying competition to shape the Black smoking market.[6]

What were RJR and DFS up to on the streets of Black St. Louis? Or to paraphrase Schindler, "what were these folks up to" as they competed aggressively for Black smokers in what was becoming known as the "inner cities"?[7] How did Big Tobacco come to pursue such a blatant influencing campaign—a new chapter in the history of menthol and racial capitalism? If Schindler refused to be placed at the scene of a crime in the 1960s, we need not follow his path. The DFS report was among thousands produced for and within the industry through the 1960s. Collectively, they flesh out the story and the actors in an impressive influence campaign taking aim at what RJR memos later referred to as "large urban Negro markets," "crowded urban Negro areas," and even as "poverty markets."[8] In cities like Newark, Chicago, Detroit, Baltimore, and many others, white out-migration to suburbs had transformed urban demographics, creating majority Black cities defined by rising percentages of people living below the poverty line. This chapter takes us deep into corporate thinking about how to sell menthol in these markets—a tour from posh tobacco industry board rooms through well-equipped marketing offices and down the nation's changing urban byways.

The DFS plan for menthol in Black St. Louis connects to a larger scheme to capitalize on poverty, or rather to extract capital from the urban poor when other markets proved too challenging. The strategy extended the industry's health claims about menthol in new directions. RJR's Salem remained the industry's leading menthol brand, but B&W's Kool brand had made enormous inroads, particularly into a Black urban consumer market. With the Camel Menthol 1967 strategy, RJR sought to carve a niche of its own to compete in a market that B&W regarded as its "Negro franchise." The memo, then, offers insight not only into an influence plan, but a moment in the intensification of business strategies that would extract dollars (and, in the long term, health) from Black Americans. Unlike Forman, we need not limit our questions to those of legal liability in understanding the 1967 St. Louis scheme. The question for us is how and why did this urban strategy come about? When did Kool's "inner-city" approach first emerge? How did it intersect with new health worries or speak to old complaints about the "smoker's cough," albeit in a new climate of race-oriented consumerism? And how did experts like those at DFS use local testimony and social studies of Black life to study, track, and shape consumption norms in St. Louis and other cities? We turn our attention, then, to the role of such studies in building a web of relationships aimed at sustaining these urban trends across the industry.

Big Tobacco's influence campaigns made extensive use of emerging sociological and psychological ideas of Black life, social norms, and attitudes in these changing American cities. "Negro allegiance to

Kools did not happen overnight," DFS's Dean observed in writing to RJR's Albanese about their arch competitor, "and our penetration of their business will undoubtedly depend on a specialized effort over and above our present advertising program." Kool's dominance was not only racial but geographical and psychological, Dean explained. The brand had built a "solid, substantial core of loyal Negro followers" particularly "in the large northern industrial centers, such as Detroit, Chicago, St. Louis, Baltimore and Cleveland," where, he reported, Kool's share of the Black market ran up to twice that of the market as a whole. To compete on Kool's home turf, Dean suggested that RJR's St. Louis campaign bypass a traditional advertising effort in favor of a "specialized Negro effort . . . tailored and designed to fit this specific market segment."[9] But before this furtive urban campaign could begin, Dean explained, it was best to "examine the Negro himself" — that is, how Black Americans perceived trustworthy and unethical merchants; where they obtained reliable information; the sociology of how news spread in their communities; and how Black men in St. Louis regarded cigarettes in relation to street knowledge, prestige, and status.

These schemes would have been utterly alien to menthol marketing only a few years earlier. How the "health cigarette" became a "race cigarette" has everything to do with government's ratcheted-up restrictions on the industry's youth marketing, the industry's loss of that lucrative outlet, and its deliberate turn to new urban exploits.

The Youthful Age of Menthol

Why did such campaigns for menthol come to focus on urban Blacks when, in the early 1960s, the youth market was by all accounts so much more economically appealing?

In 1963 few in the industry associated menthol smoking with Black Americans; rather, menthols were deemed to be popular mostly with squeamish health-conscious smokers. Industry analysts saw some menthol brands as popular with youth. They also believed that health concerns continued bolstering these brands, spanning a diverse array of worried smokers, making menthol's popularity demographically diverse. Indeed, a 1963 study of "the smoking habits of three ethnic groups" by the BBDO advertising firm even found that "Negro smokers . . . had less experience with Menthol cigarettes than have all smokers." In fact, 45 percent of African American smokers surveyed reported a dislike for the menthol taste, well above the 30 percent of all smokers who reported such a distaste.[10] That same year, the Arthur D. Little firm reported to Liggett & Myers that any ethnic variations in menthol use stemmed from "differences in promotion rather than basic radical differences in smoking desires or habits."[11] As late as 1963, then, few analysts labeled menthols as a racial preference.

A racial transformation in menthol smoking was not predictable in 1960; if anything, it was young people who drove new menthol trends. In a stand-up routine in 1960, Lenny Bruce, the acerbic thirty-five-year-old comedian, portrayed menthol smokers as hapless addicts, much to the amusement of his young audience. "Thirty per cent of you are addicted to menthol. You don't know it yet," quipped Bruce, who often smoked during his routines. "But you'll find out some night when you're out of cigarettes and you find yourself staring at the Vicks jar."[12] Menthol was an addictive ruse in his telling. But Bruce's humor also highlighted the enduring links between Salem and Kool cigarettes and the health promise that came in a jar of Vicks mentholated ointment. Bruce was not alone in understanding the medical appeal of menthol. One consultant to Philip Morris found no racial association with menthol whatsoever in 1961, based on in-depth interviews with seventy-nine smokers. Rather, Opinion Research observed that guilt, fear, and therapeutic promise continued to drive menthol's growing appeal. "The image of the menthol cigarette is that of a therapeutic cigarette, i.e., one which would be used to help repair the 'damage' done by non-mentholated cigarettes," the firm explained. And as one interview subject put it (echoing Lenny Bruce), "Menthols don't even taste like tobacco, they taste like menthols. . . . It is a strange sensation to have menthol in your throat . . . like you are inhaling Vicks Vaporub."[13]

In the years before Andrew Schindler joined RJR, if there was a target group amenable to the menthol pitch, it was young people. They drove an increase in sales of RJR's Salem, responding in part to its "distinctive springtime advertisements."[14] But menthol's health and hygiene promise also appealed widely across demographic groups—men and women, young and old. Menthol smokers were not homogeneous but fascinatingly varied. Young smokers were drawn to that promise of "springtime freshness," but many of the older smokers still clung to menthols like Kool as a strong therapeutic smoke or as something to reach for when one was congested, sick, or suffering from parched airways because of other "harsher" cigarettes.

Industry analysts believed that the menthol smoking market was segmented not by race but by age, with both older and younger smokers drawn to the health promise in different ways. The suddenly popular Salem brand found a following among the younger, hipper set; the long-standing Kool brand appealed to older people. By 1960 Kool's makers struggled to keep up with Salem's more youthful image with its own "come up to KOOL" campaign. Assessing the impact, Brown & Williamson requested a study from the Psychological Corporation and heard that they faced a steep but navigable challenge. The report *A Psychological Assessment of Viewers' Reactions to the KOOL Cigarette "Come Up" Commercial* polled adults of all ages in Paterson, New Jersey, and Atlanta, Georgia. Before watching the new ad, viewers identified Kool as for old folks; only 7 percent of viewers regarded Kool as "youthful." They also saw it as akin to medication, with 60 percent (the highest percentage) saying Kool was "good for a cold." Most users regarded it as an occasional smoke; only 5 percent said Kool was "good for steady smoking."[15] By contrast, 27 percent of respondents saw Salem as youthful, and a smaller percentage (36) said it was good for a cold, indicating that menthol still carried important health meanings to users. But a solid 38 percent said Salem was good for steady smoking, a fact that drove higher sales. To menthol smokers, Salem and Kool defined a generational divide, explained the Psychological Corporation. One represented youthful springtime freshness; the other promised therapy for the older set. Even so, for both groups menthol continued to signify health.

Figure 3.1. This 1959 Kool advertisement shows how advertisers first sought to project a youthful image for menthol smokers, to compete with Salem's appeal. The regulatory challenge to this courtship of young smokers in the early 1960s prompted the industry to cultivate other menthol markets as well. Credit: From the collection of Stanford Research Into the Impact of Tobacco Advertising (tobacco .stanford.edu).

Menthol smoking also carried a distinctively feminine meaning; in particular, many people these researchers interviewed regarded Salem as a "woman's smoke." More than a third of the respondents to the Psychological Corporation confirmed Salem's feminized image, while only 15 percent labeled Kool in the same way. Another research firm, Opinion Research, also realized that "the terms 'clean,' 'fresh,' and 'moist'" were clearly associated with menthol, and that "tied to this is the concept of a menthol cigarette as a woman's cigarette if smoked regularly." The gender associations were so potent that in one focus group discussion with nine men, one who admitted to smoking menthols "felt called upon to explain this by the fact that his wife purchases the cigarettes."[16]

Pushing back against these feminine associations earlier that year, Philip Morris sought to project a masculine image for its Alpine mentholated brand. Having successfully rebranded Marlboro as a man's smoke, the company made the case frankly and without nuance in magazine ads picturing a woman staring into the camera while lighting the cigarette for the man behind her. Their pitch phrase — "Who put the men in menthol smoking?" — was "an obvious reference to the fact that men were not menthol smokers," observed the analysts at Opinion Research.[17] The ad also provoked ridicule from a writer at the *Realist* satire magazine who joked, "To the best of our knowledge, no cigarette company has ever been so candid in telling the public what goes into its product . . . if the Philip Morris people are really putting men into their Alpines, what is the Food and Drug Administration doing about it?"[18] But highlighting the age and gender diversity of the menthol market, Opinion Research observed that Kool was "characterized to a greater degree as a male cigarette than is true of other menthols."[19] Known as a heavier or more medicated menthol cigarette, it was the only mentholated brand that defied feminine associations.

Among the many consultants studying these trends, Opinion Research insisted most strongly that advertising and packaging should proactively shape gender and age associations. Making markets was far better than waiting to respond to emerging trends. Opinion Re-

Who put the men in menthol smoking?

Alpine–that's who!

Now the menthol cigarette is as much at home in a man's shirt pocket as it is in a woman's handbag ... *The reason is Alpine.*

It always tastes rich, never smokes rough. The hearty tobaccos are specially blended for the new way of smoking. They give a man a flavor he can get hold of.

The clear, crisp flavor of Alpine will give your taste a fresh start. And your taste stays clean and moist right down to the end of the pack. *Try Alpine.*

The pleasingly new filter cigarette from Philip Morris

Figure 3.2. Philip Morris, noting the prevalence of women smokers of menthols and fresh from successfully rebranding Marlboro as a manly smoke, sought to define a new masculine image for menthol smoking with its Alpine brand in 1960 and 1961. Developing new ways to project masculinity remained an important element of the menthol appeal.
Credit: From the collection of Stanford Research Into the Impact of Tobacco Advertising (tobacco .stanford.edu).

EXAMINING a new "Men in Menthol Smoking" advertisement for Alpine mentholated filter cigarettes are Leo Burnett (left), chairman of the board, and Draper Daniels, executive vice president for Creative Services, Leo Burnett Co., Inc., Chicago, which designed the new ad campaign for Alpine's manufacturer, Philip Morris, Inc.

Figure 3.3. The men behind the image-making, Leo Burnett, chairman of the board of the advertising firm that carried his name, and Draper Daniels, the head of creative services, admire the design for the new Philip Morris Alpine brand advertisement, circa 1961.
Credit: Image courtesy of Truth Tobacco Industry Documents (https://www.industrydocuments.ucsf .edu/tobacco/).

search advised that if Philip Morris wanted to drive sales, every feature down to menthol packaging should insistently appeal to younger smokers. The consulting firm told Philip Morris that it should produce (in addition to Alpine) a light menthol for the "teenage girl" who was drawn to things "fresh" and "soothing." Young smokers were easily influenced by others—they selected brands in order "to be like his friends rather than for taste" and showed a "greater susceptibility [than their parents] to advertising." Rather than leaving choices to the "element of chance," explained the consultants, packages should be designed "to appeal to an identified market segment."[20]

Ernest Dichter, founder of the Institute for Motivational Research and now a leading psychology consultant to the tobacco industry, agreed that a distinctive youthful brand personality explained Salem's rising appeal. As he advised American Tobacco, any successful new menthol brand should "help establish the feeling that all people, young and old, men and women, all modern and active people, smoke this cigarette, thus developing a sense of liveliness and modernity which is felt to be inherent in this type of cigarette."[21] Many groups, but particularly the young, gravitated toward this "image of modernity." Like Dichter, the Student Marketing Institute (SMI) informed American Tobacco that this young adult market ("the most formidable non-TV viewing group in the nation") had become so sought after that they were "the target of more cigarette advertising, merchandising, sampling, and promotion by major brands . . . than any other market in the nation."[22]

For Dichter, cancer revealed a fascinating generational difference in health worries—and these age-related, psychological responses were ripe for exploitation. Young smokers seemed not to share their parents' worries. "The threat of cancer . . . seems to make less of an impression on young smokers and old-timers than on the middle-age groups," he observed. Old smokers, set in their habit, regarded the cancer threat "with some philosophical detachment"; younger smokers believed that "cancer is a disease of old age and they 'couldn't care less.'"[23]

Black consumers figured marginally in the menthol market in these early days of rising sales, even though African Americans were also ascending as an important cigarette buying group. Race was simply not a central concern to menthol marketers. Menthol embodied health reassurance, pure and simple, as it had when RJR's W. A. Sugg recalled that "Kool smokers tend to be hypochondriacs," and wrote about a colleague at Dancer-Fitzgerald-Sample who "told me a key idea behind the new 'Live Modern' campaign of L & M's is to reassure on the health angle."[24] Into the early 1960s, companies pitched names like Breeze for the newest menthol brands aimed at youth markets and at those smokers needing soothing reassurance.

If Dichter regarded the "Negro market" and the youth market as both growth markets, it was because they shared a common vulnerability: both groups often fell for status appeals, playing into their different kinds of insecurity. Young people were attuned to self-affirming status products, observed Dichter. Meanwhile, "the Negro market in particular has been a fruitful outlet for many status products" appealing to their "natural desire to achieve equality in every way possible." These group aspirations drove the need for symbols of status, and thus had "prompted the Negro consumer to extensive purchases of all those products which are seen as being indicative of a raised socioeconomic and cultural level," the psychologist explained. Even though the filter cigarette field was now almost a decade old and not as novel as it was in the mid-1950s, "among the young market and the Negro market they still represent a symbolic distinctiveness."[25] For Dichter, it was filtered cigarettes (not menthols) that carried status meaning for Blacks and for young people.

Of the two groups (young people and African Americans), young smokers were the overwhelming focus of marketers and company executives. As one early 1960s study noted, census data showed that "well over half of the young adults who now smoke cigarettes had firmly established the habit while still in their teens."[26] Winning over young smokers had a clear long-term appeal; the strategy meant more years of product use and profits, and carried an obvious economic and business logic. As early as 1951, SMI observed that college campuses had over half a million students enrolled, with more than half of them (375,000) declaring themselves to be cigarette smokers.[27] A decade later, SMI's president observed, "The total cigarette marketing effort in the colleges has doubled in the last five years. Now everybody is in there slugging."[28] Tobacco industry campus representatives distributed free samples; companies ran contests and advertised in campus newspapers (with college ads accounting for as much as 40 percent of the national advertising). As *Consumers Union* critically reported in 1963, the focus of such extensive advertising was to "impress one's brand both on those currently using other brands and on the wholly uninitiated. For, in the amateur psychologizing of the director of Philip Morris' college sales department, 'Students are tremendously loyal. If you catch them, they'll stick with you like glue because your brand reminds them of happy college days.'"[29] They were, in a sense, hooked early.

In 1961 and 1962, few analysts believed that the color line produced any lasting different brand preferences. Surveying African American college students and white students on segregated campuses, SMI detected only slight differences in brand popularity (and a good deal of month-by-month flux as well). Fickleness, rather than stable preferences, defined these youth markets. In its 1961 survey, for example, the researchers observed that "brand standings in the Negro college market have changed considerably again. In December, the first three positions were held by PALL MALL, Winston, and Kent, and in January, these positions are held by Marlboro, Viceroy, and Kent. . . . At the White colleges, the top three positions are held by Marlboro, Winston, and PALL MALL."[30] Salem sat in sixth place. As for menthol cigarette smoking, which was still relatively new, SMI reported only minor differences across the two types of campuses. And the overall rate of menthol smoking was nearly equivalent on both types of campuses: 16.2 percent at the Black colleges, and 14.1 percent on white-majority campuses.[31] Month by month, these researchers tracked marketing opportunities across the color line—paying attention to Black newspaper readership, exploring opportunities in Black-themed radio, and hiring representatives for Black college campuses, and so on. What was the verdict? That all students seemed to want the same thing. They insisted that Black people wanted "the same thing that anyone else does," but they remained attuned to the fact that the color line created disparities in consciousness and consumption. A few observers noted the "role and influence of the white world" on what Black buyers wanted, and acknowledged that in the context of the movement for civil rights there remained a fast-moving "relationship between purchase behavior and political and social aspirations of the Negro people."[32]

Brown & Williamson had taken all of this market flux into account in designing its innovative "Come Up to Kool" 1961 campaign—an initiative focused not on racial targeting as some scholars have argued, but on updating its old stodgy brand with a youthful image.[33] As

B&W's ad firm Ted Bates explained, the pitch sought to update Kool's old therapeutic message for the television age with vivid and bold imagery. It opened on "vague silhouettes slightly descended in foggy swirl . . . [but then] one man moves forward leaving others behind . . . on a slight ascension . . . to break through the smoke. As he reaches to top of his ascent, he comes into light."[34] As one viewer told Bates and their research collaborators at the Psychological Corporation, the "Come Up" motif "meant it was soothing and can help a sore throat. . . . It is supposed to perform a certain magic in a far-fetched way." Based on such insightful viewer reactions, the researchers concluded that the imagery "does indeed pack a highly charged emotional wallop" with a strong subconscious health message projecting both "heat-originated discomfort" and an incentive to act to relieve that unease.[35] In addition, viewers saw new things in the ads quite apart from what marketers intended; "although originally our 'Come Up' commercial was planned to ascribe a benefit to Kool's heavier menthol content, just the reverse seems to be true. The commercial actually lessens the image of Kool as 'heavily mentholated.'" Ironically, it succeeded "in increasing the 'light mentholation' image of KOOL."[36] The Psychological Corporation told Bates that smokers were looking to menthols for a resolution to their discomfort, and the psychologists encouraged Bates to continue to "experiment with new and different approaches to convey the discomfort-relief association."[37] Implicit reassurance pointed the way forward for Kool. Before watching the ad, only 5 percent perceived Kool as "good for steady smoking," but afterward that number climbed to 25 percent.

Youthfulness (that is, white youthfulness) also figured prominently in Come Up's appeal, moving aggressively into terrain occupied by Salem. For the researchers, "the *Come Up* commercial serves to operate very effectively in the very image areas where Salems show prior competitive strength," particularly on appeal to youth. The percentage of viewers saying that Kool was refreshing climbed from 29 before watching to a remarkable 98 percent afterward. And where only 7 percent saw Kool as "youthful" before seeing the ad, exposure to the cartoonish illustration convinced 22 percent of viewers to see Kool in this new light. To the psychologists and the tobacco makers, the Come Up campaign "serves to narrow the advantages ascribed to Salem rather severely on attributes such as 'gentle' . . . 'wholesome'; . . . and 'youthful.'"[38]

Tobacco's overtures to youth were intensifying in 1962 and 1963, but the industry faced increasing pushback in the states, in the US Congress, among regulators, and in the media—and it was this dynamic that ultimately drove the pivot to racial marketing. Since the 1950s, criticism for what Vance Packard had called the "psychoseduction of children" mounted. With a multitude of Dichter-like marketers developing crafty, well-placed advertising, calls for reform continued. Even in 1961, the industry's TIRC warned that "organized efforts against the use of tobacco on the basis of health are gaining increasing support at local, state and national levels." They expressed particular worry about initiatives aimed at school-aged youth: "The American Cancer Society's so-called 'school' campaign, which was discussed two years ago as posing a real threat, has now become widespread . . . , ostensibly an educational program designed for junior and senior high school students."[39] Pressure for warning labels on dangerous products and crackdowns on deceptive advertising had increased.[40] Defending modern psychology, himself, and the companies he advised in congressional testimony, Dichter explained: "Ninety percent of the clients . . . are very honest and decent and do not try to practice deceit." Using insights from modern psychology was not chicanery, he insisted; it was merely creating "the illusion of a desirable difference."[41]

While issuing public reassurance that children were not the target of marketing, the industry and its supporters played a double-sided game. Their internal studies confirmed that younger people sat in the bull's-eye of their interest, or as one study for Philip Morris noted, that "the long cigarette, the filter, and the menthol are consistently thought to appeal to young smokers."[42] Defending the industry on CBS television in late 1962, George Allen, president of the Tobacco Institute, an industry trade group, vigorously denied any youth targeting. "The great majority of the advertising, I must say in all frankness, is on the part of companies which are trying to persuade people who are already smokers to change their brand from one company to another."[43] But reformers remained skeptical, and as *Consumer Reports* observed the following year, "Several state legislatures have considered laws regulating cigarette advertising."[44] In Congress, Oregon Senator Maurine Neuberger supported the idea of a self-imposed curb on tobacco's advertising. A Minnesota bill would have banned ads showing people smoking; another bill, proposed in California, would ban tobacco ads in school and college newspapers. A few colleges had already taken action to discourage the distribution of free cigarette samples. The *Reader's Digest* (a major crusader against the cigarette's dangers) and other magazines now refused cigarette advertisements. As the cigarette scholar Richard Pollay has observed, criticism in 1963 became especially pointed as "sales among teens grew despite the growing cancer concern among scientists."[45]

Appeals to young people to take up smoking ranged from blatant to implicit; both types attracted threats from federal agencies in the early 1960s. The Federal Communications Commission and the Federal Trade Commission now scrutinized "false, misleading, and deceptive" television ads, paying close attention to a growing array of sleights of hand, camera tricks, and outright deceptions. The concern went far beyond cigarettes. In a 1962 ruling, for example, aimed at the Ted Bates Company and its client Colgate-Palmolive, the commission ordered the advertiser to cease using camera tricks, simulations, and gimmicks in their ads. In another case, the FTC ordered advertisers to cease from promoting a razor's ability to shave sandpaper; the screen trick was carried out by shaving a layer of sand scattered on plexiglass.[46] Then in the fall of 1962, the thalidomide crisis—a drug that promised to ease the pains of pregnant women only to produce miscarriages, death, or birth deformities in their offspring—made politicians, regulators, and consumers frightfully aware of the need for skepticism about overblown drug claims that hid darker truths.[47] The thalidomide scandal produced legislation enhancing the power of the FDA, and it further emboldened those who sought to protect children from harmful forms of marketing. For some critics like Senator

Neuberger, appeals to youth ("the calculated seduction of children by the smoking habit") by tobacco companies were especially egregious. The senator pushed for a self-imposed curb on tobacco advertising, echoing an idea proposed by LeRoy Collins, president of the National Association of Broadcasters. To defend children, then, new regulations seemed imminent—aimed not only at tobacco companies but at advertisers and the media most generally. As Neuberger explained, "It is inevitable that the need will eventually find expression in a Congressional mandate."[48]

Facing regulatory threats as well as billions of dollars in losses, menthol advertising geared for a major shift in focus—tilting toward making their health claims even more implicit than ever, trafficking less explicitly in outreach to young smokers, and seeking new growth markets. The implicit approach (like the warning labels soon to come on cigarette packs) carried the benefit of limiting future liability. But one outcome of increased regulation would be this: that tamping down on one market would lead industry to seek other markets to exploit and other strategies to reassure. It would be a recurring theme—heightened regulation in one sphere of the market unleashed industry energies, all the more, into the urban marketplace. The year 1964 would see the first such market pivot; later, the ban on television and radio advertising would have a similar effect. The threat of government action drove companies to test new types of pitches on new market segments, in the case of menthols ultimately toward "inner-city" segments. Faced with the threats of regulation and looking with concern at an impending Surgeon General's report, *Smoking and Health*, scheduled for release in early 1964, six major tobacco firms preemptively promised to cease directly advertising in college media.[49] The FTC also forced companies to abandon explicit health promises; the result would be implicit, and no less potent, reassuring appeals about menthols and other brands.

But as *Consumer Reports* observed, the tactical shift toward implicit health claims protected the industry from future liability; "one distinction between the explicit old-style health claims and the implicit new-style claims is that it would be far more difficult for a future lung-cancer victim to show that today's advertisements promised him long life."[50] It was as if the consumer publication could see into the future, to anticipate the difficulties that lawyers like Forman would face as they sought to fix blame. It was in 1964, then, that the industry realized that the key to the future of menthol smoking could not be youth (at least not explicitly so), and it was also that year that the menthol campaign began to tailor itself more aggressively to Black aspirations, and to cultivate new markets that might sustain the product and withstand criticism in the years ahead.

Bending toward Black Aspirations

How and when did menthol become a Black smoking preference? And why? By the time Andrew Schindler had joined RJR, the shift was already underway, led by their main rival Brown & Williamson and its brand, Kool. Marketing tactics drove the transformation, as firms sensed new opportunities at the intersection of rising health worries, youth culture, and Black demands for social justice. The shift occurred over four tumultuous years, 1963 to 1967 — crucial years in the history of cigarette politics and racial politics, years defined by civil rights protests, marches, economic boycotts, and pressure for equality. Out of this cauldron of turmoil, the industry created opportunity, and new approaches to racial marketing with menthol at its center. But the table for this transformation was set in the early 1960s, as the Black market — defined by their own internal social divisions, class tensions, and gender, age, and status dynamics — came into view for cigarette psychologists.

Racial marketing twisted marketers in knots in the very early 1960s, even if the era's events and economic activism made obvious the importance of capitalizing on some kind of racial appeal.[51] Writing in 1961, the African American sociologist and marketing scholar Henry Allen Bullock pushed for what he called a "common ground" approach to racial marketing. "The idea that separate media are required to reach Negro and white consumers is more illusion than fact," he argued in a 1961 article in the *Harvard Business Review* titled

"Consumer Motivations in Black and White."[52] Part social analysis of the psychology of race and part marketing guide, Bullock's analysis guided marketers through the treacherous terrain of stereotypes and facts about Black and white buyers. Across the color line, both groups were driven by a search for security, by fear, and motivated by desires for distinction (a "badge which the two races both wear"). Blacks and whites were more similar than different, he contended, but some divergences were notable. What was the best way to reach African Americans, Bullock asked? "Negroes seem to spend significantly more of their time with radio and magazines than do whites, while the latter apparently favor television and newspapers significantly more." These differences in media use could lead in two directions, explained Bullock—either toward separate channels of communication or toward a focus on commonalities. Bullock called for joint and integrated appeals, focusing on "motivations common to Negro and white consumers . . . appealing to both races." It is hard not to see in Bullock's writing his deeper hope for the era—a call for harmonizing Black and white ideals by emphasizing common desires over differences. Moreover, Bullock insisted, "special appeals programs do not suit Negro aspirations, and racial differences in value systems are simply not sufficient to warrant their use."[53]

White and Black needs ran along parallel roads, said Bullock, separated only because of the laws of racial segregation in many states, but they were essentially equal. The search for security defined consumer purchasing, he contended, particularly for food, automobiles, and cigarettes. With respect to cigarettes, Bullock saw health and security as among the most important questions confronting smokers, regardless of race. Across the racial divide, he insisted, "to smoke or not to smoke is not the question." Instead, every group worried about excessive smoking: "the pack-a-day habit elicits negative reactions from Negro and white consumers alike."[54]

There were, nevertheless, Black-white differences. Bullock believed that Blacks saw heavy smoking as tied to "mental disturbances and physical incapacity," while whites "associate it with lung cancer and almost certain death." The fear, however, was uniform and common to all. "At present," he argued, "people as frightened as these . . . seem to be growing in direct ratio to the dissemination of health literature about smoking." Bullock echoed the industry's conclusion following the 1950s reports linking smoking to cancer, namely, that dealing with health concerns head-on by assuring smokers that moderate smoking was best would fail: "To talk smoking moderation is to feed fear with fear. What people really want to hear is that the product has been modified according to the validated findings of medical research."[55] If people wanted to hear that cigarettes were reengineered for safety, the industry was happy to oblige.

For Bullock, these common fears across the color line about the health dangers of smoking required common gestures of reassurance from marketers. "In order to make the advertising message acceptable to Negro and white customers at the same time, sellers must cater to the common motivations that influence their buying." Tobacco marketers did not need a different pitch for white and Black smokers, but rather different ways of conveying meaningful reassurance across the color line, perhaps through cartoon rather than real images. Cartoon imagery, Bullock explained, was "most likely to appeal simultaneously to both races." Capturing astutely the tensions and possibilities of this moment, the sociologists observed, "To the extent that advertisers gain control over the human mind, they also inherit some degree of responsibility for its content. . . . [T]here are Negroes who are greatly insecure about their health or color and who are sufficiently gullible to accept some of the absurd claims of sellers of 'cure-alls.' . . . Admittedly, too, there are whites who would resent any representation of the Negro image as a human being." In this context, cartoons held an obvious appeal. Bullock could easily have cited Willie the Penguin, Kool's mascot, as a cartoon image that (whether by design or by accident) communicated precisely and effectively amid these racial and age divides while also speaking to health concerns—opening the possibility of creating new markets.[56]

Although insightful for 1961, Bullock's advice could not anticipate how—within a few years—continuing civil rights boycotts and consumer challenges against segregated establishments would compel advertisers to take African American consumerism more seriously. The rise of the economic boycott as a weapon in the civil rights struggle made clear that consumerism was being weaponized and connected directly to Black ideals of equality. But Black consumer politics also posed unique marketing challenges. The casual psychologizing on questions of status and identity that Ernest Dichter had popularized in the 1950s seemed especially urgent in this environment, as more and more consultants spawned their theories of race, consumer behavior, brand choice, and Black status aspirations.

Recognizing the market potential of the Black community, but remaining wary of alienating white consumers in an atmosphere of inflamed racial tensions, the industry bent hesitantly toward Black aspirations. In a society deeply divided on the "race question"—with marches for racial integration, pressure for a Civil Right Act, southern white defenses of segregation, economic threats to boycott segregated institutions, and so on—tobacco companies wondered how best to orchestrate market outreach to Black smokers. In the past, segregated media had provided an easy path for companies to reach Black people with a tailored message on top of the more generalized appeal that would reach them via the national media. It was one thing to advertise to Black college students in newspapers on segregated campuses, or to place ads on Black-themed radio stations, but the emergence of television and mass media alongside the integration pressures posed challenges for the tailored racial pitch. Race-oriented marketing posed a characteristically American dilemma, particularly for the larger brands wary of alienating white buyers. Marketers now turned to sociologists as well as psychologists for insights on African American and white consumer attitudes, dissecting how each group understood the health issues inherent in smoking, and charting how the broader context of struggles for representation and racial equality shaped perceptions of different products. A proliferation of consultants and market researchers like DFS, honing their skills of studying social structure and influencing behavior, pointed to Black urban communities as worthy markets for a new type of targeting. Their theories echoed insights of such sociologists as R. K. Merton on local and cosmopolitan influence, influence structures, and avenues of interpersonal influence.[57] Indeed, new firms like the Center for Research in Marketing, the Opinion Research Corporation, and the Student Marketing Institute joined old stalwarts like the Institute for Motivational Research and the Psychological Corporation, working with the tobacco industry to traffic in theories of this new, emergent Black consumer psychology.

In an early 1963 study, Dichter himself explained (in a study on the "current cigar smoking climate" requested by the Consolidated Cigar Corporation) that "more than any other ethnic group we found it important to consider the Negro buyer in dynamic not static terms . . . [as] a group striving for status and exhibiting to an ever-greater extent buying patterns at times different and at times similar to the white groups." Black buyers were not one homogeneous group, he explained, but three distinct socioeconomic groups, each defined by class, social status, and "psychological motivation." First, there was "a mass of unskilled poorly paid laborers with little or no education [whose] . . . quest for status assumes the stereotyped patterns usually assigned to the Negro." In Dichter's words, this was the type of "Negro . . . [who drives] the flashy Cadillac, wears loud clothes, and smokes big cigars." The second buying class was African Americans "entering the middle range of the socio-economic spectrum . . . [who were] better educated, better-trained." They might be postal workers, clerks, or civil servants. As Dichter saw it, their market behavior was "more closely paralleled to that of whites [than the first group] inasmuch as the drive for status is not as pressing." The third, uppermost segment of African Americans were "the better paid and better educated professionals and businessmen . . . whose patterns very closely approximate similarly situated whites." Psychologically, "these advanced segments of the Negro market" veered away from "more ostentatious symbols of the status search," Dichter observed.[58]

Despite these class variations from the high and low ends of "the Negro market," Dichter believed that, in general, Black motivations and aspirations contrasted in particular ways from so-called white "value systems." Echoing a belief among many retailers, researchers, and market experts, he said that African Americans exhibited strong brand loyalty. He similarly highlighted African Americans' supposed sensitivity to image and status; they "now are anxious to be accepted on the same value system applied to whites and they therefore are more prone to seek out brands . . . which are less susceptible to criticism than others." Good taste, reputation, and "an aura of quality" mattered to them, Dichter continued. "Here too may [be] the reason why Negroes exhibit greater brand loyalty than white consumers, a behavior pattern we found in other studies which we have conducted." Sensitive to companies who showed respect for them as buyers, African Americans were also, the psychologist explained, moving "away from [products projecting] negative stereotypes." The secret to reaching these consumers was to cater to their "sophisticated search for status."[59] These questions of brand, identity, and representation were evolving day by day, upended by both health concerns and the growing movement for rights, and made more complicated by racial tensions. As for health, Dichter observed, "the cigar is second only to the pipe as the smoke for those concerned with health." As analysts understood, race and health anxieties intersected—informing brand choice. The "subtle projection of health" had special appeal precisely "at this time when Americans generally, partly due to proselytizing by the present Administration, are becoming more and more health-oriented."[60]

Increasingly in the early 1960s, marketers and psychologists ventured carefully into these questions of race and marketing, building new partnerships with Black organizations and people of influence in the process. To support their theories, they sent researchers onto the streets of major cities to survey the attitudes of smokers and nonsmokers, with increasing attention to African Americans. In so doing, they built new relationships with smokers and others in the community. A distinctive 1963 study of 488 African American smokers (approximately fifty per city, spanning New York, Philadelphia, Chicago, Cleveland, Los Angeles, Atlanta, and St. Louis), conducted by Lennen & Newell on behalf of Lorillard, not only sought to understand Black smoking habits and attitudes, but also relied on a new partnership with *Ebony* magazine, which deployed its field staff for the survey. The absence of trained interviewers meant that the "report should be treated cautiously," noted the marketing firm, but the involvement with *Ebony* also gave the findings an aura of authenticity.[61]

Tracking Black anxiety at a moment when health concerns around smoking ran high, the survey asked smokers whether they agreed or disagreed with such statements as: "Because of what you read today, it is foolish not to smoke a safe cigarette."[62] Sixty percent of those polled said they worried about smoking's effect on health; half (49 percent) believed that smoking could cause cancer; and 39 percent of women and 28 percent of men thought it was foolish not to smoke a safe cigarette. The study also tracked "advertising penetration" in those cities, brand usage, and switching behavior. But the greatest attention was paid to "smoking anxiety." *Ebony*'s urban interviews confirmed that menthol packed an especially strong punch in promising to relieve anxiety, with a "relatively high menthol usage among Negroes—apparently traceable to the female segment." As with white women, the study found that "female Negroes tended to be more 'anxious' about smoking than male Negroes." For the Lorillard consultant, these findings pointed to "potentially profitably areas for [Lorillard brands] Newport and York, respectively."[63]

Nor was Lorillard alone in conducting such urban studies on the intersection of health beliefs, race, and the promise of menthol as a healthier cigarette. When American Tobacco, makers of Pall Mall, hired the Lawrence C. Gumbinner Advertising Agency in 1963 to conduct an extensive national study of brand trends, the firm learned that its non-menthol Pall Mall led Salem and Kool as the brand of choice among African Americans. The American Tobacco brand captured 21 percent of Black smokers, compared with only 13 percent of whites. Salem's popularity among African Americans was only 12 percent; Kool was down to 3 percent.[64] Pall Mall remained one of "the top non-filter brand[s]," noted one industry analyst, by using "what is essentially a filtration approach for some time with its message that 'Pall Mall's famous length travels the smoke naturally.'"[65] Surprisingly, the survey also revealed that whereas white smokers had slowly and systematically gravitated toward filtered cigarettes for safety, African Americans had not followed this path as rapidly. In 1963, 47 percent of "native whites" smoked filters; only 30 percent of Blacks did.[66]

Just at this moment when tobacco companies began conducting surveys and polls to track Black health worries and meet Black aspirations, civil rights activists and organizations were raising the stakes of racial marketing through boycotts and economic pressure. "If a firm persists in refusing to employ Negroes because of their race," Martin Luther King Jr. had said in January 1963, "Negroes will refuse to buy its products."[67] The converse was also true; if African Americans were loyal purchasers of a product, activists approached such firms with their own agenda. "A new development has taken place," wrote one Lorillard advertiser, A. Toft, to a colleague in September 1963, "whereby C.O.R.E. [the Congress of Racial Equality] has approached several large national advertisers asking specific question about their advertising practices and employment opportunities." By meeting with a number of firms, including Liggett & Myers and American Tobacco, the civil rights group meant to exert leverage through consumer purchasing. As the Lorillard executive explained, "C.O.R.E. did not threaten boycotts in either case, but did comment about 'Selective Buying Practices' wherein the various C.O.R.E. branches would advise their members of the cooperating firms and urge the purchase of the products of such firms."[68] In short, the civil rights organization offered to be an influencer.

The next month in a hotel room in New York City, another such meeting between CORE and representatives of Brown & Williamson suggests how, for the civil rights activists, the ability to leverage Black consumerism to advance economic goals far outstripped any health worries of cigarettes. At the Dorset Hotel, representatives from B&W and three representatives of CORE discussed particular brands. B&W executives "were asked about our policy with relation to our television commercials." Unlike the critics holding the cigarette industry to account for deceitful advertising in 1963, the civil rights leaders were not worried about health, cancer, youth marketing, or deceptive advertising. Leverage was their goal. Might the company consider casting a Black copilot in a Raleigh commercial, asked CORE. As B&W's J. W. Burgard described the meeting, the group "made it clear that their primary interest was not in securing additional jobs for Negro actors but in casting Negroes in situations portraying them in a higher status than they felt had been customary in the advertising business over the years." For their part, B&W executives explained that "we had actually refrained from casting Negroes in menial roles, even though we might well have done so under previous conditions." B&W's executives were pleased with the negotiation, convinced that CORE was receptive to their plan to "use Negroes in two KOOL commercials that were now being tested." That being said, B&W noted for the record that they would only go so far in putting African American faces on their product: "We specifically pointed out that in no instance were we using Negroes as the main characters."[69]

The search for economic opportunity underpinned much of the Black civil rights struggle—the right to a job, the right to go into a segregated business, the right to purchase goods, the right to buy a home in a whites-only neighborhood. Protests for equal opportunity drew the tobacco industry's attention to Black buying potential. Facing restrictions on youth advertising, Big Tobacco saw the Black buyer in a new light. Where Philip Morris has been skittish about openly courting African Americans in the 1950s, Brown & Williamson in 1964 made a mad rush to capture new menthol markets—and within a few years, the entire industry had set its sights on the urban Black smoker. Menthol's transformation from a health- and youth-targeted product to a Black-marketed commodity can only be fully explained in the context of these social changes working in tandem with the government's regulatory priorities to safeguard the health of youth. With youth markets under threat, the tobacco industry sensed opportunity. Within years, the industry began to cultivate deep relationships with civic organizations, Black news media, and opinion leaders—intent on cultivating Black buyers, and focusing its marketing on struggling cities.

Racial marketing of menthols neared its crucial turning point in 1964. At a time when critics of the tobacco industry were moving forcefully to restrict cigarette advertising to youth, CORE sought more, rather than fewer, Black faces in tobacco advertising. If a brand of cigarette — Salem, Raleigh, Kool — was popular among African Americans, this was not a health crisis for CORE, but an opportunity to exercise economic and political leverage. With few employment doors open to African Americans in a segregated setting, the activists reached for any rung for Blacks to climb the economic ladder, whether those opportunities took the form of tobacco factory work or televised roles in cigarette commercials.

By the end of 1963, the tactical boycotts and economic threats were winning victories, but also producing new and comprising entanglements for activists, the industry, and Black smokers. This activism created a "growing, changing, and challenging" environment, said one analyst in *Sales Management*. Black purchasing power was in flux, he noted; the pejorative image of Black "'conspicuous consumption' [i.e., buying ostentatious Cadillacs], long considered a salient trait of the Negro consumer, is declining as he expands his intellectual and social horizons."[70] With youth marketing under siege, such trends attracted increasing attention in tobacco boardrooms. Black smokers were in turn paying attention to tobacco marketing. As the meeting at the Dorset concluded, B&W executives observed that CORE "expressed satisfaction with our position but asked that we advise them on the dates on which they could see some of our new commercials using Negroes when they appeared on the air."[71] Such negotiations, formed in pursuit of civil rights and economic gains, laid the groundwork for relationships with long-term implications for advertising, menthol smoking, and the health of men like Ezell Thomas.

1964: Smoking, Health, and Race at a Crossroads

These embryonic developments in racial marketing ran headlong into a new "cancer scare" in early 1964 when Luther Terry, the US Surgeon General, issued a report on the dangers of smoking. The fallout put the industry under a new state of siege. Enhanced oversight of mass advertising and restrictions on advertising aimed at youth seemed eminent. The frenzy of 1964 spurred the industry toward new market strategies, and a new Kool image was born.

Corporate interest in Black menthol smoking surged in the tumultuous year of 1964—a year that started with a devastating Surgeon General's report and witnessed intense pressures for civil rights laws. With the release in October 1963 of a British study of smoking and disease, the US tobacco industry steadied for the fallout they knew would soon land on American shores. Tobacco companies had been here before; as late as 1962, analyst Harry Wootten had predicted that they "may continue to be faced with periodic health scares." Recalling 1953, Wootten argued that the key to "overcoming the initial health scare" was flexibility. As a result of shrewd deflection of bad news, "consumption has continued to move ahead since then despite considerable adverse health publicity." It was reasonable to assume, he concluded, that the "second major health scare which emanated from Great Britain . . . and had some repercussions here will be overcome in the long run by efforts from within the industry."[72] The fortunes of menthol brands had risen in the face of the earlier bad news. But could the industry dodge another bullet? Could such bad fortune be translated into good profits not just once, but twice? And what would be the aftereffects of this new health scare?[73]

The Surgeon General's report *Smoking and Health* offered a shocking compendium on tobacco's dangers with vast implications for the "nearly 70 million people in the United States [who] consumed tobacco regularly." The dire findings showed that "the greater the number of cigarettes smoked daily, the higher the death rate." Smoking contributed substantially to death from lung cancer, chronic bronchitis and permanent damage to the air sacs of the lung causing shortness of breath (emphysema), as well as cancers of the esophagus and urinary bladder. A smoker's illnesses might start with a cough or difficulty breathing, but the long deadly list extended across all the body's organ systems. Meanwhile, as the report explained, the factors that sustained people's smoking habit "related primarily to psychological and social drives, reinforced and perpetuated by the pharmacological actions of nicotine." The committee dismissed

Figure 3.4. Surgeon General Luther Terry announcing the findings of the Surgeon General's 1964 report *Smoking and Health*. The findings produced a wave of calamitous news for cigarette companies and for smokers. By July of that year, Brown & Williamson would begin to court Black smokers aggressively with Kool.
Credit: Courtesy of the National Library of Medicine.

the "popular hypothesis that smoking among adolescents is an expression of rebellion against authority. . . . The overwhelming evidence indicates that smoking—its beginning, habituation, and occasional discontinuation—is to a very large extent psychologically and socially determined." And finally, although the "significant beneficial effects of smoking occur primarily in the area of mental health, and the habit originates in a search for contentment," it concluded that there was no question that smoking "is a health hazard of sufficient importance in the United States to warrant appropriate remedial action."[74]

Given the sweeping gravity of the report, menthol barely warranted a single sentence. In a section on additives, it mentioned only that manufacturers in the United States used a range of additives "such as sugars . . . synthetic flavors, licorice, menthol, vanillin, and rum." In Britain, by contrast, there was a widespread "prohibition on the use of additives in tobacco manufacture."[75]

As the industry reeled and smokers responded to the second major health warning on smoking in a decade, elected officials and government agencies weighed a number of tobacco restrictions.

Many smokers quit promptly. But, as one industry observer put it, others continued to switch "not only brands but categories: from regulars to kings to filters to menthols to menthol filters."[76] The months after publication promised to be volatile for smoking behavior and for tobacco marketing, but with the promise of greater fortunes for menthol brands. The FCC and FTC quickly proposed stern public warnings, with the FCC considering a ban on tobacco advertising during the hours when young viewers watched television. "The appeal of cigarette ads to the young has been a special concern to some Government officials," noted one news report.[77] Another regulatory proposal, opposed heatedly by industry, would require all ads to carry explicit health warnings; as one FCC official speculated, "It might be better for teenagers to see it than not."[78]

Even as the industry fought publicly to refute the linkage between smoking and cancer, its confidential surveys and in-person studies gauged the effects of the news. Waves of smokers were giving up the habit, sowing seeds of anguish in the industry.[79] The African American media in Chicago and Baltimore reported that the well-known comedian and activist Dick Gregory abandoned cigarettes—they had been a regular prop for him onstage for years.[80] From 1963 to 1964, a survey conducted on behalf of American Tobacco, Brown & Williamson's parent company, found that the overall incidence of smoking among males had dropped from 56 percent to 43 percent, and incidence for younger smokers, 18–29, had declined by similar levels (55 percent to 42 percent). Smoking rates for "native whites" fell 8 percent (from 45 percent to 37 percent), and more precipitously for "Negro" smokers, from 53 percent to 37 percent.[81] How many smokers would abandon the habit, and would a rebound follow as it had in the 1950s?

Philip Morris called once again on Elmo Roper, as it had in the 1950s, to conduct a speedy survey about the effects of the Surgeon General's report on consumers and sales. The report confirmed what the tobacco firms already suspected: even as quitting had spiked, so, too, had the rate of smoking menthols edged upward. In the minds of tobacco insiders, the perceived link between menthol and health

Figure 3.5. Comedian and civil rights activist Dick Gregory, circa 1963. Following publication of the Surgeon General's report, Gregory, like many others, announced that he'd quit smoking, abandoning the cigarette as a stage prop during his routines.
Credit: Photo by Michael Ochs. Courtesy of Getty Images.

was becoming cemented, even if that linkage was out of sight of regulators, implicit in advertising copy, but well documented in private industry studies and reports. Surveying 2,000 customers in New York, Chicago, San Francisco, and Los Angeles, as well as other cities in February, the Roper Organization found evidence of a menthol "health" advantage, with "Chesterfields . . . a large loser, . . . the filter brands [getting] less than their share . . . but the menthols get somewhat more than their share." One respondent told Roper, "When the report came out I made up my mind to change to a milder cigarette. When you inhale the Kools has something in it to make you feel much cooler when you inhale the smoke. It's cooler in the head as a whole, also the throat."[82] For this smoker, the menthol coolness was more than aesthetic—it suggested health and a measure of security, as menthol usually did. In echoes of the 1950s "cancer scare," the 1964 report was driving a second menthol upsurge.

In a devastating storm, menthol's rise appeared like an economic lifeline for companies concerned about an exodus of smokers. They paid special attention to shifts in preferences in the spring of 1964, some of which were predictable. Driven by health concerns, women made up an increasing proportion of menthol smokers. Now, nearly a quarter of women smokers chose menthols, double the rate of men. But another menthol trend in the first nervous months of 1964 caught manufacturers by surprise—a small uptick in menthol consumption among African Americans. The timing suggests that the change had everything to do with the Surgeon General's report as well as the continued false health promises and health associations of menthol cigarettes. Menthol consumption among African Americans had leaped from 19 percent in the spring 1963 to 24 percent in early 1964, a dramatic increase compared to change from 16 to 17 percent of "native white" smokers during the same time period. These preference shifts were seen as "stronger among light smokers than among heavier smokers."[83] The Kool brand in particular seemed to be making particularly strong gains among Black smokers, with its share of the market spiking from 3 to 8 percent.[84] While still trailing Salem, which held steady at 12 percent, the rise was promising. The gain for menthol brands came at the expense of Camel, whose share of the market among Black smokers had dropped from 11 to 7 percent, and Lucky Strike, which declined from 10 to 6 percent.[85]

With a presidential campaign underway and as civil rights workers faced violent attacks in 1964 while trying to register Black voters, tobacco companies conducted attitudinal and "psychographic" profiling of smokers in general, including menthol smokers, as specific personality types. In a study published that eventful summer for Lorillard, the Grey Marketing and Research Department saw different psychological types of menthol smokers taking shape. Rebels, they explained, "characterized by . . . opposition to society, especially to

BRAND OF MENTHOLATED CIGARETTE SMOKED AT PRESENT

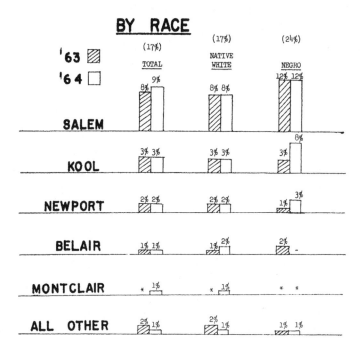

*Less than 0.5%.

Figure 3.6. One market study by Crossley S-D Surveys noticed a slight uptick in menthol cigarettes use among Black Americans, with the preference for Kool climbing from 3 percent to 8 percent from 1963 to 1964. Brown & Williamson would seize on the trend.
Credit: *National Smoking Habits Study*, vol. 2, p. 49. Image courtesy of Truth Tobacco Industry Documents (https://www.industrydocuments.ucsf.edu/tobacco/).

authority . . . and out to prove he is free to come and go as he pleases," smoked filtered cigarettes and menthols to a lesser degree.[86] The consultants told Lorillard not to fear rebellion, but to court it and channel it. If civil unrest undermined commerce for many businesses, this was not the case for tobacco. But Grey also theorized that conformists

who "conscientiously followed rules and [adapted] to prevailing realities" wanted a cigarette "which has an association with health." This
group, made up of a large share of housewives, also gravitated toward
menthols—much higher than the general market—as well as filtered
cigarettes.[87] As ever, anxieties could be good for business, if properly
understood.

Manipulation of the menthol smoker's psyche was now a major
undertaking; and there emerged a stark gap between how industry
insiders discussed persuasion and manipulation, on the one hand,
and what regulators understood about these practices, on the other.
"Show-offs" defined a third psychological type of menthol smoker,
explained Grey to Lorillard, and here, too, women figured prominently as they sought a brand that satisfied a "striving for prominence,
even if only of a transient nature."[88] Health did not appear, for them,
to be a primary motivation. But at the same time that Grey was ad-
vising Lorillard about the psychological makeup of these different
types of menthol smokers and how to market effectively to them, the
FTC lashed out at all menthol advertising as deceitful for depicting
"smoking in an essentially pure environment, in a world effectively
insulated from health hazards." The FTC took aim at specific brands
for portraying "male and female models in outdoor settings of appropriate beauty . . . with its implications that the smoke of an Alpine cigarette is as safe as exceptionally pure air at dawn."[89] What regulators
did not understand about menthols, but industry insiders did, was
what Alpine was not rising in appeal because it was pitched as *akin to*
fresh air; the menthol appeal hinged on being *better* than pure air—on
being positively therapeutic.

It was precisely at this moment of peak fear and uncertainty—as
the cancer findings threatened sales and the FTC cracked down on
misleading claims—that Brown & Williamson was reaching across
the contentious American color line with explicit Kool advertising
in African American newspapers, shaping a new market. In March
1964, the company's sales data showed a small uptick in menthol sales
among African Americans. The increase, which was tiny, would have
been unremarkable in any other context, but it took on new meaning

amid tobacco's current crisis. Where consultants had told industry a few months earlier, in November 1963, that "Negro smokers . . . had less experience with menthol cigarettes than have all smokers," B&W sensed the beginning of a new market reality.[90]

In January, the company turned to the Arthur D. Little consulting firm for insight into what was happening in the Black market. Little's report, based on consumer surveys, suggested that Kool's former heavy therapeutic appeal was expanding, changing, and winning new followers. In their view, the menthol smoker "is now an average person . . . smoking for enjoyment rather than for medicinal reasons." But if Black smokers seemed to be tilting toward menthols even slightly, the consultant argued, many were motivated by festering health concerns and the impact of advertising. Some respondents told Little that Salem provided the pleasure; Kool, by contrast, provided the discernible jolt. But as Little interpreted things, any racial differences were driven by outreach efforts. "Sales variations between races are a result of differences in promotion rather than basic radical differences in smoking desires or habits," Little explained. African American salesmen and media were a key driver of sales trends, said industry insiders. But equally important was the advertisers' grasp of ethnic group psychology regarding brands and status. "The Spanish and Negro groups like to purchase only the best of everything—they are not looking for bargains. . . . They can be reached successfully only by promotion that they understand. . . . Menthol cigarettes seem to be going well in this market. . . . [T]here must be a racial slant in the marketing efforts directed toward them." Jews, said Little, were different: "In the case of the Jewish market, this is not a requirement."[91]

By June 1964, Kool's appeal continued rising and regulators took note by criticizing the slippery therapeutic appeals—a critique that echoed the FTC's concerns from twenty years earlier when, in 1942, a cease-and-desist order prohibited B&W from claiming that "doctors know the beneficial head clearing quality of menthol."[92] Now, however, the FTC issued no such order or ban, instead merely commenting disapprovingly on Kool's now-implicit health claims. The problem, said regulators, was that these ads worked by highlighting themes of satisfaction, social desirability, and "associating smoking with individuals, groups, or ideas worthy of emulation or likely to be emulated." As the FTC observed, Kool—which had now become a top-ten brand with 3.1 percent of the total US market—had cultivated smokers with promises that heavier menthol smoking would enhance taste and bring some type of restoration. "Advertising for Kool reflects its heavy-menthol properties . . . proposed as the cigarette for the man who has smoked so many cigarettes during the day that he is no longer interested in cigarettes because, 'They don't taste like much.'" The appeal came close to crossing a line, said the regulators. For smokers who had lost a sense of taste and wanted something restorative, the FTC said, "this appeal comes close to attributing therapeutic qualities to Kool cigarettes, insofar as Kool cigarettes are claimed to be capable of restoring one's physical ability to enjoy smoking." They acknowledged that an implicit health logic lay behind the promise that "Kool's menthol magic brightens taste," but did nothing to stop the practice.[93] This was a decidedly mild critique; there would be only disapproval, but no further action against the menthol claims by tobacco companies in 1964—except to remind the public that menthol cigarettes were built on distraction and deception.

Lay observers and critics of industry well understood that a new shift to menthols was underway in the wake of the Surgeon General's warnings. Testifying before the FTC in March, for example, public health researcher Eva Salber could only decry the effects of the misleading public imagery—noting that images of manliness, sexuality, and adventure dominated cigarette advertising and that most high school students she had spoken to in Newton, Massachusetts, were convinced that "all you needed to do to be sexually attractive was to light up a particular brand . . . [and] to be manly, you smoked another brand. . . . To be an expert skier, yet another." How did these students respond to the Surgeon General's report? "Rather than give up smoking," she found, "students are turning more and more to filtered and mentholated cigarettes in the hope that these are safer. Here again television advertising is misleading."[94]

In large part, menthol sat well beneath the radar for FTC reformers. The agency's inaction stemmed from the fact that it had little deep insight into the tobacco companies' internal deliberations or knowledge of how the industry was positioning menthol as the answer to cancer worries. Critics could only speculate about what the industry consultants, with their fingers on the pulse of anxious consumers, were seeing and measuring in enormous depth, detail, and rigor month by month during this critical year. Meanwhile, menthol itself was not the FTC's primary concern. Its mission in 1964 was "to protect the youth of the nation against unfair or deceptive acts or practices in cigarette advertising," rather than taking on any particular brand or brand type.[95] Addressing the FTC, James Hundley, a physician and the Assistant Surgeon General for Operations, stressed that in the fight against "unfair and deceptive acts or practices in cigarette advertising," the agency should focus on "measures designed to prevent initiation of the habit in young people rather than attempting to motivate established smokers to discontinue or minimize the practice."[96] Television had opened the door to industry by projecting an image of smoking "as socially desirable and . . . consistent with good health and physical well-being." Regulators now sought to close that door, concerned that these images could "have great impact on impressionable young minds."[97]

As one door began to close for the industry, however, other doorways to "impressionable minds" became more appealing. Having received only the mildest critiques from the FTC, Brown & Williamson made its boldest play yet for Black smokers in the summer of 1964—launching an audacious advertising campaign for Kool in African American newspapers in major cities. The print campaign featured a Black couple in middle-class dress relaxing near an outdoor fountain. The couple smiled contentedly as water cascaded into the woman's outstretched hand. The words wove across the scene: "feel extra coolness in your throat." The campaign promised, "Through Kool's pure white filter comes the most refreshing coolness you can get in any cigarette."[98] In early June, the ad appeared in the *Los Angeles Sen-*

Through Kool's pure white filter
comes the most refreshing coolness
you can get in any cigarette.

BROWN & WILLIAMSON TOBACCO CORPORATION B&W The Mark of Quality in Tobacco Products

Through Kool's pure white filter
comes the most refreshing coolness
you can get in any cigarette.

BROWN & WILLIAMSON TOBACCO CORPORATION B&W The Mark of Quality in Tobacco Products

Figures 3.7 & 3.8. In these KOOL advertisements from 1964, couples across racial lines are shown as wanting the same qualities in the brand: "extra coolness in your throat." The Black-themed ad was a novel development in 1964, appearing in African American newspapers across the country in a major campaign that summer. The throat reference continued the therapeutic messaging that had defined menthol marketing since the 1920s.
Credit: From the collection of Stanford Research Into the Impact of Tobacco Advertising (tobacco.stanford.edu).

tinel, the *Pittsburgh Courier,* the *Cleveland Call and Post,* the *Baltimore Afro-American,* the Norfolk *New Journal and Guide,* the *Philadelphia Tribune,* and the New York *Amsterdam News.* Another set ran in July.

For B&W, the campaign opened a door into a new era of racial appeals, testing, refining, and calibrating menthol's tried-and-true health pitch in cities, many of which (at the tail end of a great influx of Black southerners) were becoming majority or near-majority African American. In 1950, St. Louis had been 17.9 percent African American; in 1960, the percentage rose to 28.6; the 1970 census would find the Black population at 40.9 percent.[99] By 1965, marketing journals announced that "Negroes are one of the most 'urbanized' segments of the country's population. . . . The 'central cities' of many U.S. urban centers are now 50 percent or more Negro-populated." The writer advised that these were not merely "scaled-down versions of urbanized whites;" these Black populations were distinctive, almost captive, clusters of consumers because segregated neighborhoods meant that "generally, they are unable to spend money for housing commensurate with incomes."[100]

If you lived in Philadelphia in 1964 and sat down to read the city's Black newspaper the *Philadelphia Tribune* on July 4th, the single issue captured a crossroads moment—a new racial politics with its promise of equality and an eye-catching new product appeal by B&W, the maker of Kool. The front page declared, "Controversial Civil Rights Bill Becomes Law," with President Lyndon B. Johnson asking all Americans to help in smashing bias.[101] Page three featured the story of a married couple turning to the NAACP for assistance after being denied housing because they were "mixed" race. Page four featured an ad for the gasoline company Esso (now Exxon) with a memorable catchphrase created by Ernest Dichter ("Put a tiger in your tank") that spoke widely to a consumer society looking to drive farther and faster. On page six, one would find news that Jackie Robinson, Major League Baseball's first African American player, had endorsed Johnson in the presidential campaign. And on page thirteen, two advertisements loomed large—one for Ballantine Beer and one for Kool with the distinctive waterfall imagery.

The Kool message—promising safety and health—would have

caught the reader's eye amidst the lingering health uncertainty and economic vulnerability of the moment. Here was a company employing Black models, advertising in the city's Black media, and reaching out for one's business at a time when such gestures of respect were fraught. Other companies kept a close eye on B&W's strategy, and in September American Tobacco noted (in an internal memo) that Kool's advertising had crossed a line—not by advertising to African Americans but by making unsupported health promises. Quoting from the existing federal regulations, American Tobacco product manager John Ulrich wrote to the company's vice president Robert Heiman that Kool's tagline, "feel extra coolness in your throat," "implies health benefit that Kools are easy on the throat. Seems to conflict with Article IV, Section 2 of Code."[102] Whether American Tobacco reported the violation to the FTC is unclear, but soon enough Brown & Williamson received a complaint, and in October they complied with the FTC's command to replace, "effective immediately," the "feel extra coolness" wording on the package.[103] So while in July and August the couple appeared in the pages of the *Philadelphia Tribune* and the *Chicago Defender* in an outdoor setting near a still pond with the copy asking readers to "feel the extra coolness in your throat," by 1965 the copy of such ads removed all references to the throat in response to competitor's claims of therapeutic deception. Now readers saw a smokers who claimed to be "sold on that extra coolness."[104]

Appearing at the same moment when other media reported widely on the industry's health woes, B&W's aggressive ad campaign in the summer of 1964 produced surprisingly few skeptics in Black communities. Perhaps this is not remarkable given the use of revered figures like Yankee catcher Elston Howard in their ads. Moreover, Black media (heavily dependent on tobacco advertising revenue) proved reluctant through these years to criticize the industry. For such local institutions like the *Philadelphia Tribune*, economic gains for African Americans were fragile; their dependence on advertising revenues effectively squelched criticism. Menthol appeals met little resistance in these media, and menthol ads and smoking flourished.

B&W's push did not go totally unchallenged by Black skeptics.

Amid the African American media's silence on tobacco's dangers, a rumor circulated in Black Chicago in 1964, coinciding with the B&W ad campaign and increasing national concern over smoking, cancer, and the Surgeon General's report. Kool, it said, was a white conspiracy against Blacks. The rumor claimed that a highly placed B&W executive was also a prominent member of the segregationist White Citizens' Council, and that racists were behind high-profile Kool's sales campaign in Black America. Adding more texture, a related rumor claimed the letter K in Kool was a secret Ku Klux Klan reference. Folklorist Patricia Turner heard from one informant, "That's what people said. They said all the brothers and sisters in the streets were smoking Kool. And that maybe the KKK had found a real good way to get them."[105] The allegation of a quiet industry-based conspiracy of white supremacists to kill Black people struck a nerve at B&W. In late September, a spokesman for the company heatedly denied the unsubstantiated claim; and the *Chicago Defender* (which, like *Ebony* and other African American publications, welcomed the advertising revenue and job opportunities of tobacco firms) publicized the company's denial. B&W, now aware of its growing Black consumer base, had found a willing platform for airing its rejection of the rumor as "totally false and . . . totally without foundation." That B&W felt compelled to respond at all, and so quickly, highlighted the company's sense of the growing stakes. Rumors could be potent if unchecked; for as psychologists Gordon Allport and Leo Postman observed at the time, "to be sure, in rumor there is often some residual particle of news, a 'kernel of truth,' but in the course of transmission it has become so overlaid with fanciful elaboration that it [truth] is no longer separable or detectable."[106] It would be foolhardy "if this were true," explained the B&W spokesman in the *Defender*. "Negro citizens throughout the nation are very good customers of ours." "No one in this company would do anything overtly or subtley [*sic*] which would in anyway [*sic*] influence Negro customers against us." The newspaper, giving a platform to the company to refute the rumormongering, also allowed B&W to broadcast its record on employment. "We have probably the best record on employment in Louisville," the company's executive insisted, "and we continue to hire Negroes for our plants."[107]

With B&W's ad campaign and its defense against any alleged Klan associations, Kool's Black urban campaign was launched. With media alliances solidified, the campaign would reap benefits and become the model for other firms, leading toward R. J. Reynolds's DFS plan for Black St. Louis and beyond. By the end of 1964, a firm linkage between the company and Black newspapers was being forged, and (in the bargain) between Black identity and Kool, ultimately solidifying in marketing imagery and also in economic relationships not only with the *Defender* and *Ebony*, but with a range of other civic groups. As F. X. Whelan, a sales manager at American Tobacco, commented in November 1964, "Negro oriented advertising, particularly on Kools . . . is a fairly recent development and I believe we can establish . . . that the brand has been showing a strong growth trend among the Negro people." Ever wary of the backlash from both Black and white people, the memo continued: "What we do not know is the negative effect, if any, this ethnic advertising may have on people who 'resent the intrusion.'" Disruptions to its strategy might come from anywhere—from Black resentment about being courted via stereotypes, from white resentment toward a brand wooing African American consumers prominently, or from more rumors of cigarettes as a white conspiracy. "How much of Kool's growth among Negroes is attributable to Negro advertising is a question I am not prepared to answer," noted the author. "But the coincidence (if that is all it is) is, at least, an interesting one."[108]

For Brown & Williamson, the government's restrictions on youth marketing enhanced the value of cultivating these new relationships with Black Americans, laying the groundwork for building a franchise; for other companies, the Kool campaign would become *the* menthol model to follow. Nothing about this transformation had happened overnight, as DFS's George Dean later observed in his 1967 memo, but the transformation had in fact been rapidly catalyzed by events in 1964. While at the start of the year, Big Tobacco envisioned the menthol smoker as a youth or college student, by year's end their gaze had shifted to the "low-income" Black smoker (many of them, of course, young). Writing in November, J. W. Edghill, a field supervisor at American Tobacco, observed that "only recently has the Negro market been pictured as a real opportunity for product cultivation and sales growth." The shift had come despite "low income and educational background, exclusion from the mainstream of American Life and conditions of segregation and discrimination in job opportunities, housing, etc. . . . [De]spite the low income and lack of opportunities for Negroes as compared to white [sic], the overall population and income of this market is tremendously large." Added to this market potential, new advertising opportunities were opening every day to allow the tobacco industry to reach 21 million Black Americans with $25 billion in annual income. The company would do well, said Edghill, to focus its energies here—where the drive for equality, freedom, and better jobs and "a bigger stake in the mainstream of American Life has created Negro Radio Appeal Stations."[109] Those stations, along with other Black media, would be valued partners in pushing menthol into the city and in helping to push back if rumors persisted that Kool was all a deceitful scam.

Menthol's "Inner City"

Over the next six years, as regulators continued to scrutinize the industry (unaware of the depth and detail of the menthol health link or the rising focus on urban marketing), the tobacco firms hunkered into a defensive crouch—protecting themselves against accusations of deceitful marketing to youth, shoring up markets under siege, and building ever-stronger relationships with media, opinion makers, and civic groups in Black America. Part of Big Tobacco's defense of menthol advertising among urban Blacks was the creation of a new, exaggerated, and fabulous conceit—that African Americans had a unique and particular love of menthol smoking, that menthol was popular because of a *pull* from Black smokers rather than a *push* from marketers. This claim was untrue, especially so at the start of 1964, but it was made increasingly plausible by year's end precisely because of the Kool campaign. As part of the push, of course, another scheme took shape in 1964—the beginning of a vast scaffolding, a web of influencers that remained hidden from public view who supported quietly, and worked to bolster, the rise of menthol smoking in Black America.

Intensified corporate competition for urban menthol smokers, with other companies quickly following B&W's example, became nothing short of a racial and commercial spectacle. In 1962 Salem led in menthols with $44 billion in total cigarette sales; Kool sales lagged at $14.5 billion. By 1965, Salem's sales were virtually unchanged, but Kool's had increased by 60 percent to $23.2 billion. And by the first half of 1968, Kool sales were on track for about $37.2 billion, only $4 billion below Salem. Kool's growth and its hold on what B&W came to regard as its "black franchise" became the envy of competitors, who emulated its strategies. "Kool's growth pattern continues. It is the fastest growing brand in the menthol segment," noted the company's marketing plan. Its success drove even more competitive advertising into Black radio, magazines, and neighborhoods. And in an added irony, Kool's success in Black America paid dividends with its outreach to the young white smokers who had once been the direct target of menthol pitches only a few years earlier. As Black music, fashion, style, and culture grew popular with white youth, in 1969 the company found that "unlike other menthols, KOOL . . . [was] male oriented, consumed in urban areas and used by younger people."[110] The courtship of Black smokers had become a profitable nexus in itself, a pathway to the young Black smoker, and increasingly to young, hip, whites as well. Kool, in short, was becoming cool.[111]

African American media figures like *Ebony* magazine's publisher, John H. Johnson, saw cigarette consumption not through the lens of health but as advertising revenue crucial for sustaining the periodical. As historian Adam Green has noted, Johnson's *Ebony* was "the most unabashed exemplar of the market turn in black culture during and after World War II."[112] Cigarette coverage reflected this fact. Where readers of *Reader's Digest* and other mainstream media had come to expect withering critiques of the tobacco industry on questions of health and marketing deception, readers of *Ebony* were treated visually to catchy images and editorial silence on such questions. Johnson did not regard the cigarette as a deadly product making inroads into Black America. Nor did he see the health questions raised by smoking as in any way comparable to the civil rights concerns of the day, such as the fight against housing segregation, refusal of public services, and denial of jobs and private accommodations to African Americans. As reported in *Sponsor*, a marketing industry journal, the *Ebony* publisher opined to a group of admen that because African Americans were "forced outside the mainstream of American life in so many ways, [they] achieve compensatory gratification in ways that often are quite surprising to the rest of America." "In some cases, [Black Americans] over-consume . . . in others, they under-consume as compare to whites."[113] Cigarettes were, in this view, merely one such area of compensatory consumption.

The magazine's April 1965 coverage of the death of singer Nat King Cole at age forty-five from lung cancer, unfolding in the shadow of the Surgeon General's report and the B&W campaign, provides a stunning case in point of *Ebony*'s silence on the smoking question. The velvet-voiced crooner had become an iconic symbol of Black accomplishment, having attained fame as a mainstream crossover entertainer in white America. His string of popular hits included "Mona Lisa," "Unforgettable," and "It's Only a Paper Moon," and Americans knew him from appearances on television and in motion pictures, and also as a businessman and as a spokesman for many consumer products. Although some African Americans criticized him for "holding himself removed" from the civil rights struggles of the day, he was adored by Black followers and even by some white fans in the segregated South. Nat King Cole was also an avid smoker, consuming three packs a day. He was rumored to prefer menthols, but officially he was widely known for his endorsement of Chesterfield. Diagnosed with lung cancer in 1964, the crooner's last months and eventual death coincided with heated public discussion about the Surgeon General's report. *Ebony*'s coverage of Cole's last days, however, focused instead on his fame (he was "by virtue of his career and modern communications media . . . the most celebrated Negro to die in world history"). The coverage dramatized how cancer had "poisoned almost every vital organ, proof that the three-hour operation for removal of his left lung on January 25 had come too late," but never linked his illness with his heavy smoking.[114] The same issue featured four prominent ads for menthol brands: Newport, showing a stylish young Black couple; Salem, portraying a couple in farm country; Montclair, featuring an elegant woman with a filtered menthol; and Kool Filter Kings, with their signature couple lingering near the outdoor pond.[115]

With Kool reaping benefits in sales in Black urban America, R. J. Reynolds grew concerned that its Salem was being "outsold by Kool in Negro areas," sometimes by a ratio of two-to-one in cities like Pittsburgh, Detroit, Baltimore, and Washington, DC.[116] In each city, the company tracked Black sales data down to the store location—the Economart on Centre Avenue in Pittsburgh, Frank's Liquor store on Georgia Avenue in DC, and the Golden Bird Patent Medicine Store on Dexter Avenue in Detroit. Such fine-grained data on sales and store location suggested a new intimate understanding that competitors were building, documenting when and where, month by month, white smokers leaned in their preferences for Salem, and in what parts of the city Black smokers gravitated toward Kool. At Philip Morris, market specialist and economist Myron Johnston marveled at the heated menthol battles, his company involved in the competition but struggling to find traction and profit with its own menthol brand. "The trend to menthol continues unabated," he wrote in 1966, even though "there is no menthol cigarette with prestige (i.e., snob appeal)."[117] Philip Morris, for all its efforts, was languishing in the market battles. For its part, in 1967 the FCC continued its critiques, accusing both R. J. Reynolds and Philip Morris of continuing to try to insulate smokers from health concerns, by projecting (through inventive advertising motifs) unique worlds of smoking pleasure, like "Marlboro Country." Even as the industry drove aggressively toward urban markets, in 1967 the Surgeon General's office struck again—closing off a captive market of soldiers by banning free cigarettes from being sent to wounded GIs in veterans hospitals. The move subject the government to fierce criticism from tobacco advocates, but such developments also made the Black city markets all the more appealing.[118]

Keen to join the competition for urban Black menthol sales,

insiders at Philip Morris turned to Tibor Koeves Associates of Sag Harbor to study race and menthol taste, or rather to invent a theory about it as a guide to branding and marketing. The firm produced the first of what would become increasingly bizarre sociocultural theories that circulated in the industry in the late 1960s and into the 1970s—theories about the different origins of what they imagined to be an innate or socially developed African American love of menthol cigarettes. This particular study rolled out a "dynamic sensory theory" about menthol as deeply entangled with the challenges and gratifications of Black ghetto life. "When we probed the underlying factor which generated the great enthusiasm for menthol cigarettes," they explained, "we found that it was based both on dynamic sensory and on psychological gratifications." In the ghetto, the report claimed, Kool was not a sissy smoke but a statement about manliness. For Black people, Tibor Koeves claimed, "in half the cases the menthol smoke was experienced as something substantial, almost a light food. It might be no exaggeration to say that quite a few of our people were 'eating' the menthol. They were inhaling slowly, and turned around, almost 'chewed' the smoke. Two of them said that menthol cigarettes were candy to them. One said it was a chewing gum. Another said it was his 'dessert' after a meal."[119] A mere four years after the Kool campaign was launched, racial marketing had coalesced around an image of menthol not as a sensory experience pushed by industry but as some kind of inherent Black taste—and thus, perversely, as a lens into the Black "inner city."

These consultants portrayed menthol as part of a Black urban food aesthetic, but the rise of menthol smoking was also a sociological phenomenon that transcended race in their view. As Tibor Koeves concluded, "There is hardly any such phenomenon as 'the Negro market,' or a unified Negro market. . . . While there are strong common traits among our respondents, first of all the general pronounced taste for menthol, many of the psychological needs and requirements are motivated by the social background, the life circumstances and personal ambitions of the smoker."[120] The study of the psychology of smoking was taking a profoundly sociological turn. In 1969 Brown &

Williamson inaugurated its own Black smoker study—a series of annual reports focused closely on tracking the shifting Black aesthetic. It was in studies like these that the company deemed Kool not only to be its "black franchise," but also to be "a perfect match with what may be the most highly valued personality trait among Negroes, i.e., savoir-faire or 'coolness.'"[121]

But yet another study, this one prepared by Motivational Programmers Inc. & Depth Research Laboratories, reminded Liggett & Myers of the fundamental therapeutic meaning of menthol for some Black smokers. Their studies showed that "smokers who switch to menthol cigarettes want to obtain relief from tobacco taste while fulfilling the needs of cigarette smoking." For those who were looking for "a change of pace or because he has a cold . . . menthol takes on the connotations of a therapeutic product." Thus, layered atop all the new, inventive, and imagined racial meanings was the quality that had driven menthol smoking's appeal from its earliest days—the enduring therapeutic promise. "Thus, we might project the possibility that smokers of menthol cigarettes are a quite individual segment of the marketplace, willing to use a medicine-like crutch to enable them to keep smoking."[122] (In a Roper survey two years earlier, 31 percent of people surveyed reported being "bothered by a cough"; 8 percent believed Kool cigarettes were safer than other brands.)[123] The menthol health appeal endured—underpinning its popularity for many anxious smokers. As Tibor Koeves explained to Philip Morris, "There are indications that menthols tend to be considered as generally 'better for one's health.'" A "typical expression of that feeling" came from one man who explained, "You see all the time how cigarettes ain't good for you but that if you smoke long cigarettes and menthol cigarettes they are not so strong and it's better than just plain tobacco without the menthol."[124]

: : :

Modern menthol smoking was reborn as a Black taste as tobacco consultants took aim at smoking in the city. Shifting focus away from white youth, they cultivated self-serving theories of Black taste that justified new forms of marketing, influence, and predation. These experts had migrated from studying African Americans as comprised of multiple social classes in the early 1960s to focusing their marketing gaze on urban, increasingly lower-income Black consumers. This transformation occurred quickly in the fraught aftermath of the Surgeon General's report *Smoking and Health* and amid growing government restrictions on youth markets. Kool was first to court the Black "inner city"; others rushed to follow. The Dancer-Fitzgerald-Sample plan for finding street-level influencers in 1967 Black St. Louis was, then, just one among an expanding genre of such schemes. Nor was Camel's menthol push exclusively focused on the city's Black smokers, for the industry continued to court other groups—women, Latinos, men, as well as those who were insecure about their health.

But in city after city, Black urbanites attracted particularly intense marketing attention. As St. Louis declined fiscally, and as businesses and some white residents left the city seeking economic security in the suburbs in the late 1960s, the cigarette industry and its consultants stayed. They kept their gaze trained on people in these cities despite worries over their worsening poverty and economic decline. The DFS study showed a deep interest in the complexities of African American sociology and culture, social structure, authority figures, generational politics, and influence making. Courting younger Black smokers remained a goal. Analyzing generational tensions, DFS noted that "Negroes don't want what Daddy used to smoke or drink—that's old fashioned." Analyzing rising Black pride, the consultants noted the growing tendency to reject white standards: "The Negroes no longer look to the white market (and its purchasing norms/habits) to set the pace in what to buy. Again, Negroes are becoming increasingly proud of the fact that they are Negroes, and they are now rejecting many of the standards or patterns set by the white community." The consultants also acknowledged street-level attitudes such as stereotypical Black wariness of con artists and salesmen, observing that "Negroes are skeptical of new consumer products. . . . They have been gouged and gypped many times by unethical merchants and con artists, and advertised products have not always lived up to their claims." They documented an urban culture beyond the reach and influence of television and traditional media—young men looking to the street for the "true word." Even as Camel advertised its new menthols in the city's widely circulated mainstream *Post-Dispatch*, DFS advised the company that shaping preferences in Black neighborhoods would depend on studying how news was spread at the neighborhood level. Success at embedding menthol preference would require, they believed, imparting "prestige and factual knowledge in a personalized, almost secret manner in addition to the product itself. . . . [W]e must aim this promotional effort at the leaders and communicators within the Negro cell groups."[125]

The years of blaxploitation had arrived. The transformation from 1963 (when Kool and Salem sought youth smokers and ran ads in college periodicals) to 1967's study of street life in St. Louis tells the story of the rise of a distinctive brand of predatory menthol marketing. These schemes also generated new theories of racial taste, as if to defend the racial outreach by claiming that Black people wanted menthols. The race-for-profit scheme, a new enterprise for making and securing urban markets, would have lasting impact on the city. Nothing was natural about this process, nor was the rise of menthol smoking in these settings driven by "Negro personality and taste." Decades later, the machinations of this era would be thrust into public view when R. J. Reynolds's CEO Schindler took the stand, challenged to transport himself back to the scene of menthol's racial transformation.

Seen in hindsight, the St. Louis plan highlighted how key actors shaped menthol consumption in boardrooms and on the street, but also how several developments in this tumultuous era—from the Surgeon General's report, to the protection of youth consumers, to the cigarette industry's own economic challenges—made this turn in menthol marketing an industry passion. These forces in tobacco capitalism and regulation led menthol makers into the city, pointing toward schemes like the Dean memo and its predatory strategies for embedding menthol cigarettes in the Black "inner city." From 1963 to 1969, aggressive marketers conducted their work in the shadows, evading scrutiny by critics, regulators, and the affected communities, their activities concealed in file cabinets and guarded as private business communications, only coming to light when RJR's CEO took the stand many decades after the work was done.

The predatory marketing in cities reflected a profound economic irony in a time of urban economic stress, civil rights victories, and demographic change. As many businesses and employers fled cities in the mid- to late 1960s, cigarette makers sensed opportunity. White flight and suburbanization in the wake of racial integration were transforming cities. At this very moment, the industry's menthol pitch unleashed a particularly predatory strain of racial capitalism, a style of "exploitation" in which companies sought to court and capitalize on people who (by their own account) were wary of "unethical merchants and con artists"—Black people of expanding aspirations who were concentrated, demographically poorer, and increasingly pathologized as "inner-city" urbanites.

Of course, not all of this was new since tobacco's business model for menthol had long capitalized on anxiety, social turmoil, and psychological stress. Personal difficulties were good for the cigarette industry's nicotine-based business. This had been true in the Depression years, and it was true in the anxious 1950s when the "cancer scare" led to rising menthol sales. In this new chapter of the menthol story, new forms of social anxiety and crisis in the tumultuous 1960s drew menthol makers toward new urban possibilities. Profit and value stood to be extracted from bodies, and the role of consultants was to develop the practices and theories to justify and inform the work of these extractive industries. In the long history of menthol smoking in America, the tobacco industry had turned another corner toward deceit, predation, and indeed into a new era of racial capitalism.

By decade's end, the industry had refined these strategies of outreach and influence—deploying them in force in Black St. Louis, Chicago, New York, Los Angeles, and hundreds of other cities. Meanwhile, the federal government, which had created elaborate barriers to reaching young white minors, now had begun to put limits on tobacco's reach via mass media, including radio and television.

What had started as a decade focused on feeding a youthful desire for kicks had turned toward cultivating a Black urban identity for menthol—where there were not only fewer regulatory barriers but also welcoming partners hungry for revenue.

A month after the assassination of Martin Luther King Jr. in 1968, two articles in the *Tobacco Reporter* captured these diverging regulatory trends and budding urban partnerships. One article, focused on the declining youth market, asked, "Is Teenage Smoking Really Falling Off?" Here, social researchers suggested that "the proportion of smokers among teenagers appears to have declined." "There is an overwhelming awareness among youth at each year of age from 12 through 18 that cigarette smoking is a health hazard," Dr. Daniel Horn said, leading to fewer high school smokers. This generational shift, making youth distinct from their parents, posed challenges for industry. "One reason for this drop in cigarette consumption," said Horn, "is the anti-smoking publicity appearing in the press, television, radio and other sectors, including the schools."[126]

In stark contrast to the public health push, a second article in the *Tobacco Reporter*, "Race Relations and Tobacco," highlighted how the sales gap was being filled. The Rev. Jesse Jackson explained why his new Operation Breadbasket was looking to tobacco firms to support Black causes. "We chose the tobacco industry as our target," said Jackson, "because . . . [s]lavery started in the tobacco fields, not in the cotton fields as many believe, and the tobacco industry still has its roots in the South." Where other critics might have pivoted from the tobacco-slavery connection to decrying a new enslavement, industry deceit, or the health consequences of smoking, Jackson challenged Lorillard to provide "more job openings and up grading of Negro employees . . . greater donations for United Negro College Fund . . . contributions to colored colleges . . . [and] to Negro magazines and other publications . . . and more creativity in creating Negro image in television advertising with black men seen as part of the American scene."[127] More advertising in Black media was Jackson's plea. Rather than recoil from these challenges to support Black causes in return for sales, such companies were now keen themselves to accept Jackson's bargain.

Ironically, the activist regulatory government of the 1960s had played a role in these trends. For as regulations on Big Tobacco became more effective at limiting mass advertising and outreach to youth and other markets, the aftershocks would be felt in urban Black America. In 1969, for example, sensing a strong movement toward banning television and radio advertisements, nine of the US cigarette companies approached Congress with a plan to voluntarily stop broadcast advertising in exchange for a grant of antitrust immunity. As the *Tobacco Reporter* observed, "The question of how much of the $240 million would be diverted to other media, how it would be spent, and what the results might be has been a hot topic." The television industry stood to lose millions in revenue; the winners, noted the magazine, would be the "'junk' publications, tabloids, movie magazines[,] and drive-in theater trailers." There would also be "boosts in the Black press.... A spokesman for the *Pittsburgh Courier*, a Negro newspaper, said it anticipates a 'definite increase.'"[128] Menthol's supporting players were now aligned; and the city was now squarely in view as the place where Big Tobacco would build its house of menthol.

4

Urban Hustles and Suburban Dreams

On November 16, 2000, Myron Johnston (a seventy-year-old retired researcher for Philip Morris and an avid menthol smoker) would not have passed any cigarette billboards on the car ride through Richmond, Virginia, into the heart of the downtown. The absence that day of public ads for Kool, Salem, or even the local Philip Morris brands would have made a stark contrast with the commercial landscape a decade earlier. Two years earlier in 1998, attorneys general from forty-six states had reached a $206 billion settlement with the four largest tobacco companies, including R. J. Reynolds, Brown & Williamson, Lorillard, and Richmond's own Philip Morris to recover the costs of caring for sick ex-smokers, deceived for years by false promises that cigarettes were safe.[1] The settlement also mandated a ban on all outdoor advertising, which had come to define the nation's highways, public transportation systems, and urban vistas, proliferating especially after 1970, when cigarette advertising was banned from television and radio.[2] By 2000, the billboard's heyday had ended.

The signs had been everywhere and evoked memories for almost all urban residents; menthol imagery was particularly visible in Black neighborhoods. Not only had tobacco companies built an imposing gauntlet of ads, but they relentlessly studied their effects on buying. The struggle between the menthol brands Kool, Salem, and Newport was perhaps the most intense. In 1974, during the early years of R. J. Reynolds's expansion of urban billboard advertising for its leading menthol, Salem, a market researcher for the company asked one middle-aged Black man in Dallas if he recalled anything about the highway signage. One stood out. "It's upon the Stemmons freeway. . . . It's got running water. It just said smoke cool. . . . Smoke Salem." Another Black man recalled another image he had seen: "It had a girl's picture on it. Just a slim colored girl. . . . Nothing but a girl and a pack of cigarettes in her hand. . . . Only that girl looked better than the cigarettes." Companies spent considerable resources studying the influence of such signage on purchasing and on urban residents' powers of recall, but they also tracked the skeptics—people who saw through Salem's visual charade. One of these included a younger Black man who commented with disdain about a Salem image he had seen, "a mountain climber hanging out from the mountain and smoking a Salem cigarette," which he regarded as "low in the scale of intellectual truth." It defied his sense of logic; "if the ads are illogical, I laugh and I dismiss it and I smoke Kools. . . . The [Salem] advertising to me was ineffectual, it just didn't work for me."[3] In the age of urban billboards, the tobacco industry and its network of experts erected a remarkable machinery to track recall, perceptions, and how to best convey "the truth" of menthol smoking. The visual imagery of Kool and Salem commanded urban vistas, particularly so from the 1970s through the 1990s when Big Tobacco's menthol hustle expanded and intensified.

In this era, billboard signage, which faced many zoning restrictions in the suburbs, was a visual front in the menthol cigarette urban battles; and as Johnston knew, their demise marked a turning point for tobacco—not only for corporate accountability but also for shaping urban preferences. Driving into a billboard-less Richmond in 2000, the retired Philip Morris researcher faced his own accountability. For three decades, Johnston had produced market research intended solely for tobacco industry eyes. Now, his once-private recommendations on how tobacco companies could use race and other forms of identity to shape smokers' preferences was being examined in legal proceedings and being greeted with damning public and legal scrutiny. On this particular morning, he was on his way to be questioned about his research in a lawsuit filed by two longtime smokers, Gloria Scott and Deania Jackson.[4] The two women alleged that their lifelong cigarette addiction was fostered by years of Philip Morris's and other companies' deceit about the addictive effects of nicotine—a concealment "designed to distort the entire body of public knowledge."[5] Their attorney, Daniel Malis, hoped to place Johnston's once-private research at the heart of the deceitful enterprise.

Johnston's research on the shaping of people's preferences had already received scathing attention in the states' lawsuit, and even his own CEO had expressed shame about Johnston's studies. The *Washington Post* had called attention to a 1981 Johnston study stating that "[today's] teenager is tomorrow's potential regular customer."[6] Shown another statement by Johnston from 1975, Philip Morris's own CEO, Geoffrey Bible, pronounced himself "ashamed" by its focus on the "teenage years . . . during which most smokers begin to smoke."[7] These studies, with titles like "Market Potential of a Health Cigarette," had become smoking guns in lawsuits alleging that the industry had used deceit and false claims of safety to lure minors into a lifelong habit. Once read only by his colleagues at PM, such corporate communications were now embarrassing public documents—legal exhibits in far-reaching questions of corporate accountability. Being deposed in 2000, it must have rankled Johnston to see how his former employer disowned his work.

Johnston epitomized the industry's surging attention to the racial demographics and urban economics of menthol smoking. To study menthol was, in large part, to study race. In his view, these trends explained the rising fortunes of Brown & Williamson's Kool not only with Black smokers but also with young white smokers. He was an astute observer of the epic battle being waged between Kool and Salem. By the mid-1980s, he noticed "strange happenings" in this warfare—a kind of backlash of racial attitudes among young whites, working against the menthol brands. The recoil against racial emulation, he explained to his colleagues, was now reaping benefits for Philip Morris, which had never found a winner in the menthol sweepstakes: "The

entire Marlboro family has been the beneficiary of the decline in menthol as an entry brand."[8] Nor was Johnston's fixation on how racial
demographics and attitudes underpinned menthol smoking unusual.
In the 1970s and 1980s, consultants at an array of marketing research
companies—Behavioral Systems, Inc., Computer Field Express, Kapuler & Associates, and D. Parke Gibson—treated menthol branding
as an area of rich racial research. Gibson's business followed many of
the strategies for developing a specific Black market, as outlined in his
1969 book, *The $30 Billion Negro*.[9] Researchers in the 1970s expanded
these racial repertoires to the new times. In a decade where residential gaps between Blacks and white widened and poverty deepened
among the Black "underclass," they casually talked about Winston's
"superfly" positioning; the need to avoid "Archie Bunker" types with
advertising; the link between Black masculinity, menthol, and drug
use; and how cultural associations should shape urban campaigns on
billboards and imagery on public transit signage.[10]

For psychologist Alvin Poussaint and other critics, 1970s racial marketing added up to a form of "blaxploitation," a term coined to capture
how films were turning stereotypes of Black life into profits. Poussaint
saw tobacco and liquor advertising in the same light. These commercial images were doing more than simply selling menthol cigarettes.
In their sweep, they created their own racial landscapes—and their
optics were so dominant that they were shaping both Black and white
attitudes about menthols, about the city, and indeed about race itself.

The New Racial Optic

In the very years that universities were creating the discipline of African American studies, firms were developing their corporate style of
"race studies." Their theories of race and the "inner city" from Richmond to Dallas would inform everything from menthol brand image
to billboard placement. This tobacco-based study of race also built
a new racial optic in cities, as billboards, public transit signage, and
point-of-purchase posters became the backdrop of urban life in the
United States.

Figure 4.1. By the 1970s, companies embraced a bolder "proud to be Black" imagery to sell menthol brands. But a backlash was brewing against what some Black critics called "blaxploitation" and some white viewers regarded as off-putting "superfly" imagery.
Credit: From the collection of Stanford Research Into the Impact of Tobacco Advertising (tobacco .stanford.edu)

If Black people had preferred Kool over Salem in the 1960s, why were Kool sales stagnant in the 1970s? Why was Newport trending upward? For analysts in the 1970s, menthol brand trends could best be explained by studying the spectrum of changing racial attitudes and anxieties at a time when "white flight" was transforming cities and suburbs. Their studies on menthol's appeal therefore tracked how the changing geography of brand preferences reflected national and region-specific racial attitudes, how the decline of menthol smoking reflected white alienation, whether Black suburbanization put a dent in sales, and what these trends meant about urban Black people and (perhaps most important) other users' perspectives on the plight of "inner cities." In study after study, researchers learned that menthol smokers were driven by social imagery like that on billboards and transit posters, and that whatever smokers might say about cigarette "taste" as the driver of their preferences, they actually cared much more about these racial optics.

Big tobacco's era of intense race branding and urban billboarding was born of economic crisis—a new direction following the loss of other markets due to stricter regulations. The pivot had first begun in the early 1960s when governments first took aim at the industry's youth marketing. Again in the late 1960s, even before the national ban on television and radio advertising took effect in 1970, industry executives anticipated that they would need to make up for the loss. Broadcast advertisements had "meant maximum penetration into virtually every home in the U.S. on a frequent basis." In 1968 R. J. Reynolds had spent $62 million on television and radio ads ($20 million of that for Salem alone). The loss would be devastating, for "this weight of exposure cannot be duplicated through any other media or media mix."[11] Magazines, newspapers, and mass transit posters offered obvious new avenues for reaching consumers—especially Black consumers.

The billboard era, then, was no accident. Industry-watchers were unsurprised by the move to billboards, point-of-purchase advertising, and print media. In adopting the TV and radio ad ban, even Congress had anticipated "a massive shift" to this sort of advertising.[12] But for the tobacco companies, the question of influence and effectiveness remained. As RJR executives worried: "Billboards can teach. But can they sell?" Research for RJR conducted by A. C. Nielsen found "that people who drive more see more billboards," but there was much uncertainty about the impact on sales. "Each of us drives to work each day. There are, undoubtedly, at least five billboards on our route. Can you describe one?" RJR executives agreed that they should approach the problem "in the same way that the liquor companies do it"—that is, through systematic research.[13] A new era in research would emerge in the wake of the "demise of TV," focused on how people navigated these new landscapes of perception. "Our question now is no longer a matter of the best TV complement but the best TV replacement."[14]

Billboards had important advantages in densely populated cities, but those advantages were yet to be fully studied. As RJR's Negro Market Study (part of an expansive 1969 "Study of Ethnic Markets") observed, billboards allowed "for showings key to concentrated Negro population centers tailored for desired markets"; public transportation also carried benefits since "like outdoor billboards, subway station billboards in Negro areas can be very effective." In this new era, "outdoor penetration" became a valued tactic, entering the lingo of the market researchers. But public signage on billboards, commuter buses, and trains also demanded something that television advertising did not—a new kind of research on how people, Black and white, moved through urban and suburban spaces, what they saw, and how those images changed purchasing behavior. RJR's study, part of an expansive "Study of Ethnic Markets," had already anticipated this question, noting the uncertainty of "effective negro-oriented media [since] seldom do routes have confinement within Negro communities."[15] Blacks and whites moved through many spaces together, making race-specific targeting quite tricky. As one study in Boston for American Tobacco noted, companies sought urban vistas that "provide[d] good geographical coverage of the market except in certain residential areas where the medium is zoned out." In cities that were becoming majority-minority, reshaped by white suburbanization ("white flight") yet still defined by suburban commuting to city centers, new research focused on "intercepting people as they passed by the ad." These new urban-suburban dynamics meant that tobacco companies needed information on movements, perception, awareness, sales, and even answers to such detailed questions as "the length of time it took to transmit the basic message to a pedestrian or driver."[16]

For the tobacco industry at large (and for menthol brands in par-

Figure 4.2. A prominent Kool billboard on Broadway and Ninth Avenue, New York City, in 1979. Urban billboards proliferated in the wake of the national ban on television and radio advertising, an example of how regulations cutting off one market in turn opened urban markets to greater exploitation while also transforming the physical landscape of cities.
Credit: Duke University, Resource of Outdoor Advertising Descriptions (ROAD). Courtesy of the Out of Home Advertising Association of America.

ticular), the new advertising terrain meant looking at the composition of communities; at urban, suburban, and racial routes; and at shifting white and Black viewpoints. In Dallas, for example, RJR analysts explained that the city's "extensive freeway system makes it a particularly strong paint [i.e., billboard] market" and that Philip Morris's "Marlboro has several excellent paint locations." Dallas's bus and taxi system was not as strong. As for neighborhood billboards, Brown & Williamson had carved out valuable territory: "Kool appears to have been particularly effective in placing their 30-sheet postings in heavy black population areas." The consumers' street-level optic as they navigated streets, highways, subways, public transit, and pedestrian byways was strikingly different than their vantage point while scanning magazines and newspapers or watching television ads.[17] Supplementing such urban ad campaigns in the 1970s and 1980s would be cultural events, music concerts, and sports clinics—all with posters and signage intended to cement the connection between brand and community.

In 1972 Myron Johnston at Philip Morris worried about how his company could compete at a menthol game dominated by B&W's Kool and RJR's Salem, and recently intensified by Lorillard's Newport. This new era of advertising promised to "further segment the cigarette market and lead to the emergence of local or regional cigarette brands, and different brand images in different markets."[18] Johnston saw older consumer patterns being challenged not only by the loss of TV and the rise of billboards, but also by increased taxes levied by state governments, increases in retail prices, and a growing threat of local regulations (such as bans on public smoking). Looking down this difficult road, the astute economist stressed the importance of paying close attention to local dynamics—from state taxes to local anti-cigarette initiatives—in assessing the future of menthol. Philip Morris executives worried specifically about their failure to compete in the urban market. Its menthol, Alpine, languished in the urban market, in stark contrast with its industry-leading national sales of Marlboro, its dominant product especially popular among white men.

Desperate to understand the perspective from the street, PM turned to Burrell-McBain Advertising in Chicago, who (in turn) hired Behavioral Systems, Inc. (BSI), a company run by African American Chicago-based entrepreneur Herbert Coverdale Jr. A psychologist by training, Coverdale's task was "to investigate the connotative significance of the Marlboro masculinity concept among black urban male cigarette smokers." In short, could cowboys help sell Marlboros to Blacks? The BSI report saw an image gap: "The contribution of masculinity to the black male's self concept is considerable, however, the associated qualities conveyed in Marlboro advertising of rugged individualism, total independence, and an intense appreciation of nature" did not resonate in the urban context, failing particularly to resonate with Black masculinity.[19] BSI concluded that PM's problem

that the nature of its appeal has been divested of <u>any</u> exploitative or manipulative connotations."[25] To be effective, the exploitation—the hustle—could never be visible.

Liggett & Myers found itself in a similar position to Philip Morris in 1970. The company's most successful non-menthol product, Chesterfield, lagged in these same urban markets. Its menthol, Oasis, had never caught on. In 1970 the company launched a new menthol, Eve, targeted at women. In 1971, hoping this time to get it right, company executives turned to the research firm Computer Field Express (CFE) for guidance—not unlike that offered by BSI—about how to build Eve's urban appeal.

CFE's advice to Liggett stressed similar themes to BSI's report to Philip Morris, but also highlighted another element that buoyed Kool's sales—the lasting associations between menthol and health, and the apparently strong new associations with urban drug use. Analyzing results from a national study of over seven hundred interviews in twenty markets (including five markets involving "special interviewer recruitment and training for working in inner city ghetto areas"), CFE found "two sources of growth for the menthols"—those who smoked it for "the kick" such as "youngsters and Black militants," and those who smoked it for "health care" by "alternating between menthol and filter-without-menthol." For some, "menthol is general health—the 'clean,' 'freshness,' a 'light, airy mouth feeling,'" or even a deeper health promise "resting . . . on a <u>medicinal emphasis to the drug</u> association . . . [with] curative benefits, soothing, numbing and relieving" the throat. These therapeutic associations, long central to menthol's appeal, had lasted. But for others, "there is a hard drug impact from menthol—the intense, pungent, icy cooling, a 'punch,' and a 'kick.'"[26] As Liggett sought to push into the urban menthol market and simultaneously build a market for a new female-oriented menthol like Eve, they learned from CFE that race, gender, health, and age were seamlessly interlinked in this urban competition.

Eve avoided competing with Kool's masculine imagery, instead pitching itself as a feminine brand—perhaps also with crossover racial appeal. Liggett's strategists turned to CFE to understand where their brands fit in this emerging racial geography, and how they should balance the competing interests of urban ghetto markets, suburban female consumerism, and white male anxieties. In 1960 there had been only a handful of menthol brands, but by the early 1970s, more than thirty brands competed for smokers' loyalties. Where could Eve make a mark? Some brands like Kool were more "male in tone than the generic menthol market," while Salem remained slightly more popular with white women in suburbs. Liggett's plan for Eve involved advertising aimed to "convince all female smokers that the Brand's uniqueness of design, packaging and good taste will enhance their femininity . . . [and] to build consumer awareness of Eve menthol as a truly feminine cigarette." In short, Eve sought to complete on Salem's terrain. This would involve mainstream advertising, but CFE also endorsed efforts to "strengthen the Brand's position in the black market through the use of special black creative and media."[27]

Could a single menthol brand achieve such a crossover appeal in the 1970s? CFE warned Liggett that it might be impossible because brand choice and racial attitudes had become so deeply entangled. If the company was looking for smokers who consumed heavily, menthols would not do the trick. CFE painted a dire picture of the heavy smoker as white, male, and averse to menthols. They were motivated by a range of psychological factors such as "male sexual image," "fatalistic acceptance of disease," "an internal self-reward, self-reliance system," and a tendency toward lower economic class status, alcoholism, and "racism and backlash."[28] Heavy smokers, regardless of brand, had distinctive racial beliefs aligned against progress for Blacks:

> Disproportionately, the heavy smokers believe blacks have gone too far in trying to achieve social equality. They are rigidly for law and order. They subscribe to the philosophy that blacks are pushing an excessive integration they are unwilling to earn by achievement and performance. Finally, George Wallace is a significant celebrity model for heavy smokers. The heavy smokers summarize as white militants.[29]

Predictably from this profile, whites were known to be heavier smokers than Blacks. Smoking trends thus reflected a shifting geography of racial ideologies.

By contrast with the so-called heavy-smoking white man skeptical of Black social equality, CFE portrayed the menthol smoker—or at least the Black menthol smoker—as increasingly racially militant and drug-oriented.[30] Those who smoked menthols to the exclusion of other kinds of tobacco harbored strong beliefs about rights and resistance. In CFE's portrait, they were "not just believers in Negro rights . . . they (far more than light smokers) take up the sword for violence." They believed that "peaceful integration is a slow, unproductive, onerous and self-defeating route."[31] These menthol-exclusive smokers also tended to be young and to associate menthol with drugs more generally:

They reach for the guitar, the "pot," the marijuana, the "grass," the cocaine, LSD, heroin, hard rock and "acid." . . . They are the "thrillists" . . . [who] want the smoke of their cigarette to travel, to circle gaily in colors, emitting a distant and exotic smell.[32]

As CFE explained to Liggett, the ideals of these menthol smokers echoed not only the pro-Black views of Coretta Scott King and actress Diahann Carroll, but also the radical activist views of Angela Davis.[33]

The CFE study reflected an increasing trend in cigarette image-making—the interlacing of politics and brand imagery. CFE stressed that "racial attitudes explain smoking menthols exclusively more so than actual race." CFE also found that more moderate ideas about race and gender drove the smoking preferences of so-called "dual smokers"—those who switched between menthols and filtered non-menthol cigarettes. Approximately one in six menthol smokers fell into this category. They tended to be white men who were "realistic health self-carists"; that is, health concerns remained a primary motivation. Their "salient characteristics are manifested in caution, precaution, constrained expression and reserve." But they, too, fit a specific political type, for "[they] would free the woman and wife from subjugation, even though they resist granting equality to the Negro."[34] They were bankers, accountants, scientists, and lawyers, and they "subscribe to the maxim that 'an ounce of prevention is worth a pound of cure.'" They saw menthol as medicine. They leaned politically toward figures like consumer activist Ralph Nader and Democratic politician Edmund Muskie.[35] As CFE saw it, menthol-smoking trends channeled social psychology, political beliefs, and views of racial and gender trends, "drawing together . . . attitudes from other sources" into preferences.[36]

Both the BSI and CFE reports stressed that menthol's health associations endured for both Blacks and whites even in the face of this complex and volatile racial climate. Smokers told the researchers again and again that, as one person noted, "I had pneumonia and decided to try a menthol cigarette. I found I coughed less and stayed with Kool." As another separate report for Lorillard stated: "The Camels began to taste harsh and bitter and hot to smoke. I switched [to Kool] for taste—it seemed milder and less burning in my mouth." A former Pall Mall smoker professed: "I had sinus trouble and I thought it would help to switch to menthol. . . . I wanted a cool smoking cigarette with a lot of taste." And as one former Chesterfield smoker admitted bluntly, "I switched because Arthur Godfrey got cancer [which had been diagnosed in the late 1950s]. He used to advertise Chesterfields. Then he told people not to smoke them. They gave him cancer." For this smoker, Kool was the answer to these cancer concerns.[37] Regardless of fractious racial attitudes and the intensifying brand competition across cities and suburbs, these health associations endured.

Race and geography aside, companies remained keenly aware of how people's health anxieties underpinned menthol smoking; this was true in the 1920s when companies deceitfully portrayed menthols as medicine, it remained an important part of the pitch in the 1950s, and it continued to do so in the 1970s. In the battle against Kool, William Esty told RJR in 1973 that Kool's rise over the past decade could be traced to "gains made in cold weather months." The practice of smoking Kool in wintertime was especially notable in the northeastern and north-central states, Esty's data suggested. Salem, Esty argued, should try to "capitalize on cold season specific copy," perhaps by using an umbrella in its ads. But, at the same time, the Esty study took note of the overwhelming urban-suburban divide that overlay these health worries, as Kool was seen as a young "big city" brand while Salem's smoker profile "tends to be somewhat older, slightly more upscale occupationally and less concentrated in big cities."[38]

The Geographical Divide: Suburban Salem and Urban Kool

A new geographical divide had opened in the United States, and with it a commercial divide separating cities from suburbs.[39] The industry was keen to track movements across these zones, maneuvering everywhere for access to public signage. Between 1960 and 1970, the white populations of US central cities declined by 16.2 percent in the Northeast and nearly 10 percent nationwide.[40] Cities like Detroit went from 70 percent white to 55 percent, on its way to 34.4 percent in 1980; meanwhile, the Black population climbed from 28.9 percent in 1960 to 43.7 percent in 1970 to 63.1 percent in 1980.[41] With suburbanization, commercial patterns also shifted, as more suburbanites drove to the shopping centers that now dotted the landscape, while urban residents continued to shop in urban commercial corridors. The same patterns that transformed residential and commercial life in the United States also transformed the market for menthol cigarettes.

Detroit was an obvious case study in the rise of new urban opportunities for researchers at R. J. Reynold as "shopping centers are springing up in or near newly developed residential districts throughout the suburban metro area . . . [and as] Blacks continue to reside downtown." With its 4.8 million residents, Detroit's greater metropolitan area still had the fifth-largest population in the country, but "like many other central cities, Detroit is suffering from the flight of Whites to the suburbs," noted the RJR analysis. The core of the city had become racially distinct: "The Black population . . . continues to be concentrated near the downtown, as it is in many major cities," and even African American out-migration from the center city was more like a "spreading action rather than one of integration." And as the study observed, "Like Blacks in other cities, they prefer menthol brands and buy cigarettes in the package in neighborhood stores. . . . Party stores, liquor stores, and drugstores."[42]

Urban point-of-sale advertising took on special significance not only because of the television and radio ad ban but also because of the era's demographic changes. As one early 1973 Philip Morris national tracking poll noted, the impact of the media bans was waning as "awareness of cigarette advertising appears to have rebounded to that prevailing just after the television ban."[43] Magazines, billboards, and transportation posters took on increased value. Demographic concentration of Black people also made for efficiencies in marketing, and "transportation and billboards seem to reach blacks best." In the 1970s, companies also expanded their intrusive urban presence in other ways—including support for fashion shows, jazz festivals, and elaborate courtship of community organizations. They sought not merely to be a visual presence in neighborhoods, but also to be seen as a product of the community itself—and to embody support for Black style and aspiration, with cultural campaigns for a "Soul 70 album" featuring performances by Ike and Tina Turner, Sly and the Family Stone, Santana, and other luminaries. Yet there remained an adversarial tone in these efforts, as B&W considered developing new brands and spending advertising dollars "against the black market."[44]

As one B&W report summarized the situation, after the ban "Kool sales had been hurt by rumors that the product was being taken off the market," but by the end of 1971, the rumors had abated. Localized ads had apparently helped the brand beat back the rumors. "The reach of Kool's advertising to lower income consumers (predominantly Negro) was particularly limited by the elimination of broadcast. Print media was less effective in relaying Kool's message to this consumer group" because of lower magazine readership. Therefore, "since Negroes are important to the brand's total smoker franchise, interior transit was used in 30 cities with large Negro populations."[45] For its part, RJR maneuvered Salem to "achieve a broad base of national advertising emphasizing message delivery in urban areas against young adult smokers[,] . . . utilize local media[, and] . . . use media vehicles in creative formats that can deliver Salem's advertising message in the most intrusive, effective, and convincing manner." In their marketing lingo, the goal was to throw "media weight against the Black, Spanish, and Jewish ethnic groups with particular emphasis on Blacks."[46]

B&W's Kool was best positioned to appeal to this increasingly "ghetto" franchise.[47] Kool was seen as a young "big city" brand, while RJR's Salem's smoker profile "tends to be somewhat older, slightly more upscale occupationally and less concentrated in big cities."[48] Year by year, Kool had been gaining ground on Salem in total sales and had in fact surpassed Salem in urban markets: Kool commanded the highest share of Black smokers (20 percent), with Salem in third place with 13 percent and Newport now placed second. A host of other competitors had emerged. By 1971, twenty-three menthol brands competed for 24 percent of the cigarette market that went to menthols. Of all the competitors, Lorillard had done increasingly well in the menthol sweepstakes with Newport. The rise had nothing to do with taste; its marketing department agreed that there was little substantive difference between Kool and Salem, except for their image. The gender, race, age, and regional trends in menthol smoking were especially notable, with Kool continuing to defy the stereotype of menthol as a female cigarette. Men accounted for 61 percent of its volume; Salem smokers, on the other hand, were split more or less evenly by gender. Regionally, Salem was strong in the Southeast; Kool was strong in the cities, but weak in the West. Kool was "youth oriented far more than other menthol brands."[49] More than any other brand, Kool's users were young, Black, urban, and male.

"Why don't our menthol brands have a larger share of the market?" wondered Peggy Martin in Philip Morris's psychology research office in June 1972. By now, industry insiders agreed that menthol *taste* was not driving preferences. "Smokers are remarkably insensitive to the amount of menthol in smoke," observed Martin.[50] As another PM psychologist noted, the relationship between actual menthol content in a cigarette and "the smoker's perception of menthol delivery is not at all veridical."[51] Although people said that they preferred Kool because it was heavier in menthol, in fact the menthol content was no higher than other brands. Even more annoying to PM psychologists, "In blind taste testing of [its menthol brand] Alpine against Kool and Salem, Alpine has generally been found to be as acceptable or even more acceptable to menthol smokers." For Philip Morris, the perplexing question was "If smokers like Alpine, then why don't they buy them?"[52]

People were poor judges of taste, but they were excellent judges of imagery. As those who ran blind taste tests knew, perception was shaped by many contextual factors. Taste was not inherent, and as one PM consultant explained, in the "continual quest to understand consumer behavior and to develop and market products to exploit his behavior . . . the psyche appears to have more effect in controlling perception of taste than does the taste buds." The path to influencing taste led though the mind, not the mouth. "The smoker . . . is basically buying not a product but an expectation of satisfaction." This view had long been commonplace in the industry, even in the early days of the menthol pitch in the 1920s and 1930s. As the consultant added, "If this expectation is created with sufficient strength, the smoker's taste buds will not let his psyche down."[53] Differences in brand preferences hinged on location, identity, and perception—not taste.

Marketers followed closely how these matters of taste related to the daily movements of Blacks and whites across the urban-suburban boundary. It appeared, demographically at least, that the average Kool smoker was considerably different than both the average Salem smoker and all other menthol smokers. At RJR the company believed their weakness "among lower income, less educated and older smokers" was due to "Kool's entrenchment, particularly among Black smokers." Salem needed a two-part strategy designed to appeal to both the market of urban Black smokers and white suburbanites. In the health-conscious suburbs, RJR would promote Salem Lights; in the city, the company believed that a "black emphasis [in Salem marketing] is justified because . . . the menthol category is significantly overdeveloped in the black market." But RJR struggled to match Kool, which was "significantly over-developed in the Black market relative to Salem." By contrast, Salem's "suburban emphasis" was due to the "expected population explosion in the suburbs"; and here, Salem Lights would be promoted strongly. These demographic divisions were also blurred, as people moved across the urban-suburban divide every day. "Suburbanites commute by automobile. . . . The principal users of buses are those Blacks in the inner city who use buses as their local mode of transportation and Blacks who work in the suburbs, primarily domestics."[54] The implications of commuting for transit advertising, highway signage, and city-based advertising were vast and constantly shifting; Black city dwellers comprised, by contrast with commuters, a more stable and "captive" market.

A wide range of stereotypes and oversimplified binaries began to flourish as researchers sought to explain the market consequences of the era's demographic shifts and characteristics of the "inner-city" consumer. "Inner city" was coded Black; suburban was defined as white. Black men preferred stronger menthols, akin to drugs carrying a "kick"; white women in suburbs preferred light menthols. The physical landscape of signage projected and reinforced these binaries, accentuating perceptions of menthol's racial divide. As billboards pervaded the city (with advertising in the suburbs far less obvious), Black urban motifs became associated more deeply than ever with menthols.

Market researchers in the early and mid-1970s interpreted menthols' appeal in the city as a reflection of what one researcher later called "the negative side of ghetto life."[55] Focus groups were telling marketers like Esty that Kool was firmly situated in a drug- and alcohol-oriented Black culture. It was, almost by definition, a drug or a drug enhancer—helping users to "retain the 'high' achieved by drinking wine and other alcoholic beverages and by using drugs. . . . Mentholated cigarettes are considered to combine well with liquor or with drugs . . . respondents say they enhance and extend the 'high.'" Kool's popularity, said RJR consultants, helped "the Black cope with his environment by continuously giving him a pleasurable experience."[56] These market consultants identified the motivation to smoke in the hardships of urban life. As one 1973 study at RJR concluded, menthol cigarettes mingled with hard drugs and liquor in the ghetto—indeed, menthols were posited to amplify the "high." "For the marijuana smoker they have an additional advantage of soothing the throat since marijuana has a harsh effect on it."[57] Meanwhile at Philip Morris, the Black-white consumer divide in menthol use seemed so firm (if not unbridgeable) that researchers concluded that starker racial marketing might be warranted; Alpine had a "nicotine and menthol characteristics . . . satisfactory to Whites but not for Blacks. This raises the possibility . . . that it might be wise for us to market a menthol cigarette just for Blacks."[58]

By the mid-1970s, the industry's internal marketing reports were filled with these facile theories of ghetto life and supposed stark divisions of racial taste. Taking stock of the suburban-urban divide, RJR insiders concluded that Salem had little chance of making inroads in the ghetto. "It is seen as a cigarette for middle aged suburban housewives or a cigarette for clean cut, blue eyed, blond-haired people who live in an 'antiseptic' world." The only hope for RJR was to focus its Salem campaigns on what consultants characterized as non-ghetto Blacks. Salem, after all, had something that Kool did not—an "upscale, sophisticated image (a factor that is usually an advantage for other product[s])." Why did some African Americans smoke Salem? The 1974 report opined that "Salem may mean to Blacks becoming 'more like whites' and 'more middle class.'"[59]

This observation that brands appeals to Blacks differently depending on their cultural aspirations offered the door to a new racial possibility for RJR by marketing to Black smokers who wanted "to make it in a new way." Esty recommended that RJR promote Salem using "a mature confident and masculine image appealing to middle-class Black Americans" and "to employ OOH [out-of-home advertising, i.e., billboards] as the primary medium to reach blacks . . . in predominantly Black areas in central cities to obtain broad reach."[60] A year later, however, RJR found that this strategy was more complicated than the company had originally anticipated since Black tastes themselves appeared in flux. In non-southern regions, "it was found that blacks . . . were smoking Salem as a way of breaking with the ghetto environment and in a sense—with their 'blackness.' In Birmingham [however], the young blacks interviewed did not want to become 'more like whites' . . . rather, they desire to strengthen their blackness and establish their own separate black identity."[61] The Esty exploratory study ended with a warning that resonated across the industry and identified a difficult puzzle of race and branding in the 1970s: Direct appeals to Black smokers risked alienating existing white Salem smokers. Another urgent worry continued to be "meaningfully reach[ing] the young smoker before he has made a final commitment to a brand for the rest of his life." "Failure to accomplish" the task "could mean the erosion of the Salem franchise."[62]

Courting Black smokers came at a cost. Executives at B&W were beginning to worry about white alienation as well. Although the company was riding high with Kool, its leaders wondered whether their "black penetration" turned white smokers away. On the one hand, B&W proudly defended its Black franchise against stiffer competition from new brands like Lorillard's Blue Ice. On the other hand, executives grew worried that Kool's bold play for Black smokers—with its posters and billboards now defining the landscape of cities, highways, thruways, and interior bus and train transit—had begun to provoke a cultural backlash among both Black and white smokers. The strategy of linking menthols to urban coolness had worked fabulously for a time in the 1960s; but by the mid-1970s, industry insiders saw danger signs for Kool's racial branding, visible on billboards, buses, and public posters across urban America.

Between Black Exploitation and White Alienation

The tobacco industry's racial-themed advertising was producing its own racial effects. In surveys and interviews with market researchers, smokers took in the message and echoed the very racial stereotypes that advertisers had used to shape brand preferences, including beliefs about the healthiness of menthols.

The views of participants in a series of RJR focus groups revealed vividly how menthol brand smoking was giving shape and texture to elemental beliefs about Black and white identities. In one group, researchers assembled Kool smokers and Salem smokers and asked them about their taste preferences. Kool smokers liked "the strong taste of the menthol [as well as] a tobacco taste strong enough to come through the menthol." They believed that Salem didn't provide "enough of a smoking sensation." Salem smokers, in turn, said that Kool was "too harsh," too heavy with "overpowering menthol." In a now-familiar refrain, eight Black men in one focus group told the interviewer that they came to menthols to reduce their coughs, but stayed for the "high." "I haven't coughed since with a cigarette," one man commented. Menthol had done its trick yet again. Another said that menthol smokes reminded him of his mother's therapies when she would "put a heaping spoon of sugar and dropped a couple of spoons of turpentine on it, and shoved it down your throat, that also soothes your throat. You've got that menthol taste you grew up with." When asked directly if menthol provides a high, the men had plenty of say. "It boosts your high a little . . . a menthol cigarette," said one man. "Maybe it's a mental thing but I'm saying nine of ten people ever used drugs or anything like that, smoke a menthol cigarette." For another man in the group, menthol, and liquor went hand in hand— "I'm an alcoholic and I smoke Kool."[63]

White women in a different RJR focus group emphasized the fundamental therapeutic appeal of menthol smoking and they also associated Kool with drug use and what one consultant called "the negative side of ghetto life." While none of these women mentioned deep associations between menthol and childhood remedies or drug use for that matter, menthol did figure for them as a temporary salve: "When I get to the point that I feel my throat is parched and that's when I go to a mentholated cigarette."[64]

Health meanings aside, racial marketing remained too lucrative to let pass by. The challenge of racial marketing in the 1970s was how to navigate the increasingly complex landscape of white alienation, even as the industry's heavily race-themed advertising produced its own echo effects. And given new patterns in urban-suburban movement, mastering this new racial optic proved to be continually challenging.

As RJR's Detroit study had noted, "Blacks travelling through predominantly white areas are exposed to general advertising and, conversely, whites are exposed to Black advertising in Black neighborhoods. . . . Segmented advertising would weaken the potential success of either effort, and could alienate whites or Blacks, especially Blacks if advertisers were perceived as viewing either group as different."[65] Racial alienation—that is, not person-to-person alienation but animus toward off-putting product imagery that stood in for race—figured prominently among the worries of these image makers.

In 1974 Harvard psychiatrist Alvin Poussaint used the term *blaxploitation* (coined by the NAACP's Junius Griffin) to capture the wider cultural phenomenon in which films, advertising, and popular culture trafficked in images of Blacks as pimps, prostitutes, and dopepushers. The critique applied to tobacco ads as well. Popular culture was turning images of self-abnegation into profit, with the "insidious message [that] blacks are violent, criminal, sexy savages." Blaxploitation was now embedded in consumer products on billboards across

Figure 4.3. Alvin Poussaint, Harvard psychiatrist and critic of blaxploitation and the profitable marketing of cheap, degraded images of Black people in American popular culture.
Credit: Courtesy of Gerth Archives and Special Collections, California State University, Dominguez Hills.

the changing city. Their message encouraged urban youth to believe that "success comes with a cool 'rap,' flashy clothes, big expensive cars, and a gun," and from heroes who "punch and kill 'whitey' and 'honkies.'" "Such vicarious thrill seeking," Poussaint insisted, "does little to touch the deep social problems that lead to black despair." It was particularly galling that "the American public, and particularly the black sector, support the new black films."[66]

At RJR, blaxploitation ran the gamut from embracing gambling motifs to positive Afrocentric ad campaigns. The company tested out these ideas on a Black focus group in August 1973. One new brand idea, Deuce, emphasized a gambling theme. Another was Shamba, a "bold menthol" blend proposed as made from "tobacco grown under the sun of the African plains." As RJR learned when testing these ideas, "The card-playing concept behind 'Deuce' was . . . well received," but the "menacing face in the visual" needed revision if the idea was worth pursuing. Shamba, by contrast, was "viewed with almost total favorable reaction," with participants reporting that the name "suggested to them peace, tranquility, gentleness, and coolness. . . . They projected these characteristics on to the cigarette and anticipated that it would be mild, smooth, and refreshing." The product, with its positive Africa-centered themes, would likely receive "a high degree of trial and acceptance in the Black marketplace," the study found.[67]

At the same time, however, RJR learned that these campaigns ran the risk of turning off the very consumers they were hoping to attract because the manipulation was all too obvious. The Shamba concept had been bandied about in RJR boardrooms before, not as a brand name but as an advertising gimmick to sell Salem in the city. In 1971 the company had asked Howard Sanders Advertising, a company "specializing in Black advertising," to conduct a study of 150 Black people in Detroit on several marketing concepts for making Salem more palatable among Black smokers. It was there that the "King Shamba" concept was first tested, seeking to "capitalize to a larger extent upon the menthol growth potential among Blacks."[68] Shamba referenced a seventeenth-century Congo leader known for promoting peace and culture. As one market researcher at RJR put it, "The purpose of the King Shamba Executions are to give Blacks reasons beyond the product for becoming familiar with Salem."[69] But late in 1971, Sanders found that the Shamba concept (in which an African figure "did such things as abolish war, invent things, and help[ed] his people in other ways") "received a relative[ly] larger number of unfavorable comments." Sanders's informants described the approach as "exploitation/patronizing Blacks" and "false/phoney/gimmick." Sanders had at that time concluded that using King Shamba to sell Salem had "many negatives that would have to be overcome, as well as a full educational program instituted informing the Blacks who King Shamba is." In short, not only did people not know Shamba, but the figure was also "too complex to be considered as a viable sales promotion vehicle."[70] As one RJR insider commented, a few respondents thought Shamba was a comical lie—that "King Shamba was not relevant to Salem, might be a fabrication, was less favorable to Blacks, and that he looked funny."[71] That was in 1971. Two years later, however, Shamba was back wearing a new African guise, and on the table

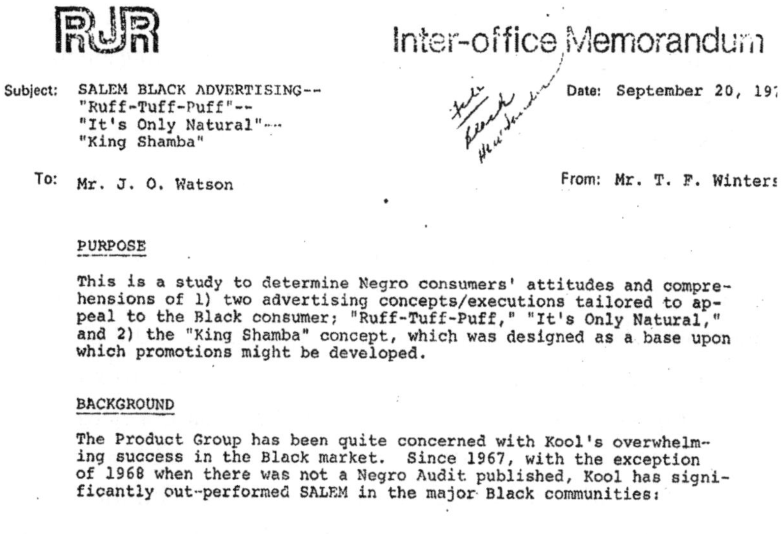

RJR   Inter-office Memorandum

Subject: SALEM BLACK ADVERTISING--   Date: September 20, 197
         "Ruff-Tuff-Puff"--
         "It's Only Natural"--
         "King Shamba"

To: Mr. J. O. Watson   From: Mr. T. F. Winters

PURPOSE

This is a study to determine Negro consumers' attitudes and compre-
hensions of 1) two advertising concepts/executions tailored to appeal to the Black consumer; "Ruff-Tuff-Puff," "It's Only Natural,"
and 2) the "King Shamba" concept, which was designed as a base upon
which promotions might be developed.

BACKGROUND

The Product Group has been quite concerned with Kool's overwhelming success in the Black market. Since 1967, with the exception
of 1968 when there was not a Negro Audit published, Kool has significantly out-performed SALEM in the major Black communities:

Figure 4.4. An R. J. Reynolds memo, dated 1971, illustrating how the company sought relentlessly to compete with Kool by steeping their brands, such as Salem, in Black and Afrocentric themes like "King Shamba" in the 1970s.
Credit: Image courtesy of Truth Tobacco Industry Documents (https://www.industrydocuments.ucsf.edu/tobacco/).

for consideration as a brand name in its own right at RJR, with the company once again asking consultants how to embed the concept in the Black market.

The line between cinematic and advertising blaxploitation had blurred. By the mid-1970s, companies began hearing that their carefully crafted images of Black coolness were off-putting to white smokers. At RJR, market researchers they had hired to do a "Negro market audit" in major metropolitan areas told them that Philip Morris's Winston brand was flailing in the city and its "Marlboro Country and cowboys mean nothing to Blacks." PM had sought to aggressively courted urban Blacks with what the researchers called "Winston's 'superfly' positioning," a losing effort.[72] The reference, of course, was to the low-budget film *Super Fly*, which focused on street life and the drug dealer as a cultural icon. Over at Brown & Williamson, having aggressively developed Kool's "downscale" associations, the company now faced the challenge of solidifying the appeal without feeding white antagonism. While Blackness had been "cool" in the eyes of young whites in the 1960s, now the "bold, cold," "blue ice," urban imagery of menthol made insiders worry both about charges of blaxploitation from critics like Poussaint and impending alienation from whites.

In focus groups, consultants began to hear white smokers voicing negative views about Black people—views that seem to have been cemented by the tobacco campaigns and imagery.[73] When Lorillard tested new brands like Blue Ice and Baron (aimed at the "heavily black oriented . . . Kool franchise" and promising a "super shot of menthol"), they courted disaster with whites even as the pitch appeared to succeed in cities. Even so, company executives worried that if the campaign was "skewed black, it is unlikely that Lorillard would proceed with a product that wins among blacks and loses among whites."[74] The industry's imagery now intertwined with the vernacular discourse of race—with animus against Black people and brand motifs feeding one another. In a particularly graphic and racist example, white high school students in Grand Rapids, Michigan, told

Philip Morris interviewers in 1974 that they liked its Marlboro Green menthol, and they also revealed the potent racial hostility underlying their brand choice. The white students in this newly integrated school disdained Kool. As the report's author put it, "racial problems" had developed since the "school is located in a White neighborhood" but 60 percent of the students were Black because of the recent and controversial policy of school busing.[75] Critics at the time regarded the issue as "an incendiary failure—an incitement to racial tension."[76] Surveying students in that setting, the report said that "the Whites in this school refer to Kools as the 'nigger cigarette' and apparently smoke other menthols so as not to be identified with Blacks." White students had also developed their own lingo, ordering "Greens" from the local seller. "'Greens,'" the study found, "apparently fit into the young White vernacular much the same way that Kools is part of the Blacks [sic] everyday language." For these white youth, Marlboro Green appealed as an accompaniment to smoking marijuana. As the study reported, "One store owner located next to a high school (Greens and Kools are his best sellers) sells 10 to 15 boxes of cigarette wrapping paper a week . . . to wrap the 'grass.'"[77]

The hostility of the Grand Rapids students to both the Kool brand and Black people was not unique; in a Chicago study, RJR also detected "a widespread feeling of racism evidenced in the segregated neighborhoods and blatant protesting of school busing." The backlash against integration and concerns about government spending (labeled as "conservative" by RJR) trickled into respondents' views about advertising imagery, noted the study:

This racist behavior appears to a greater extent among the white population, feeling that whites are better than blacks, that the races should not be mixed, and that blacks are lazy and create slums. These feelings also appear in a more widespread dislike for integrated ads. The black population has indicated a strong desire to see black people in local advertising and P.O.S. [point-of-sale advertising].[78]

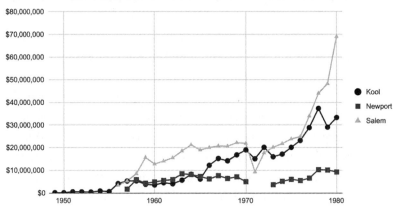

Advertising Expenditures by Brand, 1949-1980
Magazines, Newspapers, Sunday sections, Network Radio and Television

Figure 4.5. Advertising expenditures for Kool, Newport, and Salem, 1949–1980. The marketing battles between Kool and Salem escalated through the 1970s, unabated by the radio and television advertising ban.
Credit: Dov Grohsgal, data compiled from *Advertising Age*, 1954–1982.

The study concluded that "smokers in Chicago appear to be more anti black and against integration than smokers in general and this is probably more true of the City Belt segment."[79]

These toxic racial attitudes of the 1970s were reshaping the advertising landscape. In the face of such virulent attitudes in Chicago, for example, RJR began to think carefully about how imagery directed toward Black consumers could be kept out of sight of white viewers, and vice versa. Integrated ads were particularly treacherous, analysts concluded. "Because of this more prevalent racist attitude any integrated or black advertising should not penetrate the geographical areas where these white smokers predominate," the authors declared.[80] But fortunately for the tobacco industry, residential segregation and the diverging shopping patterns of Blacks and whites in Chicago made separate campaigns easier to execute. In addition, RJR's market research indicated that "lifestyles are dramatically different, being blue collar and white collar, upscale and downscale, white racist and black separates [i.e., separatists]; therefore, the copy that is applicable to one segment does not necessarily communicate to other segments."[81] Residential segregation created separate media pathways.

The findings on white alienation from Grand Rapids and Chicago were replicated in Birmingham focus group discussions with white and Black Alabamans. Seeking responses about a new high-menthol, Salem Extra, that used a street-corner scene with a hip Black smoker as its billboard motif, RJR heard more backlash:

Whites were totally alienated to Salem Extra when "super cool" blacks were included in the advertising. In fact, there was evidence to conclude that this kind of advertising showing "blacks on the corner" or the black "dude" could alienate the white franchise which is currently smoking regular Salem.[82]

One respondent stated bluntly, "Only blacks could relate to the su-perfly talk and look." "To me," said another person, referring to the Black-themed advertising, "you might as well say 'do not buy' on top of it." But Black respondents were also alienated by the superfly motif. One person advised the company to "show people in regular dress . . . casual people . . . doing their own thing . . . not just standing on the corner." "You're trying to put us in a bag, like we're still on the corner . . . a stereotype."[83]

For many in the industry, however, the truly worrisome develop-ments for sales was not racism but a broader set of challenges beset-ting its urban focus. These included the rising tide of public health initiatives such as anti-billboard agitation, steep unemployment in an economic recession, and even the emergence of Black Islam with its outright rejection of smoking. As a Bates expert wrote to B&W executives, Black unemployment hovered at 21 percent and teenage unemployment reached 36 percent: "The high national unemploy-ment rate becomes more a critical factor for Kool in light of the Brand's disproportionately high representation among black smok-ers," the advertiser observed. At the same time, "The anti-smoking forces have been making new inroads" with prohibitions on smoking in movie theaters and (in New York City) elevators and food markets. In Dallas–Fort Worth, local zoning ordinances now took aim at the proliferation of billboards. In the face of these and other pressures,

Kool's sales had declined in a number of cities, including New York, Philadelphia, and Detroit, for the first time in a decade. What affected sales in these venues, Bates concluded, was not race relations but the state of the economy.[84] And as William Esty explained to RJR, another political movement (the "Black Muslim movement") was "an entity to be recognized since their estimated followers can be expanded by family ties and non-member sympathizers to well over a million possible cigarette abstainers."[85] Cigarettes were, in Malcolm X's writing, one of the "fashionable ghetto adornments"; not only were they as addictive as any narcotic, but they were also part of an elaborate scam where "every regular priced carton . . . bought meant that the white man's government took around two dollars of a black man's hard-earned money for taxes."[86] The converging theme in all this was a rejection of the very Black imagery that had been the centerpiece of menthol's urban dominance.

The era's cultural trends and remarkably bigoted views about race and menthol were having an indisputable effect on sales. In RJR's assessment, these views were driving new preferences toward a third competitor, Lorillard's Newport. For some respondents in the RJR study, the two leading brands simply came from different worlds: as one respondent said, "The black guy would smoke Kool and the white guy Salem." Others added value judgments—that Salem was "goody-too-shoes [sic]" or that it was the brand for middle-aged women with dyed hair.[87] But others crossed over into frank anti-Black prejudice. In a study conducted for RJR, one woman expressed "rather strong and clearly defined feelings, attitudes and perceptions about Kools. . . . 'Men smoke Kools . . . Blacks smoke them . . . all the people that I see smoking Kools are always colored.'" Other women "felt obligated to 'put down' Kools because of the firmly entrenched image the brand apparently conjured up in their minds." "Let's face it," said a third survey participant, "all the blacks and Puerto Ricans I come in contact with at the bank have no class. . . . They all smoke Kools." The analyst saw these views as an expression of a deep bigotry, a "definite 'Archie Bunker' attitude tended to prevail . . . that white people are generally 'classier' than blacks." To RJR's dismay, Lorillard

Newport's popularity was being driven by these smokers who "desire to be part of the mainstream white majority."[88]

It would have been simpler for marketers if Black preferences and white preferences on these brands were completely segregated, if Blacks smoked Black brands and whites smoked white brands. But the reality was far more complicated. Menthol brands (Kool, Salem, Newport, and so on) continued to have interracial crossover appeal despite the era's polarization. Despite the decline in smoking rates across the population, menthol smoking as a percentage of total cigarette consumption continued to rise (from 22 percent in 1970 to 27 percent in 1977).[89] In 1974 Elmo Roper told PM that despite stark racial divisions and even though 36 percent of young white smokers preferred Marlboro, sales remained stable. Kool, by contrast, was smoked by 14 percent of young whites, but "it may be on the way up."[90] Racial animus aside, Kool had a white following that could not be ignored.

In the continuing battle to reach Black consumers without provoking white smokers, most companies looked to use the strong cultural signaling of Black popular music. There were many misfires in this effort. In a shockingly cynical advertising gesture, for example, a Lorillard executive named H. L. Carroll suggested that a new crossover brand might be named after the famous crossover crooner of the 1960s Nat King Cole. Carroll, apparently unaware of Cole's death from lung cancer in 1964 after years of smoking, strongly recommended "a major entry into the Menthol Market with a direct appeal to Blacks with a King Size Filter . . . named COLE." "I believe the name COLE (if not already registered) would be immediately accepted by the Blacks, as the first thought comes to mind would be Nat 'King' Cole, whose name is highly revered among Blacks and Whites alike." The suggestion went nowhere in the company; no doubt someone pointed out that Cole's widow had sued cigarette producers after his death, resulting in a rumored private settlement in 1971. Highlighting how such companies reached for partners in Black media to build such cultural resonances and markets through advertising, Carroll observed, "If there is a competent Black advertising agency, I would give them the . . . account. The promotional possibilities of marketing a brand named COLE, particularly in the Black Markets, would seem to be boundless."[91]

Creating racial optics in this setting (whether on billboards, subway posters, buses, or street corners) presented a multilayered geographical challenge for advertisers. Getting it right involved gathering local knowledge about the flows of people around the city, and between the city and the suburbs, down to specifics about bus ridership and which buses moved through which neighborhoods and the demographics of those neighborhoods.[92] As RJR's Detroit study noted, "Out-of-home [advertising] is judged to be the most effective local medium for efficiently and impactfully reaching all segments of the Detroit market, with the exception of a few upscale communities, i.e., Bloomfield, Southfield, Grosse Pointe, etc., where out-of-home is zoned out." Designing materials for display in or on local buses that crossed from the city to the suburbs posed particular challenges, "since in many cases routes pass through all Black neighborhoods as well as suburban white [neighborhoods]." In this case, any "exterior advertising should be compatible to both market segments." But since few white people used Detroit's buses within the city *or* the suburbs, the interior advertising could more explicitly call on Black-centered themes.[93]

Kool in Crisis

By 1985 young people were abandoning menthols. Myron Johnston speculated that the phenomenon could be explained by the diverging preferences between white and Black youth:

> During the late 1960s and 1970s young blacks were the trend setters and young whites were copying them in everything from clothing styles to music to language and behavior patterns. Now the civil rights movement has cooled; Alex Haley's "Roots" is nearly ten years old; peace has returned to college campuses, along with . . . an emphasis on practical courses instead of vague commitment

to social goals; and young whites have discovered that they have "roots" of their own.

In this memo, titled "The Implications of Those Strange Happenings in the Menthol Market," Johnston expressed a belief that the alienation of young whites from Black culture had produced a transformation in preferences and a decline in menthol sales.[94]

Companies had already begun noticing changes in the market in the 1970s as billboards proliferated and the competition for the urban menthol market grew heated. The relentless creation of new brands, commented the *Wall Street Journal*, had resulted in "cannibalization," with companies undercutting even their own products. A case in point was the new "low tar" Kool Super Light, which was intended "to keep health and low-tar conscious former Kool regular smokers, revitalize interest in all of the Kool brands, and capture a larger share of the menthol smokers who make up 30% of all smokers."[95] The only thing the new Super Light brand accomplished was cutting into Kool sales, which dropped in 1976 and continued sliding downward in 1977.[96] Gains by competitors like Newport came at Kool's expense. B&W now worried also about "the decline in consumption among black smokers."[97]

B&W faced a racial conundrum of its own design. Although the "inner-city" menthol market remained lucrative, B&W executives worried that "Kool's black franchise is no longer expanding."[98] Data from 1976 in B&W's Black smoker study highlighted the opportunities and challenges. The Black population over sixteen years of age was 18.4 million; roughly 52 percent, or some 8.5 million people, smoked. Kool's share of this market was large at 38 percent. These 3.25 million people accounted for more than half (55 percent) of Kool's nearly 6 million smokers in the United States. But was this trend sustainable? There were many warning signs. For one, Blacks smokers smoked "two packs per week less than White smokers." Even so, the figures were astronomical. At 8,000 cigarettes per year per person on average, the total Black consumption per year was 19.5 billion Kool cigarettes. Put another way, a subset of the Black population that accounted for

10 percent of the US population was consuming about a third of the roughly 60 billion Kool cigarettes consumed in the nation each year.[99]

And yet for all the billions in profits generated by its "inner-city" focus, Kool's heavy menthol message and expansive racial imagery also "represent an enormous vulnerability." In 1977 B&W executives came to believe that the entire menthol market was tilting toward lighter, "health-oriented" smoking. Once again, whatever the racial instabilities in menthol smoking, the underlying health meanings steadied the appeal. Company insiders believed that "the menthol segment's growth will come primarily from health-oriented brands," and that Kool needed to redouble its efforts in this area.[100] Philip Morris's advertising firm, Leo Burnett, saw similar trends, noting that RJR's new high-filtration Salem was selling particularly well. As one *New York Times* journalist put it, "With the health controversy, Salem Lights are riding to glory . . . on consumer preference for lightness." The brand was even making inroads with Black smokers.[101] In the light menthol category, Salem was clawing its way back up with 10.3 percent in the "Negro market" in 1976, then 10.8 percent in 1977, and 11.2 percent in 1978. In these same three years, Kool's market share had dropped—from 24.4 to 23.3 and 23.2 percent.[102] Despite its large lead in sales to Black smokers, Kool sensed stagnation while Salem was rising.[103]

When B&W's sales decline continued in 1978 and 1979, the company criticized its longtime advertiser Ted Bates for failing on two image-making fronts. Bates had failed to adapt the "downscale user image among all smokers and our Black image among White smokers" to new circumstances, complained B&W executives. It had also failed to reinforce Kool's fundamental, if deceptive, health message by deemphasizing its heaviness, potency, or "harshness." The company's G. T. Reid declared that too many people now saw Kool as harsh and socially unacceptable—signifiers in the register of both taste and race.[104] Newport, he observed, had developed a new "pleasure and fun of smoking" theme in its advertising aimed at Black communities, while avoiding patronizing tones or offensive jargon and offering visually positive "life-style and reference groups association." B&W insiders criticized their own ads for falling out of touch with what Blacks wanted.[105] Of course, the youth culture that had bought into Kool in the 1960s had aged; the youth of the 1970s were not drawn to Motown cool but to their own music in the disco era, and Kool had failed to keep up with the new styles. In particular, Kool imagery was criticized from inside the firm for being "rated better by Blacks than Whites on every attribute" and struggling to appeal to white smokers.[106] As one executive put it, the brand needed to "incorporate strong white user symbolism because of Kool's strong black franchise."[107] The market strategy that had worked so well for the Kool brand in the late 1960s and early 1970s was now undermining sales.[108]

In truth, no one knew why fewer young Black men were smoking Kool cigarettes, but one Lorillard executive believed it had something to do with Black suburbanization. The "black franchise" was dynamic and changing—straddling urban aspirations and suburban dreams.[109] In a memo to the company, marketer R. W. Davis offered a range of sociological insights to explain the trend, speculating that Black suburbanization, along with aversion to "inner-city" imagery and a changing health consciousness, drove Newport's rise and Kool's stagnation. Davis saw the "'inner-city' Black smoker" as "not part of the 'traditional' market. They have shown themselves basically impervious to print media exposure, outdoor availability is limited and most importantly, they have high susceptibility to peer influence." Strikingly, he said, despite "the high crime rate in these areas preclud[ing] the use of front counter displays," which were often stolen, Newport was becoming "identified as an 'entry' brand." Davis perceived a backlash against the now "passé 'hip' life-style which is somehow associated with Kool." Possibly, Newport was benefiting by connecting to a "different 'mind-set,' predominantly among males, in the Black inner city," and it was increasingly "identified as an 'entry' brand." According to Davis, health remained important because Black Newport smokers were older (ages 25–49), "more affluent and concerned with status, also more health conscious." The decline of menthol was also tied to Black suburban dreams: "As the 'inner-city' black moves to the suburbs and life-style changes, there is a new peer group influence and a desire to make a change i.e. the old car, beer, cigarette brand reminds you of where you were." In truth, said Davis, there was no sharp division between the Black "inner city" and the white suburbs, but rather Black suburban aspirations were increasingly changing the choices of those who lived in the city, even as there was a "ripple effect" of tastes migrating from the inner city to the suburbs.[110]

B&W and the Ted Bates firm were heading for a breakup over Kool's decline and the brand's apparent inability to adjust to these social, demographic, and racial realities, and over its struggle sustaining the health appeal that had bolstered menthol brands from the very beginning. The B&W-Bates relationship grew tense; as one 1979 B&W memo complained: "Our advertising needs a shot in the arm and . . . a change in focus."[111] Another memo guessed that the "Root Cause of Share Erosion" was that Kool products had "not provided sufficient health reassurance," nor had the brand "adequately adapted to changing consumer needs."[112] Bates's hold on the Kool account became untenable. From the days of Willie the Penguin in the 1940s through the "Come Up to Kool" campaign of the 1960s, Bates had been praised for its ability to offer smokers a reassuring health promise, building new audiences.[113] But sales stagnation in the late 1970s threw the corporate relationship into crisis. In 1980 B&W frustration flared over the advertisers' perceived failures in competing for urban billboard space and Kool's visual reach. While B&W executives praised Bates for the large billboards it secured "in Boston and New York inner-city areas," which were "much greater than in the metro suburban areas," one executive complained bitterly about how their failure to win space along "metropolitan, highly-traveled freeway area positions have limited our ability to convey far reaching impulses." He panned the inner-city billboards for their "lack of action depicted [which] seems out of step with today's young adult markets."[114] Worried over the future of Kool and the challenges from Salem and Newport, B&W fired Bates and began a new relationship with the Chicago-based PKG/Cunningham & Walsh firm. It also brought in other consultants who promised better insights into 1980s Black aspirations.[115]

Philip Morris's Myron Johnston sensed opportunity in B&W's struggles. In his view, menthol smoking had everything to do with politics, and politics had everything to do with menthol preferences.[116] With the Reagan Revolution's rejection of preferential treatment and its critique of political gains for Blacks, it was only to be expected that some white smokers were rejecting menthols that aligned with Black identity. In Johnston's view, menthols as a brand type had always been linked to drugs: "There has been anecdotal evidence that menthol and marijuana are particularly compatible, and marijuana use among the young peaked in 1979."[117] As he noted of the 1980s, "What I judge to be happening is that young Marlboro smokers who might otherwise have been tempted to switch to a menthol have stuck with Marlboro, while other young whites who might otherwise have started on a menthol have rejected the black image of menthols and have started with Marlboro instead."[118] The tide of smoking seemed to follow the tide of racial attitudes and race relations. "Fewer whites are starting with menthol," Johnston observed. The new data suggested a fresh day was dawning for Philip Morris; "the entire Marlboro family has been the beneficiary of the decline in menthol as an entry brand."[119]

For tobacco companies that had invested in the "black franchise," these years of "white alienation" posed challenges for their brands. But if more white-oriented brands from Philip Morris had hoped to benefit from a political shift to the right, their high hopes proved fleeting—dashed by the continuing deluge of health warnings. In 1979, for example, the Surgeon General issued a fifteen-year anniversary update of its landmark 1964 report, a stark reminder of the ongoing deadly toll of the cigarette in America. The new report confronted the industry directly about its misleading claims and presented updated data on deaths from cancer and other diseases. Its evidence sought to demolish "the claims made by cigarette manufacturers and a few others fifteen years ago and today: that the scientific evidence was sketchy; that no link between smoking and cancer was 'proven.'" "Those claims, empty then, are utterly vacuous now," concluded the Surgeon General under President Jimmy Carter.[120] The new Surgeon

General under pro-business, conservative Ronald Reagan would be no kinder, labeling smoking as "the single most preventable cause of death."[121]

A New Urban Hustle

Even as Brown & Williamson faced increased skepticism and even hostility from white smokers, the company tried to hold on to its Black franchise with a new urban hustle. Having replaced Bates, B&W looked to its new advertising partner, Cunningham & Walsh, for ways to tie the company ever closer to urban revitalization and commercialization. Regarded in the popular press as havens of poverty, unemployment, social dependency, and drug use, cities to B&W continued to be seen as vital zones for research, marketing, and sales. Two decades of both white and middle-class Black flight had left the "inner cities" more segregated and poorer. With the decline of federal funding in the 1970s and 1980s, cities had also become more vulnerable and more dependent on outside economic support. When other industries fled, tobacco stayed behind. Their continued investment in cities posed a stark choice for Black politicians and civic leaders: whether to accept tobacco support in the name of economic survival and cultural pride, or reject it in the name of health. In these difficult fiscal times for cities (some of them now majority Black and led by Black mayors), the tobacco industry trumpeted its support for all things urban as well as for Black arts, entertainment, and organizations like the NAACP.

Cunningham & Walsh pushed aggressively to control urban vistas with Kool advertising, even in cities without Black majorities. In the greater Denver metropolitan area, for example, in a city of rapid population growth, outdoor advertisers faced many obstacles due to strict zoning restrictions in the suburbs of Lakewood, Littleton, Aurora, Arvada, and Englewood; however, the central city areas were promising, including "four B&W locations . . . in dense Spanish neighborhoods . . . [and] two other locations in Hispanic areas," one at a "major N/S arterial in Denver and [the other, which] covers traffic moving toward on-ramps for Interstate 25 or continuing on to 'downtown.'"[122] B&W struggled to stabilize Kool, demanding that its consultants study ever more intensively the urban scene, showing "greater sensitivity to the Black consumer marketplace" and calling for "accurate consumer research, gathered under realistic conditions, i.e., urban studies" and "better understandings of Black consumer psychographics" as opposed to mere data gathered from existing smokers. They also sought more "creative executions" of advertisements to halt "franchise defection and . . . begin restoration by attracting new smokers."[123] The solution to share erosion led to even greater visual penetration in Kool's advertising efforts, "particularly outdoor, [which] is not sufficiently intrusive," and to increased demands by the company to communicate the "values of satisfaction and contentment." Another emphasis was stronger health messaging—exploiting Kool's "residual 'health' overtones of menthol."[124]

Encouraged by Cunningham & Walsh, B&W also reinvested in what would eventually become its marquee outreach tool for Black communities: urban jazz festivals. The marketer embraced the Kool Jazz festival and its associated imagery as a central part of Kool's revitalized branding. The company reenergized the festival by bringing major names like B.B. King and Aretha Franklin into cities like Atlanta to demonstrate Kool's affinity for Black culture and Black consumption.[125] Jazz music sales had hit $4.13 billion in 1978, noted Cunningham & Walsh, and jazz was a potent force in the music industry.[126] In late 1981, B&W announced a series of jazz festivals in twenty cities.[127] Festivals were only part of the company's $125 million push, noted the *Wall Street Journal*—it would also include advertisements in 75 magazines, 324 newspapers, 19,000 billboards, and 16,000 buses and subway cars. The new campaign would revolve around famous musicians while highlighting jazz as the "universal language which bridges the gap between countries, cultures, and attitudes."[128] A new tag line emerged with a strong jazz motif—"there's only one way to play it." While Kool's previous campaigns had involved separate ads

Figure 4.6. While employers and other industries had left the cities, the tobacco industry saw opportunity in the struggling urban neighborhoods and districts. By 1980 Brown & Williamson launched the Kool Jazz Festivals to revive flagging sales and create "authentic" connections to Black urban citizens.
Credit: From the collection of Stanford Research Into the Impact of Tobacco Advertising (tobacco .stanford.edu)

for whites and Blacks, this new jazz focus was said to be "panracial" — using Black and white models in all media.[129] Jazz, they hoped, would be the unifying theme.

Cunningham & Walsh's faith in jazz's "panracial" appeal proved difficult to sustain. By 1983 it had become clear that the results of the campaign were split along lines of race: "Blacks of all ages see jazz as part of their culture and heritage," wrote Kapuler & Associates, the firm that had done the original study on behalf of Cunningham & Walsh, and "older black people have strong nostalgic feelings about jazz . . . and they believe it is supported as much by 'intelligent' white people as by other blacks." "Most white respondents," by contrast, "were tentative in their identification of jazz." These white respondents regarded jazz as "an elitist form of music that seems to conform to no prescribed set of rules." Black listeners heard their culture echoed in the music; whites, it seemed, heard unruly nonconforming rhythms—so the stereotype went. According to the report, "White men, in particular, are disturbed by the improvisational quality of jazz, and feel it is somewhat beyond their understanding."[130] At least one Wall Street analyst agreed, saying, "That positioning attempts to support and build on their large stake among black consumers, but I think the jazz orientation is too narrow."[131] In 1984 the company tweaked the jazz festival concept, expanding the performer mix toward a "younger, White, blend of Jazz, Pop, Rock and Rhythm & Blues" (but still avoiding the "extremes of Classical or Country").[132] Two years later, acknowledging the limits of music's panracial appeal, B&W ended its sponsorship of the jazz festivals.[133]

Almost every firm with stakes in menthol had built a visual presence in the city with posters and billboards, and they launched large-scale reviews of the state of the Black menthol market and where the road ahead might lead during the 1980s.[134] Roper, for instance, conducted an expansive poll for Philip Morris that asked: Which meals were most associated with smoking?[135] Did smokers usually puff at work, while talking on the phone, or with a drink in hand? Others studied whether marketers should fear a white backlash.[136] What did lower-income Blacks think about Newport and why, Lorillard wondered, looking for clues in a study focused on Chicago, Detroit, Atlanta, Los Angeles, and Memphis?[137] The main challenge for menthol, explained one consultant to B&W, was not that Black trends were out of fashion, but that Black fashion trends of the 1960s had become mainstream and (as a result) were not "in." Simply because of the passage of time and the aging of smokers who had taken up Kool in the 1960s, the "image of Kool may be becoming that of an old brand."[138] Courting *new* young smokers in the 1980s would entail establishing fundamentally new cultural trends—staying in tune with youth, race, and the health concerns of a new generation.

For its part, B&W began thinking bigger about the social web that might sustain menthol smoking. In 1985 the company established a joint pilot partnership with the NAACP to promote a small business incubator in Hartford, Connecticut.[139] The initiative extended a relationship that had formed two years earlier, when the NAACP was struggling financially and sought deeper corporate sponsorships while aiming to promote small business development in the city. The cigarette company's promotion of economic development added to its ongoing effort to embrace multiple aspects of African American culture—supporting Black history, Black music, Black elected officials, Black artists, Black civic organizations, and singing the praises of the power of the Black consumer.[140] Nor was B&W alone in its expansive backing of Black causes as a strategy for keeping menthol smoking in place.

The Crooked Mile from City to Suburb

Menthol researchers and marketers had created a far-reaching racial optic with their 1970s advertising—a vista that was so compelling that both Blacks and whites, researchers and interview subjects, responded to Kool, Salem, and the entire menthol category as if they were proxies for the decade's racial tensions. Billboards and public transit ads had not only altered the urban landscape, but also changed perceptions of race and reshaped the urban-suburban divide in the minds of Blacks and whites alike.

With their eyes firmly focused on the Black "inner city," the consultants for industry had left far behind most formal references to psychological theory as the basis for menthol's appeal. It had been decades since the motivation psychology theories of Ernest Dichter guided marketing. In this era, companies turned to social scientists who stitched together their sociological views about race, common truisms about Black people, and varied prejudices about urban and suburban attitudes into new theories about menthol preferences. Their ideas echoed increasingly common stereotypes that were shared across politics and culture about the ugliness of the ghetto, about drugs, and about the "inner city." According to PM's Myron Johnston, young whites were abandoning menthol not because of its taste, but because of its association with downscale, menial Black images—images that, it should be said, were fabricated by the industry itself. Indeed, Blacks themselves were fleeing Kool, perceiving it as "harsh and heavy," with one focus group of young Black men explaining to B&W researchers that Kool was smoked by "thug women" and no longer seen as trendsetting. These twenty-one- to twenty-five-year-old men in Memphis had begun smoking "in adolescence or early teens, stealing cigarettes from parents or buying 'loosies.' The loosie market in Memphis seems to be a good-sized, highly available and all Kool." They had started with Kool, but then switched to Newport, perceived by them as "more hip . . . more fashionable."[141]

These impressions about race (imprinted onto the physical environment of the city and seared into the minds of white and Black viewers alike) would guide the work of in-house analysts and marketing consultants. They understood clearly that their own imagery was producing resentment and racialized reactions. They had to avoid the Archie Bunker–type white resentments, speak to shifting Black worries and aspirations, and remain ever cognizant of the impact of these images on brand preferences and sales.[142] As one analyst, C. L. Lomicka, for B&W observed, some users of other brands referred to Kool as "the brand ex-cons smoke—'the number one brand in the ghetto.'" Young Black men were also alienated by the prevailing imagery, yet Lomicka also concluded, "With minor exceptions, the cityscape scene . . . was seen by respondents as smoking appropriate and more realistic (for Blacks) . . . although there was a fantasy element that was appealing to these groups."[143]

The Kool brand, in particular, had worked its way into a vexing bind, reflecting the complexities of racial politics in the conservative-turning 1980s. As the marketing consulting firm Eaton & Associates informed the company, its Black-themed advertising was successful but flawed. It mixed powerful ideals of personal freedom, independence, and controlling of one's own destiny, with strong currents of hardship. But the consultants warned B&W that these more negative themes were overwhelming whatever positive messages Kool ads intended. Young Blacks were now "acutely aware of the obstacles of the ghetto. . . . [They] are survivors . . . [and were] looking for a way out of the ghetto mentality." Kool had invested in the image of the "frustrated" Black man who "smokes out of a need to cope with frustration rather than for satisfaction and relaxation." Focus groups were now saying that these images were out of step with Black aspirations. These smokers wanted something else — "to satisfy their desires, enjoy life to the fullest while enjoying the camaraderie of friends." For them, "the rugged, aloof individuality and seclusion depicted in the Kool ads are difficult concepts for this audience to feel related [to]." The problem, Eaton explained, was that Kool's competitors were sending more upbeat messages and their sales were rising: "There is a strong identification with the couples or small groups pictured in both Salem and Newport advertising."[144]

Alienation was said to come in shades of Black and white, according to company consultants and insiders in the 1980s. For tobacco's social scientists, racial alienation in particular had become a salient theme of cigarette consumerism at a time when Black people in the city were vilified in conservative politics as welfare queens and hoodlums, and the urban poor were being left further behind. As the columnist Juan Williams wrote following the 1988 presidential election of George H. W. Bush, "Where Reagan used the 'welfare queen' collecting checks in her Cadillac to appeal to white hostilities in the 1980 campaign, his heir, George Bush, used Willie Horton, the wild-eyed black man who raped a suburban white woman . . . appealing to the white perception that blacks are responsible for virtually all violent crime."[145] In politics as in advertising in the 1980s, branding and shaping perception were crucial to success; in both realms, there was plenty of manipulation and channeling of racial resentments. "For the most part, it appears as though Blacks who are comfortable in a racially balanced society can be comfortable smoking non-menthols," commented one analyst for PM, "while those who live a segregated existence [e.g., in inner cities] are more likely to remain smoking menthols." For PM (which had never succeeded in the urban menthol market), these realities continued to shore up its lead brand among whites, but left them struggling in Black markets. "Marlboro was viewed as a White person's brand, even among the Blacks present at the group who smoke it." But Black smokers bore no grudges against Marlboro smokers, PM analysts concluded: "There seemed to be no animosity towards the brand, despite the fact that Blacks perceived it as a brand whose advertising excluded them."[146]

Meanwhile, the Salem-Kool division had been rigidifying into a new set of racial tropes. A focus group of young people in Paramus, New Jersey, told PM researchers in blunt terms: "Salem smokers tended to be individuals who stayed at home and were somewhat 'health conscious,'" whereas "Kool smokers tended to be individuals who hung out on street corners, often drinking beer and getting into trouble. They seem to have little or no interest in getting ahead."[147] The era's attitudes on race poured out of the mouths of smokers and into the ears of interviewers, in turn coursing through company memos and research findings, and informing their theories of brand preference and racial psychology. It was a perverse feedback loop, as the industry's own imagery reacted with attitudes beyond their control, and then fed back into how and where companies advertised on billboards, buses, magazines, and newspapers.

Big Tobacco and its web of consultants left nothing to chance in shaping the racial optics on the commute from suburb to city. At Lorillard, for example, analyst Claudia Garbin looked closely at details of Black-white ridership on bus routes and local demographics when considering where and how to market Newport. In Pittsburgh's bus system, she recommended that "black creative [ads] should be utilized on 50% of Newport's interior cards on buses originating from the East Liberty Garage," because this was the only garage with a high percentage of Black ridership. In Washington, DC, with 60 percent Black ridership on buses, she also recommended Black-themed interior advertising. But in Boston, even with 60 percent Black bus ridership, Garbin recommended against "using Black creative because these buses service White areas, too." The difference hinged on understanding not just ridership but also white alienation in Boston:

> You might question why 60% was an acceptable proportion for me to recommend using Black creative in D.C. while not in Boston. This is because in the South Menthol usage is extremely Black. In Boston [where Newport had built a strong white franchise], we run the risk of alienating our White franchise/White potential users.[148]

Each city posed distinct geographic and demographic challenges, and each offered its own marketing opportunities—if one understood the racial landscape. What Big Tobacco sought from consultants was persistent insight on this question of how to control the visual landscape along the crooked mile that led from "inner city" to suburb and back again.

: : :

In the two decades from the television ad ban to the end of the 1980s, industry had colonized hollowed-out urban spaces, enhancing its commercial presence while studying racial optics in a changing society. When other industries left America's ailing cities, tobacco companies stayed behind—to sell and advertise, to support local causes, to fund politicians and political causes like the NAACP's economic development plan, and (most importantly) to nurture an image for menthol brands as intimately connected to Black culture and close to the point of purchase. From Cleveland to Philly, from Los Angeles to New York, tobacco-focused advertising supported Black magazines, newspapers, cultural programs, and jazz festivals. Menthol imagery on billboards in the 1970s had come to symbolize the social and economic chasm between the city and the suburb.

Who built this house of menthol? In 1980, with its Kool empire at risk, Cunningham & Walsh produced a Retrospective History of

KOOL" for the company—to "provide a historical background necessary for the fullest understanding of the brand's equity: what Kool
owns in the consumer's mind." The insider's document took readers
through its early days of "continued exploitation of throat comfort,"
and into the cancer years of the 1950s. Without mentioning cancer,
it acknowledged that "the early effects of the heightened personal
concern condition seemed to be helpful to Kool." Into the 1960s,
Kool's fortunes rose because "Kool was the only menthol . . . with
advertising that provided . . . situations and people with which these
groups [young males and Blacks] could identify."[149] Another internal
cultural history of Kool's rise (this one from RJR) also pointed to the
tumultuous 1960s:

> It was time for Blacks to build their own brand in the 1960's, the
> heyday of Martin Luther King and "Black Pride." Kool apparently
> capitalized on this aspect of the 1960's by simply advertising to
> Blacks before its competitors did. Kool ads were in *Ebony* consis-
> tently from at least 1962, when our records start. This was easy for
> Kool, since its early-60's penguin campaign fit either race, and it
> was effective. Kool became "cool" and, by the early 1970's, had a
> 56% share among young adult Blacks—it was the Black Marlboro.[150]

Despite B&W's insistence that Black people themselves had built
the house of menthol, the company and its web of consultants and
supporters were deeply proud of "owning the consumer's mind" and
"exploiting" personal and social conditions and health worries. Tobacco's insiders, experts, and consultants had developed an elaborate
relationship with the city; they had also constructed the elaborate
scaffolding that held up menthol's house.

For tobacco companies, the trajectory of Kool and Salem, and the
possibilities of Newport and Marlboro Green, were not about taste
but about the stiffening of white attitudes, shifting Black dreams,
the growing divide between where Black and white people lived,
how these groups saw one another, and racial alienation. Time after
time, smokers told researchers that they responded to imagery not

tobacco taste, and that the racial imagery of Kool as a "ghetto brand" had become deeply etched into the perceptions of viewers and in the industry.

In the 1980s, critics took aim at the imagery, the tactics, Big Tobacco's enablers, and the posters and billboards that now defined the industry's command over urban space. In 1989 reporters for the *Detroit Free Press* documented the stark divergence of tobacco billboards along lines of race and place: there were 154 cigarette billboards on Detroit's urban roads, 78 on the highways connecting city and suburb, and only 17 in the suburbs. Alcohol advertising followed a similar commercial divide: 128 on city roads, 28 on the highways, and 6 in the suburbs.[151] Other analysts noted that Detroit's billboards comprised only one part of a vicious web of deceit. RJR, for example, had bought the silence of Black civic organizations by generously supporting Black causes, from the popular *Ebony* magazine fashion fair to the NAACP. Those who would otherwise speak out remained muted. Philip Morris had financed the Congressional Black Caucus's national weekend of 8,000 Black leaders; some such leaders stepped forward with critiques nevertheless, but many did not. Criticism of industry's targeted urban campaigns had been muted in the 1970s. But in the 1980s, criticism of the urban marketing of alcohol products like Colt 45 malt liquor and tobacco brands began to grow from elsewhere—from public health officials, from community groups, from reformers ranging from Dallas to Detroit, and in the courts.[152] Such critics began to portray tobacco's blatant appeal to Black authenticity as a grand deception.[153]

Menthol had become a discernible eyesore, standing out for critics as a deceitful market entrapment, a colonizing project. The colonizing of ethnicity in this fashion was not confined to African Americans or Big Tobacco in these years, of course, as sociologist Arlene Davila has documented in her study on the making of Latino identity in advertising and how representations "shape people's cultural identities as well as affect notions of belonging and cultural citizenship in public life."[154] The industry relationship with civic organizations like the NAACP would pay lasting dividends as the racial politics of tobacco became ever more divisive in the 1980s. As the respected civil rights group came to rely on industry financing and economic support, tobacco companies in turn regarded the NAACP as an ally. New markets were created in the bargain. To quote anthropologists John and Jean Comaroff in *Ethnicity, Inc.* (a study of how ethnic populations remake themselves in the image of the corporation and how corporations co-opt ethnic practices to make markets): "There is no telling where a market, however modest its magnitude, might be cultivated."[155] If industry both constructed and capitalized on ethnicity, cultural pride, and images of distinctive identity, representatives of the ethnic group also gained in the bargain—ready to reinforce, support, and profit from those ethno-futurist stratagems. Menthol cigarettes had become such an ethnic project—a commodity held in place by a web of profitable relationships and secured by billboard and poster imagery across the cityscape.[156]

By the end of the 1980s, a fight brewed over the depths of this entrapment. The industry's hold on Black communities had become a wide-open secret, a standoff in an urban marketplace. The saga of tobacco and race was a tale of "help, hope, and harm," observed the *Detroit Free Press* in an extended analysis of the Black community's dilemma. On one side were the enablers like Black advertising executive Caroline Jones, who decried not the prevalence of tobacco billboards but the absence of advertising in Black communities ("so much neglect across the board of major advertisers who choose not to include minorities"). But then Reed Tuckson, DC health commissioner, spoke for a growing number of Black health officials who fervently called out the industry's cynicism, asking, "Where do the cigarette companies go to find these new recruits for the death march to the land of profit and greed? . . . They go to the vulnerable and oppressed segments of our country. They go for the people of color." In the pages of the *Detroit Free Press*, there was also a familiar testimonial from Raymond Pritchard, chairman of Brown & Williamson, defending his company as a good corporate citizen contributing "to a better quality of life in our communities . . . first and foremost to the economically disadvantaged." He disagreed strongly with the scientists and health professionals about smoking and disease; in any case, he concluded, "all smokers have the freedom of choice in the marketplace."[157]

But what kind of perverse marketplace had American "inner cities" become? What kind of consumer freedom was this? As advertising executive Gene Morris saw it, racism and segregation had allowed this exploitative system to flourish, feeding on neglect and racial disdain, and offering false hope in the form of commodities like Colt 45 malt liquor and menthol cigarettes. Blacks "since they came to this country, have been told they were inferior, lazy, stupid. . . . As a way to compensate, black people look for ways to make positive statements about themselves, ways to say they're doing well and can afford luxuries like other people."[158] This urban market was not free at all, but a trap where poverty, racism, and lack of opportunity constrained choices and made Black consumers prime targets for what another critic called "drugs of illusion."[159]

The billboard era captured this dilemma in vivid pictures. And when anti-billboard activism increased in the 1980s, NAACP spokesman James Williams defended the industry and accused critics of racism, noting, "It's racist to say black people are so malleable that they don't have the sense to decide whether to smoke or not."[160] By the early 1990s, companies like RJR continued speaking proudly of their "strong purchasing program for minority and women," their robust presence in urban neighborhoods, and their especially close relationships with "minority opinion leaders" in politics, education, economic development, professional circles, as well as civil rights.[161] A leader of RJR's effort was Benjamin Ruffin, who had credibility in the Black community as a former student at North Carolina Central University during the early days of the civil rights movement and later in state government, focusing on building opportunities for African Americans. Ruffin fondly quoted his friend the NAACP director Benjamin Hooks as saying, "The main thing tainted about the money we receive from some sources is there t'aint enough of it."[162] His role at RJR involved maintaining a web of influence that spanned from the NAACP to the National Newspaper Publishers Association, and from the United Negro College Fund to the Congressional Black Caucus.[163]

But even as Big Tobacco's web thickened, health activists and local organizers were awakening to the deadly irony of this predatory exploitation. Reaching for a graphic metaphor, Pam Miller of the American Lung Association explained that Big Tobacco's racial capitalism had enticed Black communities in a deadly snare. It was as if a Black family had a terrible accident while driving, she wrote. "The car overturns, and the wife and children are pinned in the car." Another car arrives, and with it the promise of help. "It's the KKK pickup truck. The KKK rescues the family," she continued, "and the father is very thankful to the KKK."[164] Urban Black smokers were caught in a tragic hustle—a fatal bind, indeed.

5

Uptown's Aftertaste

In early 1990, a controversy over a new brand of menthol cigarette called Uptown that was aimed unabashedly at African American buyers provoked a furious disagreement between two leading political figures. Louis Sullivan and Benjamin Hooks both claimed to speak for civil rights and the well-being of African Americans, but Sullivan (a prominent Black physician and the secretary of Health and Human Services serving in a business-friendly Republican administration) and Hooks (the leader of the NAACP) now sparred over which of them had Black people's best interests in mind when it came to tobacco. The two men's positions surprised most observers, since it was Hooks who defended Big Tobacco's racial-themed marketing and Sullivan who fiercely attacked it. The division drew attention to an open secret of race and smoking, a secret that had helped build and sustain the industry's house of menthol: Big Tobacco's success depended on cultivating powerful allies in organizations like the NAACP. But even more shocking was the fact that Sullivan's assault, a public lashing of RJR for pushing a new menthol brand exclusively at African Americans, had come from a Cabinet member in a business-friendly Republican administration.

Only recently, the two men had shared the stage at the NAACP's eightieth anniversary celebration where comity and good humor prevailed—Hooks presiding with charm and jocularity as the executive director, and Sullivan, stiffly delivering his message of good health and greetings from President George H. W. Bush. A month later, however, RJR's launching of Uptown threw the men into a nasty conflict, exposing a revealing rift over which one of them—the doctor or the civil rights leader—was being duped by the industry, and who spoke for the Black community's well-being. Sullivan accused the industry and its supporters of pushing a deadly drug and pumping money into Black institutions to buy silence; Hooks in turn accused the health regulators and activists who sought to protect Black communities by banning Uptown and tobacco billboards as nothing more than paternalistic racists.

Anger about targeted marketing and billboards in Black neighborhoods had grown through the 1980s, but even by those standards, the Uptown story was shocking. It not only pulled back the curtain on what had been common industry practice, but RJR was also surprisingly blatant—admitting with disarming candor that Uptown was meant specifically for Black smokers and would soon be test-marketed in Black Philadelphia. Where other menthol brands like Kool had made racial pitches (but had never been racially exclusive in doing so), RJR's Uptown's marketing plan admitted frankly, "What kind of smoker is Uptown targeted to? We anticipate that the brand's taste and advertising will appeal to adult black smokers."[1] Why the specific targeting? "Black smokers have some well-defined taste preferences," claimed RJR, for "a stronger tobacco flavor, less of a menthol overtone, than . . . our major menthol brand, Salem." This idea that Black smokers preferred less menthol not more was another surprise, inverting an old racial theme developed by the industry in the 1960s. For decades, the truism had been that Black people preferred stronger menthol smokes, but now the Uptown pitch suggested that they favored an even "lighter menthol concentration" than what was on offer in RJR's Salem brand—a brand that was performing below the company's hopes in Black markets.[2]

For RJR, the Uptown strategy—bold, explicit—was "an example of how highly targeted consumer products have become." They were

Figure 5.1. In 1990 the R. J. Reynolds Uptown brand intended for test marketing in Philadelphia unleashed a torrent of criticisms over the company's explicitly Black-themed branding. The legacy of the Uptown saga, including the divisions it revealed among African Americans over Big Tobacco's racial targeting, carries over through today.
Credit: From the collection of Stanford Research Into the Impact of Tobacco Advertising (tobacco .stanford.edu).

unapologetic and brazen in selling Black exclusivity. The current market was ready, RJR claimed, for "the first cigarette brand ever targeted strictly to blacks." RJR's press materials drew an analogy to the athletic shoe business and companies like Nike, "which offers running shoes, walking shoes, [and] basketball shoes." Tobacco, like "most other consumer products businesses," faced an extremely segmented market; the company had no choice, they said, except to "respond to those specific wants to remain competitive."[3] Manufacturers had to take Black tastes and habits into account even down to the package designed for Uptown. RJR's research had found, for example, "that blacks often open their packs from the bottom." Uptown was therefore packaged with this quirk in mind, with the filters facing downward.[4]

The audacity of the Blacks-only advertising plan prompted Sullivan, the founding dean of Atlanta's Morehouse School of Medicine, and now the HHS secretary, to decry the scheme as "slick and sinister."[5] It did not require health expertise to clearly see the deadly difference between targeted racial marketing of cigarettes and sneakers—Nikes had never killed any of its users. Sullivan dashed off a damning letter on agency stationery to the company's CEO, James W. Johnston, releasing a copy to the press. RJR had prepared for backlash and controversy, but not of this scope—never anticipating public outrage from someone so highly placed, let alone someone with such a bully pulpit as a Cabinet secretary in the Bush administration. Dogged by charges of deceitful marketing, luring minors, and selling a deadly product, the company was unsettled by Sullivan's vehemence. They looked for support from Benjamin Hooks; he had come to the industry's defense before. Executive director of one of the nation's oldest civil rights groups, Hooks had welcomed financial support from the tobacco industry. When the first push to ban billboards had begun in the 1980s, he defended tobacco companies' right to advertise. Now, the NAACP leader declared that he was more troubled by the outcry against RJR than the Uptown campaign itself. What was so wrong with an industry (especially one that had supported Black causes so expansively) reaching out to a targeted market, he asked. He accused anti-tobacco forces of racism in their condescending belief that Black people needed "guardian angels"—that they could not be trusted to decide these issues for themselves.[6]

Uptown and the schism between Sullivan and Hooks was a crossroads moment: it revealed the growing power of medical critics like Sullivan, speaking for a profession that had developed a deep animus toward the industry. The Uptown debacle (and it would be a debacle for the industry) also revealed the extent of Hooks's connections to Big Tobacco and the gaping hole in the NAACP'S agenda on matters of smoking and health. As the *New York Times* later observed about Hooks's tenure at the NAACP, the organization had been severely "weakened under the weight of declining membership and shaky finances." Through the 1980s, it strained to remain "an effective champion of minorities in an era of rising political conservatism."[7] How would the organization finance its work on behalf of equal opportunity, jobs, political representation, and economic opportunity? As government in the 1980s had become more of a foe than friend to the civil rights agenda, Hooks saw Big Tobacco as a stronger ally than ever. This was, of course, a Faustian bargain. In contrast, health

Figure 5.2. Louis W. Sullivan (pictured with George H. W. Bush), the first African American US Secretary of Health and Human Services, denounced the Uptown campaign as "slick and sinister." Credit: Photo by Dirck Halstead. Courtesy of Getty Images.

Figure 5.3. Benjamin Hooks, Executive Director of the NAACP. The civil rights organization received support from the tobacco industry, and Hooks rallied to support R. J. Reynolds in the Uptown controversy. In this image, Hooks speaks in Philadelphia in 1986, four years before the controversy. Credit: Photo by Robert Dias. Courtesy of Special Collections Research Center, Temple University Libraries, Philadelphia, PA.

professionals had moved forcefully in the other direction. For his part, Louis Sullivan had few ties to civil rights organizations and had inherited none of their compromises.

Unprepared for Sullivan's public ridicule, RJR quickly retreated and withdrew plans for Uptown; but the game had been exposed and the damage done. The Uptown controversy was neither a beginning nor an end, but merely another bend on menthol's crooked road. But in making menthol's supporting relationships visible, the controversy would have lasting consequences, catalyzing a move toward banning billboards while also pointing toward an extraordinary political compromise that would preserve a place for menthol smoking in the US market. As it happens, Hooks's objections and his protection of menthol cigarettes would fail in the short term, foreshadowing the demise of the billboard; but his argument would also bear fruit in long run—allowing other brands to maintain their hold in the city and allowing menthol smoking to escape from a congressional ban further down the road. The Uptown controversy, brief and tumultuous, would have a lasting legacy because it exposed a long-hidden reality in the history of menthol smoking: that menthol cigarettes' supposed association with Black smokers relied at least as much on a thick web of supportive relationships with publishers, civil rights groups, and civic officials as it did on racially targeted marketing campaigns.

How Uptown Went Down

By 1989 the sheer ubiquity of urban cigarette advertising—often featuring menthol brands alongside liquor ads—angered people in localities across the country. In Chicago a man calling himself "Mandrake" became nationally known as an anti-billboard vigilante—whitewashing tobacco and alcohol billboards in acts of guerrilla warfare. Calling into a radio debate with a tobacco spokesman, he complained, "If you live on the South Side of Chicago or the West Side . . . , or if you drive through any poor section . . . , you're going to find a disproportionate amount of billboard advertising of cigarettes in our community."[8] Mandrake's vandalism made national news in 1989, as did anti-billboard movements in other cities just before the Uptown controversy flared up. Secretary Sullivan applauded the uprising; in his letter to RJR's Johnston, he had pointedly insisted that "cigarettes are the only legal product on the market that are deadly when used exactly as intended."[9] Atlanta-based US Representative John Lewis also joined the outcry. "Every day when little children are on their way to school," he declared, "they get a message that the way to be happy and get ahead is to have a beer and smoke cigarettes."[10] Lewis had even introduced legislation that pushed cities to replace tobacco billboards with public health messages. Then RJR's Uptown came along.

The Uptown campaign effectively turned these flare-ups of discontent into a national firestorm. Facing stiff opposition, RJR's Johnston turned to Hooks, who had pushed the NAACP toward business-friendly corporate partnerships, including Big Tobacco. As a minister and a former member of the FCC, where he advocated for Black-owned media, he seized the public megaphone—loudly defending the tobacco industry's right to advertise. Any attempt to regulate billboards, he declared, was motivated by "an insidious and paternalistic attitude that is saying that blacks are just not smart enough to make up their own mind."[11] It was a scathing critique of anti-tobacco reformers from a civil rights leader, casting industry critics not only as elitists but also as condescendingly opposed to a Black person's right to self-determination. Hooks had brought the credibility of the NAACP to bear in service of the industry, even as his hands were full with other issues, which included attending the presidential signing ceremony establishing Martin Luther King Jr. Day as a national holiday and meeting with President Bush to respond to a spate of mail bombings and threats against Black leaders, judges, and NAACP offices.[12]

Hooks knew well how to use the language of civil rights to defend Black lives from threats and dangers, but he also used that language to defend the industry and advertisers. A few years earlier, Brown & Williamson had worked with the civil rights organization to establish a small business "incubator" in Hartford, Connecticut.[13] Other Black civic organizations and elected officials like US Representative Edolphus Towns of Brooklyn, New York—known on Capitol Hill as "the Marlboro Man"—also depended on industry financial support.[14] Like Hooks, they defended the industry's the right to advertise as a free speech concern. Many Black media organizations were in the same situation—dependent on the tobacco industry's advertising dollars, counted as allies, and silent on the menthol Uptown question. In the mid-1980s, for example, when regulators had threatened to restrict tobacco advertising by going beyond the existing media bans, the 165 Black newspaper publishers in the National Newspaper Publishers Association had pushed back, fearful of lost revenue. The publishers blasted any such ban as "an infringement upon first amendment rights."[15]

RJR's CEO Johnston drew on this well of Black support when he responded to Sullivan's accusations. He insisted that advertising's "function . . . is to encourage brand switching," rather than causing people to pick up the habit. The critics were wrong to claim that advertising "will cause blacks to smoke," the CEO claimed, because ads were never about recruiting new smokers, but about convincing Kool and Newport smokers to switch brands. Moreover, he said echoing Hooks, Black people were capable of making decisions for themselves about Uptown, without handholding from regulators. Standing in defense of Black self-determination, Johnston continued: "Even more troubling . . . is the implicit suggestion that blacks are somehow incapable of making their own informed decisions and need to be protected."[16] For decades, these had been shrewd and winning arguments in defense of targeted menthol advertising.

But RJR had underestimated Sullivan's strong hand. They also misjudged the growing power of the medical critique of tobacco underpinning Sullivan's assault. The HHS secretary's broadside extended far beyond the mere presence of Uptown billboards in Black Philadelphia; as a doctor and public health leader, Sullivan opposed tobacco *itself*. More to the point, as a Cabinet member in the business-friendly Republican Bush administration, Sullivan spoke from an imposing bully pulpit. RJR struck back with a barrage of questions for Sullivan: "Why did Sec. Sullivan choose Uptown as his ticket to media exposure? If black's smoking rates were troubling him, why hadn't he spoken out in the last year against the tens of other brands that blacks are currently smoking?" Why single out Uptown? And invoking their allies in the Black media, why had he singled them out for criticism? "Why hasn't he called in 'general' media to discuss the acceptance of cigarette advertising, just [as] he did the black publishers?"[17] Sullivan's fierce assault on Uptown had caused damage, generating national news about the industry's tactics. His willingness to attack reflected much more than an individual man's ire. Rather it showed how dramatically his profession had swung toward uncompromising criticism of tobacco as a drug and a danger to public health. Nor did the physician seem to be concerned about appearances of paternalism. As Sullivan had explained to Johnston, "One of my priorities has been to carry a message of better health practices and more responsible personal behavior to the American people—particularly those segments disproportionately burdened by preventable illness."[18]

Sullivan did not relent, seizing on Uptown as an opportunity to highlight his fundamental commitments as a physician and health leader. A few years earlier, he had indeed bemoaned that Black adults once smoked at far lower rates than whites, but that "by the mid-1960s . . . a higher percentage of black men than white men were smokers," while smoking among Black and white women remained roughly the same.[19] Even though smoking rates in the nation as a whole had declined over the decades, rates among Black men continued to outpace white men by roughly 9 percent.[20] Preaching the values of moderation and decrying the rising toll of smoking-related mortality, Sullivan found the RJR campaign deeply offensive; it was also a professional affront. In a follow-up speech in Philadelphia at the medical school of the University of Pennsylvania, the HHS secretary waded further into the Uptown affair—applauding the work of local activists doing battle with tobacco companies.

> They are alarmed and angered—just as I am alarmed and angered—by the plans for a new cigarette, called "Uptown." . . . At a time when we must cultivate greater personal responsibility among out citizens, "Uptown's" slick and sinister advertising proposes,

instead, a greater degree of personal irresponsibility. Just when our citizens require a new "culture of character," the maker of "Uptown" [is] promoting a culture of cancer. . . . We must resist the unworthy efforts of these tobacco merchants to earn profits at the expense of the health and well-being of our poor and minority citizens. This trade-off between profits and good health must stop!

In short, the Uptown campaign ran contrary to the administration's "personal responsibility" agenda. Uptown's message, said Sullivan, "is more disease, more suffering, more death for a group already bearing far more than its share of smoking-related illness and mortality."[21] RJR had grown accustomed to such rhetoric from liberal critics, but they had never faced such direct lashing from a Republican in high office.

The Uptown battle signaled a turning point in tobacco's fortunes; although it was only a brief skirmish in an extended war over tobacco's marketing tactics, the turmoil exposed deeper political fracture lines among Black allies and critics, and also opened the industry to withering counterattacks. For Hooks and Sullivan, Uptown forced a public reckoning about their core commitments. On one side, economic interest prevailed; on the other, protecting the public health was sacrosanct. For the citizens of Philadelphia, Chicago, New York, and other cities with large Black populations, the question was which of these men spoke for the Black community? Which of them spoke for the urban poor? Was it Hooks, who claimed that "black people don't need guardian angels"? Or was it Sullivan, who lambasted RJR for its shrewd pursuit of "blood money"? Big Tobacco's hold on Black media, civil rights leaders, and urban consumerism exposed a paradox—whether to embrace the industry's economic clout for the sake of jobs and opportunity, even if the embrace meant sacrificing health. There was also the third possibility that neither of these men—no matter how credentialed and connected—spoke for the Black consumers RJR hoped to reach. Indeed, the Uptown saga would be a catalyst for other local actors—ministers and activists like Mandrake, who attacked the local billboard scourge, taking matters into their own hands in defense of Black interests.

RJR had rolled the dice with Uptown—anticipating that an un-abashed style of racial marketing, akin to Nike's courtship of Black teens, would win adherents.[22] It remains unclear what kind of brash in-house advice had guided them in this misadventure, but a media handout announcing plans to test-market Uptown in Philadelphia suggested that the company anticipated the controversy, seeking to preemptively deflect several inflammatory questions. Black self-determination would be their best defense. Wasn't it wrong to target Blacks this way, asked the RJR media guidance rhetorically, especially since they "suffer from more 'smoking-related' diseases"? Their own talking points responded forcefully, "You know, many major corpo-rations design products to fit the preferences of the minority market." Brushing aside the criticism of targeting, RJR claimed that its effort was no different than "Sears and K-mart [which] offer a line of clothes targeted to blacks, and there are black-targeted media outlets (Ebony, Jet, Black Entertainment Network) and black-targeted music compa-nies (WEA, Motown)." Why shouldn't a menthol brand follow suit? Anticipating the inevitable health question, the company asked, "Isn't it unethical to target ads for products that the Surgeon General has said are dangerous to your health to minorities and women?" No, they insisted, the question itself "reflects bigotry on the part of the ques-tioner" because it implied that Blacks could not make up their own minds.[23] The orchestrated back-and-forth amounted to a full-throated rejection of the criticisms to come, and a bold embrace of racially tar-geted marketing as honest and a matter of Black self-determination.

RJR also knew other criticism might come, taking note of the ris-ing criticism of urban billboards. "Why is it that tobacco and liquor companies use so many OOH [out-of-home] boards in urban areas?" Their answer was simple and direct. Urban out-of-home advertising was an efficient form of marketing driven by deficiencies in other Black media, argued RJR, since "the readership of many minority publications is not as high as other general-interest publications, so it [the print periodical] is a relatively more expensive means of reaching a proportionately smaller group of readers." In the company's view, billboards and out-of-home posters got their message "to consumers as close to the time of purchase as possible" and reminded "smokers of the attributes of our brands on their way into the store as often as possible."[24] All in all, the company knew the danger it courted with Uptown. Yet they charged ahead anyway. They had arranged for video vans promoting Uptown around Black Philadelphia, an urban outreach that truly was something to be proud about.

Remarkably, RJR's media talking points also anticipated a backlash about its "guilt money" bargain with Black civic groups—buying silence about tobacco's health dangers through corporate largesse. Posing questions to itself such as "How much money does RJR Tobacco contribute to charitable causes aimed at minorities?" and "Isn't that really 'guilt money'?," RJR replied: "Over a million dollars a year . . . These contributions help organizations that are striving to improve the quality of life for minorities." This was "absolutely not" guilt money, the firm insisted; RJR had begun "contributing to the United Negro College Fund in the 1940s, long before most companies did." Its founder, Richard Joshua Reynolds, had contributed to Black causes—for example, supporting "a predominantly black college here in Winston-Salem shortly after the turn of the century." As RJR described itself, its support for Black education and charitable causes was long-standing and sincere. Uptown was merely a new chapter consistent with this history. Playing both wrongly accused victim and economic savior, the company claimed to face a "Catch-22 situation. . . . If RJR did not support minority organizations, we would be harshly criticized for being insensitive to the needs of blacks and Hispanics. But when we do support them—purely on merit—we're accused of trying to buy support for our brands." Uptown marketing itself would have a positive economic impact in Philadelphia, RJR claimed, since it had "hired a full-time local field marketing manager" along with several temporary staff and would be buying billboard ads and supplying cigarette sellers "with sales materials and promotional items that should increase their business." With Uptown, they were being a "good corporate citizen" in support of Black striving.[25]

RJR's claim to "good citizenship" rang hollow, especially to critics who were already smoldering with anger about the heavy toll of alcohol and cigarettes on Black lives. A year earlier, *Chicago Tribune* columnist Clarence Page had bemoaned the toll of billboards on cities, writing that he was "bombarded by a visual cacophony of posters and billboards" anytime he visited "the inner ghettos of our major cities."[26] Cities had started fighting back with local ordinances. Richmond, California, had proposed a tobacco billboard ban. In Oklahoma, state legislation had been introduced that banned tobacco advertisements and promotion.[27] In this context, RJR's Uptown announcement turned the embers to flames in Philadelphia. Within days of the RJR announcement, a coalition of thirty Black and Hispanic religious and community groups had organized to protest the plan. The American Cancer Society's Philadelphia chapter insisted that "promoting cigarettes among Blacks was like playing with fire, since the cancer death rate is 12 percent higher for Philadelphia Blacks than for whites."[28] The only expression of local ambivalence came, perhaps predictably, from the city's Black newspaper. Caught between dreams of increased advertising revenues from Uptown's launch and potential reader backlash, the *Philadelphia Tribune* refused to take a stand. "We don't have the right to make a choice for our readers," the paper's president stated weakly when interviewed.[29]

But Sullivan's uncompromising attack on Big Tobacco, from a Republican administration no less, threw traditional defenses radically off course. The Health secretary's brand-specific offensive did not fit the familiar scheme of attacks on the industry (that is, pitting left-leaning government regulators against right-leaning "free market" defenders). His barrage from the right did reflect just how much health experts had shifted in their anti-tobacco outlook since the early 1980s, fundamentally changing the political calculus.[30] As *Adweek* commented, "While Cabinet officers had, at times, criticized broad product categories and corporate behavior, none had ever stood up and specifically condemned a branded product. The implications—both for Sullivan personally and the black community—were far-reaching and possibly dangerous."[31] RJR complained bitterly about being singled out. But making matters hard for the tobacco industry, Sullivan carried bona fide credentials as a spokesperson for Black health, having arrived at the Bush administration after a term as president of the medical school of Morehouse, a historically Black university. His public lashing of RJR reflected a growing sense that cigarette marketing was to blame for the fact that Black men smoked at higher rates than any other demographic group, with rates of lung cancer 55 percent higher than that of their white counterparts.[32] Lung cancer, long regarded as a white male pathology, had crossed the color line.[33] As Harlem surgeon Harold Freeman commented, the ironies of caring for cancer patients in New York could be profound—working every day in a hospital dedicated to cancer care, and then walking daily past a bus stop advertising Virginia Slims. "It's terrible. . . . I looked at it in disgust. . . . How can this be?"[34] For Sullivan, too, the Uptown campaign was a direct assault on his medical work. The HHS secretary was also following in the footsteps of Ronald Reagan's own Surgeon General C. Everett Koop, who had pressed the public to confront the challenge of AIDS even when the president would not, and "who also used his highly visible post to preach against smoking."[35]

As the heat rose around Uptown, Hooks stepped forward to beat back the flames. RJR had planned for the possibility. "Should protest from the black community, the Philadelphia community at large, the legislative community or other key constituencies reach a point where broad national response is necessary," then Hooks was part of the counterattack, noted one RJR memo. "Ask Ben Hooks and others within the black community to host lunches, breakfasts, and other events with their constituents. . . . Invite the media."[36] It would be Hooks, not RJR, facing the fire. To those who criticized the civil rights group of taking tobacco money, he lashed out at what he saw as a racial double standard, insisting, "If black leaders ask for funding from the tobacco industry, we're accused of 'selling out.' Whites get billions of dollars from the same companies and for some unknown reason that's not viewed as a sellout." Hooks accused the critics of trafficking in "another form of racism."[37] In the late 1980s, the NAACP–tobacco industry partnership was growing stronger rather than weaker when the NAACP teamed with Jesse Jackson's Operation PUSH to secure industry support for Black economic development.

Industry executives proudly explained "that it's just good business to be doing business with the Black community."[38] But physicians like Alan Blum (a health consultant to the New York City schools) were disgusted, arguing that the industry had "bought the silence of black leaders on the smoking issue" and that "black leaders ought to be in the vanguard on this and not behind the times."[39] Despite the calamitous rollout, Hooks pressed on, characterizing the decision to smoke Uptown as a matter of free choice. In their efforts to stem the tide of criticism, industry defenders echoed his words across the airwaves. Their message: the NAACP's Benjamin Hooks was on their side. On CNN's *Larry King Live*, Dan Jaffe, an executive for the Association of National Advertisers, repeated Hooks's views word for word. To restrict targeted advertising in any way was to insult Black intelligence and self-determination, he said, quoting Hooks: "Buried in this line of thinking, and never really mentioned by these critics, is the rationale that blacks are not capable . . . [and] not smart enough to make up their own minds."[40]

The media battle would be lopsided and brief. The pointed critique from Sullivan had tainted Uptown's rollout; the negative media coverage mounted. Well before Uptown's promised marketing launch in February, RJR canceled the plan, giving critics a prominent victory and generating even more media coverage.[41] The industry had backed down. Insiders in other tobacco companies admitted that the rollout was disastrous—damaging not only to R. J. Reynolds but tainting the industry as a whole. As one tobacco lobbyist explained, other companies were furious with RJR for attracting Sullivan's ire. "We have been doing everything we can to keep things calm," the lobbyist noted, "but this has driven Sullivan over the edge."[42] Even with the brand launch canceled, the HHS secretary promised that he would not relent in shaming RJR for "Uptown's message."[43]

In the wake of Uptown's demise, RJR executives were backhandedly contrite, not about the brand itself but about the explicitness of its racial messaging. "Maybe, in retrospect, we would have been better off not saying we were marketing to blacks," admitted David

Fishel, the company's senior vice president of public relations. Fishel claimed that RJR was guilty only of being too upfront about an open secret within the industry: "Those were the smokers we were going after, so why shouldn't we be honest about it?"[44] For them, the sad lesson of Uptown was to keep your true intentions hidden, as the industry had done for many decades. But as the *Wall Street Journal* noted after the cancelation, the firm had debated this very question in the planning stages and made the fatal calculation that the explicit pitch was far better than the implicit messaging that had long defined urban advertising: "They would be accused of being underhanded and devious if they didn't explicitly say the brand was aimed at blacks."[45] It was a critical mistake, admitted RJR insiders. "A press release should not have been issued for the purpose of making intentions clear to the public."[46]

What RJR executives failed to understand was that the explicitness of the Uptown pitch was read as a kind of public confession, an open admission of what everyone knew but no company had so frankly admitted: menthols were aggressively, unapologetically pushed at Black people. With the demise of Uptown, the industry's tactics were now fodder for intense and highly visible debate. "RJR hasn't said they're killing the brand," commented one business professor, Rajeey Batra. "It made sense [to] kill the market test at this time, but they'll be back with the same cigarette in some form." As another marketing expert noted, the company would probably move ahead more carefully next time, modifying their tactics, and "funnel[ing] huge sums into black charities and civil rights group to quell the sort of uproar that surrounded Uptown . . . [to ensure that] these groups won't make any outcry against cigarettes."[47] Seldom before had the media, industry figures, experts, and regulators engaged in such frank assessments about the morality and tactics of targeting. In the aftermath of Uptown, local activists became more informed, but also more emboldened, more coordinated nationally, and much more effective in their fight against urban billboards. With Uptown, the exploitation at the heart of menthol brands had come fully into view.[48]

Targeting the Targeters after Uptown

After Uptown's demise, local activists were emboldened. The stealthy Chicago man who called himself Mandrake gained admirers, and other activists emulated his tactics. Well before Uptown, this "shadowy figure" had sneaked through wintery streets at dusk "with a bucket of whitewash and roller" in hand, reported *Newsweek*: "One by one, he paints over the kinds of ads that depict sultry black women smoking cigarettes or dreamboat actors with a woman in one hand and a can of malt liquor in the other." National and local media now paid increasing attention not only to Mandrake, but also to opposition groups that embodied a new style of aggressive anti-cigarette activism. Groups like the Coalition Against Billboard Advertising of Alcohol and Tobacco assailed billboards as nothing more than "24-hour pushers of legal drugs."[49] In March 1990, another vigilante act drew national press when Dallas county commissioner John Price led a group that whitewashed twenty-five billboards.[50] Price was arrested, and his case drew further media attention. In New York, Reverend Calvin Butts, pastor of the Abyssinian Baptist Church in Harlem, followed Mandrake and Price by organizing his own vigilante whitewashing attacks on liquor and cigarette billboards.[51] And back in Philadelphia, clergyman Jesse Brown, who had led the fight against Uptown, continued to speak against the industry and defend Black health. The targeted groups had grown smarter because of the controversy, and the industry was now *their* target.

The vandalism of billboards deeply troubled RJR and the industry, more so than the demise of Uptown. Billboard defacement in Black neighborhoods was not only bad press for the industry—it was an attack on their right to advertise. The lawlessness also posed the threat, if such protests should spread, that tobacco might be pushed out of view in urban neighborhoods. One commentator referred to billboards as "hidden persuaders," recycling Vance Packard's 1957 critique; but in reality, the signage was not hidden at all. With their illegal attacks, the vandals were reclaiming the public vistas, "throwing into question a basic assumption of our culture: that public space

Figure 5.4. Henry McNeil Brown, aka Mandrake, painting over a billboard in a vacant lot, circa 1992. Mandrake's vigilante protests in Chicago inspired similar tactics in other cities, spurring the national movement against tobacco and alcohol billboards in minority neighborhoods.
Credit: Photo by Steve Kagan/The LIFE Images Collection. Courtesy of Getty Images.

belongs to advertisers."[52] Congress had already legally rolled back the visibility of cigarettes—banning smoking on domestic airline flights in 1989 and contemplating new measures against the industry.[53] Sensing new danger in this new urban warfare front, industry executives framed the anti-billboard movement as part of the broad assault on freedom of speech, and on Black freedom of choice. Even as Uptown was pulled, they painted Sullivan as an enemy of these freedoms. In a Philadelphia radio debate in March 1990, one Tobacco Institute spokesperson characterized the HHS secretary as a "government bureaucrat" who was effectively saying "blacks and women cannot make the same kind of decisions that a white educated male can. That's nonsense. And it concerns a lot of people outside the industry, including Benjamin Hooks."[54] Dewitt Helm, president of the Association of National Advertisers, expanded on the "free choice" arguments on the nationally syndicated television show of John McLaughlin, accusing tobacco critics of having a "plantation mentality" and wanting a "national nanny." He revived Hooks's words: "Buried in this line of thinking and never really mentioned by these critics is the rationale that blacks are not capable of making their own free choice."[55] Defeated but unbowed, RJR's Vice President for Marketing Peter Hoult said, "We regret that a small coalition of antismoking zealots apparently believe that black smokers are somehow different" from other people.[56] This language of "free choice" became a tobacco refrain in the face of continuing attacks.

The political terrain for the tobacco industry had dramatically shifted, with industry's racial targeting practices now squarely in focus for government legislators. Emboldened members of Congress seized the opportunity to take on the industry, with some Democrats embracing the Republican HHS secretary as an urban champion. Just days after RJR relented, Cleveland's Representative Louis Stokes used Sullivan's appearance at a congressional hearing on the Health and Human Services budget to praise his response to RJR in the Uptown flare-up: "I was particularly proud of . . . your aborting the attempt by RJ Reynolds to target cigarettes towards the black community," Stokes said. "Thank god you were around and that you took the strong forceful stance you did." For Stokes and other critics in Congress, the case exemplified "how minority populations are targeted for additional death through cancer and alcoholism and things of that sort."[57]

But RJR also had allies in Congress who echoed the "free choice" warnings to stem the tide of the anti-billboard movement. In March 1990 hearings on tobacco's marketing practices, Representative Stephen Neal of Winston-Salem, North Carolina, speaking on behalf of R. J. Reynolds, referred to the company as "a bedrock industry in [his] district." "The tobacco industry is not some faceless machine pumping out packs of cigarettes," Neal insisted, but rather a large employer comprised of tens of thousands of hardworking people producing a legal product who should not be ridiculed or harassed. Industry defenders accused Sullivan of establishing a dangerous precedent for government interference in free markets and consumer choice with his condemnation of Uptown. The company was "justifiably outraged by the comments of our Secretary of Health and Human Services Louis Sullivan whose harsh speeches and comments about tobacco are unwarranted and unprecedented." Neal wondered why Sullivan was devoting so much more attention to tobacco than drug and alcohol abuse, AIDS, the elderly, the handicapped, and the homeless, especially since smoking was a matter of "individual freedom."[58]

In those same March hearings, North Carolina Representative John "Alex" McMillan also rallied to the industry's defense, portraying "targeting" in gentler terms, as a common and little-understood reality of consumer outreach. To McMillan, tobacco companies were being unfairly maligned for using standard and essential techniques used everywhere in advertising. He, too, echoed Hooks's concerns that any attempt to regulate marketing to Black consumers would be an insult to minority self-determination, and he accused the critics themselves of deceit: "those who are basically opposed to free choice in smoking should have the candor to address the issue head on . . . rather than to proceed in devious manners that basically are threats to free speech and free trade." Deflection of blame was another industry tactic used by the congressman. If cancer was Sullivan's concern, then he should devote more attention to "the health threatening aspects of *all* products, be they tobacco, alcohol, milk, dairy, prescription drugs, coffee, cholesterol, petroleum, and I could go on." But perhaps the greatest worry for McMillan and tobacco's defenders at this moment was to protect consumer-group targeting as "one of the most basic advertising and promotion principles that there is."

If you don't target your audience, you better not advertise. . . . It is
not some insidious tool as some here would undoubtedly allege. . . .
If a cigarette company targeted their product to an upper income,
WASP, male audience between the ages of 45 and 55, would there
be any clamor that we see here today? Of course not. Everyone
assumes that that target market has the capacity to make the choice
about whether or not to smoke themselves. . . . But let the target
group be a minority group or women who watch *Roseanne* or go
to tractor pulls, and automatically there are people on the anti-
smoking side who claim that these are helpless victims who do not
have the wisdom to make their own decision about whether or not
to smoke. What an insult to the individual rights of those people!
. . . Let's leave it up to the individual to make that choice and have
respect for the *capacity* of the individual to make that choice.[59]

In championing advertising and everyone's capacity for free
choice regardless of race, McMillan sought to turn the tables on
critics—accusing the anti-tobacco movement of being sanctimo-
nious, racially insensitive, and devious elites.

The Uptown debacle of 1990 had made all these public defenses
vitally necessary for an industry under siege. After decades of shrewd
marketing, one single menthol brand (Uptown, a brand that never
made it to the market) had provoked a public reckoning as never before in the history of menthol marketing. But Uptown also exposed
the many hidden players in the industry's menthol playbook, forcing them into public view for the first time. Other stark cleavages
appeared—between the representatives of tobacco states like North
Carolina and those of non-tobacco-producing states, between the
industry and the Bush administration's HHS secretary, and perhaps
most surprisingly between Black congressional representatives like
Carl Stokes, who took aim at the billboards as an assault on his community and who applauded Sullivan, and other members like Edolphus Towns and Charles Rangel of New York, who sided with Benjamin Hooks. After Uptown, the media also grew savvy to the game,
reporting that Towns and Rangel, like Hooks and the NAACP, had

Figure 5.5. Representative Edolphus Towns, D-NY, once referred to as Congress's "Marlboro Man." Towns's support for industry along with others in the Congressional Black Caucus was critical for exempting menthol cigarettes from the ban on flavored cigarettes that became law in 2009. Credit: Courtesy of the Office of the Clerk, US House of Representatives.

received large donations from the tobacco industry and built close relationships with the funders over the years.[60] Towns and Rangel would remain a particularly powerful force fighting on behalf of the industry, a vocal subset within the Black minority caucus in a House of Representatives, where tobacco's friends were still active but diminishing in numbers and political influence.[61]

Towns's stance in particular highlighted a deep division within the Congressional Black Caucus that would have lasting consequences. In a Democratic Party filled with strong industry critics like Henry Waxman, a few influential Black politicians could constrain, frustrate, and divert tobacco regulations. Their power and voice, alongside that of Hooks, was vital to the industry. In July 1990 hearings, for example, Towns worked to muddy questions of tobacco and health, introducing a range of confounding questions to cast the industry in a softer light. He distanced himself personally from cigarettes, pointing out that as a New Yorker he did not come from a tobacco-producing state and was not a smoker. Towns insisted that he only sought to be fair by not "lay[ing] all the problems of Harlem on cigarette smoking."[62] And didn't Black people know full well the risks? Towns asked Sullivan's assistant secretary, James Mason, about "studies that show that 90 to 95 percent of Americans are aware of general and specific health charges against smoking. Is there any evidence that minorities and women are less informed about these health concerns than other Americans?"[63] Many things could kill people, he said, working to distract from cigarettes as the culprit—including dirty air, starvation, and deprivation brought on by unemployment. As Towns put it, "The question is what one would like to die by." His words echoed tobacco industry talking points to a T, highlighting that the firms' strong allies in the Congressional Black Caucus could be depended upon to divert blame and sidetrack legislation harmful to the industry.

Perhaps the most important outcome of the Uptown skirmish, beyond exposing tobacco's web of supporters like Hooks and Towns, was to educate the media, newspaper readers, medical and public health experts, and the general public about Big Tobacco's strategies for maintaining a foothold in Black America. The debacle produced more public debate about these strategies than ever before. It also provoked a discussion in marketing literature about the difference between shrewd marketing and exploitation. Coca-Cola was praised, for instance, for its masterful repositioning of Sprite—geared to a market where "Blacks and Hispanics make up about one-fifth of the U.S. population but account for one-fourth of all soft-drink consumption." In two short years, its "I Like the Sprite in You" campaign "featuring homemade videos by black teenagers" had pushed the brand past 7-Up, the former leader.[64] But the literature also acknowledged the profound differences among these products. Complaints about the role of soft drink advertising in feeding child obesity was a few years off in 1990.[65] But there was the clear understanding that the cigarette was it is own class—so dangerous that even the industry would only defend it as a free choice for adults. They would never admit that they marketed to underaged teens. As for Black smokers, they maneuvered to accused opponents of intentional condescension, as if they aimed to infantilize and demean the Black smoker's capacities.

In Uptown's wake and despite these crafty maneuvers, legal scrutiny of targeted marketing tactics increased. Separate lawsuits alleged that the industry had aggressively and shrewdly targeted youth, women, and Blacks for decades. Documents in these cases also showed how tobacco industry officials and their defenders repeated the mantra that menthol smoking in Black communities was driven by adult taste preferences, not by aggressive marketing or by luring young people. In the battles to come, however, Uptown would have a lasting impact. It shifted the political and legal battlefield, energizing public health forces to move even more forcefully against targeted marketing. The industry would need Hooks, Towns, and others like them more than ever to shore up its defenses, to echo claims of menthol as a form of Black self-determination, and to characterize the anti-billboard movement as an insult to Black consumer intelligence. Menthol and the Black community were a natural fit for one another, they insisted; and racism lurked behind the effort to restrict menthol smoking. What had once been a physiological defense of menthol (it was good for colds) and then had morphed into a psychological and social defense (people were looking for safety in smoking) had how become a crassly political and racial defense.

Law, Deception, and the Crooked Road to Regulation

Louis Sullivan's self-assurance in attacking Uptown reverberated across the health professions. In contrast to earlier decades when doctors participated in cigarette advertisements assuring smokers that one brand was easier on the throat than another or endorsed menthol as therapeutic, the health professions in 1990 aligned almost unanimously against smoking. They joined health scientists, federal regulators, and even attorneys general across multiple states in decrying the cigarette's devastating effects on the body, as well as its sweeping health and economic costs. Menthol was no balm at all, only a deceiving enticement to pick up the smoking habit. With every generation, new health worries had accumulated. First it was the smoker's cough, which yielded to lung cancer concerns, and then to a stunningly vast array of breathing problems and internal diseases associated with long-term cigarette use. The costs to human life had become staggering, but the shrewd advertising continued. The industry refused to admit fault. Legal remedies were now being pursued to hold the industry accountable. As Sullivan testified on Capitol Hill, opposing Uptown was only one front in this larger battle to reduce unneeded death. "We are facing a problem when it comes to the health status of our minority communities," he said, and cigarette smoking shared a large part of the blame. As Sullivan testified on Capitol Hill, responsibility for preventable deaths fell squarely on tobacco:

> When you look at the death rate in the black community from heart disease, its one-and-a-half times higher than that of the white community. Cancer deaths are some 40 percent higher. . . . A large segment of the cancer deaths are lung cancer . . . clearly related to smoking. A large number of the deaths from heart disease are also related to smoking because of the effects of smoking on the coronary circulation and on the heart. . . . So clearly we now know irrefutably the fact that the number one preventable cause of death in our country are deaths . . . due to smoking.

To Sullivan, the free choice argument was not convincing; the industry deserved blame as pushers who could no longer feign ignorance about their product's danger. "You know, in former years, the tobacco companies had an excuse . . . 'we didn't have the data' or 'we didn't know' . . . but now we know, no question about it. To continue to push these products when we now know the death and disability resulting from them I think is unconscionable. . . . That's what led me to speak out there."⁶⁶

The legal assaults on industry marketing and deception in a growing number of liability cases developed new lines of attack: taking issue with industry's false claims that smoking is safe, questioning whether RJR used the Joe Camel cartoon image specifically to recruit minors, calling attention to specific dangerous ingredients in cigarettes, and demanding new regulations against these ingredients—among them nicotine and menthol. There were also expansive efforts by state attorneys general to force the industry to repay states for the costly health care of longtime smokers now on the Medicaid rolls.

Pressure was building in Congress to regulate cigarettes like any other dangerous drug, with attention to unsafe or toxic ingredients. In June 1990, Congress's tobacco reformer Henry Waxman proposed H.R. 5041 to give the HHS secretary sweeping new powers over tobacco products. The bill would require "the label on tobacco products to list all of the ingredients in descending order of prominence," and if the secretary found that any of the additives were unsafe, he would have the authority to reduce or eliminate the ingredients. Another provision in Waxman's bill would give HHS vast new powers to restrict the "implicit health claims" companies often used in advertising low-tar, low-nicotine, and low-smoke cigarettes. At July hearings on the bill, Kansas Representative Robert Whittaker, who had been an optometrist before running for office, emphasized that cigarettes contained a shocking number of ingredients known to be dangerous, and yet they still evaded regulation because of a "haphazard patchwork" of laws that needed repair:

> If tobacco products were to be first developed and marketed today, I cannot imagine the federal government allowing them to be sold openly and without restriction. Tobacco products contain hundreds if not thousands of chemical additives that are used as flavors and fillers. Many . . . are either known or suspected of being carcinogens

or co-carcinogens. However, no federal agency has the authority to require these additives to be disclosed or even removed if they are found to be harmful.[67]

Focusing on dangerous ingredients, Whittaker continued by pointing out the discrepancy with other product regulations. The mineral water Perrier had recent been recalled because it contained traces of benzene, yet, he argued, "the mainstream smoke in a single cigarette" contained somewhere between three and ten times the amount of benzene than an eight-ounce serving of Perrier. "I have yet not heard of a nationwide recall because of the presence of benzene in tobacco products."[68]

The attack on dangerous and deceptive ingredients opened another front in the public health war for David Kessler, the commissioner of the FDA, who set his agency's sights on nicotine. He had launched an aggressive push to bring tobacco products under FDA purview for the first time, precisely because "tobacco products function like drug delivery systems in that they contain a drug, nicotine."[69] But the focus on ingredients seemed misguided for some critics. Nicotine was the addictive agent; tobacco was the poison; menthol, it was said, was the substance that made the poison go down easier. The entire concoction was suspect, not any single ingredient by itself. But more important, the focus on nicotine risked suggesting that its removal somehow would make cigarettes less odious. In response to Whittaker's concern about benzene and the thousands of other substances in cigarettes, HHS Assistant Secretary James Mason insisted that focusing on ingredients was not the administration's primary concern. "We feel, Mr. Whittaker, that tobacco is the real culprit," he explained. "It is lethal, and we need to direct our resources fully to addressing smoking and chewing. Regulating ingredients or toxins added [to] tobacco misses the point. Nothing they put in can do more harm than the tobacco itself. The real poison is tobacco, and we really don't want to be diverted from that mission."[70]

The medical and scientific, and now political and legal, case against tobacco was expanding on multiple fronts. Individual plaintiffs had been making many of these arguments for decades, and the states—intent on recovering medical costs for the care of ailing ex-smokers—now followed suit in the 1990s. In 1988, for example, a landmark legal case was underway, launched in the name of a long-time smoker, Rose Cipollone, whose death (her husband alleged) was caused by years of market deception and a "sophisticated conspiracy to mislead."[71] Media coverage of the case focused on the industry's "motivational" and psychological studies of women, and how advertisers attempted to benefit from what they took to be women's "naivete" and emotional state. Advertisements promising better health, such as the 1954 "Just What the Doctor Ordered" campaign promoting Liggett & Myers Filters, were scrutinized anew. Personality tests conducted by McCann Erickson were entered into evidence. The firm defended itself with one simple claim: regardless of all this evidence, Rose Cipollone had the freedom to choose whether or not to continue or discontinue her habit.[72] In large part, the jury ultimately sided with Liggett—holding the firm only 20 percent culpable and choosing not to award damages for fraud.[73] Despite such industry victories, the toll of these legal battles on tobacco firms was rising. And it was not only the accumulation of individual lawsuits that did damage; now, the massive force of government was being brought to bear against the industry.

For lawmakers and critics, the cartoon figure of Joe Camel became the new public face of the tobacco industry's marketing deception and a rallying point for reform. Menthol manufacturers had been using such cartoon figures as a visual marketing strategy as far back as the 1930s, when Kool's Willie the Penguin began promising that mentholated smoking could ease the discomfort of irritated throats. Willie remained a cute branding gimmick. In the early 1960s, the scholar Henry Bullock had observed that cartoons were an effective way to avoid any type of explicit race or identity branding, reaching across the Black-white divide, for example, with a non-human mascot. In Uptown's aftermath, however, Joe Camel attracted probing attention; critics charged the industry with designing the animal figure (who had made his debut in 1987) to appeal to children. Commentators also pointed out that Joe Camel's brown skin, his wide nose, and his apparently Black facial features had all the hallmarks of a racial appeal. A 1992 study of Chicago seventh- and eighth-grade students' perceptions of such smoking icons as the Marlboro Man and Joe Camel found that Black youth did not respond as favorably as white youth to the Marlboro Man, but both groups found Joe Camel appealing.[74] As marketing consultant firm Diagnostic Research International reported to RJR, "Blacks appreciate and relate to Joe Camel; they do not relate easily to Marlboro Man."[75]

This trail of controversies (health, legal, and political) prompted the attorney general in the state of Washington to turn the entire machinery of the office to take on tobacco marketing and deceit. The state sued the industry and sought to recover the costs of caring for thousands of smokers who now depended on state programs for their care. People who had taken up smoking in the 1960s and 1970s, in the rising era of Kool, were now paying the price for their habit. By 1996 other states had begun following Washington's course, as had the US Department of Justice. Meanwhile in Congress, Senator Edward Kennedy and Representative Henry Waxman (a longtime critic of the industry) led an aggressive charge for new regulations. In the legislative minority in Congress, Democrats were fighting an uphill battle. At the FDA, the effort to regulate nicotine as a drug continued to expand as Commissioner Kessler, a Bush appointee, stayed on into the Clinton administration.[76]

The expanding legal case against killer cigarettes had one other particularly devastating effect on the industry: the lawsuits compelled the tobacco industry to produce documents in the discovery process, which then opened new vistas into the industry's decades of astute studies of consumer psychology, identity, and marketing. The inside work that had helped to build a previously unassailable empire now led to a stunning new kind of public disclosure of past practices, industry shaming, and legal liability. In these legal settings, industry insiders like Philip Morris's longtime economist Myron Johnston would be deposed and questioned about their studies and tactics over the years. As in the Cipollone case, experts in the social sciences and related health fields were called to the stand by complainants to explain how surveys, psychological studies, billboards, and race analyses had helped to create the unfolding deception.[77] In this context, a public interrogation of menthol heightened. The political tables had turned. Data from the industry's own records, which had long assisted the industry to build its markets, now helped lawyers, critics, and reform-minded policymakers to document as never before the industry's marketing tactics.

Critical attention also turned to dangerous ingredients alongside menthol's role in the industry's longtime deception. Although much of the regulatory focus was trained on nicotine manipulation to sustain addiction, menthol's expansive uses were slowly coming to light. Did menthol make it harder to quit smoking, some researchers now asked. Did it feed addiction in any way? Did its soothing quality increase the depth of inhalation? What marketing tactics led to the rising popularity of mentholated cigarette smoking among youth or African Americans? Such questions animated a growing reform-oriented public health literature. Some observers went beyond racially targeted marketing to suggest that menthol *in itself* was part of an "arsenal of weapons," newly revealed by internal documents, that were used to manipulate nicotine delivery "with extreme precision."[78] Outlets like the *Wall Street Journal* reported on the widespread use of such substances as "impact boosters"—"adding chemicals that increase the potency of the nicotine a smoker actually inhales."[79] The industry responded to attacks on menthol smoking with its own studies, insisting that no component of cigarettes had been more widely studied than menthols—and that the substance, in itself, was proven to be safe and nontoxic.[80] The results on menthol's effects were inconclusive: One independent study found, for example, decreased rather than increased inhalation by menthol smokers; another found little evidence of "central pharmacological effects."[81] Menthol smoking remained more popular than ever; but it was also squarely in the sights of reformers.

"By Any Means Necessary": Big Tobacco Reimagines Race in the 1990s

The tobacco industry's response to these legal challenges was to embrace a racial line of defense more than ever—this much is clear from the insider documents unearthed in the 1990s lawsuits. Whatever setbacks the industry faced in the Uptown controversy, the fundamentals of what can be called its Uptown marketing strategy persisted into the 1990s—redoubling its efforts in the Black market even in the face of broader regulatory challenges. Tobacco continued to build close ties with Black civic groups, to blanket urban spaces with billboards and posters, and to study African American perceptions, psychology, and smoking attitudes. In 1991, when B&W tested billboards in Atlanta, Chicago, Washington, DC, Dallas, Los Angeles, and Philadelphia, the company sought insights into "likes and dislikes," "visually aided recall," "purchase intent," and other responses by race and gender—noting, for example, that "white respondents and females were more likely to definitely remember seeing any Kool pack than black respondents and males." The company also learned that "white respondents in general were more likely to express negative feelings about the [billboard] campaign than black respondents."[82] Thirty-seven percent of Whites disliked the billboards compared to only 24 percent of Black respondents. Such tests showed a fine-grained awareness of identity and also of local markets, consumer trends, and the cultural complexities of branding.

Sponsorships of Black cultural and civic groups thrived. In New York, through 1991, Kool could be found at Black Expos, Urban League golf tournaments, and jazz benefits in Harlem. The company supported New York State Black and Puerto Rican Legislative caucus events, an international Black Writers conference, a Black arts and cultural festival, NAACP registration drives, and the West Indian Day Parade.[83] As B&W continued to cultivate its Black franchise, RJR (in the wake of the Uptown saga) was hearing from focus groups in Tampa, Florida, that its Salem imagery remained formidably white. As one report noted regarding an "all-American" poster for two surfer-themed and businessman-themed ads, "Some of the black respondents said that the surfer ad was for white people since black people don't surf. The 'Business man' ad was not particularly appealing due to its upscale impression. One respondent said it 'looks like a Donald Trump cigarette.'"[84]

Tobacco companies continued to reinforce the idea of a special menthol connection with Black smokers through various cultural marketing motifs, while also stressing menthol's sensory experience and the false promise of menthol as therapy. Identity dominated in menthol advertising, even as some of the industry's own studies found no actual differences in menthol perceptions by race. In a study of white and Black consumers in Detroit and Chicago conducted in March 1992 for Philip Morris, the firm of Marketing Perceptions found that all smokers now "expected familiar visual cues in package design and advertising that convey 'menthol,'" and that there were "few differences" between white and Black smokers. The common theme across the two groups continued to be the long-standing health appeal; they expressed similar "feelings, benefits, and descriptives of 'the menthol experience.'" It "cools the throat" and "soothes the throat." White and Black smokers alike reported that their preference for menthols was a rejection of normal cigarettes because they had a "hard, harsh," burn or were "rough on [the] throat," and left a "bad aftertaste." Interestingly, these smokers focused on menthol rather than tobacco, and "no thought [was] given to 'what is menthol' . . . where it comes from, how these are made, the interaction with tobacco."[85] In a 1997 study for R. J. Reynolds, Gene Shore Associates observed that the "menthol taste/experience" was less pharmacological than "experiential/holistic." The taste created, in the company's view, an "inner feeling of vibrancy" and was "part of the search for more experience, more awareness, and more/deeper sensations." Such marketing research continued to tell the menthol cigarette makers that identity mattered in menthol branding, as did the meanings and qualities associated with the sensations. In making menthol Black or white, imagery along with health appeal remained central.[86]

Despite finding few differences between Black and white tastes,

tobacco companies continued to generate distinctive urban terminology, urban art, and urban meanings in their approach to marketing menthols—reinforcing menthol as a Black product. In 1992
Marketing Perceptions had rejected Chill as a brand name for Philip
Morris, but learned that white and Black focus groups saw the name
as "too cold, and bring[ing] to mind 'street talk'—'chill-out.'" Three
years later, a different consulting group, Leo Burnett, learned that
Chill had a "strong positive association with hip hop culture." Ideas
that had fallen flat before could be revived, in the effort to capitalize
on new opportunities. Marketers and researchers continually studied
Black culture and Black conceptual associations, taking particular
note of generational differences and noting that "urban terminology
transcends beyond the African American community." As a hot new
trend, hip-hop caught tobacco executives' eye. As one Black man
in the study commented about Chill, "the graffiti on the pack is the
same that you would see on rap videos. . . . It's not graffiti that has no
meaning like gang symbols, this is urban art, it has meaning to it." Like
so many ideas floated within the industry, the Chill agenda itself was
never pursued, but the push into Black America with branding "tied
to identified urban smokers['] insights" remained relentless.[87] Linking
menthol to an up-to-date image of Black culture and youth identity
remained tobacco's dream and challenge; forging youthful, vibrant
Black connections, 1990s style, remained a focal point of competition
as had in the 1960s when Kool first catalyzed the inner-city race.

Brown & Williamson, R. J. Reynolds, Lorillard, and Philip Morris remained locked in battle for the loyalty of urban smokers, avidly
tracking (and shaping) consumers' racialized perceptions of different
brands. In 1994, with Kool still trailing Lorillard's Newport in overall
sales, B&W dropped its advertising firm of Campbell-Mithun-Esty
of the previous nine years in favor of Grey Advertising. "One of the
first things we have to do," said the VP at Grey, "is take a hard look at
the menthol business and the Kool franchise."[88] As B&W struggled,
Newport thrived, with a series of urban initiatives focused on studying racial gradients in menthol perception. In Philadelphia, Lorillard's
market researchers found that Kool was seen as an older man's smoke:

"I just don't see younger men smoking Kools—mostly it's old guys, people who started smoking back when cigarettes were real strong." Brand imagery remained potent. Researchers found Newport on the upswing, defying racial lines and perceived as a cigarette for people to have fun together. In contrast, informants perceived Kool as a smoke for rugged, suave men, and Salem as a menthol cigarette for tranquil white people in the country or park. Their racially inflected views of other menthol brands like "Marlboro Menthol and Camel Menthol" were almost uniformly negative, with participants indicating that these brands were "not acceptable choices for most and are seen as definitely 'for white people.'"[89]

At the moment when regulatory pressure was building and new marketing limits threatened the industry, they intensified efforts to preserve and build specific and vibrant racial markets. Restaurants, public venues, and workplaces began banning smoking; in turn, the industry studied ever more earnestly how to appeal to the smokers who were already marginalized and those who felt increasingly marginalized because of these regulations.[90] If smokers felt ostracized, how might advertising "show empathy with their plight?" asked the Melior Marketing firm in a study for Philip Morris. While race was not a central factor in these regulatory trends, Melior warned, "African-Americans are more likely to have a race-based perspective on the implications of being set aside socially." Advertising efforts in this context needed to pay attention to the fact that "Black people experience being presumptively categorized and accorded second class treatment in many public situations. One result [for advertising] is that among Black people there is an ever present watchfulness for evidences of racially-biased prejudgments, conscious or unconscious, in public circumstances." This "conditioned, self-protective wariness" should be kept in mind when formulating pitches in relation to urban ideals and Black aspirations.[91] No matter the subject, studying Black identity and Black smoking psychology remained one of tobacco's pressing marketing concerns.

Tobacco's deep economic ties to Black newspapers, politicians, and the NAACP bolstered the industry through the 1990s against charges of exploitation and aided its self-portrait as a "good corporate citizen." Philip Morris even harkened back to incidents in the 1950s, reminding its allies of how the company had stood up against racism and stood in unison with marginalized and victimized smokers. Its vice president for Corporate Affairs recounted for a gathering of lawyers at the African American National Bar Association of the time in the 1950s when the White Citizens' Council called for a boycott because the company was perceived by southern whites as too willing to hire Black workers and too keen to market to Black smokers. Their response, he said, was that Philip Morris wrote a "$1,000 check to the National Urban League." Speaking before a gathering of Black journalists seven months later, the director of Corporate Identity told the same story of how sales were "cut in half" because of the racist group's boycott, but Philip Morris "did not back down" in its support of Black opportunity.[92] The episode, exaggerating the corporation's bravery to be sure, proudly projected their unflagging commitment to "diversity in action."[93] Drawing out the meaning of this incident for the present, the company's representatives explained that "the mere fact that they [PM] 'had the nerve' to set up a program for the Black consumer market said a lot. Most White companies felt they would be labelled 'nigger companies' and would be boycotted by Whites."[94] For Philip Morris, its purported stand against the White Citizens' Council was also part of the marketing of this moment—projecting a long-standing corporate authenticity and unity with Black people and their civil rights struggles. A particularly dramatic rendering of the anecdote even came up in a court case in 2001, as the company's head of charitable giving defended the industry's outreach and bemoaned how "all sorts of allegations were levied against us." In this telling, the white boycott against the company had even "resulted in product being thrown in the streets and salesmen's cars being stoned."[95]

But in the wake of Uptown, many of these stories of past corporate heroism in the face of racism seemed transparently self-serving; they did nothing to head off the scathing critique of racially targeted marketing. Rumors once more surfaced, as they had around Kool in the 1960s, that the Ku Klux Klan was behind tobacco's conspiratorial focus on Black smokers. In response to an inquiry from folklore scholar Patricia Turner about "rumors in which the Marlboro cigarette company is ostensibly owned by the Ku Klux Klan," Thomas Lauria of the Tobacco Industry Research Committee responded, "One can assume that these lies are most-likely perpetrated by those groups or individuals who oppose tobacco interests and will say anything to disparage the industry . . . [which was] far too huge to be controlled—or even be remotely influenced—in any way by these archaic pockets of racial hatred."[96] As Turner later wrote, street informants not only claimed that the founders of Philip Morris and RJR were Klan members, but also that the "companies who market menthol cigarettes have begun to increase the menthol concentration in their formulas to accelerate the speed at which Black smokers develop lung cancer."[97] The resurgence of such rumors, alongside those explaining the rise of crack cocaine in poor Black communities as another conspiracy, reflected the "anti-tobacco mindset" that threaded through Black neighborhoods. In Los Angeles in 1991, a new brand appeared called Death—an attempt to turn the tables on the industry's shrewd messaging. Put out by a company called Death Tobacco in a Black package with a white skull and crossbones on the cover, the brand offered a stark message. "With a name like Death," said the owner Charles Southwood, "you don't really need to advertise." The Tobacco Institute dismissed the brand as a fad; but Southwood noted that he had plans to bring out a menthol version, "Green Death."[98]

No sooner had RJR withdrawn Uptown than a confidential memo leaked of RJR's plan to market another brand, Dakota, toward blue-collar women.[99] Once again, there was widespread outcry; and once again, the firm pushed back against critics, insisting that in "a declining domestic cigarette market," the fight to convince existing smokers to change brands had grown even more intense. Young adult females, age 18–24, were known to be "a major Marlboro smoker group," and RJR's intention with Dakota was to win them over. These women "should be allowed to exercise the same freedom of choice available to all other smokers," said the company. Echoing its defense of Uptown, the company insisted that it was "paternalistic at best, and, at worst,

offensive and condescending to females to imply that they are so un-
educated or weak-minded that they will react differently to marketing
than white males."[100] In Congress, the plan came under withering
attack from Representative Byron Dorgan of North Dakota, who
called the plan a "grotesque misuse" of his state's name—a state sym-
bolized by "clear air, open spaces, healthy living." He continued, "I say
to the cigarette companies, 'Don't desecrate the word Dakota with
the tar of tobacco aimed at American women. . . . If you're looking
for new names for cigarettes, call them Danger, Danger Plus, Danger
Light, Danger Menthol, . . . but don't desecrate the name Dakota . . .
to those of us who live there.'"[101]

In contrast with Benjamin Hooks's defense of Uptown in 1990, by
1994 "grassroots" vocal defenders of targeted marketing were scarce.
No women's groups came to Dakota's defense. And with the leak of
memos on tobacco's hidden relationships to Black civic leaders, such
individuals found themselves under increasing pressure to renounce
their ties with Big Tobacco. In 1994 ABC-TV reporter John Martin
challenged a Black pastor in Indiana, Charles Williams, whose Black
Expo event relied on Philip Morris support. "Tobacco money is accepted by many important Black institutions, including the Alvin Ai-
ley American Dance Theater, the NAACP, [and] the National Urban
League," explained Martin. Why then, he asked Pastor Williams, did
he and other organizations accept this money? Why did Williams use
phrases like smoking's "alleged health effects" and praised tobacco
companies as longtime "model corporate citizens"? "Does that
money affect what Black leaders say or don't say about smoking?"
Williams asked.[102] Under attack, Williams defended the company's
long-standing support for Black causes, noting that his own introduction to Philip Morris had been at an NAACP convention.

Black civic organizations with ties to Big Tobacco faced scrutiny
as never before, with the ground shifting fast under Benjamin Hooks,
the NAACP, and other groups, and the political currents tilting in
favor of local opposition, health reformers, and anti-billboard activists. Opposition to billboard advertising expanded from Chicago
to Dallas to Kansas City and beyond, feeding new coalitions among

Black clergy, local politicians, and civic groups. Industry responded as it always had, by continuing to defend its targeted advertising, supporting Black cultural activities and causes, and defending billboards on the grounds of the right to free speech. But by the mid-1990s, the anti-billboard warriors could claim numerous victories. In Mormon-dominated, smoking-averse Utah, for example, the state legislature prohibited tobacco advertising on billboards, streetcars, and buses; Mississippi also prohibited billboard and local newspaper ads for hard liquor and wine; four other states (Vermont, Maine, Alaska, and Hawaii) banned billboards outright.[103]

In a climate now highly attuned to tobacco exploitation, other companies stumbled headlong into controversy while conducting business as usual, such as when one upstart company (Star Tobacco Corporation) announced a new brand called Menthol X aimed at Black smokers. The timing, appearing not so long after Spike Lee's 1992 historical film *Malcolm X* was released, prompted another round of outrage. As one report by Philip Morris observed, the "boxes resemble a poster used to promote" the film about the assassinated Black Muslim leader, who like other adherents to Islam rejected smoking on religious grounds. Moreover, Menthol X carried an overt Black-themed design. "The pack is decorated in the [Pan-]African national flag's colors of black, red, and green which some say are symbolic of black culture."[104] The company claimed that the X motif was coincidental—only as a Roman numeral with no intended association with Malcolm X. "It was just an X," declared the company's chairman, "call us dense if you want, but [any connection to Malcolm X] didn't occur to us."[105] As with the Uptown campaign five years earlier, the pitch attracted howls of criticism for using "racial pride to lure buyers from the black community." But unlike Uptown, which never actually appeared on the market, Menthol X was marketed for a year on the East Coast before opponents took note and "California groups led the opposition."[106]

The vocal opposition to Menthol X and the Boston company's subsequent hasty retreat highlighted the increasing influence and national coordination of tobacco reform groups—a new power driven in large part by public health politics in California. In the late 1980s, Californians had passed Proposition 99, a law directing cigarette taxes toward a fund for educational media, public relations, and community outreach on tobacco's dangers. In Proposition 99's wake, the state became a leading edge of the anti-tobacco movement, and it was this West Coast campaign that mobilized against the brand.[107] As the *Los Angeles Times* framed the controversy, "With cigarette consumption falling in the United States, tobacco companies have increasingly directed their marketing at specific groups such as minorities and women."[108] As before, loss of markets drove the industry ever more intensively into race (and gender) targeting. When the Star Tobacco Corporation pulled Menthol X from the market, opponents held two news conferences—one in Boston (home of the firm and the distributor) and another in Los Angeles (the main site of protests). Representatives from an organization calling itself the National Association of African-Americans for Positive Imagery (formed in Philadelphia in the immediate wake of Uptown's demise) applauded the demise of Menthol X cigarettes as another victory for the now-national campaign against Black-themed cigarette brands.[109]

In the few years since Uptown, the Menthol X controversy showed that opposition to targeted racial marketing need not depend on a single national figure like the secretary of Health and Human Services; now, criticism of Afrocentric-themed cigarette marketing was energizing a new network to counteract the web of influencers that the industry had built to support tobacco's place in Black communities. In Boston, columnist Derrick Jackson criticized the local firm for trying to make money "by any means necessary"—a line he borrowed from Malcolm X himself. Capturing the full irony of Menthol X, Jackson also opened his essay with a 1963 quote from Malcolm X that spoke to the moment: "You are not a drug addict accidentally. Why, the white man maneuvers you into drug addiction." Jackson lambasted the firm, insisting that "a peddler who picks the motif of black liberation, whether by a miracle of subliminal, cross-cultural osmosis, ignorant random chance or a slick and sinister scheme, is seen as exploiting black people."[110] The appearance and sudden collapse of Menthol X merely solidified what had become a dominant public narrative of the 1990s: that tobacco companies (large and small) were eager to co-opt Afrocentric imagery and meanings, align themselves with great moments and figures in civil rights history, capitalize on Black pride, and even shamelessly appropriate revered Black icons—if, by doing so, they could sell a cigarette.

RJR was unbowed by the racial controversy and would make yet another bold play in the late 1990s for Black smokers with a new icon, Menthol Joe—another stunning example of how the demise of the larger market and youth-oriented appeals led companies to redouble marketing efforts in Black communities. As the *New York Times* noted, the "Joe Camel, spokes-beast to the smoking set, is trying menthol." The cartoon character now under fierce attack for its apparent appeal to youth was taking up menthol smoking—changing his name and aiming at new customers. A Paine Webber analyst commented that the new entry reflected the furious, ongoing battle for the menthol market. For RJR, mentholizing Joe Camel tried out a convenient counterargument—Menthol Joe was somehow proof that the cartoon figure was not, in fact, aimed at children. Menthol Joe was pictured doing adult things—shooting pool, riding a motorcycle, hanging out with his buddies on the front steps. "Once it [Menthol Joe] gets going, you could have a bit of a menthol war," one RJR spokesman, Frances Creighton, noted. Creighton explained the move merely in competitive terms: "The menthol smokers we talked to were very aware of Joe Camel, the personality and attitude he represents, and they liked that."[111] The campaign was conceived as a threat to Brown & Williamson's Kool. In response, B&W launched a quick response with its own B Kool campaign.

How, in this atmosphere, could Menthol Joe *not* spark outrage? Menthol Joe's appearance angered civic officials and Black clergy from North Philadelphia to South Los Angeles who blasted the cartoon figure. Once again, with California's Proposition 99 generating a steady stream of funding, the state was a hotbed of anti-tobacco public health activism. Recalling how tobacco plantations long ago had demanded the labor of African American workers, Brenda Bell

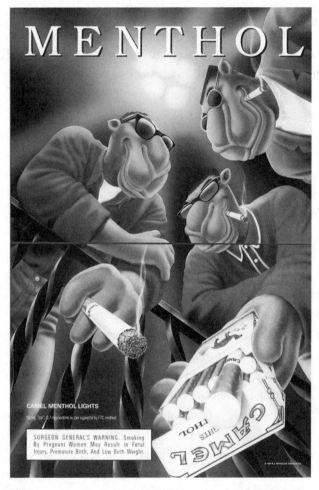

Figure 5.6. Only seven years after the Uptown controversy and the demise of the brand, a new mascot named Menthol Joe appeared. The cartoon camel was roundly attacked as an effort to target Black Americans.
Credit: From the collection of Stanford Research Into the Impact of Tobacco Advertising (tobacco .stanford.edu).

Caffee of the Sacramento-based National African American Tobacco Education Network observed, "We used to pick it, now they want us to smoke it." In other words, the racial exploitation in the tobacco fields of bygone days had returned in the new form of tobacco marketing in Black neighborhoods. "Joe Camel always looks darker when he comes to our neighborhood," Caffee observed skeptically about

Menthol Joe, "How can you believe them?" For other critics, Menthol Joe's brown facial color concerned them less than the appeal to children.[112] Led by multiple groups, the phrase "Say No to Menthol Joe" became a national rallying cry. The public legacy of Uptown, Dakota, Menthol X, and Menthol Joe was that critics were not only primed to see through the imagery and the charade, but they were organized and funded well enough to greet new launches with withering counterattacks.

However, despite the scandals, companies like RJR still had Black supporters in powerful positions who would help them withstand these attacks. Still, defending the industry was a taxing job. The wave of lawsuits and scandals had turned the once-scattered, local opposition into a formidable force. As one public relations counselor named Ofield Dukes described the situation in a March 1997 letter to RJR's vice president for Corporate Affairs, while the media had framed the battle of Philadelphia's Reverend Jesse Brown against RJR as a David and Goliath struggle, Dukes wrote, "the success of . . . Rev. Jesse Brown in Philadelphia against the corporate Goliath possibly results more from the vulnerability, timing, and circumstances of the Uptown brand marketing." In fact, "a well-funded 'Campaign for Tobacco-Free Kids' has 'resurrected' Rev. Brown from common obscurity as a hired 'human prop.'" In Dukes's view, "The highly publicized failure of Uptown . . . which now possibly haunt[s] RJR Tobacco as a ghost," even seemed to have a "psychological and social impact on RJR Tobacco's staff." The paradox, said Dukes, was that there remained plenty of quiet support for RJR in Black America. But many of Big Tobacco's supporters seemed increasingly reluctant to speak out. The trade association for the 210 Black newspapers, meanwhile, worried deeply over decreased advertising revenue if the industry pulled back. Dukes then recounted a conversation that he had had with "my good friend Bob Bogle," the publisher of Philadelphia's Black newspaper, the *Philadelphia Tribune*. According to Dukes, Bogle said, "'Rev. Jesse Brown is full of bullshit! And I told him so. He doesn't have an organization, has little respect in this city.'" As Dukes reported the conversation to RJR, "Bob said he worked with you and RJR in your marketing strategies for the Uptown brand, as you remember, and would be pleased to work with the company in clarifying issues [related to Menthol Joe] raised by Rev. Brown." He reassured the executive that relations with the Black press could be mobilized again at any time: "RJR Tobacco's corporate affairs has done an exceptional job in helping to maintain a reservoir of goodwill in the African American community for RJR Tobacco."[113] Those relationships—hidden and not nearly as critical of the tobacco industry as the mainstream media—would continue carrying the company through hard times.

The End of the Menthol Billboard

Chicago's billboard vandal Mandrake, later revealed to be Henry McNeil Brown, did not live to see the day in the late 1990s when the billboards ban came, but by the time of his death, his message defined billboard politics in cities across the country. In one 1990 Chicago City Council meeting on banning billboards, Brown called out the tactics of the tobacco industry as conniving and multipronged: first, "to sustain and expand sales to minorities, to women, and to the poor," then "to undermine the efforts to mobilize against smoking," and, perhaps most importantly, "to try to package the image of being champions of the downtrodden, the image of credibility." The scheme, he said, was a grand deceit; "the industries are the pushers of drugs of illusion."[114] By the late 1990s, Mandrake's vigilante work and Uptown had faded from the news, but the anti-billboard coalitions had gained momentum. Legal challenges for the industry expanded, for example, when in 1995 the Justice Department charged Philip Morris with using strategically placed billboards at sporting events in order to stealthily gain television exposure during fourteen baseball and fourteen football broadcasts.[115] In short, it was a tactic designed to circumvent the decades-old ban on television advertising. The company admitted no wrongdoing, but also agreed to cease advertising at televised events.

By the middle and late 1990s, these legal battles proved to be so costly for the industry that tobacco executives sought compromise.

Facing an unprecedented range of battles, including announced lawsuits from multiple states' attorneys general to recoup state expenses
for caring for former smokers, the industry began exploring ways to
cut its losses with legal settlements.[116] As Washington State Attorney
General Christine Gregoire explained in testimony before Congress
in late 1997, in April the "tobacco CEOs came to us to say they wanted
to talk about a settlement, they said they wanted to fundamentally
change the way they do business." The proposed settlement "bans
cartoon and human images such as Joe Camel or the Marlboro Man";
it also took aim at billboard, transit, and outdoor advertising.[117] In
exchange for numerous concessions, the industry sought exemption
from liability.[118] It would take a year to work out the details.

The final settlement with forty-six states, known as the Master
Settlement Agreement (MSA), signaled the demise of Joe Camel
and brought the billboard era to its end. Sweepingly, the companies
agreed to pay tens of billions of dollars to the states to cover the costly
care of former smokers. Manufacturers agreed to refrain from placing
"new outdoor advertising and transit advertising for tobacco products
in the settling States," to take down existing advertisements, and to
cease point-of-sale advertising. Beyond dropping cartoon characters,
the companies agreed not to target children in other ways or to "take
any action the primary purpose of which is to cause underage smoking." The settlement also signaled the end of decades of industry sponsorships of concerts, athletic events, or activities and events drawing
young followers. There was, however, one exception. Banned were
"any concerts (with a limited exception for two adult-oriented concert
series that have been run in the past; GPC country concerts or KOOL
jazz concerts)."[119] The internet, a powerful and emerging gateway for
advertising, was also closed. The industry also agreed not to oppose
future anti-tobacco legislation in any of the settling states and to fund
the creation of a public health foundation to promote educational and
research programs to prevent diseases associated with tobacco use.
As if to punctuate these developments, a week after the settlement
was announced, a US Supreme Court ruling handed a legal victory to
the city of Baltimore, refusing to interfere with the city's right to ban

cigarette and liquor billboard ads.[120] The court rejected free speech concerns and recognized such a ban as entirely appropriate, especially since its intent was to reduce cigarette consumption by minors.

Although the MSA marked an historic and sweeping change in the history of the cigarette, some critics—wary about the tobacco industry's ability to find new vulnerable markets—saw it as too lenient. In exchange for paying $50 billion over twenty-five years "as punishment for past actions," the industry won relief from a multitude of devastating lawsuits.[121] The formidable former Surgeon General C. Everett Koop criticized the settlement as a light penalty for decades of illegal activity, insisting that "the fine comes to a nickel a pack. An unscrupulous C.E.O. of a tobacco company could say, 'Let's market to kids all we want and raise the price by 6 cents a pack and make a fortune.'"[122]

Billboards disappeared in the wake of the settlement. Menthol Joe was no more. And yet, even as the Master Settlement Agreement altered the urban landscape, it did not fundamentally disrupt or undermine the industry's menthol market. Like the ban on TV and radio advertising nearly three decades earlier, the billboard ban was a mixed blessing. It was, after all, the television advertising ban that had led to the industry's tactical shift toward outdoor advertising in the cities, pushing cigarette advertising closer to the urban home. Critics were right to wonder what new strategies the 1998 MSA would unleash. As one legal scholar pointed out, the settlement did nothing to undo the decades of work the industry had put into building its lucrative market in Black America, for the agreement omitted "culturally specific cessation programs . . . , the funding of African-American events [to fill the space left by events] historically supported by tobacco industries . . . [and] the establishment of a Tobacco Injury Compensation Fund for addicted smokers."[123] Such community-specific smoking cessation measures or counterprogramming never made it into the settlement. Focusing primarily on children, the settlement pushed the protection of other target populations to the margins.[124] Already by the time of the settlement, for example, Philip Morris was looking into introducing Alpine menthols "into the federal prison system as we feel that there is an opportunity to grow the brand" by offering prison stores large discounts. The growth of incarceration offered new opportunities. With "the prisoner base of 85,000 . . . expanding at a rate of 8.5% per year," the captive market presented obvious appeal.[125] Newport had already established solid inroads in this burgeoning prison market, which was expanding dramatically because of increased incarceration brought about by "Tough on Crime" policies. As one journalist observed, while outdoor cigarette billboards and Joe Camel would disappear along with sponsorships at sports events, "marketing will live on."[126]

Despite the MSA, firms like RJR also continued trumpeting that they were on the side of Black smokers, and that they supported Black culture and Black social causes as they had in the 1970s and 1980s. Nurturing a web of influential Black media and political figures, its business strategies remained plain and visible. While Black media might turn a blind eye to the health ravages of cigarette smoking or help the industry to deflect blame, it was political figures like Brooklyn's US congressional Representative Edolphus Towns who were best positioned to frustrate the drive for legislative reform. Indeed, friends of the tobacco industry like Towns would prove to be crucial in the next decade when the issue of banning menthol cigarettes outright eventually rose to national prominence and the ban came up for a pivotal vote in Congress.

Meanwhile, the competition for urban smokers continued as RJR launched a new marketing appeal in New York City with its "natural" versus synthetic menthol, while simultaneously criticizing competitor B&W's new "B Kool" campaign as violating the terms of the settlement by courting underage smokers.[127] B&W rejected the RJR charge and carried on with the campaign for another two years, while themselves emulating RJR's promise of "natural" menthol.[128] Shrewdly designed images still appeared in the newspapers, even if they had been pulled from billboards and public transit. By December 1998, an advertisement in the Black *Los Angeles Sentinel* featured the

New Kool Natural, with "no artificial flavors added to the tobacco. Always a fresh, smooth taste." The image showed a clear drop of a liquid rolling off a leaf, trickling down into the Natural Menthol pack.[129]

Menthol's Great Escape and Congress's Hidden Persuaders

With the industry's supportive network severely exposed but still intact, the year 2008 set the stage for an epic effort to ban menthol cigarettes; the battle would test as never before whether the web of relationships built by Big Tobacco was strong enough to keep menthol cigarettes legal. Two decades after Uptown, the tactics of the industry were now public, legally contested, and challenged across localities, in many states, and in the federal government. The media, too, along with health professionals, reported often on the interconnected forces of influence that the industry used to maintain its markets. As well, the manipulation of nicotine and menthol to preserve those markets was widely known. By 2008, Benjamin Hooks had long since left the leadership of the NAACP; Louis Sullivan had moved on from government service to work in the health care sector. But nearly two decades after Uptown, the new menthol controversy had a familiar ring. The controversy was started this time not by a new Black-themed brand but by the rolling momentum of reformers in the US Congress, who had seized the legislative initiative and were inching toward accumulating enough power to ban menthol in cigarettes outright. This time it was not one brand, but the entire menthol market's future that hung in the balance. And as before, the division embodied by Hooks and Sullivan—over who spoke for Black health and well-being—would reemerge, this time with a reversal in outcome.

The challenge of making smoking markets had never been more difficult. Nearly one hundred years earlier, the modern competition that had been created when anti-monopoly legislation enabled the space for Kool to emerge. Now in the late 1990s, regulatory forces and litigation had wreaked such havoc on the industry that mergers offered the possibility of stability. Although menthol sales remained strong, the overall US market had been declining for decades. Cigarette smoking had been pushed from the mainstream into the margins of consumer culture, with smokers forced out of buildings, their habits increasingly stigmatized. Young people were turning away from smoking, as were older people. The litigious climate of the 1990s had put enormous legal and financial strain on companies, forcing them to consider new business plans and even to contemplate mergers that would have been unimaginable in the heyday of menthol's rise. The long, steady decline of Kool had made B&W vulnerable for a corporate takeover. So challenging had the economics of smoking become that in 2003 R. J. Reynolds acquired its longtime competitor. Now, after almost a half century of fierce brand competition vying to carve out different menthol markets (white/Black, women/men, suburban/urban), Salem and Kool sat under the same corporate roof.

For an industry in turmoil, flavored tobacco had also become a new tactic to shore up an unstable business market. Companies seized on flavors, the more extravagant the better, to captivate new markets. After all, even as overall smoking rates in the United States declined, rates of menthol smoking had held steady. Flavored tobacco seem to carry appeal, and in the 2000s companies developed new fanciful flavors of tobacco to stimulate a new demand. The newly combined company of RJR/B&W offered such brand extensions as Caribbean Chill and Midnight Berry, which one critic observed "at first hearing might be mistaken for some sort of grim drugs underworld slang," but, in fact, were colorful new brands that health campaigners feared brought glamour to nicotine addiction. They worried that these strong flavors "may mask the retch inducing effects of inhalation among first time smokers, especially young ones."[130] The industry experimented with a host of such line extension tastes, from Mocha Taboo to Sweet and Spicy. By 2004 the competition among flavored brands had grown intense — not only in the cigarette industry but also in the newly created e-cigarette industry. Companies also continued to focus on marketing that combined appeals to heritage and identity, with one Caribbean Chill advertisement showing an attractive Black women in a tropical setting, and offering to "let the alluring charm of CARIBBEAN CHILL take you on a cruise to the islands."[131]

Figure 5.7. Illinois Attorney General Lisa Madigan announces a lawsuit to stop Brown & Williamson's "Kool Mixx" campaign, 2005. Beginning in the mid-1990s, attorneys general in several states took aim at the tobacco industry's marketing, seeking to recover the costs for caring for Medicaid patients but also attacking deceitful efforts to target African American children and teenagers. Credit: Photo by Scott Olson. Courtesy of Getty Images.

Wise to these gimmicks and paying close attention to anything that seemed designed to appeal to youth, state attorneys general from Illinois, Maryland, and New York took quick legal action, forcing Brown & Williamson to end its "Kool Mixx" promotion, alleging that the hip-hop music themes violated the 1998 MSA by targeting African American children and teens. "The tobacco industry has been creative when it comes to trying to lure our children into a lifetime of addiction," declared Illinois's Attorney General Lisa Madigan. "This settlement says 'no more.' . . . For every trick the tobacco industry tries to get around the Master Settlement Agreement, we will fight back to protect the health of our children."[132]

It was clear to attorneys general, scientists, and tobacco reformers everywhere that despite the MSA, the industry seemed unbowed in its shrewd messaging. Behavioral scientist and public health scholar

Phillip Gardiner became one of the first to write an analysis of the "African Americanization" of menthol cigarettes.[133] For Gardiner and others, menthol was part of a recurring story of a defiant industry's targeting and deceit, a story that had played out again and again over many decades. The critique of menthol cigarettes resonated broadly, for it was one of a piece with other examples of urban predatory capitalism, illustrating how an oppressive and exploitative system had grown up in and around Black urban neighborhoods. Menthol's rise overlapped with the rise of "fast food oppression" and the decline of healthy food options in urban "food deserts"; part of its rise also coincided with the advent of exploitative housing policies and the rise of subprime lending and the frenzy for banks to sell unsustainable mortgages to low-income Black buyers; and the tobacco industry's tactics also mirrored other ways in which various enterprises continued to exploit the underclass created by residential segregation, and to push the boundaries on Black-specific marketing just as Uptown had done.[134] In a parallel development, a company named NitroMed would win FDA approval in 2005 for BiDil, the first drug ever approved for use specifically in self-identified Black patients.[135] Tragically, the Uptown approach had flourished, with devasting effects. For scholars like Gardiner, the vast tobacco archive allowed the story of one such enterprise to be told with evidence from the inside.

Unlike other forms of business exploitation, tobacco's practices could be seen and studied over time; and the historical evidence provided plenty of damning evidence supporting the critics' charges of sustained deceit.[136] The documents showed insiders praising menthol as a wonderful "starter product" — a way to get young smokers into the habit. They highlighted that people in the industry knew young smokers were more likely than older people to become lifelong smokers, and revealed tobacco companies' remarkable cynicism when it came to working with webs of supporters to create race-based appeals. The extraordinary resources devoted to embedding menthol and creating markets stood in stark contrast to the tobacco industry framing menthol as merely an individual preference. The evidence also pointed to a history, as documented in this volume, of employing menthol as a deceptive "therapeutic" chemical inserted to manipulate behavior and to ease initiation.[137]

Meanwhile, scientific studies in the burgeoning field of brain science suggested that menthol was far trickier than previously understood. Menthol worked not only on the throat but on the brain, one study contended.[138] Menthol, a chemical known as a terpene, was more than a flavor; as Howard Haggard had noted many decades earlier, it was a physiological deception. Like other chemicals in this class, said scientists, menthol tricks neurons in the brain, simulating the feeling of coolness by activating the same part of the brain that is triggered by cold temperatures.[139] These studies were layered atop more traditional health studies alleging the dire health implications of menthol on pregnant women.[140] Some evidence suggested that menthol's anesthetic properties made it harder for some smokers to quit. Many of these theories were speculative, but they now cast a laser-like focus on menthol as a collaborator (along with tobacco and nicotine) in the trail of cigarette death. Menthol was cast, in short, not merely as an innocuous flavor but one, in the words of historian Robert Proctor in a 2013 interview, "which makes the poison go down [easier]."[141]

These drug effects of menthol had been widely discussed ever since menthol smoking's earliest years. Menthol was a deceptive drug—a masking chemical that simulated a cooling sensation and convinced people that their airways were being opened when no such change had actually happened. For decades, menthol brands promised smokers relief from scratchy throats or congestion, weaving these claims explicitly into advertising. From the 1950s through the 1980s, however, menthol makers were pushed into a corner as regulators challenged their explicit and false therapeutic claims. It was here that menthol was reinvented as a flavor, not a drug, and therapeutic appeals became implicit. Ever since, the chemical had been discussed as a "flavor," a personal preference, and a "refreshing choice." Menthol's physiological effects had been pushed to the margins of consumer and medical debates. But now in the early twenty-first century, menthol's drug effects were resurfacing in medical and public discussion as reformers took note of menthol's share of the market and its heavy use among Black smokers, and as scientists discovered more about its chemical influence on perception. These new scientific studies of menthol's effects on the body also made their way into the courts via tobacco industry liability cases. Did menthol inhibit quitting? Did its "cooling" and numbing effect on the throat induce people to inhale more deeply? More generally, did companies use menthol to manipulate risk perception? And most important of all, did companies promote menthol as a safer cigarette?

The scientific scrutiny strengthened arguments for banning menthol. As this medical-scientific evidence pointed toward consensus, the National Cancer Institute delved into the menthol debate with a 2002 national scientific conference on the topic. Most participants concluding that the case for a ban was strong. Their findings aligned with legal arguments. Yet in 2002, politicians were not inclined to act. The industry maintained a strong network of supporters in government. The Bush administration and the Republican Congress had no appetite for new regulations; the tobacco industry still listed powerful pro-business senators and representatives as friends, including well-positioned Democrats. Yet even some tobacco supporters in Congress found it difficult to ignore the evidence of deceptive advertising, especially when evidence pointed so clearly to enticing youth.[142] Facing this new round of wrath about youth advertising, Brown & Williamson had announced in 2000 that they would discontinue the urban-focused, youth-oriented B Kool campaign featuring hip-hop music. B&W's replacement campaign was a bold and accurate slogan about the company itself—"We built the house of menthol."[143]

Banning menthol, and flavored cigarettes more generally, had been a major goal for a decade or more since the Uptown scandal—but there had been little progress. Menthols now made up over 30 percent of the US cigarette market. After the 2006 elections, with Democrats controlling the House of Representatives (though not the White House), congressional reformers now proposed sweeping federal tobacco legislation, including a comprehensive ban on characterizing flavors in cigarettes such as cherry, chocolate, and menthol, which many critics lambasted as nothing more than gimmicks designed to lure young people. But such sweeping legislation had no chance of passage.

The election of 2008—and the resulting Democratic control of the House, Senate, and White House under President Barack Obama—unleashed all of these frustrated energies. With Democrats squarely in control for the first time in decades, Henry Waxman crafted far-reaching legislation to regulate and rein in the industry. The outlines of his bill were hammered out prior to the election. Its most sweeping aspect granted FDA jurisdiction over tobacco as a drug—a designation the industry had successfully combated for the entire twentieth century. A second prong banned flavored cigarettes line extensions to Kool such as Caribbean Chill, deemed to be tasty enticements aimed at initiating young people into a life of smoking. Yet another element of the proposed legislation banned the common industry practice of handing out "loosies," or loose cigarettes, promotionally, seen as just another illegitimate method by industry to draw people—one smoke at a time—into the deadly habit.

Industry reformers had originally hoped that the bill's ban on flavored cigarettes would extend to menthols, but here the story took a predictable turn as tobacco's small cadre of Black supporters worked to save the chemical from the ban. As Waxman worked to garner support from Democrats, an all-too-familiar split appeared in the Congressional Black Caucus. Many of the main actors from the Uptown controversy two decades earlier had receded from the political stage, but not Edolphus Towns and Charles Rangel (two reliable supporters of the tobacco industry). They still remained, as did the underlying tensions. Many members of the caucus supported the ban, but some within the CBC defended menthol as a matter of free choice and as a Black preference worth championing. Bowing to their power to obstruct major tobacco reform, the version of the bill Waxman released in July 2008 treated menthol with leniency. Flavored cigarettes would be banned; menthol smokes would remain. Medical observers were outraged. But clearly, the tobacco industry's long-term cultivation of Black elected officials and organizations had paid dividends. By early 2009, shortly after Obama's inauguration, it was clear that Waxman had the votes for the landmark, if still imperfect, bill. In mid-2009, the sweeping measure became law as the Family Smoking Prevention and Tobacco Control Act.

With Congress unwilling to act against menthol, however, a new compromise had been hatched—one that would keep menthol smoking legal but deeply contested for decades to come. The 2009 law handed the power to decide its fate to the FDA. Once again, industry geared up to take on regulators to defend their lucrative product.[144] In the meantime, studies continue to highlight the lower rates of quitting by people who smoke menthols, particularly for African American and Latino smokers.

: : :

Uptown had created a stinging aftertaste. Uptown's defeat in 1990 had led to a long standoff. Despite decades of withering attacks however, by 2009, a second defeat had been averted. The menthol exemption had come about through the hard work of powerful companies and their still influential Black supporters.

Were it not for the work of men like Edolphus Towns and others in the CBC in 2009, menthol cigarettes would be banned today. The industry had cultivated these allegiances over decades, calling on them at a crucial time to save its menthol market. For Henry Waxman, with his eyes trained on the larger, long-sought prize of FDA tobacco oversight, menthol was "not a fight worth taking on." The 2009 compromise over menthol, however, set the stage for another decade of political and legal battles, as the FDA (now empowered to regulate tobacco products) became the site for legal clashes. When experts argued that menthol cigarettes made it harder to quit, the industry responded by insisting that the evidence did not support this view. Moreover, while they now admitted that cigarettes were hazardous to one's health, the companies insisted that menthol did not increase the danger. Menthol, they argued, was nothing more than a flavor. When an FDA panel was formed to consider a ban, the tobacco industry took the agency to court, alleging that the makeup of the committee had been biased. The industry claim (ultimately rejected) tied up the menthol question in courts for years.[145] And as a result of the tobacco industry's successful challenges to the FDA over the next decades, the menthol ban hung in the balance, hovering like a thick smog that would not dissipate. Critics and defenders of the tobacco industry staked out the same familiar positions that they had been articulating since Benjamin Hooks and Louis Sullivan crossed swords in 1990. Was the menthol cigarette a "sick and sinister" product fomenting a culture of cancer? Or was menthol smoking a free choice, an act of Black self-determination? There would be no clear legal answer coming from the FDA at least for another decade, a standoff that benefited industry.

Twenty years after the Uptown travesty and the ensuing demise of tobacco billboards, menthol cigarette smoking remained legal and firmly embedded in American society—but also deeply controversial and at risk for being banned. With the FDA stymied, movement toward bans picked up in cities and states, and in other countries as well. The aftertaste of Uptown still lingered. Black civic groups continued to criticize menthol producers. The tobacco industry, bowed but not broken and with well-positioned supporters, continued to defend its menthol smoking markets in Black America by any means necessary.

"And they all lived together in a little crooked house"

Conclusion

Deception by Design
The Long Road to "I Can't Breathe"

In 2020, menthol smoking collided brutally with police killing and COVID-19 deaths—linked by the resounding cry, "I can't breathe." Two metaphors come to mind in describing the grim convergence of these modern American tragedies. One is the image of a layered deception. The second is that of a web that entangled urban Black people in a long-standing deceit, too often resulting in lung disease, difficulty breathing, and slow suffocating death.

By this conclusion's writing, menthol's story of exploitation ending often with the muffled gasps for breath had taken a horrifying set of turns. Menthol's rise was never a singular, isolated affair of one industry pushing one product, resulting in one kind of deprivation and death. It was also a revealing through line in the annals of racial capitalism and urban exploitation. Then in mid-2020, tobacco-related deaths in Black America suddenly took on new meaning with the onslaught of the coronavirus pandemic and the murder of George Floyd. Black people seemed to be disproportionately victimized; deep-rooted insults now took their toll. Mr. Floyd was killed by a Minneapolis policeman who held his knee on the Black man's neck for over eight minutes ignoring his pleas, "I can't breathe." As the *New York Times* reported, his death occurred "in the waning light of a Memorial Day evening, outside a corner store known as the best place in town to find menthol cigarettes."[1] As Mr. Floyd pleaded for his life, he carried coronavirus, which was taking its own disproportionate toll on Black lives. Here was a murderer's row—culprits arrayed as if in a lineup, menthol cigarettes alongside police chokeholds and the coronavirus—all agents depriving Black people disproportionately of life and breath.

How do we make sense of this tragic convergence? What does it mean that Black lives are suffocated in incidents like this, playing out over different time scales—minutes, weeks, years, and decades? The stories of menthol, coronavirus, and policing reveal different aspects of layered exploitation, discrimination, long-term poverty, and the ills of racial capitalism. How they are conjoined sheds light on the forces that deprive Black people of breath. This conclusion looks back at menthol's road to 2020, with attention to recent calls for a ban. The question of banning menthol has taken on new urgent meaning with the rise of the e-cigarette, and because of persisting Black health crises in cities, scrutiny of the web of influencers that keeps the menthol market in place, and tragically because of COVID-19.

COVID-19—the disease caused by coronavirus—preys on pre-existing ailments, weakens the lungs, and targets disproportionately those who are afflicted by diseases like asthma, high blood pressure, and pulmonary disease, and also those who live in vulnerable conditions where viral transmission was brutally efficient. Densely populated neighborhoods, housing, and transportation networks made social distancing difficult in many contexts—from nursing homes and meatpacking plants, to prisons and congested cities. These social conditions created the context in which the pathology of COVID-19 could thrive. The deprivation that became COVID-19, then, was layered upon other unrelenting damages to Black health. These layered deprivations had taken years to produce. As historian Gregg Mitman has written, "The truth of America's urban ghettos—overcrowded conditions, decaying housing, high infant mortality, crime, poverty, and disease—began to well up in the early 1960s. So too did asthma."[2]

So it was not entirely surprising that within weeks of the first deaths from coronavirus in the United States, COVID-19 would strike Black and Latino people, the elderly, and Native Americans disproportionately. Laborers in congested workplaces, including Latinos in meatpacking plants, and nursing home residents also experienced disproportionately high rates of infection and death. But the racial disparities stood out. In June, for example, Black Americans were 6 percent of the population in Wisconsin, yet they accounted for 14 percent of the state's COVID-19 cases and 33 percent of its deaths—many residing in the larger cities, working in jobs that increased their exposure, and living in multigenerational households.[3] The same disparities appeared in state after state. The moral was clear. Pathologies of this kind were not accidental; they revealed underlying problems. In cities, they thrived amid the residual "legacies of segregation and white flight, practices of gentrification and environmental racism, and local zoning ordinances."[4] COVID-19 became embedded where asthma flourished, and asthma flourished where there was confinement and demographic concentration, noxious pollutants waging assaults on breath and life and putting people at increased risk of death.

Like asthma, the menthol cigarette also thrived in the post-1960s city, their histories coinciding tragically. But they differ in important ways. Menthol's rise tells a tale of willful exploitation, driven by a new chapter in Big Tobacco's predation. The urban setting and demographic concentration that made asthma and the coronavirus so deadly for African American communities were precisely what appealed to tobacco marketers. Urban zoning laws made it easier for the aggressive push of marketers, easing the way for billboards to flourish, for example. If bodies were transformed by these urban environments and toxins, leading to the rise of asthma rates, they were also transformed by menthol cigarette smoking, with lung pathology following close behind. Menthol cigarettes became part of the confinement of Blacks "in residential areas where we are disproportionately exposed to toxins and pollutants."[5] Over these decades, the spectrum of pulmonary complaints expanded in the city.

Then in 2020 came the infamous police choking of George Floyd, which replayed the horrific circumstances of Eric Garner's death by chokehold six years earlier; and this all happened amid the coronavirus pandemic, which was sending sufferers to hospitals, many of them dying on ventilators that strained to assist their breathing. Asthma and coronavirus, systemic racism and a police officer's knee on the neck, targeted marketing and menthol smoking all assaulted Black urban health, albeit along different time horizons. Whether over seconds, minutes, months, or decades, the effects have been devastatingly similar: African Americans struggling to breathe, gasping for air, deprived of life by forces beyond their immediate control.

The history of menthol smoking tells us that there are architects of this unequal state of affairs, exploiting lives at different scales. In the horrifying case of Mr. Floyd, we have an obvious perpetrator caught on video, but the larger system of policing also bears responsibility—a layered system that took decades to develop.[6] Like biased urban policing, the system of selling menthols also unfolded over decades. With menthol, however, there is no knee on the neck, no video. The evidence of smoking's systemic harm had been long known; but the corporate system creating the harm came more clearly to light with the lawsuits of the 1990s, and the actors involved in the slowly developing, layered tragedy became easier to see. The deprivation of breath—caused by emphysema, damaged air sacs in the lungs, chronic bronchitis, respiratory disease, and lung cancer—has been relentless and steady.[7] This book brings that exploitative and expropriative system into view by focusing on marketers, consultants, tobacco executives, and their supporting networks.[8]

The preceding pages pull back the curtain to reveal how a predatory, profit-seeking race-oriented enterprise took shape over decades, how its web of influence grew, and how its effects stretch into our time. The deprivation of breath came slowly, aided by canny deceit. Menthol smokers were never agents of truly free choices; they were subject to relentless nudges, marketing, messaging, and the skewing of choices: being offered menthol as a safer cigarette or sold menthols as a tool of Black self-determination.[9] These pages add historical texture to what tobacco consultants themselves called "exploitation" and show how these agents worked hard to manipulate the structured circumstances of the "truly disadvantaged."[10] But the prevalence of menthol in the city was not preordained. Menthol smoking was never an inherent racial taste preference. The presence of menthol cigarettes at the scene of George Floyd's murder had come about by design; it was no accident. In this book, we see how Big Tobacco sought out, cultivated, and protected these "poverty markets." We also see how marketers studied Black life and social anxieties, as well as the insecurities around health, identity, and status to understand how their product could thrive. Menthol smoking flourished not despite poverty, but precisely because marketers discovered how to exploit the vulnerabilities of Black life. Menthol smoking was manufactured by forces intent on profiting from poverty. It was *created* by forces outside the "inner city" that successfully capitalized on urban distress—doing so by an elaborate form of predation I call "pushing cool."

The Shrewd Science of Mentholated Distraction

The relationship of race and menthol is less about the pull of desire than about a relentless push, when a particular strain of predatory capitalism turned Big Tobacco's attention to these ailing cities. That relationship was historically contingent—shaped by the social circumstances and opportunities of the 1960s, by the geography and economy of cities, by how migration created (in the eyes of businesses) new markets, and by the laws and regulations that segregated and stratified these markets—closing off some opportunities, and opening up others to systemic exploitation.

Today's relationship of urban Black consumers and menthol cigarettes was made possible by the new segregation of urban Black life via white flight, urban economic decline, and the slow rise of a minority underclass. Decades ago, sociologist Doug Massey described this reality as a new American apartheid.[11] As the history of menthol smoking shows, not only were tobacco firms alert to the opportunities being created, but government action (that is, escalating but uneven tobacco regulation) also played a role in developing these

Figure C.1. We built the house of menthol. For much of its history, Brown & Williamson was proud of building the "house of menthol." The book explores how that house was fabricated and expanded over many decades with the help of a web of supporters, psychologists, marketers, and influencers. Credit: From the collection of Stanford Research Into the Impact of Tobacco Advertising (tobacco .stanford.edu).

new poverty markets. When regulators sought to deny the tobacco industry the youth market it so desperately wanted, the urban market became a new and unguarded space. Its appeal grew even more after the banning of television ads in the early 1970s. An intensive form of "inner-city" preference formation emerged. The rise of the billboard was one of the vehicles that helped tobacco companies push into this consumer market; so, too, was the special relationship that Big Tobacco created with African American publishers—Black newspapers around the nation and magazines like *Ebony*. As the preceding pages have shown, the web was spun broad, the layers of influence were thick.

The rise of Kool as a Black-identified product was the third act in menthol smoking's layered deception as the product moved through US consumer culture—a history that began with *health* deception and bent slowly in the 1960s toward urban *racial* exploitation. Menthol's feel on the throat started Kool on its way, carrying the promise of health protection. Blatant in the early decades, the promise of therapeutic relief drew smokers in. From its inception, menthol was a mask—a "perversion of sensation," to use the words of the Yale researcher Howard Haggard in the mid-1930s.[12] The chemical deceives the senses in multiple ways, convincing smokers that their airways have been opened, providing a false "cooling relief" for parched throats, and projecting a medicinal appeal. From the start, experts in the tobacco industry studied menthol's feel on the throat, and their marketing evoked the idea of physiological and health benefits for users—deceptively so. It would be decades before regulators became wise to the game. In 1941 the Federal Trade Commission ordered Brown & Williamson to "cease and desist" from explicitly claiming that "doctors know the beneficial head-clearing qualities of menthol."[13] But the industry merely moved on to implicit pitches, using different words to carry the same therapeutic message. At first, the healing message of menthol had gained traction as a balm to the "smoker's cough" in the 1930s and 1940s. In the 1950s, the discovery that smoking caused lung cancer sent worried smokers running even faster toward any cigarettes deemed "safer." Industry obliged with two false promises: filters and menthols. A second lucrative act for menthol smoking opened. Buoyed by menthol's carefully cultivated health associations, the fortunes of Kool and Salem grew. African Americans were merely one small and completely unremarkable part of the mass market for menthol, not yet the industry's primary target.

In the 1950s, the youth market beckoned. Young smokers promised greater opportunities—a long-term investment, promising years of consumption and profits. The health costs would be borne by them years down the road.

Menthol's racial transformation came in the wake of this grander deceit. It would not have been possible without the existing success of health messaging in an increasingly cancer-conscious era, without escalating regulations on youth-oriented marketing, and without an intensified, exploitative business focus on making new urban markets. While these factors built the new menthol market, it would take influencers from within the Black community to sustain it. The "African Americanization" of menthol smoking, as Phillip Gardiner called it, came as a third act of this economic and business drama—a new scheme built atop enduring health messaging. Increasingly closed off from youth consumers, tobacco companies searched for other markets to create. It was in this context that Brown & Williamson launched aggressive Kool campaigns in Black newspapers.[14] Other companies soon followed, capitalizing on health worries by deploying new advertising schemes in Black markets. At a time when mass media like *Reader's Digest* waged war against smoking, calling public attention to its dangers, the tobacco industry's increasing support for Black magazines and local newspapers with advertising dollars bought silence and ambivalence on the smoking question. At the same time, Big Tobacco expanded its support for Black education initiatives, music, fashion, and elected officials in the civil rights era, signaling respect for Black consumers and creating a visible presence for the companies in Black communities.

A vast web of "hidden persuaders" took shape, far broader than the narrow cadre of psychologists and marketers Vance Packard had decried in 1957. The web included a stunningly larger array of supporting players helping to make menthol popular—politicians, consultants, civil rights activists buoyed by industry support, the billboard owners who defended menthol ads as acts of "free speech," and the smokers themselves.[15] Whenever critics of its racial marketing have gained momentum, cigarette makers have mobilized this network. When billboards came under attack in the 1980s and 1990s and in the 1990 Uptown controversy, it was the NAACP and Benjamin Hooks who stepped forward to defend RJR's right to advertise. As Hooks insisted, it was infantilizing to suggest that Black people needed "guardian angels" to protect them.

Advocates for Black civil rights would play an oversize role in shoring up a place for menthol smoking in Black America, often defending menthol as if it were an act of Black self-determination. In the 1990s, the argument was made by Benjamin Hooks. In recent years when menthol cigarettes came under fire, the Reverend Al Sharpton stood where Hooks once did. Reacting to the New York City Council's proposed citywide ban on menthol cigarettes in 2019, the media-savvy activist lashed out at ban advocates. Leading a tobacco industry–funded organization called the National Action Network, Sharpton rallied to the defense of menthol producers using carefully crafted arguments about personal rights and freedom from surveillance, much like Hooks had done.

In a deadly irony, Sharpton defended menthol smoking with a new argument amplified for the era of Black Lives Matter and protests over unwarranted police killings of Black people. He claimed that a ban would put Black lives at risk by driving menthol smoking underground, handing police another reason to aggressively harass and potentially kill Black people. It was an argument that gained traction amid intense public concern about the police killings of innocent Black men: Michael Brown, Philando Castile, Walter Scott, and others. For years, Sharpton's network had sponsored town hall meetings in Black churches around the country in cities like Oakland, Los Angeles, and, yes, in Minneapolis, aiming to undercut any local momentum for menthol bans with this message.[16] Often the activist invoked Eric Garner, who had been strangled in 2014 by a police officer's chokehold in Staten Island, New York—killed for the crime of selling illegal cigarettes on a street corner, "loosies" as they are often known. "We don't want another Eric Garner situation," Sharpton exclaimed. A ban would drive menthol cigarette selling underground, he insisted, and produce more bootlegging on street corners. It would lead to more harassment and more deaths of Black people by police.[17]

Such artful street-level theories served one primary purpose; like menthol itself, they aim to distract from the role that influencers play in menthol consumption. As this book has shown, the scientists themselves—the psychologists, sociologists, and market researchers—have also been crucial players in these shrewd games of menthol messaging, pushing menthols while arguing that it was not the push at all but the individual's own love of menthol that explained its popularity. Meanwhile, their work had assisted the tobacco industry in creating the web by studying human psychology, tracking health fears, and understanding how poverty and anxiety drew smokers to menthol as the antidote for their worries. If Black people loved menthol, marketers argued, the reasons were internal to Black identity or the African American social condition or to inherent Black tastes, and not connected at all to the push.

In 2019 this type of argument took a bizarre genetic turn, as one study speculated, against all evidence to the contrary, that there existed "genetic factors predisposing vulnerable populations to mentholated cigarette smoking."[18] The headlines suggesting that some African Americans carried a "gene variant"—MRGPRX4, found in a group of Black people in Dallas and Washington, DC, who smoked menthols that the researchers claimed made some of them love menthol more than whites—could be read as another quiver in industry's defense. Of course, the finding was ridiculous, which even its authors admitted. Despite the blaring headlines, the study came with many caveats: only 8 percent of the Black smokers in Dallas and 5 percent of those in DC had the gene. One of the lead authors, Dennis Drayna, admitted the limits: "I don't think there are any extremely large genetic contributions" to the preference for menthol smoking, he explained. The finding, Drayna said, was "a far cry from explaining this phenomenon in its entirety."[19] Commenting on the weakness of the finding, epidemiologist Jay Kaufman observed that "the headline could have just as easily been: 'More than 98% of black menthol smokers make this choice for reasons *other than* the influence of an African-specific haplotype in MRGPRX4.'"[20]

The genetic framing paid no heed to the obvious historical and overwhelming social drivers of consumer preferences—the health promotion of menthols, the cancer "scare," the history of billboards and industry-sponsored jazz festivals, the Black-themed magazine advertisements, or the promises of status so prevalent in menthol ads. Nor could genetics explain the decades preceding menthol's rise as a Black preference, when industry had pursued a health marketing rationale before it pivoted to seeking out the Black market. The role of government regulation had no place in this genetic narrative about why some people smoke menthols more than others. Ignorant of this complex social history of predation, race, and capitalism, the study pointed to a gene. The scientific trope fit into a larger strategy of distraction—attempting to individualize the love of menthol, pointing to an imagined inner Black biology, suggesting with little evidence that science might have the answer to "why do Black people love menthol so much," and in so doing distracting our gaze from the obvious decades-long exploitation: the push.

Quitting the Menthol Markets: The Steep, Winding Road

Sharpton's defense of menthol smoking was urgently needed by the industry in 2019 because of two imminent threats to their sales—first, a wave of local initiatives to ban the sale of menthol cigarettes, and second, a larger sweeping movement by the FDA in November 2018 toward a nationwide ban. Just as HHS Secretary Louis Sullivan's assault on RJR's Uptown had caught the industry off guard in 1990, so too did FDA Commissioner Scott Gottlieb's effort—also within a business-friendly Republican administration—do the same in 2018. Gottlieb—a physician like Sullivan—stunned the industry when he announced that menthol cigarettes "represent one of the most common routes by which kids initiate on combustible cigarettes" and "disproportionately and adversely affect underserved communities."[21] The industry needed a full-throated response to the threat.

The FDA's surprise action was long in the making. Once slated for a total ban, menthol smoking's continuing legality owed much to flawed compromises crafted a decade earlier in 2009 — in which menthols had been exempted from the blanket national ban on flavored cigarettes. But the 2009 Family Smoking Prevention and Tobacco Control Act had given the FDA the power to decide the ultimate fate of menthol cigarettes. "Congress punted the question of a menthol ban to the FDA," recalled Henry Waxman, the law's chief architect. A decade of frustration followed. The law created the FDA's Tobacco Products Scientific Advisory Committee (TPSAC) to study "the impact of the use of menthol in cigarettes on the public health, including such use among children, African-Americans, Hispanics, and other racial and ethnic minorities."[22] In 2011 the TPSAC concluded that "removal of menthol from the marketplace would benefit public health in the United States," but it refrained from recommending a ban.[23] Years of litigation followed. Tobacco companies challenged the committee's legitimacy in court, charging that some of its members harbored conflicts of interest that sullied the committee's findings. In 2014 a US district court agreed that the committee lacked authority; but a 2016 federal appeals court overturned that ruling. For the next two years, the FDA—stymied by industry attacks and conflicted on the road ahead—remained reluctant to act.

As the tenth anniversary of the FDA's menthol smoking struggles neared, Gottlieb surprised observers by announcing the agency's intention to move ahead with a ban. The tobacco industry responded predictably. It claimed there was no scientific support for such an action, threatened more litigation, and mobilized its supporters.[24] Speaking from the floor of the US Senate in support of the industry, North Carolina Republican Richard Burr predicted that the proposal, if implemented, would produce dire effects. It was a slippery slope, he said, and "eerily similar to Canada a few years ago when they banned menthol products. How did they follow that up? This year they legalized cannabis."[25] He also charged that a ban would produce a massive loss in tax revenue amounting to $15.2 billion for federal, state, and local governments, "all under the belief that this will stop youth usage of tobacco. Bull!" In the face of attacks, the FDA rule-making process slowed. Gottlieb's resignation as FDA commissioner in 2019, amid an industry fight over e-cigarettes, ensured another agency retreat. It seemed the standoff between FDA and the industry would continue.

But events in 2019 surrounding e-cigarettes suddenly strengthened the hand of those calling for bans. A spate of deaths among young healthy e-cigarette users renewed calls for banning the flavored nicotine products, and these calls swept the menthol cigarette ban into the mix. The e-cigarette controversy contained eerie echoes of the early years of menthol smoking. The menthol cigarette had begun its crooked journey as a balm to the health concerns surrounding regular cigarettes. The e-cigarette was also touted as the therapeutic answer to conventional smoking. Marketers in the 1950s saw menthol smokers as people looking for solutions to their addiction, who "can neither give up smoking easily nor smoke without feeling some threat. . . . [T]hey therefore compromise. They smoke but take some measures to protect their physical well-being."[26] E-cigarettes also offered smokers a compromise: keep your nicotine use, but without the dangers of tobacco. E-cigarette firms touted their products as smoking cessation tools, promising safety that tobacco cigarettes could not offer. In shunning tobacco as an ingredient, vaping companies like Juul also avoided the messy, contentious political, health, and legal battles that afflicted the maligned tobacco market. Like menthols, the very design of e-cigarettes had been fabricated for health.

The major cigarette companies had taken note of e-cigarettes' growing popularity and had acquired significant financial interest in the upstart firm Juul.[27] In 2015 R. J. Reynolds created its own vaping company and embraced "smoking cessation" and harm reduction as a new marketing motif, seeking to diversity from the combustible cigarette market. The move was reminiscent of the rise of filters and menthol smoking in the 1950s, as companies sought to present their products as reengineered for the security and safety of smokers. RJR embraced the e-cigarette as a "major public health opportunity to reduce the harm associated with smoking."[28]

If critics saw menthol smoking as a health charade that eventually became caught up in charges of deceit, luring minors, and manipulation, they saw the e-cigarette as repeating the deception. E-cigarette messaging, its courtship of underage users, and its health effects had now become targets for reformers. By 2014, the Centers for Disease Control and Prevention estimated that about 2.4 million middle and high school students used e-cigarettes, and that 69 percent of these youth were exposed to e-cigarette ads in retail stores, on the Internet, in magazines, or on television or at the movies.[29] Soon after becoming commissioner in 2017, Gottlieb decried youth vaping, but he accepted the idea that e-cigarettes were part of the solution to smoking addiction, not a new problem.[30] Still, rising rates of minors vaping provoked growing concern.[31] Savvy social media ads posted on YouTube, Twitter, Instagram, and other platforms used by young people made the product a "runaway success." Critics learned that the e-cigarette makers played a duplicitous game. On the one hand, they benefited from a positive public image as a smoking cessation tool—one that did not damage lungs or threaten bystanders with obtrusive secondary smoke—while, on the other hand, they secretly cultivated multitudes of new young adherents to an addictive nicotine-based product.

For years, critics worried over whether the industry manipulated nicotine to feed addiction; in the e-cigarette, reformers saw a sadly familiar game of predation. Serving as FDA commissioner under Presidents G. H. W. Bush and Bill Clinton more than two decades earlier, David Kessler had sought to classify nicotine as an addictive drug in a bold effort to bring tobacco products under the agency's authority. The cigarette was little more than a nicotine-delivery device, he insisted. Speaking at a 1970s conference, Philip Morris's experts agreed. Without nicotine, "the cigarette market would collapse. P.M. [Philip Morris] would collapse, and we'd all lose our jobs and our consulting fees."[32] Yet the industry had launched a successful self-defense in response to Kessler's assertion of FDA jurisdiction. After years of litigation, the US Supreme Court sided with the tobacco industry, affirming that Congress had "created a distinct regulatory scheme for tobacco products [that] squarely rejected proposals to give the FDA jurisdiction." This had all changed in 2009, when the Obama-era law handed the FDA the authority Kessler had long sought—a stunning victory in the long quest to regulate tobacco products, flavors, and nicotine. Even so, over the next decade the FDA would pull back from nicotine oversight, watching as the new e-cigarette industry emerged.

Then came the deaths of vapers in 2019, pushing the regulation of flavors like menthol back into the public spotlight. E-cigarettes came in a range of elaborate flavorings, including menthol. The rash of lung-related deaths and pulmonary injury associated with e-cigarettes attracted national outrage. The CDC tracked 850 lung injury cases across forty-six states; twelve deaths were associated with e-cigarette use. Sixteen percent of these cases involved people under the age of eighteen. Many of the incidents involved products containing THC, the psychoactive ingredient in cannabis, but 16 percent involved products containing only nicotine. The specific chemical exposure causing these injuries and deaths remained unclear.[33] The FDA acted swiftly against Juul, issuing a warning letter and reprimanding the company for promoting its product—without agency approval—as "safer than cigarettes" (doing so, for example, in one "presentation given to youth at a school").[34] The FDA had warned another company, Electric Lotus, LLC, a year earlier against advertising its e-cigarette with flavors resembling children's cereals—with names like Cereal Treats Crunch, Cereal Treat Krispies, and Jammin Berries Blueberry Jam.[35]

The wave of deaths, in which the lungs of young e-cigarette smokers suddenly failed, tipped the scales of public outrage against the industry. Officials believed that most of the deaths involved counterfeit vaping products comprised of suspect ingredients. As Gottlieb (who had resigned as FDA commissioner months earlier) explained on CNBC's *Nightly Business Report*, the deaths seemed linked to a new type of e-cigarette that used unregulated ingredients and therefore "fell into a regulatory no-man's-land." Should all vaping products be banned, observers asked. Gottlieb warned that "banning the vaping products is probably going to exacerbate the black market for the illegal vaping products," increasing the risk of other tainted products and more lung injury. Yet Gottlieb characterized the vaping industry as "in trouble right now":

> Had they acted more responsibly when the issues around the youth epidemic first arose in 2018 . . . you wouldn't see so many people jumping on and willing to conflate these . . . lung injuries with the legally sold products. It may well be that the legally sold products are causing some of these lung injuries, but it does appear that the majority of the lung injuries are the result of illegal products.[36]

In Gottlieb's assessment, Juul and other e-cigarette producers had invited public outrage by reneging on their promises to work to limit e-cigarette use by minors—traveling down the same deceptive path as the tobacco industry had done for decades.[37] They had "behaved so badly in the first crisis," said the former commissioner, "that now that they're facing the second crisis, they're garnering very little consideration."[38]

By the fall of 2019, the movements to restrict both flavored e-cigarettes and menthol cigarettes had merged into one—with pressures building in cities, states, and at the FDA for all-out bans. E-cigarettes had come full circle, from being cast as a solution to the smoking problem to a deadly problem in itself. In the tragedies of 2019, death from lung damage came quickly and suddenly, not (as with the cigarette) with a slow progression over many years from coughs to bronchial damage to emphysema or cancer. But like menthol cigarettes, e-cigarettes were now haunted by claims that they fomented addictions, deceptively lured youth, fostered lung pathology and death, and deserved stricter regulation if not an outright immediate ban. The distinction between the e-cigarette and the cigarette blurred further when Altria (owners of Philip Morris) announced that it was taking a 35 percent interest in Juul.[39]

It was in these years that Al Sharpton's intervention, his vocal de-

fense of menthol smoking in Black communities, became vitally necessary for the industry. Arguments for bans on both e-cigarette and
tobacco-based menthol products gained momentum especially at the
state and local levels. Amid the vaping crisis, the state of Michigan announced an emergency ban on menthol vaping products, declaring its
intention to make the ban permanent. New York State had acted a day
earlier with its own statewide emergency ban on flavored vaping, followed by an announcement that the state planned to ban menthol cigarettes as well.[40] Industry defenders responded with a by now-familiar
list of concerns. Jiles Ship, president of a group called the National
Organization of Black Law Enforcement Executives (NOBLE)—with
R. J. Reynolds as a key funder—sang from the Hooks-Sharpton script,
portraying the threat to ban menthol smoking as leading toward more
Eric Garners. The bans might well be racist, exclaimed one commentator.[41] Valerie Yerger, a founding member of the African American
Tobacco Control Leadership Council, dismissed this cynical ploy. As
she and other reformers knew, the true victims were not those who
might be inconvenienced by a ban or those who might be policed
for buying black-market menthol products; the true victims were the
millions of people who currently smoked and vaped these menthol
products.[42]

The two products were joined closely in other ways, for regulators now understood that if they banned menthol vaping without also
acting against menthol cigarettes it would open the door for youth
(deprived of vaping) to migrate to menthol tobacco smoking. At the
same time, Yerger noted, "Vaping makes kids four times more likely
to start smoking combustible products. They'll go to flavored ones, so
if menthol cigarettes remain on the market, which flavored product
do you think kids will use?"[43]

Menthol's Suffocating, Resilient Web

Yoking Eric Garner's tragic death to R. J. Reynolds's menthol cause,
Sharpton equated support for menthol smoking with a stand against
police violence. In this account, menthol cigarettes were not killers

of Black people as the critics claimed. Rather, banning them criminalized daily acts and put Black lives at risk. Sharpton's group was not alone in mobilizing on this front. Another was the National Black Chamber of Commerce, whose former chair, Mark Little, insisted as early as 2011 that such a ban would produce a new illicit market that could quite possibly be "controlled by organized crime" or increase "unregulated sales to minors."[44] Sharpton pushed that argument one step further, alleging that the hostile policing of any resulting illicit market would put Black smokers at risk. It was a shrewd argument tailored to resonate with protests over police violence, but it was also another thread in the vast web that had kept menthol cigarettes entangled with urban life for so long.

But in a sign of the changing times in the menthol debates, the NAACP did not go along, rejecting Sharpton's and RJR's arguments and themselves pointing an accusing finger at Big Tobacco. Long friendly to the tobacco industry and dependent on its financial support, the civil rights organization had slowly shifted position in the few years from 2016 to 2018 to embrace a menthol ban.[45] Precisely because Black lives mattered (and Big Tobacco dollars ceased to matter as much), the organization parted ways with their occasional financers. How many Eric Garners had died slowly over many decades, deprived of air and unable to breathe not because of a police officer's chokehold, but because long-term cigarette use had slowly destroyed their lungs, their ability to breathe, and their bodies?

Two kinds of Black deaths defined the debate—by police and by cigarette. Which would prevail? In New York, the two sides squared off on the question of whether to ban menthol cigarettes. Reflecting on the massive death toll caused by targeted marketing to African Americans, Lorraine Braithwaite-Harte, the health chairman of the state's NAACP chapter, testified in favor of the New York City ban.[46] The debate between Braithwaite-Harte and Sharpton on the menthol ban put onstage two competing narratives of "I can't breathe." One of these narratives had been crafted over many decades by the tobacco industry, projecting Black masculinity and self-determination as a central aspect of menthol smoking. To be Black and male was to *smoke*

Kool and to *be* cool; to smoke menthol cigarettes was also to be "free" to do as one wished in a society where racism and barriers to progress stood in one's way. To smoke menthols was also to be one's own man, to define oneself, and to be "true" to oneself, to echo the words of one Kool advertisement.[47] This branding of Black authenticity worked not only via billboard imagery and point-of-sale messaging, but also by enlisting Black men—leaders of major organizations from the NAACP to *Ebony* magazine to major newspapers, as well as "kingfish" in communities—in these stylized defenses of Black manhood. Companies vied with one another for what one consultant called "superfly positioning," cultivating the association between menthol smoking, hard drugs, and the cultural iconography of drug dealing.[48] The rise of billboards made this message ubiquitous in the urban setting from the 1960s through the 1990s. Menthol smoking thus came to signify powerfully these men's identity. Even if everyone understood that cigarettes were dangerous, it was for men to decide whether to take the risk. Black women often figured in tobacco advertisements of menthols as supporting actors—admiring the manly smoker, participating secondarily in his pleasure, supporting his dreams. While the tobacco industry courted Black men most aggressively, now in 2019 it was a number of Black women reformers who called out the manly charade. Indeed, the new politics of banning menthol in 2019 hinged on another narrative of Black identity: Black women's defense of Black children and family. As Braithwaite-Harte wrote amid the New York banning debate, "The industry constantly needs 'replacement smokers' to keep profits soaring. That's why they target black youth in their advertising—with deadly consequences. . . . [T]his is a matter of health justice for our families, our loved ones and our children."[49]

As the 2019 New York City debate on ban menthol cigarettes unfolded, Sharpton's argument gained the upper hand. One report noted that the bill's demise was "a testament to Sharpton's political sway." Had the proposed ban made it to a full City Council vote, it would have had a veto-proof majority and wide backing, but first it needed to clear a health committee vote. Key figures on that committee echoed Sharpton's narrative, concerned "with criminalizing menthol smokers who are predominantly African-American." The bill never emerged from the committee. With the ban defeated, one assemblywoman accused Sharpton of being "bought by tobacco companies."[50] Learning from the defeat, advocates for a statewide ban sought to blunt the Sharpton defense by inserting language into proposed legislation that would bar police from stopping, questioning, or arresting a person for smoking menthol cigarettes or merely possessing a pack.[51] In hundreds of other cities, however, bans on either flavored vaping or menthol cigarettes, or both, succeeded. In November 2019, Massachusetts became the first state to ban menthol cigarettes outright. In 2020, California became the second.[52]

Sharpton's strategy illuminates much about the forces that had long assisted the tobacco industry in holding firm to its menthol smoking markets in Black communities. Sharpton's campaign in New York City also revealed the maneuvers that have been necessary to make menthol smoking "authentic," that is, to create a credible connection between Black identity and menthol cigarettes.

The city could be a deadly and suffocating place in 2020, for many reasons. The question was which forms of deadly suffocation were most urgent. At George Floyd's funeral in June 2020, it was none other than Al Sharpton who took center stage to speak eloquently about the lesson of Floyd's death. He called for justice, insisting that someone must "pay the cost" for taking Floyd's life, and that there was "intentional neglect to make people pay for taking our lives."[53] On that day of mourning, Sharpton was willing to call out the culprits who callously deprived Black men and women of life and breath, pointing to the systemic web that victimized people and subjected them to demeaning loss of life. On other occasions, however, Sharpton was part of the very web—the one created by Big Tobacco—that had woven itself around the men, women, and children of the city—tightening its grip over the decades, slowly and quietly depriving them of air.

As the anti-billboard activist who called himself Mandrake once observed, central to the industry's success in pushing and embedding these "drugs of illusion" were their deceitful claims to understand the urban Black psyche, to speak for Black people. They found Black leaders who defended their products and knew well how "to package the image of being champions of the downtrodden, the image of credibility."[54] Mandrake was right to call attention to the deception by design—the web that deprived Black people of life and breath. The drugs of illusion on urban billboards were manufactured by exploitative enterprises and designed to provide a temporary nicotine lift. They moved through urban markets guided by careful study and stealthy promotion, and aimed at slow extraction of wealth—and, indeed, surplus value—from bodies over the long haul. This menthol web was sustained by decades of studying Black urban life; and when under attack, it was defended by "credible" influencers who presented themselves as champions of the people while pushing cool on behalf of the tobacco industry. The social and economic conditions of the often struggling cities had presented ample opportunities for this brand of exploitation to flourish—a predatory system propped up over the years by uneven regulations, racial marketing, local influencers, and what some scholars have identified as "laissez-faire racism."[55] Over time—in the space of minutes, months, years, and decades—the cumulative impact of this system has been devastating, leading to disproportionate suffering that ends, all too frequently, with the plea: "I can't breathe."

Acknowledgments

The idea for this book originated in a course I have taught for nearly a decade, Race, Drugs, and Drug Policy in America, in which the menthol cigarette was only one tiny part of the complex story of how substances become part of the lives of specific consumers, and how those markets were created and sustained. In that course, the history of mentholated cigarette smoking connects to other narratives of ethnicity, commerce, and policy—opium and Chinese immigration, alcohol and stereotypes about the Irish in the nineteenth century, and the rise of OxyContin as "hillbilly heroin" over the past two decades.

Studying drugs, I have benefited greatly from working with Dov Grohsgal, an extraordinary scholar who was a teaching assistant in that course and who also worked with me on this project as a postdoctoral fellow. Dov's tireless research and ready commentary helped keep this project on track—particularly when I took on the administrative burden of chairing my department. Dov was a brilliant collaborator in the historical research, while also staying alert to the constantly unfolding debates over menthol and vaping. At earlier stages, the project also benefited from spirited research assistance from Andrew Griffin and Brittany Holom. As the project moved toward fruition, two outstanding graduate students provided exceptional assistance: Mikey McGovern, an historian of science, law, and race, gave insightful commentary on multiple chapters, while also providing detailed fact-checking to shore up the book's solid research foundations; Jay Stone, an historian of drugs in the United States, provided strong editorial insight, commented on many chapters, and also did exceptional fact-checking. Thanks to them all. Although the book has benefited from their brilliant contributions, any errors are my own.

Of the many readers, commenters, and editors who have also enriched this book by their observations and critiques, two stand out. Sincere thanks to Audra Wolfe for her always strong and steady editorial advice on the manuscript. Deep appreciation to my editor at the University of Chicago, Karen Merikangas Darling, whose insightful, patient, thoughtful, and engaged comments have made this a stronger book. It is impossible to acknowledge every last person whose insights have shaped one or another aspect of this project, but I will try. Thanks to my terrific colleagues in History of Science at Princeton, Erika Milam, Michael Gordin, Angela Creager, Graham Burnett, Katja Guenther, and Jennifer Rampling, as well as so many current and former graduate students including Genie Yoo, David Robertson, Pallavi Podapati, Felix Rietmann, Ronny Regev, Ezelle Sanford, and Wangui Muigai. There are many others, too numerous to list. At one point or another, I received brilliant suggestions and feedback from colleagues at Princeton spanning multiple units—from the Department of History and the School of Public and International Affairs to the Department of African American Studies, the Center for Health and Wellbeing, and the Mellon Initiative in Architecture and Humanities. My deep appreciation goes out to Olivier Burtin, Ruha Benjamin, Josh Guild, Tera Hunter, Leslie Gerwin, Margot Canaday, Regina Kunzel, Devanne Brookins, Betsy Armstrong, Betsy Levy Paluck, Eldar Shafir, Janet Currie, Miguel Centeno, Phil Nord, Aaron Shkuda, Devanne Brookins, Ashlie A. Sandovall, Priti Narayan, and Danielle Stewart. Others whose insights and suggestions have helped improve this work include Bridget Gurtler, Naa Oyo Kwate, and Projit Mukharji. Caley Horan provided particularly cogent remarks at an early stage of the project. Thanks to you all.

The book has also benefited from smart suggestions from colleagues at institutions where I presented this work. They include Jacqueline Goldsby, Crystal Feimster, Daphne Brooks, Gerald Jaynes, Jason Stanley, Charles Rosenberg, Allan Brandt, Lisa Berkman, Nancy Krieger, Adam Goldstein, Sharon Kaufman, Stanton Glantz, Valerie Yerger, Carol McGruder, Elena Conis, Pamela Ling, Carol Runyan, Des Runyan, Jeremy Greene, Randall Packard, Nathaniel Comfort, Mary Fissell, Marta Hanson, Dan Todes, Graham Mooney, Sam Scharff, Ayah Nuriddin, Lloyd Kramer, Don Reid, Lisa Lindsay, Terry Macintosh, Raul Necochea, Aaron Kesselheim, and Howard Koh. A sincere word of gratitude to Robert Proctor for serving as a reader for this manuscript for the publisher, as well as to a second anonymous reader.

Support for the research in this project was provided by the Princeton Center for Health and Wellbeing, as well as the Princeton Center for Digital Humanities.

Finally, I must thank (as always) my partner, Alison Isenberg, for her always loving support, pointing me often toward new things to read, asking smart insightful questions, and being a patient, ready, steady interlocutor on all aspects of history, cities, race, and American life. Thanks also to Elliot and Myla Wailoo, who indulged me by reading, listening to, and approving some of the many musings found in these pages.

Notes

Prologue

1. Purchase Point, Inc., to American Tobacco Co., "Permanent Paint Recommendation," August 31, 1976, available at Truth Tobacco Industry Documents, UCSF Library, https://www.industrydocuments.ucsf.edu/tobacco (hereafter TTID), item ID: thhx0017.

2. C. A. Jackson Jr. to C. R. McKeever, "Inspection of 30 Sheet Posters—New York Metro," April 7, 1975, TTID, item ID: gjvf0010.

3. Mason, "The New Films," 60.

4. Mason, 68.

5. William Esty Co., Inc., *Salem and "Coolness" Segment Competitors Advertising/Marketing Review*, prepared for R. J. Reynolds Tobacco Co., 1983, 6, 16, 37, TTID, item ID: mnjh0096. The poverty market data was taken by Esty from *Sales and Marketing Management* magazine, July 25, 1983, available at TTID, item ID: mnjh0096.

6. Korn, *Illusions of Reality*, 159.

Introduction

1. "Chappelle's Show—I Know Black People Pt. 1," Comedy Central, YouTube video, https://www.youtube.com/watch?v=oDcA9BIB_NQ.

2. Computer Field Express, Inc., *New Opportunities in the Menthol Cigarette Market*, Book II, prepared for Liggett & Myers, Inc., June 1971, 288, available at Truth Tobacco Industry Documents, UCSF Library, https://www.industrydocuments.ucsf.edu/tobacco (hereafter TTID), item ID: yqwn0006; on CFE, see "Computer Gets $500,000 Pact," *Broadcasting: The Businessweekly of Television and Radio*, December 15, 1969, 40.

3. For more on the role and impact of psychologists in consumerism,

311

advertising, and marketing in the United States across the twentieth century and particularly in the post–World War II era, see, for example, Horowitz, *The Anxieties of Affluence*; Samuel, *Freud on Madison Avenue*; and Packard, *The Hidden Persuaders*.

4. On targeting, see, for example, Pollay, "Targeting Youth and Concerned Smokers"; and Pollay, "The Dark Side of Seemingly 'Light' Cigarettes."

5. The logic of tobacco capitalism in relation to race has focused on racialized labor in tobacco production as well as the role of race in consumption. A recent work that smartly straddles this line in a global study is Enstad, *Cigarettes, Inc.* See also Benson, *Tobacco Capitalism*.

6. Scholarship on race, capital, marketing, and racial markets is rich and expanding. See, for example, Bay, Fabian, and Kwate, *Race and Retail*; Weems, *Desegregating the Dollar*; Connolly, *A World More Concrete*; Isenberg, *Downtown American*; and Cohen, *A Consumers' Republic*. On "predatory inclusion" in the housing market, see Taylor, *Race for Profit*; and on predatory exclusion, see Satter, *Family Properties*. On the broader cultural history of advertising, of which the story of menthol's rise is but one part, see Frank, *The Conquest of Cool*; Lears, *Fables of Abundance*; and Marchand, *Advertising the American Dream*. And for a wider view of advertising's reach, see Burke, *Lifebuoy Men and Lux Women*; and Cochran, *Chinese Medicine Men*.

7. Computer Field Express (CFE), Inc., "Highlights and Findings," in *New Opportunities in the Menthol Cigarette Market*, prepared for Liggett & Myers, Inc., June 1971, xvii, TTID, item ID: fxgn0006. For the reference to the Kool "drug franchise," see CFE, *New Opportunities in the Menthol Cigarette Market*, Book II, 344, TTID, item ID: yqwn0006.

8. CFE, 288, xvii, 288.

9. CFE, 289.

10. CFE, 289, 275, xvi.

11. Kopytoff, "The Cultural Biography of Things," 83.

12. Greene and Watkins, *Prescribed*.

13. On race-making in the drug industry, see Kahn, *Race in a Bottle*; Pollock, *Medicating Race*; Netherland and Hansen, "White Opioids"; Courtwright, "The Rise and Fall and Rise of Cocaine in the United States"; Kahn, "How a Drug Becomes 'Ethnic'"; and Inda, *Racial Prescriptions*. The scholarship on the American drug trade has grown significantly with especially important works examining the interplay of cultural politics, urbanization and suburban trends, and drug markets—both for illicit drugs like heroin, legal commodities like tranquilizers and opioids, and other substances that cross the line between licit and illicit. See, for example, Herzberg, *Happy Pills in America*; Schneider, *Smack*; Murch, *Racist Logic*; Cohen, "Jim Crow's Drug War"; Alexander, *The New Jim Crow*; Enstad, *Cigarettes, Inc.*; Courtwright, *The Age of Addiction*; and Wailoo, "OxyContin Unleashed."

14. Meryl Kornfield, Christopher Rowland, Lenny Bernstein, and Devlin

Barrett, "Purdue Pharma Agrees to Plead Guilty to Federal Criminal Charges in Settlement over Opioid Crisis," *Washington Post*, October 21, 2020, https://www .washingtonpost.com/national-security/2020/10/21/purdue-pharma-charges/.

15. The Truth Tobacco Industry Documents, referenced through this book as TTID, is "an archive of 14 million documents created by tobacco companies about their advertising, manufacturing, marketing, scientific research and political activities" that is available and searchable through a website created in 2002 by the University of California, San Francisco Library (https://www .industrydocuments.ucsf.edu/tobacco/). As the website notes, it was "built to house and provide permanent access to . . . internal corporate documents produced during litigation between the US States and the seven major tobacco industry organizations," thus providing "a view into the workings of one of the largest and most influential industries" in the nation. Such an archive is, of course, at once insight into the workings of an industry and (as all archives are) a product of a moment when power was shifting and new forms of law and social power were producing new kinds of transparency. Ann Laura Stoler's comments on colonial archives applies here as well, in this story of consumer colonization. Archives, she observes, are both things and processes—they are both "transparencies on which power relations were inscribed and [also] intricate technologies of rule in themselves." Stoler, *Along the Archival Grain*, 20.

16. Myron Johnston to Dr. Carolyn Levy, "Strange Happenings in the Menthol Market," Inter-Office Correspondence, Philip Morris U.S.A., March 20, 1985, TTID, item ID: qtmn0189.

17. Johnston to Levy.

18. Interview with "a young negro man, about thirty" in a "small cigar store newsstand in the upper west Harlem area, 145th street near Amsterdam avenue," in Elmo Roper, "Examples of Depth Interviews with Tobacco Retailers in Negro Residential Areas," in *Progress Report on Negro Market Study*, prepared for Philip Morris & Co., September 1954, 24, TTID, item ID: nqym0109. On the role of such pollsters in US society, see Igo, *The Averaged American*. On psychology and Madison Avenue advertising, see Samuel, *Freud on Madison Avenue*.

19. "Why Menthols: A Meandering Rationale Relating Certain Phenomena about Menthol Smokers to an Interesting Opportunity for Newport," Lorillard Market Research Memo, April 1970, TTID, item ID: ssvh0055.

20. Maxwell, *F.B. Eyes*, 62.

21. Among the most insightful synthetic histories produced in the aftermath of this extraordinary opening into the internal machinations of the industry are the following works: Brandt, *The Cigarette Century*; Proctor, *Golden Holocaust*; and Kessler, *A Question of Intent*. An astute study predating the Master Settlement Agreement archive is Kluger, *Ashes to Ashes*; another study based on documents revealed by whistleblowers is Glantz, Slade, Bero, Hanauer, and Barnes, *The Cigarette Papers*. See also Milov, *The Cigarette*; and Tate, *The Cigarette Wars*. While there has been no prior book-length study of menthol cigarette marketing,

two important articles have focused on the 1960s transformation in race and marketing: Gardiner, "The African Americanization of Menthol Cigarette Use in the United States"; and Jain, "'Come Up to the Kool Taste.'"

22. On the jazz festivals, I rely on a range of archives, including the Steiner Collection, University of Chicago; on the history of billboards, I use Outdoor Advertising Association of America (OAAA) Archives, David M. Rubenstein Rare Book & Manuscript Library, Duke University; on consumer psychologists like Ernest Dichter and his arch-critic, Vance Packard, I use the Ernest Dichter Papers (accession no. 2407), Hagley Museum and Library, Wilmington, Delaware; and the Vance Packard Papers (accession no. 2414), Rare Books and Manuscripts, Special Collections Library, Pennsylvania State University. On billboards and the urban marketing landscape, see Kwate, "Take One Down, Pass It Around"; and Yerger, Przewoznik, and Malone, "Racialized Geography."

23. To be sure, this is a different story of science and tobacco than many others have told. Many scholars have focused on how the industry obstructed and muddied the growing scientific consensus about the cigarette's dangers and addictiveness. The story here is different. In developing menthol, the tobacco industry cultivated social scientists not to muddy questions, but rather to study social and psychological aspects of consumer fears and behaviors so as to embed more effectively their product in consumer society. The story of menthol puts onstage a new set of scientists working for industry—the psychologists and marketing specialists who focused on the consumer psyche and helped to elevate menthol smoking to its current market dominance.

24. Henry McNeil Brown, in City Council of Chicago, Committee on Finance, July 19, 1990, Council Chambers, City Hall, Chicago, Illinois, prepared by McGuire's Reporting Service, 96, TTID, item ID: fgyj0135.

25. Duff Wilson, "Congress Passes Measure on Tobacco Regulation," *New York Times*, June 12, 2009, https://www.nytimes.com/2009/06/13/business/13 tobacco.html.

26. Stephanie Saul, "Blacks in Congress Split over Menthol Cigarettes," *New York Times*, July 25, 2008, https://www.nytimes.com/2008/07/25/business/25 menthol.html.

27. Matt Furber, Audra D. S. Burch, and Frances Robles, "What Happened in the Chaotic Moments before George Floyd Died," *New York Times*, June 10, 2020, https://www.nytimes.com/2020/05/29/us/derek-chauvin-george-floyd-worked -together.html.

Chapter One

1. The case of menthol highlights the complexities of classifying and regulating commodities. Since menthol had so many different identities, its history intersects with the story of anesthetics and antiseptics, of germ-killing agents, of hygiene products, and other more potent commodities. On the history of such commodities, see, for example, Rasmussen, *On Speed*; Tomes, *The Gospel of*

Germs; Lesch, *The First Miracle Drug*; and Schivelbusch, *Tastes of Paradise*. On BBDO, advertising, image-making, and public relations in this era, see Meyers, "Two Agencies"; Marchand, *Creating the Corporate Soul*; and Lears, *Fables of Abundance*.

2. On the cultural interests of applied physiology laboratories of the era, as these scientists sought to extend the study of the body's workings to culture, social policy, industrial hygiene, business, drugs, and commerce, see, for example, Appel, "Physiology in American Women's Colleges"; Scheffler, "The Power of Exercise and the Exercise of Power"; Sellers, "Factory as Environment"; Borell, "Organotherapy"; and Park, "Physiologists, Physicians, and Physical Educators."

3. On the formidable and growing power of the tobacco industry in the 1920s and 1930s, see Brandt, *The Cigarette Century*; Kluger, *Ashes to Ashes*; Proctor, *Golden Holocaust*; and Tilley, *The R.J. Reynolds Tobacco Co.*

4. Carl L. Spier to BBDO, June 8, 1934, available at Truth Tobacco Industry Documents, UCSF Library, https://www.industrydocuments.ucsf.edu/tobacco (hereafter TTID), item ID: szpj0137.

5. Spier to BBDO, June 8, 1934.

6. Spier to BBDO, June 8, 1934.

7. Spier to BBDO, June 8, 1934. The literature on deception as a feature of nineteenth- and twentieth-century American business, and in marketing and advertising in particular, is expansive. In the nineteenth century, see Halttunen, *Confidence Men and Painted Women*; Fabian, *Cardsharps, Dream Books, and Bucket Shops*; Cook, *The Arts of Deception*; Young, "Federal Drug and Narcotic Legislation"; and Young, *The Toadstool Millionaires*. On twentieth-century business and advertising, see Lears, *Fables of Abundance*; Ewen and Ewen, *Channels of Desire*; Stuart Ewen, *Captains of Consciousness*; and Scanlon, *The Gender and Consumer Culture Reader*. Among historians of psychology, the theme of deception has attracted considerable attention as well. See Korn, *Illusions of Reality*; and Pettit, *The Science of Deception*. On fraud in US history, see, for example, Balleisen, "Consumerism and the Reorientation of Antifraud Policy"; and Tedlow, "From Competitor to Consumer."

8. Spier to BBDO, June 8, 1934.

9. Howard W. Haggard, MD, *Report of Investigation to Determine the Physiological Effects of Menthol Derived from Smoking Kool Cigarettes*, prepared for Brown & Williamson, 1935. TTID, item ID: pgr46b00.

10. Charles Bloomingdale Jr., "Caruso's Throat Bath a Long Ceremony," *Baltimore Sun*, February 8, 1914, 6.

11. Curtis, "The Treatment of Singers' Laryngitis," 1233.

12. "The 'Cold' Season," *New York Times*, December 22, 1901, 10.

13. Heise, "Pulmonary Tuberculosis," 420.

14. Nicholls, "Observations and Deductions on the Matter of Epidemic Pneumonia," 542.

15. Brown, "The Home Medicine Closet," 195–97.

16. On drug regulation in the 1910s, 1920s, and 1930s, see Carpenter, *Reputation and Power*; see also Young, "Federal Drug and Narcotic Legislation."

17. Stewart, "Address in Medicine, the Nature and Treatment of Influenza," 249. "Inhalations of many antiseptics have been recommended for this purpose: eucalyptus and menthol have been, perhaps, among the most popular."

18. "Triumphs in Medicine and Surgery," *New York Times*, April 4, 1897, 22.

19. Alexander Graham Bell witnessed the cataract surgery of his mother-in-law in 1897, noting how the eye (under the influence of cocaine) could be operated upon as never before. See Spillane, *Cocaine*.

20. Semon, "Two Lectures," 1318. See also "Menthol and Saffrol in Neuralgias."

21. Short and Salisbury, "The Action of Cutaneous Anaesthetics," 562.

22. "Record of the Dispensing of Cocaine," 229.

23. On the 1906 law, see Johnson, "Nationalizing Regulation"; and Thomas, "Escape from the Jungle."

24. On tobacco and consumerism in the 1920s, see Brandt, *The Cigarette Century*; Tate, *Cigarette Wars*; and Proctor, *Golden Holocaust*.

25. Kluger, *Ashes to Ashes*, 52.

26. Tate, "The Little White Slaver Goes to War," in *Cigarette Wars*, 65–92.

27. Tobacco Merchants Association of the U.S., "Resume of Anti-Tobacco Activities," December 1920, 7, TTID, item ID: xrgx0096.

28. Tate, *Cigarette Wars*, 77.

29. Marguerite E. Harrison, "Sorority of Smoke on Wheels," *New York Times*, July 2, 1922, 32.

30. "A French War Prisoner," *North-China Herald and Supreme Court and Consular Gazette*, May 11, 1918, 368.

31. "Don't Let That Cold Turn into 'Flu,'" *New York Times*, March 8, 1922, 9. See also "Medical Diseases in the Mediterranean War Area."

32. "Don't Let That Cold Turn into 'Flu.'"

33. Advertisement, "Lucky Strike—It's Toasted," *Washington Post*, October 7, 1926, 19.

34. "Spuds," 52.

35. US Patent No. 1,555,580 granted to Lloyd F. Hughes, September 29, 1925. Discussed in letter from J. Granville Meyers to J. K. Crow of American Tobacco Co., February 17, 1931, TTID, item ID: zklj0012.

36. "Menthol Production in Japan," 204: "The crystal finds its chief market in America, whereas the peppermint oil is sold mostly to England."

37. "Wholesale and Retail Prices," 212.

38. "Science News," xii.

39. "Japanese Peppermint Developed," *Los Angeles Times*, August 15, 1926, G13.

40. Of course, the mentholated lozenges, ointments, and balms were only a subset of a wider array of personal hygiene products appealing to Americans

embracing new standards and ideals. For more on these themes, see Lears, *Fables of Abundance*; Marchand, *Advertising the American Dream*; and Sivulka, *Stronger Than Dirt.*

41. Advertisement, "Something New in Town from 'The Land of the Long Leaf Pine,'" *St. Louis Post-Dispatch*, March 21, 1915, 11B.

42. Advertisement, "Drives Away Cold," *Chicago Daily Tribune*, November 2, 1919, C16.

43. In 1911, for example, the Anglo-American Pharmaceutical Co. produced a Menthol and Winter Green Cream that exhibited a "pleasant-smelling, non-greasy ointment for the alleviation of rheumatic pains" at the annual meeting of the British Medical Association. *British Medical Journal* 2, no. 2647 (September 23, 1911): 355; see also Atkinson, "Some Uses of Menthol," 433.

44. Advertisement, "Stop That Cough!" *Detroit Free Press*, April 5, 1911, 7.

45. *Liberty Magazine*, November 1928.

46. Marchand, *Advertising the American Dream*; Sivulka, *Soap, Sex, and Cigarettes.*

47. Ewen, *Captains of Consciousness*, 201.

48. Advertisement, "I Am a Teacher," *Journal of Education* 104 (October 11, 1926): 319.

49. Advertisement, "Something New in Town," 11B.

50. "Letters, Notes, and Answers," 248.

51. Advertisement, "Something New in Town."

52. Advertisement, "Drives Away Cold," C16.

53. Advertisement, "Don't Let That Cold Turn into 'Flu,'" *Chicago Defender*, April 7, 1923, 18.

54. "Spuds," 55.

55. "Spuds," 107.

56. "Spuds," 107.

57. Ted Bates & Co., *Copy of a Study of Cigarette Advertising Made by J.W. Burgard, 1953*, prepared for Brown & Williamson, 1953, 49, TTID, item ID: qymm0104.

58. Ted Bates & Co., 10, 11.

59. Ted Bates & Co., 11; see also "Menthol Smokes Turnout Small," *Wall Street Journal*, March 16, 1934, 1.

60. Ted Bates & Co., *Copy of a Study*, 31, 36.

61. Ted Bates & Co., 39.

62. Ted Bates & Co., 30.

63. "I, personally, am somewhat of the opinion that probably menthol, with esthers of menthol and rum, certainly would be perfectly clear of any infringement," wrote J. A. Crowe (assistant to the president) to H. R. Hammer in the American Tobacco Research Department, J. A. Crowe to H. R. Hammer, December 7, 1932, TTID, item ID: ssdy0050.

64. "Menthol Smokes Turnout Small," 1.

65. Fox, "The Effect of Camphor, Eucalyptol and Menthol on the Nasal Mucosa."

66. J. V. Necas, Purchasing, Lorillard General Office to E. F. Harpring, Middletown Branch, March 16, 1934, TTID, item ID: qsgg0121.

67. Spier to BBDO, June 8, 1934.

68. "Do Difficulties Double Your Cigarette?" 31; letter from patent attorney J. Granville Meyers to assistant to the President J. K. Crow on American Tobacco Co., February 17, 1931, TTID, item ID: zklj0012.

69. "Do You Smoke Furiously in Excitement"; "Say What You Think of Spud Cigarettes," 59.

70. Kenyon, *Theory and Facts of Cigarette Smoking*, 28, available at TTID, item ID: yfbm0228.

71. J. A. Bradford, Comments on Publication of Axton-Fisher Tobacco Co., September 14, 1934, TTID, item ID: ltmg0179.

72. Bradford, 3.

73. Advertisement, "If You Have a Cold See Your Doctor!," *Time*, February 17, 1930, 39.

74. On the cultural prominence of germaphobia and the commercialization of microbe killers, see Tomes, *The Gospel of Germs*.

75. Howard W. Haggard to H. M. Robertson, September 17, 1934, TTID, item ID: xzpj0137.

76. Howard W. Haggard to A. L. Prichard, November 26, 1934, TTID, item ID: ttpj0137.

77. Haggard, *Report of Investigation*, 100.

78. Haggard to Prichard, November 26, 1934.

79. "Pittsburgh Cops in Raids Seeking Doped Cigarettes," *Baltimore Afro-American*, November 4, 1933, 1; "Had Doped Cigarettes," *New Journal and Guide* (Norfolk, VA), October 23, 1933, A20; Advertisement, "Hormone Twin Youthifiers," *Los Angeles Times*, February 17, 1933, A5; "Radium Water May Cost Lives of 100 Patients," *Minneapolis Star*, April 1, 1932, 11.

80. BBDO, "Notes from the Haggard-Henderson Report," May 23, 1935, TTID, item ID: jjfv0133.

81. Carleton Spier to Howard W. Haggard, April 8, 1936, TTID, item ID: xjfv0133.

82. Howard W. Haggard to Carleton L. Spier, April 15, 1936, TTID, item ID: hjfv0133.

83. Howard Haggard to H. M. Robertson, Brown & Williamson, April 18, 1936, TTID, item ID: zxfv0133.

84. Carleton Spier to Howard W. Haggard, April 17, 1936, TTID, item ID: gjfv0133; and Haggard to Spier, April 18, 1936, TTID, item ID: fjfv0133.

85. Carleton Spier to Howard W. Haggard, May 19, 1936, TTID, item ID: rxfv0133.

86. H. M. Robertson to Howard W. Haggard, April 22, 1936, TTID, item ID: txfv0133.

87. Brandt, *The Cigarette Century*, 81; Kluger, *Ashes to Ashes*, 78. As Kluger has noted, "Bernays was allowed to engage the services of psychiatrist A. A. Brill, who counseled Bernays that cigarettes were symbols of freedom for women as well as 'a sublimation of erotic eroticism; holding a cigarette in the mouth excites the oral zone.' As a phallic symbol, men ought to be offering it to women, not the other way around."

88. Advertisement, "What You Must Do to Get Mouth-Happiness," *Time*, June 27, 1932, 31.

89. Advertisement, "Do You Smoke More When the Gang Gathers?" *Literary Digest*, November 2, 1929, 31.

90. Ted Bates & Co., *Copy of a Study*.

91. Edna K. Freeman, Department of Public Relations to Ruby Hurley, April 9, 1952 letter with "Digest of Activity in Campaign Against 'Nigger Head' trademark—NAACP," "Publicity Protests 'Nigger Head Shrimp . . .'" 1942–1953, NAACP Papers, Library of Congress, Manuscript Division. See also Proctor, "The Triumph of the Cigarette," in *Golden Holocaust*, 84.

92. Advertisement, "Do You Smoke Anxiety Away?" *Time*, February 18, 1929, 33; Advertisement, "Do Long Hours Unleash Your Cigarette Appetite?" *Literary Digest* (March 15, 1930): 43.

93. Advertisement, "All Whittington Had Was a Cat," *Literary Digest*, 1936, 6.

94. Managing Director of the Psychological Corp. to S. Clay Williams, President, RJR, August 7, 1937, TTID, item ID: qrkp0081.

95. On the Psychological Corporation, applied psychology, and ideals for the "rational control of human behavior" at this moment in the cultural history of psychology, see "The Psychological Corporation"; on "rational control," see Morawski, "Organizing Knowledge and Behavior at Yale's Institute of Human Relations"; Capshew, *Psychologists on the March*; and Loss, "Reorganizing Higher Education in the Shadow of the Great War."

96. On diethylene glycol and glycerin, see Proctor, *Golden Holocaust*, 175; "Activities of the Research Department for 1938," from Research Director to O. H. Chalkley, President, Philip Morris, January 1939, TTID, item ID: srd38e00.

97. "Activities of the Research Department for 1938"; see also "Research Department: Proposed Activities, September 1936–1937," Philip Morris, August 20, 1936, TTID, item ID: pju76b00.

98. "Research Department: Proposed Activities, September 1936–1937."

99. Blum, "When 'More Doctors Smoked Camels.'"

100. Dr. Sol Wiener Ginsburg, MD, to Dr. Wendell Phillips, September 14, 1934, TTID, item ID: pkyh0112.

101. Compton Advertising, Inc., formerly Blackman Advertising, Inc., "Notes

taken in talk with Dr. Hamner in Richmond, VA, February 15, 1937," March 3, 1937, TTID, item ID: ysph0139.

102. *Modern Medicine*, October 1938. See "Clipping Appearing in October Issue of MODERN MEDICINE," Brown & Williamson Records, October 1938, TTID, item ID: peu04f00.

103. George Cooper to Othoway Chalkey, December 2, 1938, TTID, item ID: kxfv0133.

104. On the FTC and FCC, see, for example, Ringold and Calfee, "The Informational Content of Cigarette Advertising: 1926–1986."

105. On the tar derby era, see Brandt, *The Cigarette Century*, 245–48.

106. Young, "Federal Drug and Narcotic Legislation." See also Kay, "Healthy Public Relations"; and (on a subsequent, related scandal) Swann, "The 1941 Sulfathiazole Disaster."

107. Brandt, *The Cigarette Century*, 242.

108. "Research Department, Proposed Activities, September 1936–1937," 1.

109. "Research Department, Proposed Activities, September 1936–1937," 3.

110. Wootten, "Big 3 Gain in Cigarette Sales," 60. As Wootten put it, "More people are smoking . . . people (individually) are smoking more . . . millions of new smokers acquired the cigarette habit during the war—and the horizon for the cigarette is no more discernible than Shangri-la."

111. Brown & Williamson 1940 Campaign: "Switch When Sick," Stanford University, Research into the Impact of Tobacco Advertising website: http://tobacco.stanford.edu/tobacco_main/images.php?token2=fm_st072.php&token1=fm_img1732.php&theme_file=fm_mt005.php&theme_name=Menthol%20Medicates&subtheme_name=Switch%20When%20Sick.

112. Daniel Crean, *The Cigarette Racket: You Are Being Drugged!*, 22, TTID, item ID: sgyl0056.

113. Haggard, *Report of Investigation*, 99.

114. Geo. F. Gouge, BBDO Interoffice Memorandum, subject: Dr. Haggard article on Menthol, May 26, 1938, TTID, item ID: znlg0138.

115. Haggard and Greenberg, "Concentration of Menthol in the Smoke from Mentholated Cigarets."

Chapter Two

1. Packard, *Hidden Persuaders*, 3.

2. "On Radio," *New York Times*, May 6, 1957, 41.

3. Kreuzer, Prechtl, and Steiner, *A Tiger in the Tank*.

4. "Conversation" [between Vance Packard and Dr. Ernest Dichter, moderated by Clifton Fadiman], NBC Radio Transcript, May 6, 1957, Vance Packard Papers, Penn State University Archives, box 21, folder 15, "T.V.-Radio, 1957–1958."

5. Packard, *Hidden Persuaders*, 266.

6. "Conversation," NBC Radio Transcript, May 6, 1957, Vance Packard Papers, 6.

7. Dichter, "A Psychological View of Advertising Effectiveness." See also Britt, "The Strategy of Consumer Motivation."

8. "The human mind can be seen as a projector and a receiver of the things which surround it," wrote Dichter in 1952—focusing on the "tyranny of things." "The Psychology of T.V. Commercials—A Research Study," undated, box 6, folder 112C, Ernest Dichter Papers, Series I: Research Proposals and Reports (accession no. 2407A), Hagley Museum and Library, Wilmington, Delaware. For more on Dichter and motivation research, see Samuel, *Freud on Madison Avenue*; Kreuzer, Prechtl, and Steiner, *A Tiger in the Tank*; and Herman, *The Romance of American Psychology*.

9. Dichter, "The Psychology of T.V. Commercials."

10. Horowitz, *Anxieties of Affluence.*

11. Horowitz.

12. "NBC Radio: Conversation—The Art of Persuasion," May 6, 1957.

13. Britt, "The Strategy of Consumer Motivation," 671–74.

14. Dichter, "Why People Smoke," 128–30.

15. James C. Goodson, "Caprice as an Element of Cigarette Brand Selection," memo prepared for Brown & Williamson Co., October 9, 1953, available at Truth Tobacco Industry Documents, UCSF Library, https://www.industrydocuments.ucsf.edu/tobacco (hereafter TTID), item ID: ggvh0141.

16. "The Uproar in Cigarettes," *Fortune*, December 1953, 164, available at TTID, item ID: psyf0189.

17. Smith, "Product Differentiation and Market Segmentation."

18. Goodson, "Caprice," 7.

19. Igo, *The Averaged American.* See particularly chapter 3, "Polling the Average Populace."

20. Elmo Roper, *A Study of People's Cigarette Smoking Habits and Attitudes*, vol. 1, prepared for Philip Morris & Co., August 1953, ix–x, TTID, item ID: rqym0109.

21. Hoffmann, Djordjevic, and Brunnemann, "Changes in Cigarette Design and Composition," 11.

22. Wootten, "Cigarette Sales 2% under 1952."

23. Elmo Roper, "Special Tabulations of Benchmark Study," in *Progress Report on Negro Market Study*, September 1954, 3–8, TTID, item ID: nqym0109.

24. Roper, *Study of People's Cigarette Smoking Habits*, vol. 1, viii, xii.

25. Roper, *Progress Report on Negro Market Study*, 7.

26. Roper, *Study of People's Cigarette Smoking Habits*, vol. 1, vii–viii.

27. Wynder and Graham, "Tobacco Smoking as a Possible Etiologic Factor in Bronchiogenic Carcinoma."

28. Doll and Hill, "A Study of the Aetiology of Carcinoma of the Lung."

29. Glienka and Kress, "The Cancer Patient."

30. Schneider, "If You See Blood."

31. Norr, "Cancer by the Carton."

32. Walter Winchell, *Walter Winchell*, ABC Network, December 13, 1954. Transcript appears in "How the News Has Been Handled in Periodical and Radio," 3, TTID, item ID: zyfp0042.

33. Wootten, "In Changing Cigarette Market . . . ," 27, available at TTID, item ID: kpvn0011.

34. "Beyond Any Doubt," 63.

35. Winchell, *Walter Winchell*, December 13, 1954.

36. "Cigs and Cancer," available at TTID, item ID: zgnb0015; "Tobacco Trade Maps War on Cancer Scare," *New York Herald Tribune*, December 31, 1953, 18, available at TTID, item ID: kfpw0000. See also Brandt, "The Causal Conundrum," in *Cigarette Century*; and Proctor, *Golden Holocaust*.

37. See Brandt, *Cigarette Century*; Proctor, *Golden Holocaust*; "Tobacco Industry, Upset by Link to Cancer, Starts Own Research," *New York Times*, January 4, 1954, 1, 27; and "Tobacco Firms Set Up Cancer Research Board," *New York Herald Tribune*, January 4, 1954, 1, 11.

38. Packard, *Hidden Persuaders*, 51–52.

39. Ted Bates & Co., *Copy of a Study of Cigarette Advertising Made by J.W. Burgard, 1953*, prepared for Brown & Williamson, 1953, 58, TTID, item ID: qymm0104.

40. Pollay Ads for Brown & Williamson, Willie the Penguin, 1951, TTID, item ID: xnxl0037.

41. By 1953 a new tactic emerged as B&W offered relief from a psychological habit: "Don't be chained by the hot cigarette habit." Ted Bates & Co., *Copy of a Study*, 50.

42. On Bates winning the Kool account, see "News in the Advertising Field," *New York Herald Tribune*, April 9, 1948, 33. On believable copy, see Ted Bates & Co., *Copy of a Study*, 58.

43. "Cigarette Scare," 62.

44. Harry M. Wootten, *Confidential Report on Quarterly Cigarette Output by Brands*, 1954, 1, 8, TTID, item ID: jnpk0034; see also Wootten, "In Changing Cigarette Market . . ."

45. Packard, *Hidden Persuaders*, 52.

46. "Uproar in Cigarettes," 133; Wootten, *Confidential Report*.

47. Ganger, "New Trends in the Cigarette Field: A Talk Delivered by Robert M. Ganger, President, P. Lorillard Tobacco Co., before the New York Society of Security Analysts," November 13, 1952, 4, TTID, item ID: yfw60a00.

48. Roper, *Study of People's Cigarette Smoking Habits*, vol. 1, xvii. See also vol. 3.

49. Earl B. Chamberlain to R. J. Reynolds, April 23, 1954, TTID, item ID: mco23a00.

50. Von Pauli, "A Psychologist Looks at the Cigarette Scare," 63, available at TTID, item ID: qnjv0015.

51. "Uproar in Cigarettes," 164.

52. Packard, *Hidden Persuaders*, 32.

53. Ted Bates & Co., *Copy of a Study*.

54. Ted Bates & Co.

55. "Cigarette Scare," 68.

56. Wootten, *Confidential Report*; see also Wootten, "In Changing Cigarette Market . . ."; see also "Uproar in Cigarettes," 133.

57. Wootten, *Confidential Report*; see also Wootten, "In Changing Cigarette Market . . ."

58. Roper, "Special Tabulations of Benchmark Study," 3.

59. William Esty Co., radio ad copy, July 31, 1957, 3, TTID, item ID: gqfc0102.

60. *Brand Name for a Mentholated Cigarette*, 1959, 6, TTID, item ID: qsmk0190.

61. Letter from George Weissman to Joseph F. Cullman, March 12, 1956, TTID, item ID: qngp0105.

62. Elmo Roper, *A Look at the Cigarette Industry and Philip Morris' Role in It*, prepared for Philip Morris & Co., February 26, 1957, TTID, item ID: ynkc0122.

63. George Weissman, Philip Morris memo, "Status of Project Dups," March 12, 1956, 2, TTID, item ID: qngp0105.

64. Roper, *A Look at the Cigarette Industry*, 26.

65. Liggett & Myers Tobacco Co., Inc., *1957 Annual Report*, 1958, 12, TTID, item ID: xkkb0175.

66. Roper, xv.

67. "Negroes Get More 'Brand Conscious' as Income Rises," 30.

68. Roper, *Study of People's Cigarette Smoking Habits*, vol. 1, xv–xvi.

69. Roper, vol. 1, xvi.

70. Roper, *Progress Report on Negro Market Study*, iv.

71. Roper, ii, 15.

72. Roper, 24, 28. Several other respondents mentioned the impact of Arthur Godfrey. "Even though I can't stand Arthur Godfrey, I think he's done the most good for Chesterfields on the racial side. . . . I mean the fact that he uses Negroes on his program, in his quartet and on his talent shows, without making a special comment about it," stated one forty-year-old respondent—the wife of an investigator for the New York State Commission against Discrimination. Roper, 42. Another respondent gave credit to Philip Morris for sponsoring another musical TV show hosted by Horace Heidt, "the talent show he used to put on for Philip Morris. . . . Well, they had a lot of colored winners on that. It really went over big, and some of those kids have gone along. And I don't think people—colored people—have forgotten it." Roper, 44.

73. Overhearing an interview conversation on the positive effects of an amber-colored poster instead of images that "make us look—inky black, or

like comedians most of the time," one proprietor interjected: "He's telling you right. That advertising is what gets it—and the kind of advertising is what means something to colored people." Roper, 25.

74. Roper, 36.

75. Roper, 45, 17–18.

76. George Weissman, "Pardon Us While We Change Our Dress: Q&A," presentation, Region II Sales Meeting, Fort Lauderdale, FL, January 1956, 11, TTID, item ID: rsln0116.

77. Vanessa E. Broussard, "Abstract of interview with George Weissman," interview by Scott Ellsworth, Marlboro Oral History Project Interview #59, National Museum of American History, April 27, 1987, 3, TTID, item ID: qhvh0045.

78. Roper, *Progress Report on Negro Market Study*, 36–37.

79. Higginbotham, *Righteous Discontent*.

80. Roper, *Progress Report on Negro Market Study*, 37.

81. Roper, 48, 40.

82. Redbook Magazine, Marketing Research Department, *Cigarettes: Notes on the Industry, Cigarette Consumption and Smoking Habits: Market Reports—Redbook Magazine*, April 1956, 26, TTID, item ID: ghvm0103. "The three top cigarette brands were found to be the most clearly defined. 'Camels' were regarded as masculine, strong and irritating, 'among the top cigarettes' and 'for ordinary working people.' 'Lucky Strike' cigarettes had a similar reputation—strong, irritating, for men, for 'ordinary working people, but less the working man's.' 'Chesterfields' were considered to be for both men and women, on the mild side as compared to 'Camels' and 'Luckies' and were not 'class bound.'"

83. Britt, "The Strategy of Consumer Motivation," 673–74.

84. Market Planning Corp., *A Motivation Study for Liggett & Myers*, vol. 1, October 1957, 1, 121, TTID, item ID: zlbm0016. This document redacts the names of all brands, but despite the blacked-out letters it is possible to discern the brands being discussed—particularly Kool vs. Salem—from the broader context of the discussion.

85. Market Planning Corp., 76.

86. "With few exceptions, smokers expressed the earnest desire that their children never smoke, especially their daughters." Market Planning Corp., 15.

87. Market Planning Corp., 6–7.

88. Market Planning Corp., 29.

89. Market Planning Corp., 18. On tranquilizers, see Herzberg, *Happy Pills in America*.

90. Market Planning Corp., *Motivation Study*, vol. 1, 17, 2.

91. "In periods of tension, smoking constitutes a compensation." Market Planning Corp., 18.

92. Market Planning Corp., 46.

93. Market Planning Corp., 126.

94. Market Planning Corp., 129, 130.

95. Market Planning Corp., 133, 142, 144.

96. Market Planning Corp., 19–20, 146–47.

97. Market Planning Corp., 137, 149, 138, 153.

98. Market Planning Corp., 188–89, 155, 156–57.

99. Market Planning Corp., 19.

100. Packard, *Hidden Persuaders*, 258.

101. *False and Misleading Advertising (Filter-Tip Cigarettes): Hearings before a Subcommittee of the Committee on Government Operations*, 85th Cong. 1 (July 18, 19, 23, 24, 25, and 28, 1957).

102. "Filter-Tip Ads Hit by House Unit," *New York Herald Tribune*, February 20, 1958, 7.

103. "News of the Advertising and Marketing Fields," *New York Times*, April 6, 1955, 42.

104. "FTC Opens Campaign on TV Ads," *Washington Post and Times Herald*, April 1, 1957, B11.

105. "Tranquilizer Pill Sales Worry FDA," *Washington Post and Times Herald*, May 8, 1957, B1. For scholarship on drugs for the alleviation of anxiety in the 1950s from the rise of tranquilizers to the appearance of antipsychotic drugs, see Tone, *The Age of Anxiety*; Metzl, *Prozac on the Couch*; Rasmussen, *On Speed*; and Herzberg, *Happy Pills in America*.

106. "Cigarettes," *Consumer Reports*, March 1957, 99–110.

107. "Cigaret Psychology," *Wall Street Journal*, November 11, 1958, 9.

108. "Food Packaging: Industry, Consumer Spokesmen Differ on Rationality in the Supermarket," 1408.

109. Dichter, "Seven Tenets of Creative Research," 4.

110. "Adman Rips 'Mumbo-Jumbo,'" *Detroit Free Press*, May 29, 1958, 25.

111. Lieb, *Safer Smoking*, 79.

112. Market Planning Corp., *Motivation Study*, vol. 1, 128.

113. Market Planning Corp., 150.

114. Social Research, Inc., *Cigarettes: Their Role and Function*, prepared for the Chicago Tribune, April 30, 1952, 12, TTID, item ID: qrlc0014.

115. *Brand Name for a Mentholated Cigarette*, 1959, 12.

116. Alexander R. Hammer, "Menthol Smokes Burning Brightly," *New York Times*, November 20, 1960, F1.

117. Richard Rutter, "Personality: Change a Habit to Tobacco Man," *New York Times*, September 18, 1960, F3; Harry M. Wootten, *Confidential Report on Cigarette Sales by Brands*, May 18, 1960, 4, TTID, item ID: ynww0003.

118. Hammer, "Menthol Smokes Burning Brightly."

119. Wootten, *Confidential Report*, 4.

Chapter Three

1. The Mississippi Attorney General was the first to launch a Medicaid lawsuit in 1994, followed by Minnesota and West Virginia that same year. In 1995 Florida

filed its lawsuit. In 1996 Massachusetts, Louisiana, Texas, Maryland, Washington, Connecticut, Arizona, Kansas, Michigan, New Jersey, Utah, and Oklahoma all filed suits. The Kansas Attorney General Carla Stovall estimated that her state spent $100 million per year to cover smoking-related illnesses. Discussed in Charles F. Gay Jr., "Lawyers for Civil Justice: Medicaid Reimbursement Litigation & Legislation," 1996, TTID, item ID: jyyn0088.

2. Transcript of videotaped deposition of Andrew J. Schindler, September 18, 2000, in Ezell Thomas v. R.J. Reynolds Tobacco Co., Civil Action No. 96-0065 (Circuit Ct., Jefferson County, MS), TTID, item ID: mjcy0019.

3. Deposition of Andrew J. Schindler, 61; George A. Dean (DFS, Inc.) to J. A. Albanese (R. J. Reynolds Tobacco Co.), "Camel Menthol and the Negro Market," November 9, 1967, TTID, item ID: tqyh0099.

4. Deposition of Andrew J. Schindler, 62.

5. Deposition of Andrew J. Schindler, 63.

6. R. J. Reynolds Tobacco Co., *Product Research Report: Salem vs. Kool among Negroes*, Marketing Research Department, April 28, 1969, 2, TTID, item ID: qpxp0085.

7. Writing in 1964, one public school educator observed that "for many people the term 'inner city' and 'cultural deprivation' have become synonymous with Negro." Stewart, "Correcting the Image of Negroes in Textbooks," 30. Because the term functioned as a euphemism in this fashion to signify urban, Black, and people living in poverty or with low incomes, I use scare quotes around "inner city" throughout whenever that is the implied meaning. On the euphemistic use of "cultural deprivation" in the same era, see Raz, *What's Wrong with the Poor?*

8. Arthur G. Weber to William Esty Co., letter, September 4, 1968, TTID, item ID: nrjx0016; William Esty Co., Inc., *Salem and "Coolness" Segment Competitors Advertising/Marketing Review*, prepared for R. J. Reynolds Tobacco Co., 1983, TTID, item ID: mnjh0096.

9. Dean to Albanese, "Camel Menthol and the Negro Market," 1.

10. Batten, Barton, Durstine & Osborn, Inc., *Smoking Habits among Three Ethnic Groups—Negro, Puerto Rican, Mexican*, prepared for the American Tobacco Co., November 1963, 16, 52, TTID, item ID: hykl0134.

11. Arthur D. Little, Inc., *Development of Cigarette Packaging*, prepared for Liggett & Myers, October 14, 1963, 6, TTID, item ID: sfbl0011.

12. "Menthol on My Back," 8.

13. Opinion Research Corp., *Smoking Behavior and Smoker Motivation—Their Implications for Packaging*, Pilot Study for Research and Development Department, Philip Morris, Inc., November 1961, 30, 31, TTID, item ID: hqmx0045.

14. *Brand Name for a Mentholated Cigarette*, 1959, TTID, item ID: qsmk0190.

15. The Psychological Corp., *A Psychological Assessment of Viewers' Reactions to the KOOL Cigarette "Come Up" Television Commercial*, prepared for Ted Bates & Co., March 22, 1961, 19, 21, TTID, item ID: rtbv0132.

16. Opinion Research Corp., *Smoking Behavior and Smoker Motivation*, 30.

17. Opinion Research Corp., 31.

18. Kitman, "Report from an Independent Research Laboratory," 15. In another piece, Kitman professed to have firsthand information on a revolutionary new cigarette, "the first all-filter-tip cigarette . . . the last word in the continuing battle against lung cancer." It was 72 millimeters of filter, "not a trace of tobacco." Kitman, "I Was a Spy in the Cigarette Revolution," 7.

19. Opinion Research Corp., *Smoking Behavior and Smoker Motivation*, 30.

20. Opinion Research Corp., 59, 62. Opinion Research also heard smokers' strong social class associations with products. Echoing the words of one person surveyed, the report noted that "a laborer would choose a more masculine ciga-rette, say a nonfilter cigarette, than, say an office person" (61). Another explained: "The society-type person would smoke the filter tips. . . . This is even more true of women than men" (61).

21. Ernest Dichter, *A Motivational Research Study on the Potentials of a 100mm Cigarette*, prepared for the American Tobacco Co., August 1962, 18, TTID, item ID: mmhl0134.

22. See Table V: Comparison of Negro to Other Campaign Colleges, Share of Type Market—January 1961, in American Tobacco Co., *The American Tobacco Company Campus Campaign Audit Analysis*, January 1961, TTID, item ID: gzvw0141. Note: quoted text comes from appended document: *The American Tobacco Company Campus Campaign Activities, September, October, November, 1957—Recommendations for 1958*, 16, section "New Facts about the College Mar-ket," TTID, item ID: gzvw0141. See also Harry W. Wootten, *Confidential Report on Cigarette Competition: Brand Sales through Third Quarter 1962*, November 30, 1962, TTID, item ID: yfkv0090.

23. Dichter, *The Motivations of Cigarette Smoking: A Creative Memorandum*, 35.

24. W. A. Sugg to Bowman Gray, July 2, 1956, TTID, item ID: rtkp0085.

25. Dichter, *The Motivations of Cigarette Smoking*, 40.

26. Lawton, "Psychosocial Aspects of Cigarette Smoking," 165.

27. Student Marketing Institute, *Lucky Strike Campus Campaign: Analysis of Smoking Survey and Store Audit*, 1951. TTID. Item ID: pswb0020.

28. Quoted in Brecher et al., *The Consumers Union Report on Smoking and the Public Interest*, 165, available at TTID, item ID: gzwm0178.

29. Brecher et al., 165.

30. American Tobacco Co., *The American Tobacco Company Campus Campaign Audit Analysis*, 3. See also Wootten, *Confidential Report on Cigarette Competition*.

31. American Tobacco Co., *The American Tobacco Company Campus Cam-paign Audit Analysis*, 3.

32. The Center for Research in Marketing, Inc., "A Prospectus for a Third Study of the Dynamics of Purchase Behavior in the Negro Market," 1962, TTID, item ID: ntfy0010.

33. See Jain, "'Come Up to the Kool Taste.'" Jain offers an astute analysis of African American upward mobility themes in Kool advertising. The campaign, however, began with very different ideals playing for a different group of youthful buyers.

34. Psychological Corp., "Appendix A: Come Up Script," in *A Psychological Assessment of Viewers' Reactions*, 24, TTID, item ID: gylx0045.

35. Psychological Corp., *Psychological Assessment of Viewers' Reactions*, 23, 12, 20.

36. Brown & Williamson, "Market Research Summary," 1961, TTID, item ID: fyvv0132.

37. Psychological Corp., *A Psychological Assessment of Viewers' Reactions*, 6.

38. Psychological Corp., 20.

39. The Tobacco Institute, Inc., "Organized Anti-Smoking Campaigns Gaining," Spring Meeting, May 18–20, 1961, 1, TTID, item ID: mfvv0043.

40. For example, on May 15, 1962, acting FTC chairman Sigurd Anderson assured US Senator Maurine Neuberger that "the Commission has engaged in a constant endeavor to prevent advertisements and commercials for cigarettes from being deceptive or misleading." *Congressional Record*, vol. 108, Session 87-2 (1962), p. 1979.

41. "Food Packaging," 1408–9.

42. Opinion Research Corp., *Smoking Behavior and Smoker Motivation*, 62.

43. "Allen Protests CBS Program on Tobacco," *Evening Star* (Washington, DC), September 20, 1962, available at TTID, item ID: hqnk0000; see also "Tobacco Man Hits Network Smoking Show," *Los Angeles Times*, September 20, 1962, available at TTID, item ID: hqnk0000.

44. Brecher et al., *Consumers Union Report on Smoking and the Public Interest*, 191.

45. Pollay, "Targeting Tactics in Selling Smoke," 5, available at TTID, item ID: hjhx0149.

46. Lawrence Laurent, "Fadeout Is Ordered for Ad Trickery on TV," *Washington Post*, January 4, 1962, A1; Anthony Lewis, "FTC Ruling Bars Deceptive TV Ads," *New York Times*, January 4, 1962, 22.

47. "Victory on Drug Regulation," *New York Times*, October 5, 1962, 32.

48. "Sen. Neuberger Warns TV Over Television Advertising," *New York Times*, December 8, 1962, 54; Lawrence Laurent, "Collins's Stand Praised and Attacked," *Washington Post*, December 17, 1962, A19.

49. "Billions in Smokes at Stake in Federal Study"; Pollay, "Targeting Tactics in Selling Smoke," 7.

50. Brecher et al., *Consumers Union Report on Smoking and the Public Interest*, 167.

51. For more insight on the early 1960s and how civil rights transformed the politics and business calculus of advertising and consumption, see Isenberg,

Downtown America; Weems, *Desegregating the Dollar*; and Cohen, *A Consumers' Republic*.

52. Bullock, "Consumer Motivations in Black and White—I"; Bullock, "Consumer Motivations in Black and White—II," 114. See also Bullock, *Pathways to the Houston Negro Market*; and Bullock, "Racial Attitudes and the Employment of Negroes."

53. Bullock, "Consumer Motivations in Black and White—II," 121, 116, 110, 110–11.

54. Bullock, 113.

55. Bullock, 113.

56. Bullock, 118, 124.

57. Merton, "Patterns of Influence."

58. Dichter, *Executive Summary and Supplemental Analysis of a Motivational Research Study of the Current Cigar Smoking Climate*, 86–89.

59. Dichter, 89, 90. For brands like Muriel cigars, for example, Dichter urged the "development of future ads that dramatically illustrate the 'initiation' elements of the brand's personality" (that is, Muriel as a good starter product), but doing so in a way that would not alienate the "experienced smoker" (114).

60. Dichter, 13, 104.

61. Lennen & Newell, Inc., *Negro Smoking Habit Study*, prepared for Lorillard Tobacco Co., June 1963, Table 8: Extent to which Smokers Agree with "Anxiety" Statements, 4, TTID, item ID: rrhh0055.

62. Lennen & Newell, 13.

63. Lennen & Newell, 5.

64. Lawrence C. Gumbinner Advertising Agency, *Study of the Filter Tip Cigarette Market*, prepared for the American Tobacco Co., July 1963, 19, TTID, item ID: hynn0174.

65. Dodd, "Cigarettes: The Splintered Market," 26, available at TTID, item ID: ktnf0143. On the popularity of Pall Mall among Black smokers, see Lennen & Newell, *Negro Smoking Habit Study*, 15.

66. Lawrence C. Gumbinner, *Study of the Filter Tip Cigarette Market*, 43.

67. "King Announces Boycott Plans to Stop Bias," *Pittsburgh Courier*, January 19, 1963, 12.

68. A. Toft to D. Ladd, General Office communication, P. Lorillard Co., Advertising Department, September 3, 1963, TTID, item ID: qxwp0015.

69. J. W. Burgard, "Memorandum of Meeting between Mr. W. S. Cruthins and J. W. Burgard with the Following Representatives of CORE: Miss Breslin, Mr. Robinson, Mr. Mullet, in Mr. Cruthins' Room at the Dorset Hotel in New York," October 21, 1963, 1–2, TTID, item ID: xqlp0132.

70. Black, "The Negro Market," 46.

71. Burgard, "Memorandum of Meeting," 2.

72. Wootten, *Confidential Report on Cigarette Competition*, 10, 6.

73. "While consumers are still interested in 'healthier' cigarettes," Dichter noted in a report to advertising firm Young & Rubicam, "our evidence . . . indicates that the cigarette smoker shows considerable anxiety about coughs and other respiratory symptoms." Dichter, *Motivations of Cigarette Smoking*, 10.

74. US Department of Health, Education, and Welfare (HEW), *Smoking and Health* (1964). See particularly, chapter 4, "Summaries and Conclusions," 23–42.

75. HEW, *Smoking and Health* (1964), 62.

76. Dodd, "Cigarettes: The Splintered Market," 23, 21.

77. Anthony Lewis, "F.C.C. Maps Action on Cigarette Ads," *New York Times*, January 20, 1964, 12.

78. Lewis, 12.

79. William Clark, "March of Dimes Physician Advises Pregnant Women," *Atlanta Daily World*, January 3, 1964, 2; "'Quit Cigarettes' but Not Cigars, Fasi Told Board," *Hartford Courant*, January 25, 1964, 9; Ruth Brecher and Edward Brecher, "How to Give Up Smoking," *New York Times*, January 26, 1964, SM16.

80. "Dick Gregory Deserts Favorite Cigarette Prop," *Baltimore Afro-American*, January 25, 1964, 11; "Comic Quits Cigarets: Gregory Nixes Butts," *Chicago Daily Defender*, January 14, 1964, 3.

81. Crossley S-D Surveys, Inc., *National Smoking Habits Study*, vol. II, prepared for the American Tobacco Co., Spring 1964, 1, 5, TTID, item ID: ghxc0010.

82. Elmo Roper and Associates, *A Study of Reactions to the Surgeon General's Report on Cigarette Smoking*, prepared for Philip Morris, Inc., February 1964, vi, 28, TTID, item ID: stck0112.

83. Crossley S-D Surveys, *National Smoking Habits Study*, 23, 12, 20.

84. Sullivan, Stauffer, Colwell, and Bayles, Inc., *The Market for Menthol Cigarettes: Implications for Montclair*, prepared for the American Tobacco Co., September 1964, 60, TTID, item ID: kxvx0017.

85. See Sullivan, Stauffer, Colwell, and Bayles, 60; and Crossley S-D Surveys, *National Smoking Habits Study*, 46.

86. Grey Marketing and Research Department, *A Marketing Target-Buying Incentive Study of Cigarette Market*, Summer 1964, II-3, 6, 12, 15, TTID, item ID: xmwv0116.

87. Grey Marketing, 22, 23, 24.

88. Grey Marketing, II-27.

89. US Federal Trade Commission (FTC), *Statement of Basis and Purpose of Trade Regulation Rule for the Prevention of Unfair or Deceptive Advertising and Labeling of Cigarettes in Relation to the Health Hazards of Smoking* (1964), 68, 69, available at TTID, item ID: xxwx0147.

90. Batten, Barton, Durstine, & Osborn, *Smoking Habits among Three Ethnic Groups*, 16.

91. Arthur D. Little, *Development of Cigarette Packaging*, 5–6.

92. FTC, *Statement of Basis and Purpose*, appendix A, 3.

93. FTC, 53, 68.

94. Official Transcript of Proceedings before the Federal Trade Commission, Washington, DC, March 16, 1964, 155, 157, TTID, item ID: fnnl0190.

95. FTC, *Statement of Basis and Purpose*, appendix C, 5.

96. Official Transcript of Proceedings before the Federal Trade Commission, 12.

97. FTC, *Statement of Basis and Purpose*, appendix C, 5.

98. See, for example, advertisement, *Pittsburgh Courier*, June 6, 1964: 3; advertisement, *Philadelphia Tribune*, July 4, 1964, 13.

99. Gibson and Jung, "Historical Census Statistics on Population by Race, 1790 to 1990, and by Hispanic Origin, 1970 to 1990, for Large Cities and Other Urban Places in the United States," table 26, p. 71.

100. "New Marketing Profile of U.S. Negro Emerges," 38–43.

101. "Controversial Civil Rights Bill Becomes Law," *Philadelphia Tribune*, July 4, 1964, 1.

102. John A. Ulrich to Robert K. Heiman, Vice President, Memorandum of the American Tobacco Co., September 14, 1964, TTID, item ID: spkb0146.

103. J. W. Burgard, "Changes in Wrapping Material," Brown & Williamson Tobacco Co., October 27, 1964, TTID, item ID: jgpp0138.

104. Kool advertisement, *Philadelphia Tribune*, May 4, 1965, 6.

105. Turner, *I Heard It through the Grapevine*, 98.

106. Allport and Postman, *The Psychology of Rumor*, 33. On rumor, see also Shibutani, *Improvised News*; and Odum, *Race and Rumors of Race*.

107. "Ciggy Exec. Denies Racist Connections," *Chicago Daily Defender*, September 23, 1964, 4.

108. F. X. Whelan, Executive Sales Manager, to E. F. Mooney, Director of Sales, November 23, 1964, TTID, item ID: qfgx0136.

109. J. W. Edghill to E. F. Mooney, November 30, 1964, TTID, item ID: hpgb0015.

110. Brown & Williamson Tobacco Corp., Marketing Plans, 1969, 24, TTID, item ID: mnyd0139. Statistics found on p. 12.

111. On the rise of the word "cool" as a potent cultural signifier for this generation, see Frank, *The Conquest of Cool*. Note also the appearance of the film *The Cool World* in 1963, directed by Shirley Clarke.

112. Green, *Selling the Race*, 129.

113. "Patronizing a first class eating establishment in a comfortable manner is not always easy. Outlays of money for country clubs, resorts and similar recreation in most instances is out of the question," Johnson explained. Quoted in "New Marketing Profile of U.S. Negro Emerges," 38.

114. Robinson, "The Life and Death of Nat King Cole," 123, 125.

115. *Ebony*, April 1965, 59, 87, 89, 155. In March 1964, the makers of Montclair menthols advertised a new design innovation, highlighting that they were the "first to put the menthol in the [filter] tip" rather than spraying it onto the tobacco. The tobacco smoke was said to be drawn through the menthol in the

filter, mingling and combining as the smoke moved into the mouth, throat, and lungs. "First to Put the Menthol in the Tip," 66.

116. R. M. Odear Jr., Market Research Department, R. J. Reynolds to A. G. Weber, "Salem Negro Problem Markets," March 24, 1966, 1, TTID, item ID: gjvv0019.

117. Myron Johnston to Dr. H. Wakehan, Inter-Office Correspondence, Philip Morris, May 2, 1966, TTID, item ID: lslw0115.

118. Alice Widener, "Cigarets Welcomed by War-Worn GIs," *Memphis Commercial Appeal*, November 25, 1966.

119. Tibor Koeves Associates, *A Pilot Look at the Attitudes of Negro Smokers toward Menthol Cigarettes*, prepared for Philip Morris, Inc., September 1968, 3–4, TTID, item ID: shby0189.

120. Tibor Koeves Associates, 10–11.

121. R. J. Reynolds Tobacco Co., *Product Research Report: Salem vs. Kool among Negroes*, 2.

122. Motivational Programmers Inc. and Depth Research Laboratories, *An In-Depth Exploratory Study on Cigarette Smoking Habits and Attitudes*, prepared for Liggett & Myers, Inc., January 1969, 69, TTID, item ID: gmwg0009.

123. Roper Research Associates, Inc., *A Study of Cigarette Smokers' Habits and Attitudes in 1967*, prepared for Philip Morris, Inc., December 1967, 68, survey on p. 106, TTID, item ID: qqdv0125.

124. Tibor Koeves Associates, *A Pilot Look*, 7.

125. Dean to Albanese, "Camel Menthol and the Negro Market," 3–4.

126. Hampton, "Is Teenage Smoking Really Falling Off?," 28–29, available at TTID, item ID: qxcf0000.

127. "Race Relations and Tobacco," 22–25, 47, available at TTID, item ID: qxcf0000.

128. "Here Comes the Senate Bill," 19, 21, available at TTID, item ID: nhcf0000.

Chapter Four

1. Miyo Geyelin, "States Agree to $206 Billion Tobacco Deal," *Wall Street Journal*, November 23, 1998, B13.

2. "Creative Time for Marketers of Cigarettes," *New York Times*, December 11, 1998, B26.

3. R. J. Reynolds Tobacco Co., *(Confidential) Advertising Research Report: Salem "Brown" vs. "Brown/Red Haired Man in Water" (#50) Outdoor Recall Test*, 6, 13, available at Truth Tobacco Industry Documents, UCSF Library, https://www.industrydocuments.ucsf.edu/tobacco (hereafter TTID), item ID: zrch0099.

4. Transcript of videotaped deposition of Myron E. Johnston Jr., vol. 1, November 16, 2000, in Scott v. American Tobacco Co., Civil Case No. 96-8461 (Dist. Ct. La., Orleans Parish, 2004), TTID, item ID: pljp0180.

5. Gloria Scott and Deania M. Jackson, Plaintiffs, v. The American Tobacco

Company, Inc., et al., Appeal from Civil District Court, Orleans Parish, Judge David S. Gorbaty, 23, TTID, item ID: jpjp0180.

6. John Schwartz, "Philip Morris Memos Detail Teen Habits," *Washington Post*, January 30, 1998, A15; Myron E. Johnston, *Young Smokers: Prevalence, Trends, Implications, and Related Demographic Trends*, prepared for Philip Morris U.S.A., March 31, 1981, 1, TTID, item ID: jynj0191.

7. "Philip Morris Head 'Ashamed' over '75 Youth-Sales Memo," *Los Angeles Times*, March 4, 1998; "Cigarette Mogul: 'Ashamed' of Trying to Lure Teens," *Alexandria Daily Town Talk*, March 4, 1998, A4.

8. Myron Johnston to Tom Goodale, Inter-Office Correspondence, Philip Morris U.S.A., September 18, 1985, 2, TTID, item ID: qslk0037.

9. Gibson, *The $30 Billion Negro*.

10. Wilson, *The Truly Disadvantaged*.

11. A. J. Berger, *RJR Non-Broadcast Media Posture*, prepared for R. J. Reynolds Tobacco Co., August 15, 1968, 8, TTID, item ID: gqhx0091.

12. "Here Comes the Senate Bill," 13, available at TTID, item ID: nhcf0000.

13. Berger, *RJR Non-Broadcast Media Posture*, 12–18. "RJR will, undoubtedly, purchase billboards after the demise of TV," concluded one industry observer.

14. Berger, 20.

15. R. J. Reynolds Tobacco Co., *A Study of Ethnic Markets*, September 1969, 30, TTID, item ID: jrgc0035. As one B&W memo later noted, "Since Negroes are important to the brand's total smoker franchise, interior transit was used." Brown & Williamson Tobacco Corp., *Domestic Brands, Product Designs and Sales*, [date unknown], 279, TTID, item ID: hgdj0037.

16. "A large segment of the population, to avoid downtown vehicular traffic, drive to the end of the transit line where they change to mass transportation." Batten, Barton, Durstine & Osborn, Inc., *The American Tobacco Company 1976 Review and Recommendations, Out-of-Home Media (13 Markets)*, prepared for American Tobacco Company, September 17, 1975, 18, TTID, item ID: jfdy0142. Concerns about suburban zone-out restrictions were frequently voiced. As one 1992 Buffalo study noted, "Buffalo's media offer great visibility and excellent coverage . . . even where other traditional out-of-home is zoned out. 30 Sheet & Paints are located mostly on the highways and are zoned out of the suburbs therefore missing a substantial % of the population of people working and living in the suburbs." TDI, "Buffalo Market Facts," prepared for Philip Morris, January 1992, TTID, item ID: gglx0025.

17. As RJR observed for its Winston brand, "Panel locations will be restricted to core areas of ethnic concentrations, will frequently be close to the point of sale . . . and reflect WINSTON's presence and importance in the black community." Posters were meant to evoke a sense of being part of the community. While such a campaign could never have the impact of a TV campaign, posters "in 61 major markets with large Negro concentrations [could still reach] 58% of the total U.S. Negro population." William Esty Co., Inc., *Winston Cigarettes Marketing Plan*

Negro Market, prepared for R. J. Reynolds Tobacco Co., January 1972), 12–13, TTID, item ID: nlwf0083.

18. Myron Johnston, *Economic Forecast, 1973–1977*, prepared for Philip Morris U.S.A., April 7, 1972, 7, TTID, item ID: rxdk0112.

19. Behavioral Systems, Inc. (BSI), *The Marlboro Image Revisited*, prepared for Burrell-McBain Advertising, June 1971, 1, TTID, item ID: gxby0189.

20. BSI, 13. See also White, Oliffe, and Bottoroff, "From Promotion to Cessation," e44–e55.

21. BSI, *The Marlboro Image Revisited*, 34, 15, 17.

22. BSI, 39.

23. BSI, 35.

24. BSI, 38.

25. BSI, 42–43.

26. Computer Field Express, Inc. (CFE), *Existing Market for Menthol Cigarettes*, prepared for Liggett & Myers, Inc., June 1971, 101, 109–10, TTID, item ID: gxgn0006.

27. Liggett & Myers, Inc., *Cigarette and Tobacco Division: 1972 Annual Plan*, December 1971, 15, TTID, item ID: mgyy0011.

28. CFE, *Existing Market for Menthol Cigarettes*, 13. In terms of health, heavy smokers were said to recoil from health fantasies—and were realistic in a way that light smokers were not. Light smokers were "self-righteously proud of their minimal (or non-existent) smoking habits—all lulled into these dreams of physical safety, building up a rationalized concept of immunity and protection," the anti-tobacco warnings "lulling them into a false unrealistic sense of health confidence." CFE, 36.

29. CFE, 14.

30. Among the eleven themes for understanding these smokers were "youth," "classical female sexual imagery," the lack of self-reliance, absences of anxiety, as well as a "fantasy of excellent, ever-continuing health." Race also figured in light smoking, since "Negroes are the light smokers," and "disproportionately, the light smokers" held liberal or even militant pro-Black views, "promoting interracial marriage," and even believing that "peaceful means of gaining civil rights is Uncle Tomism." CFE, 29–32.

31. CFE, 57–58.

32. CFE, 59.

33. CFE, 58.

34. CFE, 57, 65, 67, 70.

35. CFE, 70.

36. CFE, 92.

37. Lorillard Market Tobacco Co., *The Menthol Cigarette Market: A Summary, Job #9016*, February 1972, 51, 53, 55, TTID, item ID: hlnc0129.

38. William Esty Co., Inc., *Salem Task Force Presentation*, prepared for R. J. Reynolds Tobacco Co., December 1973, 88, 126, 58, TTID, item ID: yrlj0088.

39. Luke, Esmundo, and Bloom, "Smoke Signs"; Kwate and Lee, "Ghetto-izing Outdoor Advertising."

40. Blakeslee, "'White Flight' to the Suburbs"; Frey, "Population Movement and City-Suburb Redistribution."

41. Gibson and Jung, "Historical Census Statistics on Population Totals by Race, 1790 to 1990," Table 23: Michigan—Race and Hispanic Origin for Selected Cities and Other Places: Earliest Census.

42. Lee Yancey, *Detroit Metro Plan*, prepared for R. J. Reynolds Tobacco Co., February 1976, 9, TTID, item ID: xndf0091.

43. Market Research Department, PM-USA, *The Cigarette Market: The National Tracking Study* (January–February 1973), 6, TTID, item ID: flvv0106.

44. "B&W-New Products," memo from Wyatt Williams to Mr. J. Doherty et al., November 11, 1974, 3, TTID, item ID: lkmy0132.

45. "Brand Histories—B&W Brands," undated, 279, TTID, item ID: hgdj0037.

46. RJR, *Menthol Fact Book*, January 16, 1973, 32, TTID, item ID: zqhg0091.

47. They also took aim at Salem's popularity among women with a new "Lady Be Cool" campaign, which adapted television ads from before 1970 (featuring long-haired blond woman in slacks and green sweater, leaning against a tree in a verdant woods with a "stylishly long, tastefully cool" cigarette in her hand) for magazine formats. For television ads, see: https://www.youtube.com/watch?v=OTFtciWa618 For print ads, see "The Longer You Smoke, the more you'll like Kool super longs . . . Lady be Kool." TTID, Item ID: hmxj0227. Another 1971 advertising featured a racially integrated band and asked viewers: "Have you heard about KOOL? It's everywhere." To assist in the effort, advertiser Ted Bates scripted ads with titles like "uptight" "extra cool," "groovin'," and "shilly-shally" to capture the appeal. "Have you heard about Kool?" (advertisement), *Daily News*, April 14, 1971, TTID, item ID: tylx0022.

48. William Esty Co., *Salem Task Force Presentation*, 58.

49. Lorillard Market Research Department, *The Menthol Cigarette—A Summary*, February 1972, 2, TTID, item ID: hlnc0129.

50. P. G. Martin to R. N. Thomson, "Memo: Philip Morris Menthol Market Inquiry," June 8, 1972, 1, TTID, item ID: xjpc0107.

51. T. R. Schori, *Confidential: Menthol Cigarettes as Seen by Menthol Smokers*, Philip Morris, March 1973, 10, TTID, item ID: lzpx0037.

52. T. R. Schori, P. G. Martin, and B. W. Jones, *Menthol Cigarette Preferences of Blacks and Whites*, Philip Morris, 1975, 2, TTID, item ID: rqfw0118.

53. Brand, Gruber, Stander, and Company, "The Perceptual Context of Smoking: Phase 1 of a Study to Vitalize the Multifilter Brand," for Philip Morris, Inc., October 1971, 17, 18, TTID, item ID: ttjf0028.

54. Yancey, *Detroit Metro Plan*, 54, 55, 65.

55. Eaton & Associates, *Kool Inner City Research Project: Focus Group Reports 1985*, prepared for Brown & Williamson, January 1986, 3, TTID, item ID: zpyj0141.

56. R. J. Reynolds Tobacco Co., *Exploratory Research for Salem Cigarettes*, February 1974, 27, TTID, item ID: gmvc0102.

57. William Esty Company, *Salem Cigarettes Black Market—Current New Product Directional Copy Research*, August 9, 1973, 7, TTID, item ID: qjhj0016.

58. Schori, Martin, and Jones, *Menthol Cigarette Preferences of Blacks and Whites*, 5. Yet Philip Morris concluded in 1973 that "prudence . . . dictates that we reaffirm the validity of our findings before any conclusions of far-reaching consequences are drawn."

59. R. J. Reynolds Tobacco Co., *Exploratory Research for Salem Cigarettes*, 31, 29.

60. William Esty Company, Inc., *Salem Cigarettes: Ethnic Market Report*, prepared for R. J. Reynolds Tobacco Co., March 1976, 18, TTID, item ID: nkll0096.

61. Rosenfield, Sirowitz, and Lawson, Inc., *Exploratory Focus Group Research for Salem Extra—Birmingham, Alabama*, prepared for R. J. Reynolds Tobacco Co., January 1975, 12, TTID, item ID: xlmh0091. As another RJR study noted, building on these themes, "While Salem appears to have an undefined image for many young, white smokers, the Black Salem smoker seems to know exactly who he wants to be when he smokes this brand. Salem appears to be the Blacks' way of breaking out of the ghetto environment and obtaining a new status." R. J. Reynolds Tobacco Co., "The Black Market and the Menthol Category," in *Black Market Study*, June 14, 1976, 15–16, TTID, item ID: lqbp0093. For contemporary analyses on "ghetto marketing" and the urban Black consumer, see Joyce and Govoni, *The Black Consumer*.

62. R. J. Reynolds, *Exploratory Research*, 31.

63. R. J. Reynolds Tobacco Co., *Brand Image Survey: Black Male Smokers "Menthol," White Women Smokers "High Flavor,"* December 6, 1972, TTID, item ID: lsnf0091.

64. R. J. Reynolds Tobacco Co., *Brand Image Survey*.

65. Yancey, *Detroit Metro Plan*, 61.

66. Poussaint, "Blaxploitation Movies," 22, 30. See also Poussaint, "A Negro Psychiatrist Explains the Negro Psyche."

67. William Esty Co., *Salem Cigarettes: Black Market Current/New Product Directional Copy Research*, prepared for R. J. Reynolds Tobacco Co., August 9, 1973, 50, TTID, item ID: klpw0083.

68. T. F. Winters to J. O. Watson, "Salem Black Advertising," Inter-Office Memorandum, R. J. Reynolds, September 20, 1971, TTID, item ID: hndv0019.

69. J. H. Sherrill Jr. to Ellen Monahan, "Copy Research—Special Negro Effort in Detroit," April 2, 1971, TTID, item ID: sqck0037.

70. Winters to Watson, "Salem Black Advertising."

71. G. E. Harlow to J. O. Watson, *Salem Black Advertising "Ruff-Tuff-Puff"—"King Shamba,"* Advertising Research Report, August 24, 1971, TTID, item ID: tnbv0102.

72. Tatham-Laird & Kudner, Inc., *A Summary of the Black Cigarette Market*,

prepared for R. J. Reynolds Tobacco Co., January 29, 1974, 11, TTID, item ID: rgdl0094. The study's observations depended on a number of recent sales reports, as well as a recent paper in *Advertising Age*: Wall, "Positioning Your Brand in the Black Market."

73. Choudhury and Schmid, "Black Models in Advertising to Blacks."

74. Mary Ann Riffon to Scott Crump, "Proposal on the Baron/Blue Ice Menthol Product Test #11047," Inter-Office Memorandum, Lorillard, January 25, 1974, TTID, item ID: kmfm0126.

75. James Spector to R. Fitzmaurice, "Marlboro Menthol Analysis—Grand Rapids," Inter-Office Correspondence, Philip Morris U.S.A., September 12, 1974, TTID, item ID: pgmy0219.

76. Kevin P. Phillips, "Racial Politics: Rhetoric, Reality," *Hartford Courant*, May 27, 1974, 22.

77. Spector to Fitzmaurice, "Marlboro Menthol Analysis—Grand Rapids."

78. R. J. Reynolds Tobacco Co., *Chicago Metro Market*, 1974, 2, TTID, item ID: jghh0091.

79. R. J. Reynolds Tobacco Co., *Chicago Metro Market: Objective/Strategies/ Rationale*, 1975, 71, TTID, item ID: xjgl0094.

80. R. J. Reynolds Tobacco Co., *Chicago Metro Market*, 71.

81. N. W. Glover to D. A. Cummins, J. O. Watson, and D. F. Pearson, "Re: Metro Market Plans," September 30, 1975, 35, TTID, item ID: tpwx0091. The study observed that more than half of whites in the Chicago area bought cigarettes from supermarkets and drugstores, with far fewer sales from small groceries or liquor stores. For Blacks, purchases were evenly distributed between supermarkets, drugstores, liquor stores, and small groceries.

82. Rosenfield, Sirowitz, and Lawson, *Exploratory Focus Group Research for Salem Extra*, 21.

83. Rosenfield, Sirowitz, and Lawson, 22, 23.

84. Ted Bates & Co., Inc., *Kool "Project Task Force": A Marketing Recommendation*, prepared for Brown & Williamson, June 23, 1975, 2, TTID, item ID: mkgn0140.

85. William Esty Company, Inc., *Salem Cigarettes: Ethnic Market Report*, A-26. As the company noted, "The Muhammad Speaks, newspaper of the group, is said to have a circulation of 500,000 to 950,000, making it the largest Black weekly in the world."

86. Malcolm X, *The Autobiography of Malcolm X*, 64, 283.

87. R. J. Reynolds Tobacco Co., *Exploratory Research for Salem Cigarettes*, 20. Kool, in contrast, was said to be "the brand" for younger people and the "in" cigarette. In the 1970s, Esty concluded that the "Come up to Kools" motif now had both status and drug implications—it communicated "status and a sense of achievement" and promised a "high" or "rush" to others who were surveyed (21, 25).

88. Abby Ellison, *An Overview: A Qualitative Profile of the Newport Smoker*,

prepared for R. J. Reynolds Tobacco Co., November 1976, 9, 10, TTID, item ID: ysyf0091.

89. J. W. Isaacs to Jon Zoler, "Menthol Cigarettes," Inter-Office Correspondence, Philip Morris U.S.A., November 18, 1977, 2, TTID, item ID: ghbj0037. As PM executives observed, this menthol trend "contain[ed] a strong black influence"—notable among people who earned "slightly downscale incomes." If there was one downside, it was that Black people tended to smoke fewer packs per week than whites.

90. Roper Organization, Inc., *A Study of Smoking Habits among Young Smokers*, prepared for Philip Morris U.S.A., July 1974, 3, TTID, item ID: qjvk0191. Brand image dominated preferences, and "whites differ so greatly from blacks in their smoking habits—and in their images of brands."

91. H. L. Carroll to A. J. Bass Jr., "Product Information—Suggestion for New Cigarette Brand," February 10, 1976, Lorillard, TTID, item ID: ptvx0055.

92. As one William Esty study for RJR noted, the Black community was not monolithic: there were four elements to the Black community: the "satisfied element," committed to the American way of life; the "optimistic moderates," who recognized problems but saw the American system as basically sound; "troubled/unhopeful" people, who were tolerant of violence and separatism but unsure of next steps; and "radicals" who saw violence and/or separatism as the way to resolve problems. This was the backdrop for understanding which Blacks sought out menthol smokes, and why. William Esty Co., *Salem Cigarettes: Ethnic Market Report*, A-22.

93. Yancey, *Detroit Metro Plan*, 52.

94. Myron Johnston to Tom Goodale, "The Implications of Those Strange Happenings in the Menthol Market," Inter-Office Correspondence, Philip Morris U.S.A., September 18, 1985, 4, TTID, item ID: yqmn0189.

95. "B.A.T. Unit to Spend $32 Million to Unveil Kool Super Lights," *Wall Street Journal*, June 20, 1977, 13.

96. In 1977 another new entry in the menthol market was Tareyton. See George Lazarus, "Tareytons to Enter Menthol Cigaret Race," *Chicago Tribune*, July 25, 1977, E8.

97. Stephen G. Yates to Frank E. McKeown, "Re: Kool, Black Smoker Study," August 25, 1976, TTID, item ID: nmnm0128.

98. Brown & Williamson, "New Products Brand Group," in *New Products—Marketing Plan—1977 Marketing Plans*, 7, TTID, item ID: srcp0042.

99. Memo from I. R. Holmes Jr. to G. T. Reid, B&W, "Black Smokers in the Kool Franchise," May 4, 1978, 1, TTID, item ID: ymnx0102.

100. Brown & Williamson, 6.

101. Philip H. Dougherty, "Advertising: Inside a Menthol Cigarette Campaign," *New York Times*, March 31, 1977, 86; on "status seeking" etc., see R. J. Reynolds Tobacco Co., *Vantage: Developing Unique Black Marketing/Advertising Strategies through Life Style Consumer Analysis*, 1978, 5, TTID, item ID: ltbd0102.

102. R. J. Reynolds Tobacco Co., *Results of the 1978 Negro Market Audits*, prepared by T. F. Fields, Marketing Research Department, November 2, 1978, 2, TTID, item ID: tjbj0045.

103. George Lazarus, "Kool Readies Hot Ad Plans," *Chicago Tribune*, June 20, 1977, E10; George Lazarus, "Salem Broadens Attack on Kool's Slim Lead," *Chicago Tribune*, July 31, 1980, C8.

104. G. T. Reid to Phil Weinseimer, "Subject: Kool Low 'Tar' Parent Advertising Strategy," July 10, 1978, TTID, item ID: ksjh0145.

105. G. T. Reid to John Moss, "Kool vs. Newport—Marketing to Black Smokers," October 12, 1978, 2, TTID, item ID: slkd0135.

106. Brown & Williamson, *Final Report: Menthol 84 Pack Test*, January 13, 1978, 10–12, TTID, item ID: rrch0145.

107. Stephen G. Kates to Frank McKeown, "Re: Kool Competitive Copy," March 30, 1977, TTID, item ID: ymjk0133.

108. E. A. Kully, "File Note: cc: F.E. McKeown. Subject: Meeting with Ted Bates—4/10/78," April 25, 1978, TTID, item ID: hlpw0138. When executives proposed a new advertising approach equating Kool with a "Hint of Mint" in a blue pack, Bates objected that it lacked "vitality"; "Kool stands for menthol."

109. See, for example, Zikmund, "A Taxonomy of Black Shopping Behavior."

110. R. Davis to J. R. Ave et al., "Black Marketing Research—Findings and Recommended Actions to Date," Lorillard Memo, June 9, 1978, 3, TTID, item ID: xsfj0045.

111. W. Roberson to F. E. McKeown, "Field Observations Boston/New York," B&W Memorandum, March 7, 1979, TTID, item ID: yyyp0134.

112. Brown & Williamson, "Kool Parent Styles: Business Problem," 1978, 2, TTID, item ID: hfxf0126.

113. F. E. McKeown to W. F. Scholz, May 23, 1978, TTID, item ID: fpng0137. "This is the third time we have had problems in this area with KOOL Americana creative," complained McKeown about mistakes in Bates's urban marketing plan. See also Natalie Katz, *A Summary of Group Discussions among Menthol Cigarette Smokers Regarding Proposed New Advertising*, prepared for Brown & Williamson, March 8, 1980, TTID, item ID: nxvy0139.

114. Roberson to McKeown, "Field Observations Boston/New York."

115. Lazarus, "Salem Broadens Attack on Kool's Slim Lead"; George Lazarus, "B&W Seeks New Menthol Cigaret Winner," *Chicago Tribune*, March 1, 1979, E8; Philip H. Dougherty, "Ted Bates Loses Kool Cigarettes," *New York Times*, May 9, 1980, D13. On Black aspirations, see also Brown & Williamson Tobacco Corp., *1979 Marketing Plans: Complete Brand Plans*, 29, TTID, item ID: tzfj0136.

116. These comments echoed remarks Johnston had made in 1981, when he said, "For over fifteen years certain demographic and social trends have been moving in directions favorable to industry growth. Now, one by one, these powerful social and demographic factors are turning against us, and by 1985 all will be operating against us." Johnston, *Young Smokers*, 1.

117. Johnston to Goodale, September 18, 1985, 4. If this relationship was true (and he admitted that it was speculative), this drug trend "may be a partial explanation" for menthol's decline. One other possibility was that menthol smokers were quitting faster than non-menthol smokers, but the evidence here was confusing since some people in focus groups "reported that they switch to a menthol thinking that it would be easier to quit from something they did not really like, only to wind up liking menthol."

118. Myron Johnston to Dr. Carolyn Levy, "Strange Happenings in the Menthol Market," Inter-Office Correspondence, Philip Morris U.S.A., March 20, 1985, TTID, item ID: qtmn0189.

119. Johnston to Goodale, September 18, 1985, 2.

120. US Department of Health, Education, and Welfare, *Smoking and Health* (1979), ii.

121. Daniel Greenberg, "Smoke," *Baltimore Sun*, November 8, 1982, A9.

122. Wig Wigmore to Pat Kaminski, "Denver, CO—Re G. Gratta's 1-10-83 Memo to Jim Coleman," Inter-Office Memorandum, Cunningham & Walsh, February 3, 1983, TTID, item ID: ykcw0134.

123. M. W. Steele to D. S. Johnston and R. D. Sharp, "Minority Ad Agency Project," Internal Correspondence, Brown & Williamson, April 6, 1984, TTID, item ID: zghx0102.

124. G. T. Reid to R. A. Pittman, "Parent KOOL Future Marketing Strategy," December 18, 1978, 11, 13, TTID, item ID: lkhj0145. See also G. T. Reid to A. R. Nagie et al., "Kool New Product Objectives," Memorandum, June 19, 1978, TTID, item ID: nnhn0133.

125. "Kool Jazz Fete Slated for Atlanta June 29," *Atlanta Daily World*, June 15, 1979, 3. See also "Kool Pro Balloon Tour," *Atlanta Daily World*, August 28, 1979, 2.

126. Cunningham & Walsh, *Kool, Jazz and the Recording Industry*, prepared for Brown & Williamson Tobacco Corp., September 1981, 1, TTID, item ID: jxxv0100.

127. Philip H. Dougherty, "Advertising: Jazz Promotion Set for Kool Cigarettes," *New York Times*, December 1, 1981, D26.

128. "B&W Plans Big Kool Push," *Wall Street Journal*, December 3, 1981, 31; Kapuler & Associates, Inc., *Final Report: Kool Campaign Qualitative Evaluation*, prepared for Brown & Williamson Tobacco Corp., 7, TTID, item ID: zfdx0145. "The proposed advertising is designed for outdoor and print media. It represents a dramatically different campaign, and would feature a wide variety of musical instruments with dark backgrounds. Each advertising execution would portray a single musical instrument, for example, a soprano saxophone, an acoustic guitar, an electric guitar ... part of a player, a package of Kools, and the headline: 'There's only one way to play it.' The campaign's objective would be to affect [*sic*] change in attitudes toward the Kool family brand." The report examined closely white and Black attitudes about Black and white artists, as well as various

instruments and genres. See T. G. Sommers to S. A. Wallace et al., "Kool Copy Evaluation," April 29, 1981, TTID, item ID: kzcn0143.

129. "B&W Plans Big Kool Push," *Wall Street Journal*, December 3, 1981, 31.

130. Kapuler & Associates, Inc., *Consumer Reactions to 1983 Kool Executions*, prepared for Brown & Williamson Tobacco Corp., February 17, 1983, 40, 38–39, TTID, item ID: yyvy0143.

131. John (Jay) Nelson, Manager in Investment Research Dept of Brown Brothers Harriman, in "Tobacco Industry Roundtable," *Wall Street Transcript*, June 13, 1983, 11.

132. Brown & Williamson Tobacco Corp., *1984 Kool Operational Plan*, 23, TTID, item ID: trlx0045.

133. Duncan, "No Longer Kool, but Just as Hot; JVC Jazz Festival," 33.

134. William Esty Co., Inc., *The Black Menthol Cigarette Market*, prepared for R. J. Reynolds Tobacco Corp., February 1979, TTID, item ID: gmlj0103.

135. Roper Organization, *A Study of Smokers' Habits and Attitudes with Special Emphasis on Low Tar and Menthol Cigarettes*, vol. 1, prepared for Philip Morris U.S.A., March 1979, TTID, item ID: thvx0045.

136. Bush, Hair, and Solomon, "Consumers' Level of Prejudice and Response to Black Models in Advertisements."

137. Newman-Stein, Inc., *Cigarette Attitude Study among Lower Income Blacks*, prepared for Lorillard Tobacco Co., March 1979, TTID, item ID: ttyl0115. See also *Newport Brand Analysis*, prepared for Lorillard Tobacco Co., 1979, TTID, item ID: lkfx0096.

138. Tri-Ad Plus 2 Consultants, Ltd., *Final Report on Reactions to Cigarette Advertising by Black Consumers*, prepared for Brown & Williamson Tobacco Corp., April 1979, 40, 39, TTID, item ID: jmgd0135.

139. "NAACP and Brown and Williamson Establish Small Business Enterprise," *New Journal and Guide* (Norfolk, VA), August 7, 1985, 3; "NAACP Joins B&W in Economic Development," *Atlanta Daily World*, August 4, 1985, 2.

140. "B&W Exec Sees Minority Marketing as Continuing Rewarding Challenge."

141. C. L. Lomicka to L. R. Lewis et al., "Observations/Comments on Kool Ethnic Focus Groups," Internal Correspondence, Brown & Williamson, October 28, 1985, TTID, item ID: jllg0134.

142. The irony was that, for all of Johnston's sophistication at PM, the company's Alpine cigarette performed poorly—consistently so.

143. Lomicka to Lewis et al., "Observations/Comments." See also Michael Amoroso, Inc., *An Analysis of the Menthol Market*, prepared for Lorillard Tobacco Co., September 1986, TTID, item ID: qpkv0108.

144. Eaton & Associates, *Kool Inner City Research Project*, 3–5.

145. Juan Williams, "Divided We Fell: Race and the '88 Election," *Washington Post*, November 20, 1988, D4.

146. Jeanne Bonhomme to Nancy Brennan, "Appeal of Marlboro among

Black Male Non-Menthol Smokers," Philip Morris Marketing Research Department Report, May 13, 1987, TTID, item ID: ptmx0045.

147. Bamundo Qualitative Research, *Qualitative Research Exploring the Popularity of Newport among 18 to 24 Year Old Smokers*, prepared for Philip Morris U.S.A., December 1987, 10, TTID, item ID: qrcn0058.

148. Claudia G. Garbin to Roland D. Hammer, "Black Transit," Lorillard Memorandum, February 12, 1986, TTID, item ID: smfh0055.

149. Cunningham & Walsh, *A Retrospective View of Kool*, November 10, 1980, 3, 7, 14, 33, TTID, item ID: stfk0141.

150. Diane S. Burrows, *Young Adult Smokers: Strategies and Opportunities*, prepared for R. J. Reynolds Tobacco Co., February 29, 1984, 22–23, TTID, item ID: ntxb0099.

151. Roger Chesley and Duane Noriyuki, "Billboards Aim Drinks, Smokes at City Blacks," *Detroit Free Press*, February 5, 1989, 1A.

152. There had always been criticism, but it grew with the widening chasm between urban and suburban advertising. See, for example, Russo, Metcalf, and Stephens, "Identifying Misleading Advertising"; Reiss, "Black Media Association Cites Offensive Ads," 78; "Cigarette Maker Accused of Enticing Youths, 'Sowing Doubt' about Hazards," *Baltimore Sun*, July 7, 1981, A6; Garfield, "Colt 45 Ads a Black Day for Blacks," 84; and Hacker, Collins, and Johnson, *Marketing Booze to Blacks*.

153. See, for example, Cummings, Giovino, and Mendicino, "Cigarette Advertising and Black-White Differences in Brand Preference."

154. Davila, *Latinos, Inc.*, 2. On ethno-futures, see Comaroff and Comaroff, *Ethnicity, Inc.*

155. Comaroff and Comaroff, *Ethnicity, Inc.*, 145–46.

156. Letter from Charles L. Merin, The Tobacco Institute, to Congressman Edolphus Towns, May 21, 1984, TTID, item ID: qpkw0047; Ian Fisher, "On Tobacco Lobby List, Two Unlikely Names," *New York Times*, November 20, 1995, 41; "NAACP Joins B&W in Economic Development," *Atlanta Daily World*, August 4, 1985, 2.

157. "Special Report: Part One—Uneasy Alliance," *Detroit Free Press*, July 23, 1989, 1B, 6B–7B.

158. "Special Report," 7B.

159. Henry McNeil Brown, also known as Mandrake, discussed in the next chapter. Patrick Donoho, "Chicago City Council Transcript," August 3, 1990, 95–96, TTID, item ID: fscb0034.

160. Joan Tyner, "Tobacco Ads Geared toward Blacks Spur Controversy: Groups Like NAACP Get Industry Funds," *Baltimore Sun*, November 16, 1987, 6A.

161. "1990 Corporate Affairs Plan Outline," R. J. Reynolds, TTID, item ID: shpb0082.

162. Quoted in memo from John Singleton to Maura Payne, "Minority and

Women Business Magazine Cover Story—Benjamin Ruffin," March 1991, 5, TTID, item ID: rrdv0087.

163. RJR's proposed discussions "with small groups of key minority leaders . . . to discuss Company objectives and mutual benefits" included the NAACP's Benjamin Hooks, the National Urban League's John E. Jacob, Christopher F. Edley of the United Negro College Fund, Dr. Leon H. Sullivan of the Opportunities Industrialization Center, and Steve Davis of the National Newspaper Publishers Association. Ben Ruffin, "Final Presentation: 1990 Corporate Affairs Plan," February 27, 1990, TTID, item ID: glcb0082.

164. Epstein, "Sending Smoke Signals to Minorities," 18, available at TTID, item Id: nzll0029.

Chapter Five

1. "Proposed Media Q&A, Project UT," 1990, available at Truth Tobacco Industry Documents, UCSF Library, https://www.industrydocuments.ucsf.edu/tobacco (hereafter TTID), item ID: ylcb0082.

2. Anthony Ramirez, "Reynolds, after Protests, Cancels Cigarette Aimed at Black Smokers," *New York Times*, January 20, 1990, A1.

3. "Proposed Media Q&A, Project UT."

4. Morgan, "'Uptown' May Be Up in Smoke, but Targeted Groups Are Smarter for It," 16; Anthony Ramirez, "A Cigarette Campaign Under Fire," *New York Times*, January 12, 1990, D1; James R. Schiffman, "After Uptown, Are Some Niches Out?" *Wall Street Journal*, January 22, 1990, B1.

5. Louis Sullivan to James W. Johnston, January 17, 1990, TTID, item ID: mxlv0082. For "slick and sinister," see "Remarks by Louis W. Sullivan, Secretary of Health and Human Services," January 18, 1990, TTID, item ID: grpk0094.

6. Carol Jouzaitis, "Billboards as Battleground," *Chicago Tribune*, April 30, 1990, 1.

7. Steven A. Holmes, "Benjamin L. Hooks, Leader of N.A.A.C.P. for 15 Eventful Years, Is Dead at 85," *New York Times*, April 16, 2010, A19.

8. Karen Dennard interview with Gary Miller, Tobacco Institute, and Mandrake, *Talk of Chicago*, WGCI-FM Radio, September 15, 1989, TTID, item ID: pmdj0140.

9. Louis Sullivan to James W. Johnston, January 17, 1990, TTID, item ID: mxlv0082.

10. "An Uproar Over Billboards in Poor Areas," *New York Times*, May 1, 1989, D10.

11. Hooks quoted by Dan Jaffe, Executive Vice President of the Association of National Advertisers, *Larry King Live*, February 22, 1990, CNN-TV. Transcript created for the Tobacco Institute by Radio TV Reports, Inc., TTID, item ID: xrxj0191; quote is from p. 4 of transcript.

12. Benjamin Hooks News Conference, January 9, 1990, C-SPAN, https://www.c-span.org/video/?10568-1/benjamin-hooks-news-conference.

13. "NAACP and Brown and Williamson Establish Small Business Enterprise," *New Journal and Guide* (Norfolk, VA), August 7, 1985, 3.

14. Ian Fisher, "On Tobacco Lobby List, Two Unlikely Names," *New York Times*, November 20, 1995, 41.

15. News release, "Black Newspaper Publishers on Tobacco Advertising Ban," March 24, 1986, TTID, item ID: jqhl0049.

16. James W. Johnston to Louis W. Sullivan, January 23, 1990, TTID, item ID: flv0082. This is Johnston's reply to Sullivan's January 17 letter.

17. RJR, "Proposed Questions for Sec. Sullivan," date unspecified, TTID, item ID: zhry0080. This document was presumably prepared as talking points, circulated to defenders of RJR as the Uptown controversy unfolded.

18. Louis Sullivan to James W. Johnston, January 17, 1990, TTID, item ID: mxlv0082.

19. Quoted in "Health Issues Spark Debate Over Industry Ties," *Detroit Free Press*, July 23, 1989, 1B, 7B.

20. The smoking rate had declined for Black men from 60 percent in 1965 to 40 percent in 1987; in those same years, the smoking rate for white men had dropped from 51 percent to 31 percent. Data from National Health Interview Surveys, Department of Health and Human Services. Displayed in "Health Issues Spark Debate," *Detroit Free Press*, 1989, 7B.

21. Louis Sullivan speech at University of Pennsylvania, January 1990. See also Selwyn, "Sullivan Assails Cigarette Aimed at Black Buyers," 5.

22. Randall Rothenberg, "Advertising: Shift Sought from 'Black' to 'Urban,'" *New York Times*, November 30, 1989, D19; Joseph Cosco, "African-Americans: In the Era of Nike, Uptown and Quaker Oats, Companies Are Finding It's Harder to Do the Right Thing," 18.

23. "Proposed Media Q&A, Project UT."

24. "Proposed Media Q&A, Project UT."

25. "Proposed Media Q&A, Project UT."

26. Clarence Page, "The 'Good Life' Is Billboard-Size in Our Inner Cities," *Chicago Tribune*, January 11, 1989, 19.

27. Patrick Media Group, "Outdoor Industry Position Paper, Chapter 9.44: Advertisement of Tobacco Products and Alcoholic Beverages," 1990, TTID, item ID: smlg0101.

28. Paul Baker, "Philadelphians Want Tobacco Firm to Avoid Other Cities," *New Pittsburgh Courier*, February 3, 1990, 6; see also "Antismokers Fuming Over Cigarette Campaign for Blacks," *Chicago Tribune*, December 26, 1989, 18; John Hoeffel, "Mixed Reviews: Uptown Causes a Ruckus, but Not in Winston-Salem," *Winston-Salem Journal*, January, 21, 1990, TTID, item ID: xnvl0094.

29. Ramirez, "A Cigarette Campaign under Fire," D1.

30. Rhein, "Minority Targeting of Cigarettes under Fire," 214.

31. Koeppel, "In Philadelphia, R.J. Reynolds Made All the Wrong Moves," 20, available at TTID, item ID: mxdx0049.

32. Holden, "Uptown Goes Down," 530.

33. See Wailoo, *How Cancer Crossed the Color Line.*

34. Koeppel, "In Philadelphia," 21.

35. "'Uptown' Feeds War on Smoking," *Miami Herald*, January 20, 1990, 1C, available at TTID, item ID: qxkk0154.

36. Maura Payne, Interoffice Memorandum, R. J. Reynolds, "Uptown Update of January 12," January 16, 1990, TTID, item ID: sshy0080.

37. Lena Williams, "Blacks Debate the Influences of Tobacco Industry," *New York Times*, January 17, 1987, 9.

38. Kendall Wilson, "Groups Fight for Econ. Welfare of Blacks," *Philadelphia Tribune*, January 10, 1989, 2A.

39. Williams, "Blacks Debate the Influences of Tobacco Industry," 9.

40. Hooks quoted by Dan Jaffe, Executive Vice President of the Association of National Advertisers, *Larry King Live*, CNN-TV, February 22, 1990. Transcript created for the Tobacco Institute by Radio TV Reports, Inc. TTID, item ID: xrxj0191.

41. Mark Wagenveld, "Plan for Test of Cigarette Here Halted," *Philadelphia Inquirer*, January 21, 1990, 1-A; "Black-Targeted Cigarette Test Snuffed by Attacks," *Detroit Free Press*, January 20, 1990, 4A; "R.J. Reynolds Cancels Test of Cigarette Aimed at Blacks," *Los Angeles Times*, January 20, 1990, D2; "Firms Snuff Test of Cig for Blacks," *New York Daily News*, January 20, 1990, 26; "'Uptown' Cigarette Trials Snuffed Out by Black Community," *Boston Herald*, January 20, 1990, 3; "Tobacco Firm Drops Black-Oriented Push," *Chicago Tribune*, January 20, 1990, 1; "Cigarette Targeted at Blacks Dropped," *St. Louis Post Dispatch*, January 20, 1990, 6A; "R.J. Reynolds Withdraws New Cigarette for Blacks," *Seattle Post-Intelligencer*, January 20, 1990, A3; "Firm Cancels Test-Marketing of Cigarette Aimed at Black Smokers," *Atlanta Journal and Constitution*, January 21, 1990, A7; "'Black' Cigarette Killed," *Denver Rocky Mountain News*, January 21, 1990, 65; "R.J. Reynolds Cancels Uptown Cigarette Test Marketing," *Houston Post*, January 20, 1990, C2, available at TTID, item ID: xnvl0094.

42. "'Uptown' Feeds War on Smoking," 1C.

43. Schiffman, "After Uptown."

44. Ramirez, "Reynolds, after Protests, Cancels Cigarette"; see also Michael Specter, "Reynolds Cancels Plan to Market New Cigarette," *Washington Post*, January 20, 1990, A3.

45. Schiffman, "After Uptown,"

46. Memo from Uptown Interdepartmental Task Force to J. W. Johnston, "Uptown Review," January 30, 1990, 3, TTID, item ID: lqjm0042.

47. Griggs, "RJR's 'Uptown' May Be Down, but It's Not Out—Yet," 17.

48. A thoughtful analysis of the anti-Uptown campaign in Philadelphia is Marshall, "The Uptown Coalition."

49. Mabry, Click, and Lewis, "Fighting Ads in the Inner City," 46.

50. Wildavsky, "Tilting at Billboards," 19–20.

51. Stephanie Strom, "Billboard Owners Switching, Not Fighting," *New York Times*, April 4, 1990, B1.

52. "Confronting the Hidden Persuaders," 70; see also "Consumers Are Getting Mad, Mad, Mad, Mad at Mad Ave.," 70–71.

53. Ken Fireman, "Flying Cold-Turkey: Health Groups Cheer Planned Cigarette Ban on Most U.S. Flights," *Newsday*, October 18, 1989, 5.

54. Thomas Lauria, Assistant to the President of the Tobacco Institute on the *Diane Raymond Show*, WWDB-FM, March 7, 1990, Philadelphia, PA, TTID, item ID: grdj0140.

55. Dewitt Helm on *McLaughlin*, CNBC, March 6, 1990, TTID, item ID: qnlf0132. In April, the vice president of the Tobacco Institute quoted Hooks again in a letter to *Newsday*, noting that "the NAACP's Benjamin Hooks put the issue into perspective recently when he wrote, 'This is an insidious form of paternalism. Blacks, like the rest of the populace, can make the choice of whether to smoke or not." Merriman, "Smokers' Right to Choose," C2.

56. Rhein, "Minority Targeting of Cigarettes under Fire," 214.

57. "Health and Human Services Budget, Part 1," House Appropriations Subcommittee on Labor, Health and Human Services, and Education, February 8, 1990, C-SPAN, https://www.c-span.org/video/?11080-1/health-human-services -budget-part-1. Stokes's comments begin at 1:06:00.

58. "Marketing Practices of Tobacco Companies," House Energy Committee, Subcommittee on Transportation and Hazardous Materials, March 1, 1990, C-SPAN, https://www.c-span.org/video/?13732-1/marketing-practices-tobacco -companies. The hearing focused on H.R. 1250, the Protect Our Children from Cigarettes Act, and discussed tobacco marketing aimed at young people, women, and minorities. Neal's comments begin around 26:30.

59. "Marketing Practices of Tobacco Companies." McMillan's remarks appear at roughly 17:30–20:25.

60. Fisher, "On Tobacco Lobby List," 41.

61. Schiffman, "After Uptown."

62. Edolphus Towns, "Tobacco Advertising" subcommittee hearing, July 12, 1990, C-SPAN, https://www.c-span.org/video/?13874-1/tobacco-advertising (at 2:36:00 and 1:28:30). The subcommittee heard testimony on H.R. 5041, a proposed bill to regulate labeling and advertising for tobacco products.

63. Mason responded that there was, in fact, "a difference in information . . . about the lethal effects of tobacco" shaped by education levels, and that advertising targeting had also reinforced these differences. "Tobacco Advertising" subcommittee hearing, starting near 1:29:00.

64. Gallant-Stokes, "Black Marketing Marksmanship."

65. Kotz and Story, "Food Advertisements during Children's Saturday Morning Television Programming"; and Nestle and Jacobsen, "Halting the Obesity Epidemic."

66. Hearings on Health and Human Services Budget, House Appropriations

Subcommittee on Labor, Health, and Human Services, and Education, February 8, 1990, C-SPAN, https://www.c-span.org/video/?11080-1/health-human -services-budget-part-1; quote begins near 1:07:25.

67. "Tobacco Advertising." Whittaker's quote begins at 21:55. Earlier quotes, as noted in main text, come from Whittaker at 23:46 and 23:25.

68. "Tobacco Advertising." Whittaker at 23:10.

69. Quoted in Givel, "Philip Morris' FDA Gambit," 450.

70. James Mason testimony, "Tobacco Advertising," appears around 1:16:53.

71. Joseph R. Tybor, "Tobacco Firm Found Liable in Smoker's Death," *Chicago Tribune*, June 14, 1988.

72. Morton Mintz, "Ad Agency's Study Cites Strong Dependency of Smokers," *Washington Post*, March 9, 1988, F3.

73. Kluger, *Ashes to Ashes*, 674.

74. Huang et al., "Black-White Differences in Appeal of Cigarette Advertisements among Adolescents," available at TTID, item ID: mgph0049.

75. DR International, *Camel Menthol Image Evaluation*, prepared for R. J. Reynolds, November 11, 1993, TTID, item ID: kxgb0079.

76. Kessler, *A Question of Intent.*

77. Pollay, "Targeting Tactics in Selling Smoke"; Chen, "Smoking and the Health Gap in Minorities."

78. Douglas, "Taking Aim at the Bull's-Eye"; Treise et al., "Ethics in Advertising."

79. Alix M. Freedman, "'Impact Booster': Tobacco Firm Shows How Ammonia Spurs Delivery of Nicotine," *Wall Street Journal*, October 18, 1995, A1.

80. Kabat and Hebert, "Use of Mentholated Cigarettes and Oropharyngeal Cancer."

81. Pritchard et al., "Little Evidence That 'Denicotinized' Menthol Cigarettes Have Pharmacological Effect"; McCarthy et al., "Menthol vs. Nonmenthol Cigarettes."

82. Brown & Williamson Tobacco Corp., *Kool Billboard Test*, 1991, TTID, item ID: qqjg0081.

83. "Kool Cigarettes to Test New Campaign in Ohio," *New York Times*, September 30, 1991, D10; "Menthol Initiative Program, New York/New Jersey Region," December 18, 1991, TTID, item ID: srvc0103.

84. Memo from Warner Hall to Laura Bender and Emily Etzel, "Salem Gold Focus Groups July 17–18, 1991, Tampa," August 9, 1991, 3, TTID, item ID: lmpn0061.

85. Marketing Perceptions, Inc., *Understanding Menthol Smokers and Opportunities for a Sub-Generic Menthol Concept: A Qualitative Research Study*, prepared for Philip Morris, March 1992, 4, 8, 11, 8, 15, TTID, item ID: tfvf0017.

86. Gene Shore Associates, "Salem and Menthol Emotional Benefits," January 1997, 2, TTID, item ID: rlkj0188.

87. Leo Burnett Co., Inc., *Menthol "Creative Platform" Exploration Research*, prepared for Philip Morris, December 11, 1995, 31, TTID, item ID: jgbb0152.

88. Kevin Goldman, "Saatchi's Campbell Mithun Loses Kool," *Wall Street Journal*, March 31, 1994, B6.

89. Analytic Insight, Inc., "Project Look: Smokers' Perceptions of the Menthol Market—A Presentation of Research Results," prepared for Brown & Williamson Tobacco Corp., October 4, 1996, 22, TTID, item ID: hkyd0191.

90. "Comments of the Tobacco Institute in Opposition to Petition for an Emergency Temporary Standard Prohibiting Indoor Workplace Smoking," September 25, 1987, TTID, item ID: rrdw0019; Warren E. Leary, "U.S. Agency Urges Ban on Workplace Smoking," *New York Times*, July 18, 1991, B7; The Tobacco Institute, State Activities Division, "Confidential: Tobacco Issues in the Northeast," December 1, 1992, TTID, item ID: jgyj0148. On the targeting of other vulnerable populations, see Hirschbein, *Smoking Privileges*.

91. Melior Marketing Research/Forecasting/Consulting, *Evaluation of Benson & Hedges "Creative Solutions" Advertising Concepts: Prospects for African-American Reactions and Interpretations*, prepared for Philip Morris, January 1994, 3, TTID, item ID: htvk0025.

92. Alfonso L. Carney Jr., Speech before National Bar Association, August 11, 2000, TTID, item ID: jtgk0073; see also Rodney Walker, Director, Corporate Identity, Strategies and Programs, speech before National Association of Black Journalists—Region VII, Friday, March 9, 2001 (San Antonio, TX), TTID, item ID: nyjb0055.

93. "Diversity Timeline," Philip Morris, January 6, 2000, TTID, item ID: gxbd0061.

94. "Corporate Involvement with the Black Community," 1992 (PM), 4, TTID, item ID: hhjg0089.

95. Deposition of George Knox, In the matter of *Thomas v. R. J. Reynolds*, April 20, 2001, 123, TTID, item ID: nrcv0184.

96. Thomas Lauria to Patricia Turner, March 12, 1990; Patricia Turner to Tobacco Institute, February 26, 1990, TTID, item ID: rjmb0037.

97. Turner, "Ambivalent Patrons," 431. These rumors were not confined to Black America. As one February 1992 Philip Morris memo noted, "A pamphlet prepared by the British Health Education Authority to discourage smoking by school children . . . included three depictions of the Marlboro pack, including one which showed the Ku Klux Klan (KKK) initials where the Marlboro crest and name would appear." Lee Pollak to Aleardo G. Buzzi, "Pamphlet by British Health Education Authority," February 18, 1992, TTID, item ID: xklp0101.

98. "A New Cigarette You'll Love to Death," 51.

99. R. J. Reynolds Tobacco Company Executive Preparation/Briefing Notebook, February 19, 1990, 52, TTID, item ID: llxn0174.

100. RJR Briefing Notebook, 52.

101. House Pro Forma Session, February 22, 1990, C-SPAN, https://www.c-span.org/video/?11227-1/house-pro-forma-session&start=1423&transcript Query=menthol. Quote begins around 23:06; Dorgan speech at 23:58.

102. *Day One*, ABC-TV, July 1, 1994, TTID, item ID: trng0122.

103. Kelly, "The Target Marketing of Alcohol and Tobacco Billboards to Minority Communities," 55n179.

104. "Competitor Review—March 1995," PM-USA Business Planning, April 11, 1995, TTID, item ID: jhxf0172.

105. Samuel Sears, chairman of Star Tobacco Corp., quoted in "Banned X," *Washington Post*, March 18, 1995, D3.

106. Peter Hong, "Maker of Menthol X Cigarettes Agrees to Pull It after Protests," *Los Angeles Times*, March 17, 1995, A4.

107. "Waiting for the Smoke to Clear," available at TTID, item ID: pqnh0102.

108. Hong, "Maker of Menthol X."

109. "X Cigarettes Pulled Off Market," *Boston Globe*, March 17, 1995, 35.

110. Derrick Z. Jackson, "Making Money by Any Means Necessary," *Boston Globe*, February 1, 1995, 13.

111. Stuart Elliott, "Joe Camel, Spokes-Beast to the Smoking Set, Is Trying Menthol," *New York Times*, January 17, 1997, D4.

112. Tony Perry, "New Camel Cigarette Draws Protest; Smoking Activists Say Black Youth Are Focus of Ad Campaign Touting Menthol Variety," *Los Angeles Times*, March 16, 1997, A26.

113. Ofield Dukes to Benjamin S. Ruffian, March 18, 1997, TTID, item ID: ffpk0094.

114. Patrick Donoho, "Chicago City Council Transcript," August 3, 1990, 95–96, TTID, item ID: fscb0034.

115. Paul Farhi, "Tobacco Moving Out of Spotlight," *Washington Post*, June 7, 1995, F1; "Marlboro Man Lassoed in Deal on Stadium Ads," *Chicago Tribune*, June 7, 1995, L4.

116. Milo Geyelin, "Tobacco Faces Year of Courtroom Drama," *Wall Street Journal*, February 10, 1997, B1.

117. The Tobacco Settlement: Views of the Administration and the State Attorneys General; Hearing before the Committee on Commerce, House of Representatives, 105th Congress, 1st sess., November 13, 1997, TTID, item ID: frpl0078.

118. John Schwartz and Saundra Torry, "Tobacco Firms Negotiating Package Settlement of Suits," *Washington Post*, April 17, 1997, A1.

119. "Principal Terms of Attorney General Settlement," Brown & Williamson, TTID, item ID: mrlh0081.

120. Edward Felsenthal and Yumiko Ono, "Outdoor Ads for Tobacco Can Be Curbed," *Wall Street Journal*, April 29, 1997, B1. See *Penn Advertising vs. Mayor and City Council of Baltimore*, US Court of Appeals 4th Circuit, November 13, 1996, 101 F 3rd 332. The Supreme Court upheld the 4th Circuit Court's ruling.

121. John Schwartz and Saundra Torry, "Tobacco Pact Calls for Strict Federal Controls," *Washington Post*, June 21, 1997, A1; John M. Broder, "Major Concessions," *New York Times*, June 21, 1997, 1.

122. John M. Broder, "Tobacco Critics Begin Heavy Attack on Settlement, Calling It Soft on Cigarette Makers," *New York Times*, June 24, 1997, A17.

123. Randall, "Smoking, the African-American Community, and the Proposed National Tobacco Settlement," 678.

124. Hirschbein, *Smoking Privileges*.

125. John Murphy to David Himmel, (Philip Morris) "Alpine Prison Program," February 27, 1995, TTID, item ID: yjjd0025. See also PM-USA Business Planning, "June 1994 Competitor Review," July 14, 1994, 11, which calls attention to "Newport's Prison Program," which "for eight years . . . has distributed thousands of free cigarettes . . . at the Washington, D.C. District's Lorton prison." On trend in race and incarceration in this era, see Alexander, *The New Jim Crow*.

126. Dana Canedy, "Cigarette Ads May Disappear, but Marketing Will Live On," *New York Times*, April 18, 1997, D1.

127. Melanie Wells, "Kool Cigarettes to Get Ad Makeover," *USA Today*, October 21, 1998, 3B.

128. Landau, "Trend toward Natural Flavors Boosts Menthol in Cigarettes," 19, available at TTID, item ID: phdb0190.

129. Display ad, *Los Angeles Sentinel*, December 31, 1998, A10.

130. Simpson, "USA/Brazil," 105–6.

131. Brown & Williamson, "Sample Report: Report for 2004 YTD," November 15, 2004, TTID, item ID: frwh0226. See also Connolly, "Sweet and Spicy Flavours," 211–12.

132. "Landmark Settlement of 'Kool Mixx' Tobacco Lawsuits," press release, New York State Office of the Attorney General, October 6, 2004, https://ag.ny.gov/press-release/2004/landmark-settlement-kool-mixx-tobacco -lawsuits.

133. Gardiner, "The African Americanization of Menthol Cigarette Use in the United States."

134. Freeman, "Fast Food: Oppression through Poor Nutrition." See also Taylor, *Race for Profit*; see also Massey and Denton, *American Apartheid*.

135. Kahn, *Race in a Bottle*; Pollock, *Medicating Race*.

136. Pollay and Dewhirst, "The Dark Side of Marketing Seemingly 'Light' Cigarettes."

137. Hanson and Kysar, "Taking Behavioralism Seriously."

138. Travis, "Cool Discovery," 101–2; Glaeske and Boehlke, "Making Sense of Terpenes."

139. Seydel, "How Neurons Know That It's C-c-c-c-cold Outside," 1451–52.

140. Savitz et al., "Smoking and Pregnancy Outcome among African-American and White Women in Central North Carolina."

141. Robert Proctor, discussion of the Golden Holocaust, April 24, 2013, C-SPAN, https://www.c-span.org/video/?312354-5/golden-holocaust&start= 1086; quote from around 18:30.

142. Connolly, "Sweet and Spicy Flavours."

143. Stuart Elliott, "The Kool Cigarette Brand Starts a Campaign to Emphasize That It 'Built the House of Menthol,'" *New York Times*, June 7, 2000, C8.

144. Wailoo, "The FDA's Proposed Ban on Menthol Cigarettes," 995–97.

145. Ibid.; see also Public Health Law Center, "Important Appeals Court Decision Means FDA Now Free to Use Scientific Committee Recommendation on Menthol: R.J. Reynolds v. FDA," https://www.publichealthlawcenter.org /blogs/2016-02-15/important-appeals-court-decision-means-fda-now-free-use -scientific-committee-recomm; press release, Statement of Matthew L. Myers, President, Campaign for Tobacco-Free Kids, "In Victory for Health, Appellate Court Overturns Misguided Ruling Regarding FDA's Tobacco Advisory Committee," January 15, 2016, https://www.tobaccofreekids.org/press-releases/2016_01 _15_fda.

Conclusion

1. Matt Furber, Audra D. S. Burch, and Frances Robles, "What Happened in the Chaotic Moments before George Floyd Died," *New York Times*, June 10, 2020, https://www.nytimes.com/2020/05/29/us/derek-chauvin-george-floyd-worked -together.html.

2. Mittman, *Breathing Space*, 134.

3. By December 2020, in the wake of a massive statewide surge in cases the disparities had dropped, with Black Wisconsinites accounting for 6.8 percent of the cases and 8.0 percent of the deaths. Wisconsin Department of Health Services, "COVID-19: Wisconsin's Summary Data," https://www.dhs.wisconsin .gov/covid-19/data.htm#race.

4. Hardeman, Medina, and Boyd, "Stolen Breaths."

5. Hardeman, Medina, and Boyd.

6. Balto, *Occupied Territory*.

7. Centers for Disease Control and Prevention, *How Tobacco Smoke Causes Disease*, chap.7, "Pulmonary Diseases."

8. Fraser, "Expropriation and Exploitation in Racialized Capitalism: A Reply to Michael Dawson."

9. On choice architecture and the study of nudges in service of improving health, see Thaler and Sunstein, *Nudge*.

10. Wilson, *The Truly Disadvantaged*. Singer, *Drugging the Poor*. For a new theory of ghettos and of the "political ethics of the unjustly disadvantaged," see Shelby, *Dark Ghettos*.

11. Massey, "American Apartheid."

12. Howard W. Haggard, MD, *Report of Investigation to Determine the Physiological Effects of Menthol Derived from Smoking Kool Cigarettes*, prepared for Brown & Williamson, 1935, TTID, item ID: pgr46b00.

13. Before the US Federal Trade Commission, "File No. 1-14737, In the Matter of Brown & Williamson Tobacco Corporation," May 22, 1942, TTID, item ID: mrdc0136.

14. Gardiner, "The African Americanization of Menthol Cigarette Use."

15. The relationship of ethnic authenticity to markets is commented upon by Davila in her book, *Latinos, Inc.*, 9, in which she calls attention to "research [that] now ponders the political implications of the commercial imagination of particular populations and the significance of the individuation of tastes, issues, debates, and desires for contemporary processes of identity creation."

16. Levin, "Blowing Smoke."

17. Rich Calder and Carl Campanile, "Al Sharpton Raises Concerns about Ban on Menthol-Flavored Cigarettes," *New York Post*, January 30, 2019, https://nypost.com/2019/01/30/al-sharpton-raises-concerns-about-ban-on-menthol-flavored-cigarettes/.

18. Kozilitina et al., "An African-Specific Haplotype in MRGPRX4 Is Associated with Menthol Cigarette Smoking"; Abbasi, "Gene Variant Associated with Menthol Cigarette Smoking in Some African Americans."

19. Abbasi, "Gene Variant Associated with Menthol Cigarette Smoking in Some African Americans."

20. Personal communication, Jay Kaufman to Keith Wailoo, February 18, 2019.

21. Scott Gottlieb, "Statement from FDA Commissioner Scott Gottlieb, M.D., on Proposed New Steps to Protect Youth by Preventing Access to Flavored Tobacco Products and Banning Menthol Cigarettes," November 15, 2018, FDA, https://www.fda.gov/NewsEvents/Newsroom/PressAnnouncements/UCM625884.htm.

22. Family Smoking Prevention and Tobacco Control Act, Pub. L. No. 111-31, 123 Stat. 1776 (2009), https://www.govinfo.gov/content/pkg/PLAW-111publ31/html/PLAW-111publ31.htm.

23. US Food and Drug Administration, "Preliminary Scientific Evaluation of the Possible Public Health Effects of Menthol Versus Nonmenthol Cigarettes," https://permanent.access.gpo.gov/gpo39032/Preliminary%20Scientific%20Evaluation%20Menthol%20508%20reduced.pdf.

24. The following paragraphs are based on Wailoo, "The FDA's Proposed Ban on Menthol Cigarettes."

25. "Senator Burr (R-NC) Floor Speech on FDA Ban on Menthol Cigarettes," January 31, 2019, C-SPAN, https://www.c-span.org/video/?c4777366/senator-burr-floor-speech-fda-ban-menthol-cigarettes; see also Steven T. Dennis, "GOP Senator Lights Up Trump's FDA Chief on Menthol Cigarette Ban," *Bloomberg News*, January 31, 2019, https://www.bloomberg.com/news/articles/2019-01-31/gop-senator-lights-up-trump-s-fda-chief-on-menthol-cigarette-ban.

26. Market Planning Corp., *A Motivation Survey for Liggett & Myers Tobacco Company*, vol. 1, October 1957, 128, TTID, item ID: zlbm0016.

27. By 2018 R. J. Reynolds Vapor Co. was second to Juul in the vaping market with its Vuse brand, which had 10 percent of the total market, a decline from 20.7 percent in 2017. Richard Craver, "Juul Ends 2018 with 76 Percent Market

Share," *Winston-Salem Journal*, January 8, 2019, https://www.journalnow.com /business/juul-ends-with-percent-market-share/article_6f50f427-19ec-50be -8b0c-d3df18d08759.html.

28. Pinney Associates, "The Truth about E-Cigarettes (ECs) and Tobacco Harm Reduction," confidential memo to RJR, March 1, 2016, TTID, item ID: hxpn0227. See also transcript of Deposition of Robert N. Proctor, in "Joyce Hardin v. R.J. Reynolds," Case No. 12-29000-CA, Thursday, June 15, 2017, 22, TTID, gtbn0225.

29. Centers for Disease Control and Prevention, "E-Cigarette Ads and Youth," https://www.cdc.gov/vitalsigns/ecigarette-ads/index.html.

30. Angelica LaVito, "FDA Chief Gottlieb's Departure Might Not Actually Be a Good Thing for Vaping Industry," CNBC.com, March 10, 2019, https://www .cnbc.com/2019/03/10/fda-chiefs-departure-might-not-be-a-good-thing-for -vaping-industry.html.

31. Brodwin, "$15 Billion Startup Juul Used 'Relaxation, Freedom, and Sex Appeal' to Market."

32. William L. Dunn and Tom Osdene, "Smoker Psychology Program Review," October 19, 1977, 5, TTID, item ID: ysmp0042.

33. Centers for Disease Control and Prevention, "Outbreak of Lung Injury Associated with E-Cigarette Use, or Vaping," https://www.cdc.gov/vitalsigns /ecigarette-ads/index.html.

34. Ann Simoneau to Kevin Burns, "Warning Letter," September 9, 2019, https://www.fda.gov/inspections-compliance-enforcement-and-criminal -investigations/warning-letters/juul-labs-inc-590950-09092019.

35. Ann Simoneau to Christopher M. Davis, "Warning Letter: Electric Lotus, LLC," November 29, 2018, https://www.fda.gov/inspections-compliance -enforcement-and-criminal-investigations/warning-letters/electric-lotus-llc -568710-11292018.

36. Scott Gottlieb, "Potential Future of E-Cigarettes," *CNBC Nightly Business Report*, September 26, 2019, http://nbr.com/2019/09/26/potential-future-of-e -cigarettes/.

37. Sheila Kaplan, "F.D.A. Accuses Juul and Altria of Backing Off Plan to Stop Youth Smoking," *New York Times*, January 4, 2018, https://www.nytimes.com /2019/01/04/health/fda-juul-altria-youth-vaping.html.

38. Gottlieb, *CNBC Nightly Business Report*.

39. Ben Tobin, "Altria Purchases 35% Stake in Juul in Deal Worth $12.8 bil- lion," *USA Today*, December 20, 2018, https://www.usatoday.com/story/money /2018/12/20/altria-buys-stake-juul-deal-worth-12-8-billion/2373663002/. As Juul CEO Kevin Burns commented, "We understand the controversy and skepticism that comes with an affiliation and partnership with the largest tobacco company in the U.S. We were skeptical as well," but had become convinced that "this partnership could help accelerate our success switching adult smokers."

40. Mary Beth Griggs, "Michigan Becomes the First State to Ban Flavored

E-Cigarettes," *The Verge*, September 4, 2019, https://www.theverge.com/2019
/9/4/20849051/michigan-e-cigarette-flavor-ban; "Michigan Bans Flavored
E-Cigarettes a Day after New York," WIBW, September 18, 2019, https://www
.wibw.com/content/news/Michigan-bans-flavored-e-cigarettes-a-day-after
-New-York-560699301.html; "Governor Looks to Expand Flavored E-Cig Ban to
Include Menthol Flavors," WHAM, September 26, 2019, https://13wham.com
/news/local/governor-looks-to-expand-flavored-e-cig-ban-to-include-menthol
-flavors.

41. Castillo, "Banning Menthol Cigarettes Criminalizes Black Communities";
Alex Norcia, "Banning Flavored Vapes Might Be Good for Teens. It Also Might
Be Racist," *VICE News*, September 19, 2019, https://www.vice.com/en_us/article
/8xw5n3/banning-flavored-juul-vapes-might-be-good-for-teens-it-also-might
-be-racist.

42. See, for example, McCandless, Yerger, and Malone, "Quid Pro Quo:
Tobacco Companies and the Black Press"; Yerger, "Menthol's Potential Effects on
Nicotine Dependence"; Yerger and McCandless, "Menthol Sensory Qualities and
Smoking Topography"; and Yerger, Przewoznik, and Malone, "Racialized Geog-
raphy, Corporate Activity, and Health Disparities"; and Yerger and McCandless,
"African American Leadership Groups."

43. Quoted in Norcia, "Banning Flavored Vapes."

44. Little quoted in *The Industry Menthol Report, Menthol Cigarettes: No
Disproportionate Impact on Public Health*, submitted to FDA by the Non-Voting
Industry Representatives on TPSAC and Other Tobacco Industry Stakeholders,
March 23, 2011, 221, https://www.webcitation.org/63dghRH1B.

45. "NAACP Statement on FDA Plan to Ban Sale of Menthol and E-Cigarettes,"
November 14, 2018, https://www.naacp.org/latest/naacp-statement-fba-plan-ban
-sale-menthol-e-cigarettes/.

46. Calder and Campanile, "Al Sharpton Raises Concerns"; see also J. David
Goodman, "When Big Tobacco Invoked Eric Garner to Fight a Menthol Cigarette
Ban," *New York Times*, July 14, 2019, https://www.nytimes.com/2019/07/14
/nyregion/fur-menthol-bans-lobbyists.html. The NAACP's Marjorie Innocent,
senior director of its health program, also spoke out in defense of the ban, testifying that "there are ten times more menthol advertisements and retail promotions
in black communities than in other neighborhoods." Marjorie Innocent, "Black
Communities Suffer without a Ban on Menthol Cigarettes," *The Hill*, November 21, 2018, https://thehill.com/opinion/healthcare/417543-black-communities
-suffer-without-a-ban-on-menthol-cigarettes.

47. See "Introduction," fig. I.3.

48. Tatham-Laird & Kudner, Inc., *A Summary of the Black Cigarette Market*,
prepared for R. J. Reynolds Tobacco Co., January 29, 1974, 11, TTID, item
ID: rgdl0094. The study's observations depended on a number of recent sales
reports, as well as a 1973 paper in *Advertising Age*; Wall, "Positioning Your Brand
in the Black Market."

49. Lorraine Braithwaithe-Harte and Chirlane McCray, "Ban Menthol Cigs to Protect Our Kids: Stop Using Flavors to Create More Addicts," *New York Daily News*, May 10, 2019, https://www.nydailynews.com/opinion/ny -oped-stop-the-sale-of-menthol-cigarettes-to-protect-our-kids-20190510-k37 holgkybcvvosz5pgyc4enva-story.html.

50. Eisenberg, "After Defeating Menthol Ban, Sharpton Sought Out by Former Foes."

51. Denis Slattery, "N.Y. Proposed Ban on Menthol Cigarettes Could Go Up in Smoke: Critics," *New York Daily News*, March 7, 2020, https://www.nydailynews .com/news/politics/ny-menthol-cigarette-ban-enforcement-20200307 -load5jvh5fe5heulebduf2utei-story.html.

52. As of November 2020, over 300 localities had passed restrictions on the sale of flavored tobacco products, with significant differences by type. Over 110 had banned menthol cigarettes outright. See Campaign for Tobacco-Free Kids, "States and Localities That Have Restricted the Sale of Flavored Tobacco Products," https://www.tobaccofreekids.org/assets/factsheets/0398.pdf.

53. "Reverend Al Sharpton Delivers Eulogy at George Floyd's Funeral," *ABC News*, June 9, 2020, https://www.youtube.com/watch?v=clcgUZ7VIYo.

54. Henry McNeil Brown, in City Council of Chicago, Committee on Finance, July 19, 1990, Council Chambers, City Hall, Chicago, Illinois, prepared by McGuire's Reporting Service, 96, TTID, item ID: fgyj0135.

55. Bobo, Kluegel, and Smith, "Laissez-Faire Racism." See also Issar, "Listening to Black Lives Matter."

Bibliography

The Truth Tobacco Industry Documents, referenced through this book as TTID, is "an archive of 14 million documents created by tobacco companies about their advertising, manufacturing, marketing, scientific research and political activities" that is available and searchable through a website created in 2002 by the University of California, San Francisco Library (https://www.industrydocuments.ucsf.edu/tobacco/).

Abbasi, Jennifer. "Gene Variant Associated with Menthol Cigarette Smoking in Some African Americans." *JAMA* 321, no. 24 (June 5, 2019): 2391–92.

Alexander, Michelle. *The New Jim Crow: Mass Incarceration in the Age of Colorblindness.* New York: New Press, 2010.

Allport, Gordon W., and Leo Joseph Postman. *The Psychology of Rumor.* 1947. Reprint, New York: Russell and Russell, 1965.

Analytic Insight, Inc. *Project Look: Smokers' Perceptions of the Menthol Market—A Presentation of Research Results.* Prepared for Brown & Williamson Tobacco Corporation, October 4, 1996. TTID, item ID: hkyd0191.

American Tobacco Co. *The American Tobacco Company Campus Campaign Audit Analysis,* January 1961. TTID, item ID: gzvw0141.

Appel, Toby A. "Physiology in American Women's Colleges." *Isis* 85 (March 1994): 26–56.

Arthur D. Little, Inc. *Development of Cigarette Packaging.* Prepared for Liggett & Myers, October 14, 1963. TTID, item ID: sfbl0011.

Atkinson, F. P. "Some Uses of Menthol." *British Medical Journal* 2, no. 3016 (October 19, 1918): 433.

Balleisen, Edward J. "Consumerism and the Reorientation of Antifraud Policy." In *Fraud: An American History from Barnum to Madoff.* Princeton, NJ: Princeton University Press, 2017.

Balto, Simon. *Occupied Territory: Policing Black Chicago from Red Summer to Black Power*. Chapel Hill: University of North Carolina Press, 2019.

Bamundo Qualitative Research. *Qualitative Research Exploring the Popularity of Newport among 18 to 24 Year Old Smokers*. Prepared for Philip Morris U.S.A., December 1987. TTID, item ID: qrcn0058.

"B&W Exec Sees Minority Marketing as Continuing Rewarding Challenge." *Gibson Report* 20, no. 2 (June 15, 1979): 1–4.

Batten, Barton, Durstine & Osborn, Inc. *The American Tobacco Company 1976 Review and Recommendations, Out-of-Home Media (13 Markets)*. Prepared for American Tobacco Company, September 17, 1975. TTID, item ID: jfdy0142.

Batten, Barton, Durstine & Osborn, Inc. *Smoking Habits among Three Ethnic Groups—Negro, Puerto Rican, Mexican*. Prepared for the American Tobacco Company, November 1963. TTID, item ID: hykl0134.

Bay, Mia, Ann Fabian, and Naa Oyo Kwate, eds. *Race and Retail: Consumption Across the Color Line*. New Brunswick, NJ: Rutgers University Press, 2015.

Behavioral Systems, Inc. *The Marlboro Image Revisited: An Exploration of the Masculinity Concept among Black Urban Male Cigarette Smokers*. Prepared for Burrell-McBain Advertising, June 1971. TTID, item ID: gxby0189.

Benson, Peter. *Tobacco Capitalism: Growers, Migrant Workers, and the Changing Face of a Global Industry*. Princeton, NJ: Princeton University Press, 2012.

Berger, A. J. *RJR Non-Broadcast Media Posture*. Prepared for R. J. Reynolds Tobacco Company, August 15, 1968. TTID, item ID: gqhx0091.

"Beyond any Doubt." *Time*, November 30, 1953, 63.

"Billions in Smokes at Stake in Federal Study." *Sponsor*, September 30, 1963, 25–30.

Black, Lawrence E. "The Negro Market: Growing, Changing, Challenging." *Sales Management*, October 4, 1963, 46.

Blakeslee, Jan. "'White Flight' to the Suburbs: A Demographic Approach." *FOCUS: Institute for Research on Poverty Newsletter* 3, no. 2 (Winter 1978–79): 1–4.

Blum, Alan. "When 'More Doctors Smoked Camels': Cigarette Advertising in the *Journal*." *New York State Journal of Medicine* 83 (December 1983): 1347–52.

Bobo, Lawrence, James R. Kluegel, and Ryan A. Smith. "Laissez-Faire Racism: The Crystalization of a Kinder, Gentler, Antiblack Ideology." In *Racial Attitudes in the 1990s: Continuity and Change*, ed. Steven A. Tuch and Jack K. Martin, 15–42. London: Praeger, 1997.

Borell, Merriley. "Organotherapy and the Emergence of Reproductive Endocrinology." *Journal of the History of Biology* 18 (Spring 1985): 1–30.

Brand Name for a Mentholated Cigarette. 1959. TTID, item ID: qsmk0190.

Brandt, Allan M. *The Cigarette Century: The Rise, Fall, and Deadly Persistence of the Product That Defined America*. New York: Basic Books, 2007.

Brecher, Ruth, Edward Brecher, Arthur Herzog, Walter Goodman, Gerald Walker, and Editors of *Consumer Reports*. *The Consumers Union Report on*

Smoking and the Public Interest. Mt. Vernon, NY: Consumers Union, 1963. TTID, item ID: gzwm0178.

Britt, Steuart Henderson. "The Strategy of Consumer Motivation." *Journal of Marketing* 14, no. 5 (1950): 666–74.

Brodwin, Erin. "$15 Billion Startup Juul Used 'Relaxation, Freedom, and Sex Appeal' to Market." *Business Insider,* October 26, 2018. https://www.businessinsider.com/juul-e-cig-marketing-youtube-twitter-instagram-social-media-advertising-study-2018-10.

Brown, M. M. "The Home Medicine Closet." *American Journal of Nursing* 4 (December 1903): 195–97.

Brown & Williamson Tobacco Corp. *Domestic Brands, Product Designs and Sales.* [Date unknown]. TTID, item ID: hgdj0037.

Brown & Williamson Tobacco Corp. *Final Report: Menthol 84 Pack Test—Project #77-118.* January 13, 1978. TTID, item ID: rrch0145.

Brown & Williamson Tobacco Corp. *Kool Billboard Test.* 1991. TTID, item ID: qqjg0081.

Brown & Williamson Tobacco Corp. "New Products Brand Group." *New Products: Marketing Plan—1977 Marketing Plans.* 1977. TTID, item ID: srcp0042.

Brown & Williamson Tobacco Corp. *1979 Marketing Plans: Complete Brand Plans.* 1979. TTID, item ID: tzfj0136.

Brown & Williamson Tobacco Corp. *1984 Kool Operational Plan.* 1984. TTID, item ID: trlx0045.

Bullock, Henry Allen. "Consumer Motivations in Black and White—I." *Harvard Business Review* 39 (May–June 1961): 89–104.

Bullock, Henry Allen. "Consumer Motivations in Black and White—II." *Harvard Business Review* 39 (July–August 1961): 110–24.

Bullock, Henry Allen. *Pathways to the Houston Negro Market.* Ann Arbor, MI: J. W. Edwards, 1957.

Bullock, Henry Allen. "Racial Attitudes and the Employment of Negroes." *American Journal of Sociology* 56 (1951): 448–57.

Burke, Timothy. *Lifebuoy Men and Lux Women: Commodification, Consumption, and Cleanliness in Modern Zimbabwe.* Durham, NC: Duke University Press, 1996.

Burrows, Diane S. *Young Adult Smokers: Strategies and Opportunities.* Prepared for R. J. Reynolds Tobacco Co., February 29, 1984. TTID, item ID: ntxb0099.

Bush, Ronald L, Joseph F. Hair Jr., and Paul L. Solomon. "Consumers' Level of Prejudice and Response to Black Models in Advertisements." *Journal of Marketing Research* 16, no. 3 (August 1979): 341–45.

Capshew, James H. *Psychologists on the March: Science, Practice, and Professional Identity in America, 1929–1969.* New York: Cambridge University Press, 1999.

Carpenter, Daniel. *Reputation and Power: Organizational Image and Pharmaceutical Regulation at the FDA.* Princeton, NJ: Princeton University Press, 2010.

Castillo, Tessie. "Banning Menthol Cigarettes Criminalizes Black Communities,

Say Advocates." *Filter*, September 24, 2019. https://filtermag.org/menthol -ban-black-criminalize/.

Centers for Disease Control and Prevention (US); National Center for Chronic Disease Prevention and Health Promotion (US); Office on Smoking and Health (US). *How Tobacco Smoke Causes Disease: The Biology and Behavioral Basis for Smoking-Attributable Disease: A Report of the Surgeon General.* Atlanta: Centers for Disease Control and Prevention (US), 2010. https:// www.ncbi.nlm.nih.gov/books/NBK53021/.

Chen, Vivien W. "Smoking and the Health Gap in Minorities." *Annals of Epidemiology* 3 (1993): 159–64.

Choudhury, Pravat K., and Lawrence S. Schmid. "Black Models in Advertising to Blacks." *Journal of Advertising Research* 14. no. 3 (June 1974): 19–22.

"Cigarette Scare: What'll the Trade Do?" *Business Week*, December 5, 1953, 62.

"Cigs and Cancer—Ad $ to the Upped to Refute Charge." *The Billboard*, December 5, 1953, 3. TTID, item ID: zgnb0015.

Cochran, Sherman. *Chinese Medicine Men: Consumer Culture in China and Southeast Asia*. Cambridge, MA: Harvard University Press, 2006.

Cohen, Lizbeth. *A Consumers' Republic: The Politics of Mass Consumption in Postwar America*. New York: Vintage, 2003.

Cohen, Michael M. "Jim Crow's Drug War: Race, Coca Cola, and the Southern Origins of Drug Prohibition." *Southern Cultures* 12 (Fall 2006): 55–79.

Comaroff, John L., and Jean Comaroff. *Ethnicity, Inc.* Chicago: University of Chicago Press, 2009.

Computer Field Express, Inc. *Existing Market for Menthol Cigarettes.* Prepared for Liggett & Myers, Inc., June 1971. TTID, item ID: gxgn0006.

Computer Field Express, Inc. *New Opportunities in the Menthol Cigarette Market.* Book II. Prepared for Liggett & Myers, Inc., June 1971. TTID, item ID: yqwn0006.

"Confronting the Hidden Persuaders." *Business Week*, April 30, 1990, 70.

Connolly, G. N. "Sweet and Spicy Flavours: Brands for Minorities and Youth." *Tobacco Control* 13 (September 2004): 211–12.

Connolly, Nathan. *A World More Concrete: Real Estate and the Remaking of Jim Crow South Florida*. Chicago: University of Chicago Press, 2014.

"Consumers Are Getting Mad, Mad, Mad, Mad at Mad Ave." *Business Week*, April 30, 1990, 70–71.

Cook, James W. *The Arts of Deception: Playing with Fraud in the Age of Barnum.* Cambridge, MA: Harvard University Press, 2001.

Cosco, Joseph. "African-Americans: In the Era of Nike, Uptown and Quaker Oats, Companies Are Finding It's Harder to Do the Right Thing." *Adweek* 32 (January 21, 1991): 18.

Courtwright, David T. *The Age of Addiction: How Bad Habits Became Big Business.* Cambridge, MA: Belknap, 2019.

Courtwright, David T. "The Rise and Fall and Rise of Cocaine in the United

States." In *Consuming Habits: Global and Historical Perspectives on How Cultures Define Drugs*, ed. Jordan Goodman, Paul E. Lovejoy, and Andrew Sherratt, 215–35. New York: Routledge, 2007.

Crean, Daniel. *The Cigarette Racket: You Are Being Drugged!* TTID, item ID: sgyl0056.

Crossley S-D Surveys, Inc. *National Smoking Habits Study*. Vol. II. Prepared for the American Tobacco Company, Spring 1964. TTID, item ID: ghxc0010.

Cummings, K. Michael, Gary Giovino, and Anthony J. Mendicino. "Cigarette Advertising and Black-White Differences in Brand Preference." *Public Health Reports* 102. no. 6 (November–December 1987): 698–701.

Cunningham & Walsh. *Kool, Jazz and the Recording Industry*. Prepared for Brown & Williamson Tobacco Corp., September 1981. TTID, item ID: jxxv0100.

Cunningham & Walsh. *Kool, 1933–1980: A Retrospective View of Kool*. Prepared for Brown & Williamson Tobacco Corp., November 10, 1980. TTID, item ID: stfk0141.

Curtis, Holbrook. "The Treatment of Singers' Laryngitis." *British Medical Journal* 2 (October 22, 1989): 1233.

Davila, Arlene. *Latinos, Inc.: The Marketing and Making of a People*. Berkeley: University of California Press, 2001.

Davila, Arlene M. "Making and Marketing National Identities." In *Sponsored Identities: Cultural Politics in Puerto Rico*, 1–23. Philadelphia: Temple University Press, 1997.

Dichter, Ernest. *Executive Summary and Supplemental Analysis of a Motivational Research Study of the Current Cigar Smoking Climate*. Report submitted to Consolidated Cigar Corp., February 1963. Ernest Dichter Papers, box 061, 1252C.1, Hagley Museum and Archives, Wilmington, DE.

Dichter, Ernest. *A Motivational Research Study on the Potentials of a 100mm Cigarette*. Prepared for the American Tobacco Company, August 1962. TTID, item ID: mmhl0134.

Dichter, Ernest. *The Motivations of Cigarette Smoking: A Creative Memorandum*. Report submitted to Young & Rubicam, Inc., March 1961. Ernest Dichter Papers, box 065, 1400E, Hagley Museum and Archives, Wilmington, DE.

Dichter, Ernest. "A Psychological View of Advertising Effectiveness." *Journal of Marketing* 14, no. 1 (1949): 61–66.

Dichter, Ernest. "Seven Tenets of Creative Research." *Journal of Marketing* (April 1961): 4.

Dichter, Ernest. "Why People Smoke." *Coronet*, August 1944, 128–30.

Dodd, Allen R., Jr. "Cigarettes: The Splintered Market." *Printer's Ink*, September 6, 1963, 26. TTID, item ID: ktnf0143.

"Do Difficulties Double Your Cigarette?" *Literary Digest*, December 30, 1930, 31.

Doll, Richard, and A. Bradford Hill. "A Study of the Aetiology of Carcinoma of the Lung." *British Medical Journal* 2, no. 4797 (December 13, 1952): 1271–86.

Douglas, Clifford E. "Taking Aim at the Bull's-Eye: The Nicotine in Tobacco Products." *Tobacco Control* 7 (Autumn 1998): 215–18.

"Do You Smoke Furiously in Excitement." *Literary Digest.* April 1, 1929.

DR International. *Camel Menthol Image Evaluation.* Prepared for R. J. Reynolds, November 11, 1993. TTID, item ID: kxgb0079.

Duncan, Amy. "No Longer Kool, but Just as Hot. JVC Jazz Festival." *Christian Science Monitor,* July 3, 1986, 33.

Eaton & Associates. *Kool Inner City Research Project: Focus Group Reports 1985.* Prepared for Brown & Williamson, January 1986. TTID, item ID: zpyj0141.

Eisenberg, Amanda. "After Defeating Menthol Ban, Sharpton Sought Out by Former Foes." *Politico,* December 4, 2019. https://www.politico.com/states /new-york/albany/story/2019/12/04/after-defeating-menthol-ban-sharpton -sought-out-by-former-foes-1230523.

Ellison, Abby. *An Overview: A Qualitative Profile of the Newport Smoker.* Prepared for R. J. Reynolds Tobacco Co., November 1976. TTID, item ID: ysyf0091.

Elmo Roper and Associates. *A Study of Reactions to the Surgeon General's Report on Cigarette Smoking.* Prepared for Philip Morris, Inc., February 1964. TTID, item ID: stck0112.

Enstad, Nan. *Cigarettes, Inc.: An Intimate History of Corporate Imperialism.* Chicago: University of Chicago Press, 2018.

Epstein, Nadine. "Sending Smoke Signals to Minorities." *American Medical News,* December 9, 1988, 18. TTID, item ID: nzll0029.

Ewen, Stuart. *Captains of Consciousness: Advertising and the Social Roots of the Consumer Culture.* New York: McGraw Hill, 1976.

Ewen, Stuart, and Elizabeth Ewen. *Channels of Desire: Mass Images and the Shaping of American Consciousness.* New York: McGraw Hill, 1982.

Fabian, Ann. *Cardsharps, Dream Books, and Bucket Shops: Gambling in Nineteenth-Century America.* Ithaca, NY: Cornell University Press, 1990.

False and Misleading Advertising (Filter-Tip Cigarettes): Hearings Before a Subcommittee of the Committee on Government Operations. 85th Cong. 1, July 18–28, 1957.

Family Smoking Prevention and Tobacco Control Act. Pub. L. No. 111-31, 123 Stat. 1776 (2009). https://www.govinfo.gov/content/pkg/PLAW-111publ31 /html/PLAW-111publ31.htm.

"First to Put the Menthol in the Tip." *BioScience* 14 (June 1964): 66.

"Food Packaging: Industry, Consumer Spokesmen Differ on Rationality in the Supermarket." *Science* 134 (November 3, 1961): 1408–9.

Fox, Noah. "The Effect of Camphor, Eucalyptol and Menthol on the Nasal Mucosa." *Archives of Otolaryngology* 11 (1930): 48–54.

Frank, Thomas. *The Conquest of Cool: Business Culture, Counterculture, and the Rise of Hip Consumerism.* Chicago: University of Chicago Press, 1997.

Fraser, Nancy. "Expropriation and Exploitation in Racialized Capitalism:

A Reply to Michael Dawson." *Critical Historical Studies* 3, no. 1 (Spring 2016): 163–78.

Freeman, Andrea. "Fast Food: Oppression through Poor Nutrition." *California Law Review* 95 (December 2007): 2221–59.

Frey, William H. "Population Movement and City-Suburb Redistribution: An Analytical Framework." *Demography* 15, no. 4 (1978): 571–88.

Gallant-Stokes, Trudy. "Black Marketing Marksmanship." *Marketing Insights* 2 (March 1, 1990): 101–4.

Ganger, Robert M. "New Trends in the Cigarette Field: A Talk Delivered by Robert M. Ganger, President, P. Lorillard Company, before the New York Society of Security Analysts." November 13, 1952. TTID, item ID: yfw60a00.

Gardiner, Phillip S. "The African Americanization of Menthol Cigarette Use in the United States." *Nicotine and Tobacco Research* 6, Supplement 1 (February 2004): S55–S65.

Garfield, Bob. "Colt 45 Ads a Black Day for Blacks." *Advertising Age*, November 10, 1986, 84.

Gay, Charles F., Jr. "Lawyers for Civil Justice: Medicaid Reimbursement Litigation & Legislation." 1996. TTID, item ID: jyyn0088.

Gene Shore Associates. "Salem and Menthol Emotional Benefits." Prepared for R. J. Reynolds Tobacco Co., January 1997. TTID, item ID: rlkj0188.

Gibson, Campbell, and Kay Jung. "Historical Census Statistics on Population by Race, 1790 to 1990, and by Hispanic Origin, 1970 to 1990, for Large Cities and Other Urban Places in the United States." US Census Bureau, Population Division, Working Paper No. 76 (February 2005).

Gibson, D. Parke. *The $30 Billion Negro*. London: Macmillan, 1969.

Givel, Michael. "Philip Morris' FDA Gambit: Good for Public Health?" *Journal of Public Health Policy* 26 (2005): 450.

Glaeske, Kevin W., and Paul R. Boehlke. "Making Sense of Terpenes: An Exploration into Biological Chemistry." *American Biology Teacher* 64 (March 2002): 208–11.

Glantz, Stanton A., John Slade, Lisa A. Bero, Peter Hanauer, and Deborah Barnes. *The Cigarette Papers*. Berkeley: University of California Press, 1996.

Glienka, Franziska, and Louis C. Kress. "The Cancer Patient: Giving Bedside Care in the Home." *American Journal of Nursing* 44 (May 1944): 435–36.

Green, Adam. *Selling the Race: Culture, Community, and Black Chicago, 1940–1955*. Chicago: University of Chicago Press, 2007.

Greene, Jeremy, and Elizabeth Siegel Watkins. *Prescribed: Writing, Filling, Using, and Abusing the Prescription in Modern America*. Baltimore: Johns Hopkins University Press, 2012.

Grey Marketing and Research Department. *A Marketing Target-Buying Incentive Study of Cigarette Market*. Summer 1964. TTID, item ID: xmwv0116.

Griggs, Robyn. "RJR's 'Uptown' May Be Down, but It's Not Out—Yet." *Adweek*, January 29, 1990, 17.

Gumbinner Advertising Agency. *Study of the Filter Tip Cigarette Market.* Prepared for the American Tobacco Co., July 1963. TTID, item ID: hynn0174.

Hacker, George A, Ronald Collins, and Michael Johnson. *Marketing Booze to Blacks.* Washington, DC: Center for Science in the Public Interest, 1987.

Haggard, Howard W. *Report of Investigation to Determine the Physiological Effects of Menthol Derived from Smoking Kool Cigarettes.* Prepared for Brown & Williamson, 1935. TTID, item ID: pgr46b00.

Haggard, Howard W., and Leon A. Greenberg. "Concentration of Menthol in the Smoke from Mentholated Cigarets: A Study of Local and Systemic Effects." *Archives of Otolaryngology* 33 (1941): 711–16.

Halttunen, Karen. *Confidence Men and Painted Women: A Study of Middle-Class Culture in America, 1830–1870.* New Haven, CT: Yale University Press, 1982.

Hampton, Lloyd. "Is Teenage Smoking Really Falling Off?" *Tobacco Reporter* 95 (May 1968): 28–29.

Hanson, Jon. D., and Douglas A. Kysar. "Taking Behavioralism Seriously: A Response to Market Manipulation." *Roger Williams University Law Review* 6 (Fall 2000): 259–392.

Hardeman, Rachel R., Eduardo M. Medina, and Rhea W. Boyd. "Stolen Breaths." *New England Journal of Medicine* 383 (July 16, 2020): 197–99. https://www.nejm.org/doi/full/10.1056/NEJMp2021072?query=race_and_medicine.

Hearings on Health and Human Services Budget. February 8, 1990. House Appropriations Subcommittee on Labor, Health, and Human Services, and Education. https://www.c-span.org/video/?11080-1/health-human-services-budget-part-1.

Heise, Fred H. "Pulmonary Tuberculosis." *American Journal of Nursing* 27 (June 1927): 420.

"Here Comes the Senate Bill." *Tobacco Reporter* 96 (August 1969): 19, 21. TTID, item ID: nhcf0000.

Herman, Ellen. *The Romance of American Psychology: Political Culture in the Age of Experts.* Berkeley: University of California Press, 1995.

Herzberg, David. *Happy Pills in America: From Miltown to Prozac.* Baltimore: Johns Hopkins University Press, 2010.

Higginbotham, Evelyn Brooks. *Righteous Discontent: The Women's Movement in the Black Baptist Church, 1880–1920.* Cambridge, MA: Harvard University Press, 1994.

Hirschbein, Laura. *Smoking Privileges: Psychiatry, the Mentally Ill, and the Tobacco Industry in America.* New Brunswick: Rutgers University Press, 2015.

Hoffmann, D., M. V. Djordjevic, and K. D. Brunnemann. "Changes in Cigarette Design and Composition Over Time and How They Influence the Yields of Smoke Constituents." *Journal of Smoking-Related Disease* 6 (1995): 11.

Holden, Constance. "Uptown Goes Down." *Science* 247, no. 4942 (February 2, 1990): 530.

Horowitz, Daniel. *The Anxieties of Affluence: Critiques of American Consumer Culture, 1939–1979.* Amherst: University of Massachusetts Press, 2004.

Huang, Philip P., et al. "Black-White Differences in Appeal of Cigarette Advertisements among Adolescents." *Tobacco Control* 1 (1992): 249–55. TTID, item ID: mgph0049.

Igo, Sarah. *The Averaged American: Survey, Citizens, and the Making of a Mass Public.* Cambridge, MA: Harvard University Press, 2007.

Inda, Jonathan Xavier. *Racial Prescriptions: Pharmaceuticals, Difference, and the Politics of Life.* Surrey, UK: Ashgate, 2014.

The Industry Menthol Report, Menthol Cigarettes: No Disproportionate Impact on Public Health. Submitted to FDA by the Non-Voting Industry Representatives on TPSAC and Other Tobacco Industry Stakeholders. March 23, 2011. Available at https://www.webcitation.org/63dghRH1B.

Isenberg, Alison. *Downtown American: A History of the Place and the People Who Made It.* Chicago: University of Chicago Press, 2004.

Issar, Siddhant. "Listening to Black Lives Matter: Racial Capitalism and the Critique of Neoliberalism." *Contemporary Political Theory* (2020). https://doi.org/10.1057/s41296-020-00399-0.

Jain, Sarah S. Lochlann. "'Come Up to the Kool Taste': African American Upward Mobility and the Semiotics of Smoking Menthols." *Public Culture* 15 (2): 295–322.

Johnson, Kimberly S. "Nationalizing Regulation: The Pure Food and Drug Act of 1906." In *Governing the American State.* Princeton, NJ: Princeton University Press, 2007.

Johnston, Myron E. *Economic Forecast, 1973–1977.* Prepared for Philip Morris U.S.A., April 7, 1972. TTID, item ID: rxdk0112.

Johnston, Myron E. *Young Smokers: Prevalence, Trends, Implications, and Related Demographic Trends.* Prepared for Philip Morris U.S.A., March 31, 1981. TTID, item ID: jynj0191.

Joyce, George, and Norman A. P. Govoni. *The Black Consumer: Dimensions of Behavior and Strategy.* New York: Random House, 1971.

Kabat, Geoffrey C., and James R. Hebert. "Use of Mentholated Cigarettes and Oropharyngeal Cancer." *Epidemiology* 5 (March 1994): 183–88.

Kahn, Jonathan. "How a Drug Becomes 'Ethnic': Law, Commerce, and the Production of Racial Categories in Medicine." *Yale Journal of Health Policy, Law, and Ethics* 4 (Winter 2004): 1–46.

Kahn, Jonathan. *Race in a Bottle: The Story of BiDil and Racialized Medicine.* New York: Columbia University Press, 2013.

Kapuler & Associates, Inc. *Consumer Reactions to 1983 Kool Executions: Final Report.* Prepared for Brown & Williamson Tobacco Corp., February 17, 1983. TTID, item ID: yyvy0143.

Kapuler & Associates, Inc. *Final Report: Kool Campaign Qualitative Evaluation.* Prepared for Brown & Williamson Tobacco Corp. TTID, item ID: zfdx0145.

Katz, Natalie. *A Summary of Group Discussions among Menthol Cigarette Smokers Regarding Proposed New Advertising.* Prepared by NVK Qualitative Research, Inc., for Brown & Williamson Tobacco Corp., March 8, 1980. TTID, item ID: nxvy0139.

Kay, Gwen. "Healthy Public Relations: The FDA's 1930s Legislative Campaign." *Bulletin of the History of Medicine* 75 (Fall 2001): 446–87.

Kelly, Kathryn A. "The Target Marketing of Alcohol and Tobacco Billboards to Minority Communities." *University of Florida Journal of Law and Public Policy* 5 (1992–1993): 33–72.

Kenyon, Otis Allen. *Theory and Facts of Cigarette Smoking.* Louisville, KY: Axton-Fisher Tobacco Company, 1934. TTID, item ID: yfbm0228.

Kessler, David. *A Question of Intent: A Great American Battle with a Deadly Industry.* New York: Public Affairs, 2001.

Kitman, Marvin. "I Was a Spy in the Cigarette Revolution." *The Realist*, no 18 (June 1960): 7.

Kitman, Marvin "Report from an Independent Research Laboratory." *The Realist*, no. 29 (September 1961): 15.

Kluger, Richard. *Ashes to Ashes: America's Hundred-Year Cigarette War, the Public Health, and the Unabashed Triumph of Philip Morris.* New York: Vintage, 1996.

Koeppel, Dan. "In Philadelphia, R.J. Reynolds Made All the Wrong Moves." *Adweek*, January 29, 1990, 20. TTID, item ID: mxdx0049.

Kopytoff, Igor. "The Cultural Biography of Things: Commoditization as Process." In *The Social Life of Things: Commodities in Cultural Perspective*, edited by Arjun Appadurai. New York: Cambridge University Press, 1986.

Korn, James H. *Illusions of Reality: A History of Deception in Social Psychology.* Albany: SUNY Press, 1997.

Kotz, Krista, and Mary Story. "Food Advertisements during Children's Saturday Morning Television Programming: Are They Consistent with Dietary Recommendations?" *Journal of the American Dietetic Association* 94 (November 1994): 1296–1300.

Kozilitina, Julia, et al. "An African-Specific Haplotype in MRGPRX4 Is Associated with Menthol Cigarette Smoking." *PLoS Genetics* 15 (February 15, 2019). https://doi.org/10.1371/journal.pgen.1007916.

Kreuzer, Franz, Gerd Prechtl, and Christoph Steiner. *A Tiger in the Tank: Ernest Dichter, an Austrian Advertising Guru.* Riverside, CA: Ariadne Press, 2007.

Kwate, Naa Oyo. "Take One Down, Pass It Around, 98 Alcohol Ads on the Wall: Outdoor Advertising in New York City's Black Neighborhoods." *International Journal of Epidemiology* 36 (October 2007): 988–90.

Kwate, Naa Oyo, and Tammy Lee. "Ghettoizing Outdoor Advertising: Disadvantage and Ad Panel Density in Black Neighborhoods." *Journal of Urban Health* 84. no. 1 (January 2007): 21–31.

Landau, Peter. "Trend toward Natural Flavors Boosts Menthol in Cigarettes." *Chemical Market Reporter*, December 28, 1998, 19. TTID, item ID: phdb0190.

"Landmark Settlement of 'Kool Mixx' Tobacco Lawsuits." Press Release. New York State Office of the Attorney General. October 6, 2004. https://ag.ny.gov /press-release/2004/landmark-settlement-kool-mixx-tobacco-lawsuits.

Lawton, M. Powell. "Psychosocial Aspects of Cigarette Smoking." *Journal of Health and Human Behavior* 3 (1962): 165.

Lears, Jackson. *Fables of Abundance: A Cultural History of Advertising in America.* New York: Basic Books, 1994.

Lennen & Newell, Inc. *Negro Smoking Habit Study.* Prepared for Lorillard, June 1963. TTID, item ID: rrhh0055.

Leo Burnett Co., Inc. *Menthol "Creative Platform" Exploration Research.* Prepared for Philip Morris, December 11, 1995. TTID, item ID: jgbb0152.

Lesch, John. *The First Miracle Drug: How the Sulfa Drugs Transformed Medicine.* New York: Oxford University Press, 2006.

"Letters, Notes, and Answers: Mosquito Bite." *British Medical Journal* 1, no. 3344 (January 31, 1925): 248.

Levin, Myron. "Blowing Smoke: Tobacco Giant Uses Al Sharpton, Other Black Leaders to Combat Menthol Restrictions." *Salon*, February 12, 2017. https:// www.salon.com/2017/02/12/blowing-smoke-r-j-reynolds-uses-al-sharpton -other-black-leaders-to-combat-menthol-restrictions_partner/.

Lieb, Clarence William. *Safer Smoking.* New York: Exposition Press, 1953.

Liggett & Myers, Inc. *Cigarette and Tobacco Division: 1972 Annual Plan.* December 1971. TTID, item ID: mgyy0011.

Liggett & Myers Tobacco Co., Inc. *1957 Annual Report.* 1958. TTID, item ID: xkkb0175.

Lorillard Market Tobacco Company. *The Menthol Cigarette Market: A Summary, Job #9016.* February 1972. TTID, item ID: hlnc0129.

Loss, Christopher P. "Reorganizing Higher Education in the Shadow of the Great War." In *Between Citizens and the State: The Politics of American Higher Education in the Twentieth Century.* Princeton, NJ: Princeton University Press, 2012.

Luke, Douglas, Emily Esmundo, and Yael Bloom. "Smoke Signs: Patterns of Tobacco Billboard Advertising in a Metropolitan Region." *Tobacco Control* 9, no. 1 (March 2000): 16–23.

Mabry, Marcus, Daniel Click, and Shawn D. Lewis. "Fighting Ads in the Inner City." *Newsweek*, February 5, 1990, 46.

Malcolm X. *The Autobiography of Malcolm X as Told to Alex Haley.* 1965. Reprint, New York: Ballantine, 1992.

Marchand, Roland. *Advertising the American Dream: Making Way for Modernity, 1920–1940.* Berkeley: University of California Press, 1985.

Marchand, Roland. *Creating the Corporate Soul: The Rise of Public Relations and*

Corporate Imagery in Big Business. Berkeley: University of California Press, 1998.

"Marketing Practices of Tobacco Companies." House Energy Committee, Subcommittee on Transportation and Hazardous Materials, March 1, 1990. https://www.c-span.org/video/?13732-1/marketing-practices-tobacco -companies.

Marketing Perceptions, Inc. *Understanding Menthol Smokers and Opportunities for a Sub-Generic Menthol Concept: A Qualitative Research Study.* Prepared for Philip Morris, March 1992. TTID, item ID: tfvf0017.

Market Planning Corporation. *A Motivation Survey for Liggett & Myers Tobacco Company.* Vol. 1. October 1957. TTID, item ID: zlbm0016.

Marshall, David R. "The Uptown Coalition: A Case Study of the Intersection of Media Advocacy, Media Literacy, and Social Change." PhD diss., Temple University, 2003.

Massey, Douglas S. "American Apartheid: Segregation and the Making of the Underclass." *American Journal of Sociology* 96 (September 1990): 329–57.

Massey, Douglas S., and Nancy A. Denton. *American Apartheid: Segregation and the Making of the Underclass.* Cambridge, MA: Harvard University Press, 1993.

Maxwell, William J. *F.B. Eyes: How J. Edgar Hoover's Ghostreaders Framed African American Literature.* Princeton, NJ: Princeton University Press, 2015.

McCandless, P. M., V. B. Yerger, and R. E. Malone. "Quid Pro Quo: Tobacco Companies and the Black Press." *American Journal of Public Health* 102, no. 4 (April 2012): 739–50.

McCarthy, William J., et al. "Menthol vs. Nonmenthol Cigarettes: Effects on Smoking Behavior." *American Journal of Public Health* 85 (January 1995): 67–72.

"Medical Diseases in the Mediterranean War Area." *British Medical Journal* 1, no. 2883 (April 1, 1916): 500.

Melior Marketing Research/Forecasting/Consulting. *Evaluation of Benson & Hedges "Creative Solutions" Advertising Concepts: Prospects for African-American Reactions and Interpretations.* Prepared for Philip Morris, January 1994. TTID, item ID: htvk0025.

"Menthol and Saffrol in Neuralgias." *British Medical Journal* 1, no. 1486 (June 22, 1889): 1419.

"Menthol on My Back." *The Realist,* no. 18 (June 1960): 8.

"Menthol Production in Japan." *Journal of the Royal Society of Arts* 70 (January 27, 1922): 204.

Merton, Robert K. "Patterns of Influence: Local and Cosmopolitan Influentials." In *Social Theory and Social Structure.* 1949. Reprint, New York: Free Press, 1968.

Metzl, Jonathan. *Prozac on the Couch: Prescribing Gender in the Era of Wonder Drugs.* Durham, NC: Duke University Press, 2003.

Meyers, Cynthia B. "Two Agencies: Batten Barton Durstine & Osborn, Crafters of the Corporate Image, and Benton & Bowles, Radio Renegades." In *A Word from Our Sponsors: Admen, Advertising, and the Golden Age of Radio*. New York: Fordham University Press, 2014.

Michael Amoroso, Inc. *An Analysis of the Menthol Market*. Prepared for Lorillard, September 1986. TTID, item ID: qpkv0108.

Milov, Sarah. *The Cigarette: A Political History*. Cambridge, MA: Harvard University Press, 2019.

Mittman, Gregg. *Breathing Space: How Allergies Shape Our Lives and Landscapes*. New Haven, CT: Yale University Press, 2007.

Morawski, J. G. "Organizing Knowledge and Behavior at Yale's Institute of Human Relations." *Isis* 77 (June 1986): 219–42.

Morgan, Richard. "'Uptown' May Be Up in Smoke, but Targeted Groups Are Smarter for It." *Adweek*, January 29, 1990, 16.

Motivational Programmers Inc. and Depth Research Laboratories. *An In-Depth Exploratory Study on Cigarette Smoking Habits and Attitudes*. Prepared for Liggett & Myers, Inc., January 1969. TTID, item ID: gmwg0009.

Murch, Donna. *Racist Logic: Markets, Drugs, Sex*. Cambridge, MA: MIT Press, 2019.

"NAACP Statement on FDA Plan to Ban Sale of Menthol and E-Cigarettes." November 14, 2018. https://www.naacp.org/latest/naacp-statement-fba -plan-ban-sale-menthol-e-cigarettes/.

"Negroes Get More 'Brand Conscious' as Income Rises." *Advertising Age*, March 18, 1946, 30.

Nestle, Marion, and Michael F. Jacobsen. "Halting the Obesity Epidemic: A Public Health Approach." *Public Health Reports* 115 (January–February 2000): 12–24.

Netherland, Julie, and Helena Hansen. "White Opioids: Pharmaceutical Race and the War on Drugs That Wasn't." *Biosocieties* 12 (2017): 217–38.

"A New Cigarette You'll Love to Death." *Newsweek*, May 13, 1991, 51.

Newman-Stein, Inc. *Cigarette Attitude Study among Lower Income Blacks: Awareness, Attitudes, and Usage*. Prepared for Lorillard Tobacco Co., March 1979. TTID, item ID: ttyl0115.

"New Marketing Profile of U.S. Negro Emerges." *Sponsor* 19 (July 26, 1965): 38–43.

Newport Brand Analysis. Lorillard Tobacco Co., 1979. TTID, item ID: lkfx0096.

Nicholls, Albert G. "Observations and Deductions on the Matter of Epidemic Pneumonia." *Public Health Journal* 10 (December 1919): 542.

Norr, Roy. "Cancer by the Carton." Condensed from the *Christian Herald*, in *Reader's Digest*, December 1952, 7–8.

Odum, Howard W. *Race and Rumors of Race: Challenge to American Crisis*. Chapel Hill: University of North Carolina Press, 1943.

Opinion Research Corporation. *Smoking Behavior and Smoker Motivation—Their*

Implications for Packaging. A Pilot Study for Research and Development
Department, Philip Morris, Inc., November 1961. TTID, item ID: hqmx0045.

Packard, Vance. *The Hidden Persuaders.* New York: David MacKay, 1957.

Park, Roberta. "Physiologists, Physicians, and Physical Educators: Nineteenth-
Century Biology and Exercise, 'Hygienic' and 'Educative.'" *Journal of Sport
History* 14 (Spring 1987): 28–60.

Pettit, Michael. *The Science of Deception: Psychology and Commerce in America.*
Chicago: University of Chicago Press, 2013.

Pollay, Richard. "Targeting Tactics in Selling Smoke: Youthful Aspects of 20th
Century Cigarette Advertising." *Journal of Marketing Theory and Practice* 3
(Winter 1995): 1–22. TTID, item ID: hjhx0149.

Pollay, Richard. "Targeting Youth and Concerned Smokers." *Tobacco Control* 9
(2000): 136–47.

Pollay, R. W., and T. Dewhirst. "The Dark Side of Marketing Seemingly 'Light'
Cigarettes: Successful Images and Failed Fact." *Tobacco Control* 11 (March
2002): i18–i31.

Pollock, Anne. *Medicating Race: Heart Disease and Durable Preoccupations with
Difference.* Durham, NC: Duke University Press, 2012.

Poussaint, Alvin F. "Blaxploitation Movies: Cheap Thrills That Degrade Blacks."
Psychology Today 7, no. 9 (February 1974): 22.

Poussaint, Alvin F. "A Negro Psychiatrist Explains the Negro Psyche." In *Being
Black: Psychological-Sociological Dilemmas,* edited by Robert V. Guthrie. San
Francisco: Canfield Press, 1970.

Pritchard, Walter W., et al. "Little Evidence That 'Denicotinized' Menthol Cigarettes Have Pharmacological Effect: An EEG/Heart-Rate/Subject-Response
Study." *Psychopharmacology* 143 (1999): 273–79.

Proctor, Robert. *Golden Holocaust: Origins of the Cigarette Catastrophe and the
Case for Abolition.* Berkeley: University of California Press, 2011.

Psychological Corporation. *A Psychological Assessment of Viewers' Reactions to the
KOOL Cigarette "Come Up" Television Commercial.* Prepared for Ted Bates &
Company, March 22, 1961. TTID, item ID: rtbv0132.

"The Psychological Corporation." *Science* 55 (February 17, 1922): 169–71.

"Race Relations and Tobacco." *Tobacco Reporter* 95 (May 1968): 22–25, 47.
TTID, item ID: qxcf0000.

Randall, Vernellia R. "Smoking, the African-American Community, and the
Proposed National Tobacco Settlement." *University of Toledo Law Review* 29
(Summer 1998): 678.

Rasmussen, Nicholas. *On Speed: The Many Lives of Amphetamines.* New York:
NYU Press, 2008.

Raz, Mical. *What's Wrong with the Poor: Psychiatry, Race, and the War on Poverty.*
Chapel Hill: University of North Carolina Press, 2016.

"Record of the Dispensing of Cocaine." *British Medical Journal* 2, no. 2902
(August 12, 1916): 229.

Redbook Magazine, Marketing Research Department. *Cigarettes: Notes on the Industry, Cigarette Consumption and Smoking Habits: Market Reports—Redbook Magazine.* April 1956. TTID, item ID: ghvm0103.

Reiss, Craig. "Black Media Association Cites Offensive Ads." *Advertising Age,* September 19, 1983, 78.

Rhein, Reginald, Jr. "Minority Targeting of Cigarettes under Fire." *British Medical Journal* 300, no. 6719 (January 27, 1990): 214.

Ringold, Debra Jones, and John E. Calfee. "The Informational Content of Cigarette Advertising: 1926–1986." *Journal of Public Policy and Marketing* 8 (1989): 1–23.

R. J. Reynolds Tobacco Co. "The Black Market and the Menthol Category." In *Black Market Study.* June 14, 1976. TTID, item ID: lqbp0093.

R. J. Reynolds Tobacco Co. *Brand Image Survey: Black Male Smokers "Menthol," White Women Smokers "High Flavor."* December 6, 1972. TTID, item ID: lsnf0091.

R. J. Reynolds Tobacco Co. *Chicago Metro Market.* 1974. TTID, item ID: jghh0091.

R. J. Reynolds Tobacco Co. *Chicago Metro Market: Objective/Strategies/Rationale.* 1975. TTID, item ID: xjgl0094.

R. J. Reynolds Tobacco Co. *(Confidential) Advertising Research Report: Salem "Brown" vs. "Brown/Red Haired Man in Water" (#50) Outdoor Recall Test.* April 16, 1974. TTID, item ID: zrch0099.

R. J. Reynolds Tobacco Co. *Exploratory Research for Salem Cigarettes.* February 1974. TTID, item ID: gmvc0102.

R. J. Reynolds Tobacco Co. *Product Research Report: Salem vs. Kool among Negroes.* Marketing Research Department, April 28, 1969. TTID, item ID: qpxp0085.

R. J. Reynolds Tobacco Co. *Results of the 1978 Negro Market Audits.* Prepared by T. F. Fields, Marketing Research Department, November 2, 1978. TTID, item ID: tjbj0045.

R. J. Reynolds Tobacco Co. *Vantage: Developing Unique Black Marketing/ Advertising Strategies through Life Style Consumer Analysis.* 1978. TTID, item ID: ltbd0102.

Robinson, Louie. "The Life and Death of Nat King Cole." *Ebony,* April 1965, 123, 125.

Roper, Elmo. *A Look at the Cigarette Industry and Philip Morris' Role in It—In the Immediate Past, Present, and Future.* Prepared for Philip Morris & Co., February 26, 1957. TTID, item ID: ynkc0122.

Roper, Elmo. *Progress Report on Negro Market Study.* Prepared for Philip Morris & Co., September 1954. TTID, item ID: nqym0109.

Roper, Elmo. *A Study of People's Cigarette Smoking Habits and Attitudes.* Vol. 1. Prepared for Philip Morris & Co., August 1953. TTID, item ID: rqym0109.

Roper Organization, Inc. *A Study of Smokers' Habits and Attitudes with Special*

Emphasis on Low Tar and Menthol Cigarettes. Vol. 1. Prepared for Philip Morris U.S.A., March 1979. TTID, item ID: thvx0045.

Roper Organization, Inc. *A Study of Smoking Habits among Young Smokers*. Prepared for Philip Morris U.S.A., July 1974. TTID, item ID: qjvk0191.

Roper Research Associates, Inc. *A Study of Cigarette Smokers' Habits and Attitudes in 1967*. Prepared for Philip Morris, Inc., December 1967. TTID, item ID: qqdv0125.

Rosenfield, Sirowitz, and Lawson, Inc. *Exploratory Focus Group Research for Salem Extra — Birmingham, Alabama*. Prepared for R. J. Reynolds Tobacco Co., January 1975. TTID, item ID: xlmh0091.

Russo, J. Edward, Barbara L. Metcalf, and Debra Stephens. "Identifying Misleading Advertising." *Journal of Consumer Research* 8 (September 1981): 119–31.

Samuel, Lawrence R. *Freud on Madison Avenue: Motivation Research and Subliminal Advertising in America*. Philadelphia: University of Pennsylvania Press, 2010.

Satter, Beryl. *Family Properties: Race, Real Estate, and the Exploitation of Black Urban America*. New York: Metropolitan Books, 2009.

Savitz, David A., et al. "Smoking and Pregnancy Outcome among African-American and White Women in Central North Carolina." *Epidemiology* 12 (November 2001): 636–42.

"Say What You Think of Spud Cigarettes." *Literary Digest*, March 10, 1929, 59.

Scanlon, Jennifer. ed. *The Gender and Consumer Culture Reader*. New York: NYU Press, 2000.

Scheffler, Robin Wolfe. "The Power of Exercise and the Exercise of Power: The Harvard Fatigue Laboratory, Distance Running, and the Disappearance of Work, 1919–1947." *Journal of the History of Biology* 48 (Fall 2015): 391–423.

Schivelbusch, Wolfgang. *Tastes of Paradise: A Social History of Spices, Stimulants, and Intoxicants*. New York: Vintage, 1993.

Schneider, Eric. *Smack: Heroin and the American City*. Philadelphia: University of Pennsylvania Press, 2011.

Schneider, Louis. "If You See Blood." *American Journal of Nursing* 53 (February 1953): 204–5.

"Science News." *Science* 62 (July 3, 1925): xii.

Sellers, Christopher. "Factory as Environment: Industrial Hygiene, Professional Collaboration and the Modern Sciences of Pollution." *Environmental History Review* 18 (Spring 1994): 55–83.

Selwyn, Jeremy. "Sullivan Assails Cigarette Aimed at Black Buyers." *University of Pennsylvania Daily Pennsylvanian*, January 19, 1990, 5.

Semon, Felix. "Two Lectures on Some Thoughts on the Principles of Local Treatment of Diseases of the Upper Air Passages." *British Medical Journal* 2, no. 2131 (November 9, 1901): 1318.

Seydel, Caroline. "How Neurons Know that It's C-c-c-c-cold Outside." *Science* 295 (February 22, 2002): 1451–52.

Shelby, Tommie. *Dark Ghettos: Injustice, Dissent, and Reform.* Cambridge, MA: Harvard University Press, 2016.

Shibutani, Tamotsu. *Improvised News: A Sociological Study of Rumor.* New York: Bobbs-Merrill, 1966.

Short, A. Rendle, and Walter Salisbury. "The Action of Cutaneous Anaesthetics." *British Medical Journal* 1, no. 2566 (March 5, 1910): 562.

Simpson, David. "USA/Brazil: The Flavour of Things to Come?" *Tobacco Control* 13 (June 2004): 105–6.

Singer, Merrill. *Drugging the Poor: Legal and Illegal Drugs and Social Inequality.* Long Grove, IL: Waveland Press, 2008.

Sivulka, Juliann. *Soap, Sex, and Cigarettes: A Cultural History of American Advertising.* Boston: Wadsworth, 1999.

Sivulka, Juliann. *Stronger Than Dirt: A Cultural History of Advertising Personal Hygiene in America, 1875–1940.* Amherst, NY: Humanity Books, 2001.

Smith, Wendell R. "Product Differentiation and Market Segmentation as Alternative Business Strategies." *Journal of Marketing* 1 (July 1956): 3–8.

Social Research, Inc., *Cigarettes: Their Role and Function.* Prepared for the Chicago Tribune, April 30, 1952. TTID, item ID: qrlc0014.

Spillane, Joseph. *Cocaine: From Medical Marvel to Modern Menace in the United States.* Baltimore: Johns Hopkins University Press, 2000.

"Spuds." *Fortune,* November 1932, 51–55, 107.

Stoler, Ann Laura. *Along the Archival Grain: Epistemic Anxieties and Colonial Common Sense.* Princeton, NJ: Princeton University Press, 2009.

Stewart, Charles E. "Correcting the Image of Negroes in Textbooks." *Negro History Bulletin* 28 (November 1964): 29–30, 42–44.

Stewart, Thomas Grainger. "Address in Medicine, the Nature and Treatment of Influenza." *British Medical Journal* 2, no. 1753 (August 4, 1894): 249.

Student Marketing Institute. *Lucky Strike Campus Campaign: Analysis of Smoking Survey and Store Audit.* 1951. TTID, item ID: pswb0020.

Sullivan, Stauffer, Colwell, and Bayles, Inc. *The Market for Menthol Cigarettes: Implications for Montclair (A Report Based on the 1964 National Consumer Study).* Prepared for the American Tobacco Company, September 1964. TTID, item ID: kxvx0017.

Swann, John P. "The 1941 Sulfathiazole Disaster and the Birth of Good Manufacturing Practices." *Pharmacy in History* 41 (1999): 16–25.

Tate, Cassandra. *The Cigarette Wars: The Triumph of the "Little White Slaver."* New York: Oxford University Press, 1999.

Tatham-Laird & Kudner, Inc. *A Summary of the Black Cigarette Market.* Prepared for R. J. Reynolds Tobacco Co., January 29, 1974. TTID, item ID: rgdl0094.

Taylor, Keeanga-Yamahtta. *Race for Profit: How Banks and the Real Estate Industry Undermined Black Homeownership.* Chapel Hill: University of North Carolina Press, 2019.

Ted Bates & Co., Inc. *Copy of a Study of Cigarette Advertising Made by J.W.*

Burgard, 1953. Prepared for Brown & Williamson, 1953. TTID, item ID: qymm0104.

Ted Bates & Co., Inc. *Kool "Project Task Force": A Marketing Recommendation.* Prepared for Brown & Williamson, June 23, 1975. TTID, item ID: mkgn0140.

Tedlow, Richard S. "From Competitor to Consumer: The Changing Focus of Federal Regulation of Advertising, 1914–1938." *Business History Review* 55 (Spring 1981): 35–58.

Thaler, R. H., and C.R. Sunstein. *Nudge: Improving Decisions about Health, Wealth, and Happiness.* New Haven, CT: Yale University Press, 2008.

Thomas, Courtney I. P. "Escape from the Jungle." In *In Food We Trust: The Politics of Purity in American Food Regulation.* Lincoln: University of Nebraska Press, 2014.

Tilley, Nannie M. *The R.J. Reynolds Tobacco Co.* Chapel Hill: University of North Carolina Press, 1985.

Tomes, Nancy. *The Gospel of Germs: Men, Women, and the Microbe in American Life.* Cambridge, MA: Harvard University Press, 1998.

Tone, Andrea. *The Age of Anxiety: A History of America's Turbulent Affair with Tranquilizers.* New York: Basic Books, 2009.

Travis, John. "Cool Discovery." *Science News* 161 (February 16, 2002): 101–2.

Treise, Debbie, et al. "Ethics in Advertising: Ideological Correlates of Consumer Perceptions." *Journal of Advertising* 23 (September 1994): 59–69.

Tri-Ad Plus 2 Consultants, Ltd. *Final Report on Reactions to Cigarette Advertising by Black Consumers.* Prepared for Brown & Williamson Tobacco Corp., April 1979. TTID, item ID: jmgd0135.

Turner, Patricia. "Ambivalent Patrons: The Role of Rumor and Contemporary Legends in African-American Consumer Decisions." *Journal of American Folklore* 105 (Autumn 1992): 431.

Turner, Patricia A. *I Heard It through the Grapevine: Rumor in African-American Culture.* Berkeley: University of California Press, 1993.

"The Uproar in Cigarettes." *Fortune,* December 1953, 164. TTID, item ID: psyf0189.

US Department of Health, Education, and Welfare. *Smoking and Health: Report of the Advisory Committee to the Surgeon General of the Public Health Service.* Washington, DC: Public Health Service Publication No. 1103, 1964.

US Department of Health, Education, and Welfare. *Smoking and Health: A Report of the Surgeon General.* Washington, DC: US Government Printing Office, 1979.

Von Pauli, T. "A Psychologist Looks at the Cigarette Scare." *Popular Medicine,* April 1955, 63. TTID, item ID: qnjv0015.

Wailoo, Keith. "The FDA's Proposed Ban on Menthol Cigarettes." *New England Journal of Medicine* 380 (March 14, 2009): 995–97.

Wailoo, Keith. *How Cancer Crossed the Color Line.* New York: Oxford University Press, 2010.

Wailoo, Keith. "OxyContin Unleashed." In *Pain: A Political History*. Baltimore: Johns Hopkins University Press, 2014.

"Waiting for the Smoke to Clear." *Reputation Management* (May/June 1995): 45–51. TTID, item ID: pqnh0102.

Wall, Kevin A. "Positioning Your Brand in the Black Market." *Advertising Age*, June 18, 1973.

Weems, Robert. *Desegregating the Dollar: African American Consumerism in the Twentieth Century*. New York: NYU Press, 1998.

White, Cameron, John Oliffe, and Joan L. Bottoroff. "From Promotion to Cessation: Masculinity, Race, and Style in the Consumption of Cigarettes, 1962–1972." *American Journal of Public Health* 103, no. 4 (April 2013): e44–e55.

"Wholesale and Retail Prices." *Monthly Labor Review* 25 (November 1927): 212.

Widener, Alice. "Cigarets Welcomed by War-Worn GIs." *Memphis Commercial Appeal*, November 25, 1966.

Wildavsky, Ben. "Tilting at Billboards." *New Republic*, August 20 and 27, 1990, 19–20.

William Esty Company, Inc. *The Black Menthol Cigarette Market*. Prepared for R. J. Reynolds Tobacco Corp., February 1979. TTID, item ID: gmlj0103.

William Esty Company, Inc., *Salem and "Coolness" Segment Competitors Advertising/Marketing Review*. Prepared for R. J. Reynolds Tobacco Co., 1983. TTID, item ID: mnjh0096.

William Esty Company, Inc. *Salem Cigarettes: Black Market Current/New Product Directional Copy Research*. Prepared for R. J. Reynolds Tobacco Co., August 9, 1973. TTID, item ID: klpw0083.

William Esty Company, Inc. *Salem Cigarettes: Ethnic Market Report*. Prepared for R. J. Reynolds Tobacco Co., March 1976. TTID, item ID: nkll0096.

William Esty Company, Inc. *Salem Task Force Presentation*. Prepared for R. J. Reynolds Tobacco Co., December 1973. TTID, item ID: yrlj0088.

William Esty Company, Inc. *Winston Cigarettes Marketing Plan Negro Market*. Prepared for R. J. Reynolds Tobacco Co., January 1972. TTID, item ID: nlwf0083.

Wilson, William J. *The Truly Disadvantaged: The Inner City, the Underclass, and Public Policy*. Chicago: University of Chicago Press, 1987.

Wootten, Harry M. "Big 3 Gain in Cigarette Sales; All Others Lose." *Printer's Ink*, January 31, 1947, 60.

Wootten, Harry M. "Cigarette Sales 2% under 1952." *Printer's Ink*, January 15, 1954.

Wootten, Harry M. *Confidential Report on Cigarette Competition: Brand Sales through Third Quarter 1962*. November 30, 1962. TTID, item ID: yfkv0090.

Wootten, Harry M. *Confidential Report on Cigarette Sales by Brands*. May 18, 1960. TTID, item ID: ynww0003.

Wootten, Harry M. *Confidential Report on Quarterly Cigarette Output by Brands.* 1954. TTID, item ID: jnpk0034.

Wootten, Harry M. "In Changing Cigarette Market . . ." *Printer's Ink*, December 31, 1954, 27. TTID, item ID: kpvn0011.

Wynder, Ernest L., and Evarts A. Graham. "Tobacco Smoking as a Possible Etiologic Factor in Bronchiogenic Carcinoma: A Study of Six Hundred and Eighty-Four Proved Cases." *Journal of the American Medical Association* 143, no. 4 (1950): 329–36.

Yancey, Lee. *Detroit Metro Plan.* Prepared for R. J. Reynolds Tobacco Co., February 1976. TTID, item ID: xndf0091.

Yerger, V. B. "Menthol's Potential Effects on Nicotine Dependence: A Tobacco Industry Perspective." *Tobacco Control* 20, Suppl. 2 (May 2011): 29–36.

Yerger, V. B., and P. M. McCandless. "African American Leadership Groups: Smoking with the Enemy." *Tobacco Control* 11. no. 4 (December 2002): 336–45.

Yerger, V. B., and P. M. McCandless. "Menthol Sensory Qualities and Smoking Topography: A Review of Tobacco Industry Documents." *Tobacco Control* 20, Suppl. 2 (May 2011): 37–43.

Yerger, Valerie B., J. Przewoznik, and R. E. Malone. "Racialized Geography, Corporate Activity, and Health Disparities: Tobacco Industry Targeting of Inner Cities." *Journal of Health Care of the Poor and Underserved* 18, no. 4, Suppl. (November 2007): 10–38.

Young, James Harvey. "Federal Drug and Narcotic Legislation." *Pharmacy in History* 37 (1995): 59–67.

Young, James Harvey. *The Toadstool Millionaires: A Social History of Patent Medicines in America Before Federal Regulation.* Princeton, NJ: Princeton University Press, 1961.

Zikmund, William G. "A Taxonomy of Black Shopping Behavior." *Journal of Retailing* 53, no. 1 (Spring 1977): 61–72.

Index

Page numbers in italics refer to illustrations.